THE
LANDSCAPE
AND
THE LOOKING
GLASS

Winner of

the New England Quarterly

Literary Fellowship Award

in American Studies

THE

LANDSCAPE

AND

THE LOOKING

GLASS

Willa Cather's Search for Value

BY

JOHN H. RANDALL III

HOUGHTON MIFFLIN COMPANY BOSTON
THE RIVERSIDE PRESS CAMBRIDGE
1960

Grateful acknowledgment is due the following authors and publishers for permission to use quotations from the works cited:

Mildred R. Bennett
The World of Willa Cather by Mildred R. Bennett. Published by Dodd, Mead & Company. Copyright, 1951, by Mildred R. Bennett. All rights reserved.

Houghton Mifflin Company
Alexander's Bridge by Willa Cather. Copyright 1912, by Willa Sibert Cather. All rights reserved.
My Ántonia by Willa Cather. Copyright 1918 by Willa Sibert Cather. All rights reserved.
O Pioneers! by Willa Cather. Copyright, 1913, by Willa Sibert Cather. All rights reserved.
The Song of the Lark by Willa Cather. Copyright, 1915, by Willa Sibert Cather. All rights reserved.

Alfred A. Knopf, Inc.
Death Comes for the Archbishop by Willa Cather. Copyright 1926, 1927, by Willa Cather. All rights reserved.
A Lost Lady by Willa Cather. Copyright 1923 by Willa Cather. All rights reserved.
Lucy Gayheart by Willa Cather. Copyright 1935 by Willa Cather. All rights reserved.
My Mortal Enemy by Willa Cather. Copyright 1926 by Alfred A. Knopf, Inc. All rights reserved.
Not Under Forty by Willa Cather. Copyright 1922, 1933, 1936, by Willa Cather. All rights reserved.

ALFRED A. KNOPF, INC. *cont'd*
Obscure Destinies by Willa Cather. Copyright 1930, 1932 by Willa Cather. All rights reserved.

The Old Beauty and Others by Willa Cather. Copyright 1948 by Alfred A. Knopf, Inc. All rights reserved.

On Writing by Willa Cather. Copyright 1920, 1924, 1925, 1926 by Alfred A. Knopf, Inc. Copyright 1936 by Willa Cather. Copyright 1927, 1931, 1938, 1949 by the Executors of the Estate of Willa Cather.

One of Ours by Willa Cather. Copyright 1922 by Alfred A. Knopf, Inc. All rights reserved.

The Professor's House by Willa Cather. Copyright, 1925, by Willa Cather. All rights reserved.

Sapphira and the Slave Girl by Willa Cather. Copyright 1940 by Willa Cather. All rights reserved.

Shadows on the Rock by Willa Cather. Copyright 1931 by Willa Cather. All rights reserved.

Willa Cather, a Critical Biography by E. K. Brown and Leon Edel. Copyright 1953 by Margaret Brown. All rights reserved.

Youth and the Bright Medusa by Willa Cather. Copyright 1920 by Willa Cather. All rights reserved.

J. B. LIPPINCOTT COMPANY
Willa Cather: A Memoir by Elizabeth Shepley Sergeant. Published by J. B. Lippincott Company. Copyright 1953 by Elizabeth Shepley Sergeant. All rights reserved.

To the memory of

Irwin Edman

FOREWORD

THE IDEA for this book came from an experience I had while teaching Freshman English at a midwestern university. I was teaching F. Scott Fitzgerald's *The Great Gatsby,* and, since at that time I was a graduate assistant earning twenty-two dollars a week, one of the questions that proposed itself to me was of what does the good life consist? This was soon followed by two other questions: what do Americans think constitutes the good life, and are they right?

The usually somnolent students in my 8:30 section awoke with a start. Gatsby made my questions meaningful to them; he managed to bring home the relevance of the questions to their personal lives. The class soon developed a divided and, I think, typically American mentality: they readily admitted the limitations of money and romantic love as ultimate goals, and yet felt them to be the most potent lures they knew.

At this point I turned to the teaching of Willa Cather's "Paul's Case." Much to my surprise, I found it embodied the same divided mentality that had already been demonstrated by my class. This story of a deranged boy who wants to lead the comely life, steals money to achieve his end, and commits suicide when his funds run out suggests that the search for the good life can turn out to be not only elusive but criminal, that the pursuit of beauty, however desirable, may lead to disaster. In particular it embodied Fitzgerald's motif of that peculiarly perplexing link that exists between beauty and money. My class seemed as deeply moved by this as Broadway audiences are said to have been by *Death of a Salesman,* and for much the same reason. It posed for them an intensely modern problem: how, in a society largely divorced from human needs, can abstract and impersonal means be utilized to bring about highly personal ends?

At the same time I was casting about for a possible author to study for a doctoral dissertation. I had long been curious to know just what it was that differentiated the twentieth century from the nineteenth; it seemed to me that somewhere around 1914 there existed a watershed

ix

in American history and culture, with currents sweeping forward toward the present on one side of the divide and backward to the past on the other. I wanted to find an author whose career spanned the peak to serve as a subject for study in exploring this problem; someone whose artistry was sufficient to make him interesting and whose values were held by a large enough group to make him representative. When I considered the historical problem together with the problem of the connection between beauty and money, I decided that the writer for me to study was Willa Cather.

I soon found that the author with whom I was dealing had her own peculiar reaction to the historical problem. It seems to me that the chief distinction between the age of optimism and humanitarianism and the age of anxiety and intolerance is the different evaluations they place upon that creature man. To the nineteenth century, he was endowed with dignity and worth and sufficient power to in some sense shape his own destiny. To the twentieth century he all too often seems to have no stature at all, to be at best pathetic and at worst squalidly selfish, and to be driven by forces beyond his control. Willa Cather started out a firm believer in the nineteenth-century conception of the dignity of man. But the First World War and subsequent events developed in her an excruciating awareness that this whole lofty concept might be groundless. The effect was to make her vehemently assert that the habit of heroism, where it still existed, had no chance whatsoever against the cash register complex which she saw as the prevailing credo of the twentieth-century American.

When I started to study Willa Cather my ideas were fairly representative of one school of critics who have written about her. I thought of her as a fulfilled artist whose career showed a steadily rising curve of satisfying achievement. Upon closer examination I became convinced that the best work she ever did belonged to her relatively early prairie period, and found that she herself preferred *My Ántonia* to such a latter-day best seller as *Death Comes for the Archbishop*. The pessimism about the present which is so striking a feature of everything she wrote after about 1922 runs directly counter to the values she cherished first and last, so that it now seems to me her artistic career was anything but fulfilled. I had thought of her as being a conscious artist and highly polished stylist who knew just how she achieved her effects. It was clear from the first that she was a conscious contriver of the smaller units of style, the sentence and the paragraph, but deeper study convinced me that the larger elements — overall structure, general theme, and drive behind her work — were

almost entirely unconsciously determined. She did not know where
she was going until she got there. This trait is demonstrated by the
fact that it took her the first forty years of her life to find her appropriate subject and tone. The break between her apprenticeship
pieces and the work of her early maturity is a decisive one and represents a complete change of values; about the most one can say of it
is that suddenly, almost instinctively, she hit her stride and found her
métier. Similarly her later work embodies another shift in values from
those of her prairie period, and yet the old values of the prairie novels
keep cropping up over and over again as the really desirable even if
unattainable ones. It seems clear that she did not control her material
as much as her material controlled her. Because the conscious and unconscious areas of her mind were working together only part of the
time, I believe that only a fraction of her work represents her best
effort. But this is in no sense to be construed as detracting from the
value of that fraction.

The title of this book deserves a word of comment, as does the
form in which it is cast. My search for a unifying factor in Willa
Cather's work led me to conclude that she herself was engaged in a
search, a lifelong quest for value; and I called the book *The Landscape
and the Looking Glass* because those were the two places where she
most often sought it. The form is a little more difficult to explain.
When I first began to work on Willa Cather I thought I would write
a short study concentrating on the development of her ideas. But I
soon discovered that she wrote a prose so poetic as to demand extensive
imagistic analysis before I could even begin to determine what her
ideas were like. Consequently I employed many of the techniques usually associated with the name of the New Criticism — study of imagery,
structure, theme, and tone — to discover the author's basic preoccupations, then traced the development of her attitudes from book to book
throughout her career, and finally showed how her attitudes fitted in
with those of her time, which themselves underwent a change. Thus
what started out as literary criticism became a foray into the domain
of cultural history. If I have been successful, I may have helped a
little to throw some light on other authors than Willa Cather herself
by revealing something of the cultural conditions under which they
worked.

How important is Willa Cather? Opinions vary widely about this,
ranging from those which consider her a creative genius of supreme
distinction to those which hold her to be a mere painter of pretty pictures of a nostalgically remembered past. At various stages in the

writing of this book I have held each of these opinions. The picture I finally formed of her work is neither so flattering as the one nor so damning as the other, since to me the defining characteristic of her vision is that it is deep but not broad. But if she does not emerge from this study as incredibly great, she does emerge as believably human. For the search she made for value is the search we all make. If the defects of her life were matched by defects in what she sincerely hoped was better than her life — her art — it merely shows that what she wrote and was has relevance to the aspirations and travails of all of us.

Many people have helped me with this study. I want particularly to mention Professor Bernard Bowron, my thesis director at the University of Minnesota, who kept my nose to the grindstone and slashed to ribbons anything he thought was shoddy and inferior; Miss Elizabeth Shepley Sergeant, who graciously consented to an interview which set me thinking about some of the central problems connected with Willa Cather; the late Mr. Ferris Greenslet, Miss Cather's editor at Houghton Mifflin, whose anecdotes about her confirmed many impressions I already had of her personality; and Professor Lionel Trilling, whose *New Republic* article started me thinking about Willa Cather's theory of history. I also want to mention Professors Samuel Holt Monk, Henry Nash Smith and Leo Marx, the latter two formerly of the University of Minnesota, and Professor Walter Rideout of Northwestern University, all of whom kept my morale simmering in different ways. I particularly want to thank my wife, Lois, who not only typed up the manuscript but engaged in and listened to my endless discussions on Willa Cather, and helped me in other ways more than I can say.

JOHN H. RANDALL III

Wellesley, Massachusetts
August 1959

CONTENTS

THE

LANDSCAPE

AND

THE LOOKING

GLASS

CHAPTER I

FORMATIVE INFLUENCES

But then the battle had claimed him; the desire had come upon him to bring some message of repose and peace to the youth of this work-driven, joyless people, to cry the name of beauty so loud that the roar of the mills could not drown it.

— *"The Professor's Commencement"*

ART FOR ART'S SAKE

In a letter to Michael Williams of *The Commonweal* Magazine dated April 17, 1936, Willa Cather writes: "You were asking me what I thought about a new term in criticism: the Art of 'Escape.' Isn't the phrase tautological? What has art ever been but escape?" [1] She could hardly have stated her position more succinctly. This utterance, coming in the middle of the socially conscious thirties, during the era of the proletarian novel (which she abhorred), expressed a view which she had adhered to through nearly forty years of writing, from the day when, a recent graduate of the University of Nebraska, she had stepped on board the train at Lincoln, bound for a magazine job in Pittsburgh, full of the hope of conquering the East. Great changes had come over the world since that summer day in 1896; a civilization caught up in a world war had been brought to the verge of collapse, and many older people, including Willa Cather, thought that it had gone over the edge. But, in the turmoil of the postwar period, amidst the wholesale rejection of old values and the experiment with radically new forms in painting, literature, and music, Willa Cather's concept of art and of the mission of the artist did not change. She grew to literary awareness in the eighteen-nineties; it was the nineties that shaped her artistic consciousness, and she remained a child of the nineties for the rest of her life.

Not that Miss Cather was indifferent to the changes going on around her. She was painfully aware of them and for the most part fiercely resented them. The mood expressed by Lord Grey when he spoke of the lights going out all over Europe on the eve of the First World War was felt even more strongly by this daughter of the plains; for her the lights never did go on again, nor did she live to recover. "But," as she continued in the above-mentioned letter, "the world has a habit of being in a bad way from time to time, and art has never contributed anything to help matters — except escape." [2] She held that for the writer to assume the burden of solving the problems of society was wrong. Art could not be measured by the yardstick of social utility as other forms of human endeavor can be; Citizen Shelley may have been interested in social reforms of his time, but it is as a poet that he is remembered. "He was 'useful,'" she said, "if you like that word, only as all true poets are, because they refresh and recharge the spirit of those who can read their language." [3]

Since it was in the nineties that Willa Cather acquired her artistic training, it is to this period we must turn if we want to understand her artistic ideas. One of the leading literary movements of the time was the aesthetic movement, whose rallying cry, "Art for art's sake," had first been popularized in England in the late eighteen-sixties by a young Oxford don named Walter Pater. It appealed first and foremost to people for whom the most important thing in life was the experience of beauty. Looking around late nineteenth-century England they found very little which could feed their sense of the beautiful; the prevailing temper of the time was usually utilitarian or puritanical, and both tendencies were hostile to art. The utilitarian movement on the one hand came from a rationalistic tradition which denied that art was a way of expressing truth, and the evangelical movement, associating beauty with sin, thundered against poetry and fiction as beguilements to entice men away from the moral and religious path. To these movements the aesthete found himself unalterably and sometimes defiantly opposed. He reminded the Puritan that art was an independent realm and was to be judged by its own intrinsic standards, not by the standards of an intransigent morality; as Oscar Wilde put it, "The business of art is not to do good on other people's ground, but to be good on its own." [4] He reminded the utilitarian that there is a world of difference between means and ends, that art is an end in itself and therefore valuable for its own sake. Oscar Wilde expressed this viewpoint succinctly in his preface to *The Picture of Dorian Gray* which concludes:

> We can forgive a man for making a useful thing as long as he does not admire it. The only excuse for making a useless thing is that one admires it intensely.
> All art is quite useless. [5]

The aesthetic movement, for Pater, was an attempt to assert the independence of art from both morality and the utilitarian tradition, in the interest of the fullest possible expression of beauty. Although hostile to any insistence on the primacy of scientific truth, it was, nevertheless, allied to the scientific spirit insofar as it made use of the relativism fostered by the empirical sciences to undermine any belief in an absolute. Religious systems come and go, Pater said, and schools of art rise and fall; the only thing that does not change is the existence of beautiful sensations, the experience of art. He held that the one thing we can be sure of is the reality of our sense impressions, and that it is the business of the aesthete to gather as many beautiful sensations as he possibly can, whether in art or in nature. In this way life might be made comely, might itself become a work of art. It can be seen that this view of life was impressionistic and subjective in the extreme; its entire attention was centered on the reaction of the individual in isolation from all other individuals. Pater thought that, faced by life's essential transience and unintelligibility on the one hand and its undoubted capacity for producing beauty on the other, the wise man would do well to spend his life in pursuit of loveliness, for it is the search for beauty alone that refreshes the soul. The phrase "art for art's sake" is thus something of a misnomer; the emphasis is on the percipient and is more accurately indicated by the term "art for the individual's sake."

The most eloquent statement of this view of life is found in Walter Pater's conclusion to *The Renaissance:*

> The service of philosophy, of speculative culture, towards the human spirit, is to rouse, to startle it to a life of constant and eager observation. Every moment some form grows perfect in hand or face; some mood of passion or insight or intellectual excitement is irresistibly real and attractive to us — for the moment only. Not the fruit of experience, but experience itself, is the end. A counted number of pulses only is given to us of a variegated, dramatic life. How may we see in them all that is to be seen in them by the finest senses? How shall we pass most swiftly from point to point, and be present always at the focus where the greatest number of vital forces unite in their purest energy?
>
> To burn always with this hard, gemlike flame, to maintain this ecstasy, is success in life. In a sense it might even be said that our failure is to form habits: for, after all, habit is relative to a stereotyped world, and meantime it is only the roughness of the eye that makes any two persons, things, situations, seem alike. While all

melts under our feet, we may well grasp at any exquisite passion, or any contribution to knowledge that seems by a lifted horizon to set the spirit free for a moment, or any stirring of the senses, strange dyes, strange colours, and curious odours, or work of the artist's hands, or the face of one's friend. Not to discriminate every moment some passionate attitude in those about us, and in the very brilliancy of their gifts some tragic dividing of forces on their ways, is, on this short day of frost and sun, to sleep before evening.[6]

Most of this doctrine was taken over wholly by Willa Cather and can be found on almost any page of her critical writings. Pater had said, "Not the fruit of experience, but experience itself, is the end"; Willa Cather was fond of quoting an expression of Michelet's: *"Le but n'est rien; le chemin c'est tout."* [7] With Pater she believed in the doctrine of beautiful sensations, especially in her early career; she too accepted the romantic exaltation of the individual and his sensations and impressions, holding that nothing else is knowable. Walter Pater had tried in his criticism to find out the distinctive characteristics of an art object, to discover the essence or "virtue" of a thing; Willa Cather had written in a similar vein, "The higher processes of art are all processes of simplification." [8] Pater, in his writings, aimed at romantic evocativeness or suggestion rather than direct statement; Willa Cather wrote, "Whatever is felt upon the page without being specifically named there — that, one might say, is created." [9] Finally, Pater expressed his suggestive charm through the medium of a rich sensuous prose learned largely from Flaubert; Willa Cather likewise wrote a poetic prose and acknowledged Flaubert as her master.[10]

But the greatest similarity between Pater and Willa Cather lay in the stern, monastic dedication which each assumed was necessary to a life of art.[11] True aestheticism, according to Pater, required rigid self-discipline and the constant schooling of oneself to discriminate between what was exquisite in experience and what was not; it was ascetic in the extreme and left no room for self-indulgence. Willa Cather expresses the same idea in a contribution to the *Nebraska State Journal* written during her college years, in which she outlines what was to be the aesthetic of a lifetime:

> The further the world advances the more it becomes evident that an author's only safe course is to cling to the skirts of his art, forsaking all others, and keep unto her as long as they two shall live. An artist should not be vexed by human hobbies or human

follies: he should be able to lift himself into the clear firmament of creation where the world is not. He should be among men but not of them, in the world but not of the world. Other men may think and believe and argue, but he must create.[12]

Walter Pater had great influence in the nineties, and in calling Willa Cather a child of the nineties I mean chiefly that she was his disciple. But in that decade Pater had other literary offspring as well. These were sometimes known as the decadents, and in many ways they misunderstood or chose to ignore certain implications in the work of their master. There is, for instance, a considerable difference in emphasis between the writings of Pater and the work of a man like Wilde. Pater and the aesthetes insisted that beauty could be found in all sorts of sensations, some of which might fall beyond the bounds of traditional morality. The decadents, who were out to shock people, sometimes insisted that beauty could be found only beyond the pale. Many people found this perverse, and the decadents, anxious to show their independence of utilitarian and evangelical enemies, eagerly seized upon this and made perversity one of their chief values. Again, the aesthetes did not discriminate between beautiful sensations induced by art and those induced by nature; one was as good as the other as far as the aesthetic response was concerned. The decadents on the other hand were bored by the nineteenth century cult of nature worship and concentrated on art; to them the great glory of art was that it was *artifice,* and had a design and polish and style which nature lacked. As Wilde put it in *The Critic as Artist,* "Art is art because it is not nature." With great gusto he carried the idea even further, writing:

> Art is our spirited protest, our gallant attempt to teach Nature her proper place. . . . All bad art comes from returning to Life and Nature, and elevating them into ideals. Life and Nature may sometimes be used as part of Art's rough material, but before they are of any real service to Art they must be translated into artistic conventions. . . . Life imitates Art far more than Art imitates Life. This results not merely from Life's imitative instinct but from the fact that the self-conscious aim of Life is to find expression, and that Art offers it certain beautiful forms through which it may realize that energy.[13]

This declaration of the out-and-out superiority of the artistic over the natural merely because it is artificial shows the lengths to which the

6   FORMATIVE INFLUENCES

decadents would push a half truth in order to combat what they considered to be a half lie.[14]

Now Willa Cather had a good deal of sympathy with the spirit of the decadents, especially in her early days when she was struggling to outgrow her home environment and wanted to shock the prim and proper citizens of Red Cloud. Perversity and artificiality as ideals play a large part in such an early story as "Paul's Case," and even in a late work like *Death Comes for the Archbishop* they make their appearance in the episode entitled "The Legend of Fray Baltazar." For the most part, however, Willa Cather had far more in common with the aesthetes than with the decadents. Her main points of difference with the latter group were that she was interested in people as people,[15] whereas the decadents on the whole were not; and (after the first few years at least) she valued the natural over the artificial: her finest work, the prairie novels and tales, is based on an abiding love for nature.[16] In her regard for people she resembles Pater; what Pater was finally interested in was the humanity of the artist behind the art object; in the last analysis the man was more important for him than the man's work.[17] The regard for nature on the other hand was the result of her childhood in Nebraska.[18] Willa Cather managed to combine these two interests: she felt that the greatest artists themselves felt an impulse to abandon their craft and turn to nature itself for their real satisfactions:

> Some very great artists have outgrown art, the men were bigger than the game. Tolstoi did, and Leonardo did. When I hear the last opuses, I think Beethoven did. Shakespeare died at fifty-three, but there is an awful veiled threat in *The Tempest* that he too felt he had outgrown his toys, was about to put them away and free that spirit of Comedy and Lyrical Poetry and all the rest he held captive — quit play-making and verse-making for ever and turn his attention — to what, he did not hint, but it was probably merely to enjoy with all his senses that Warwickshire country which he loved to weakness — with a warm physical appetite.[19]

THE POPULIST MOVEMENT

In addition to art-for-art's-sake, another influence on Willa Cather was destined to be of lifelong importance. This was the Populist movement. To appreciate its full impact on her it is necessary to consider certain biographical and historical facts. First, in a well-known interview given in 1921 she stated that the "formative period in a writer's life, when he unconsciously gathers basic material," are the "years from eight to fifteen." [20] Second, roughly the same period in her own life — her tenth to her sixteenth years — she spent in the farm region of Webster County, Nebraska. Third, the beginning of this period coincided with the great Western land boom, a time of intense speculation in the appreciation of land values, which eventually collapsed so that at the period's end Nebraska and the other farm states, because of drought, overmortgaging of farms, and the falling price of wheat, hogs, and cattle in the world market, fell into the throes of the worst agricultural depression the country had ever had. Such was the background against which the Populist agitation took place. As Willa Cather describes it in her essay "Nebraska: the End of the First Cycle," written in 1923, the state "was arrested in the years 1893-1897 by a succession of crop failures and by the financial depression which spread over the whole country at that time — the depression which produced the People's Party and Free Silver agitation." [21] The suffering was acute, and Willa Cather's own family was not spared. Her father, like most of his neighbors, had indulged in undue speculation and owned a great deal of heavily mortgaged land. He was, according to her biographer, E. K. Brown, "in desperate straits." [22]

The Populist movement brought to a head a long series of agrarian protests against the impact of the Industrial Revolution on rural America. Some of the things the Populists complained about were due to human greed, such as high interest rates on mortgages, abuse of the Homestead Act, and speculation by railroads on government-granted lands. Others, such as the fall in farm prices due to the world-wide agricultural depression extending from the eighteen-seventies to the eighteen-nineties, were not clearly anybody's fault. Nevertheless the Populists, who had a tendency to personify abstract issues, tended to fix the blame for their predicament on specific groups of people: Eastern capitalists, Wall Street bankers, the gold crowd. What emerged was a fairly well-defined Populist folklore in which the Populists cast themselves in the role of heroes and victims, with the Eastern bankers as villains. This folklore can be summed up in three concepts: idealization of the virtuous yeoman tilling an agrarian Garden of Eden, a dualistic view of social struggles as occurring between the forces of light and the forces of darkness, and the idea of history as a conspiracy against agrarian virtue. [23]

Now Willa Cather had no use for politics, and the few remarks she makes in her work about the art of government are invariably uncomplimentary. Nevertheless she was a child of her place and time, and in the eighteen-eighties and nineties the whole Midwest was seething with political ferment. Although she hated politics, she was apparently unable to resist the Populist folklore. As we shall see, it formed the basis for all of her best work, in both its positive and negative aspects. *My Ántonia* and *O Pioneers!* are both based squarely on the concept of the virtuous farmer dwelling in a Garden of Eden.

The idea of the agrarian Garden of Eden is an old one, having roots in such classical writers as Vergil and Horace, as well as in the Bible; its extensive application to America first occurred in the latter half of the nineteenth century. It was fundamental to the thought of Thomas Jefferson, who wrote, "The small land holders are the most precious part of the state," [24] and "Those who labor in the earth are the chosen people of God." [25] As Richard Hofstadter puts it:

> The yeoman, who owned a small farm and worked it with the aid of his family, was the incarnation of the simple, honest, independent, healthy, happy human being. Because he lived in close communion with beneficent nature, his life was believed to have a wholesomeness and integrity impossible for the depraved popula-lations of cities. His well-being was not merely physical, it was moral; it was not merely personal, it was the central source of civic virtue; it was not merely secular but religious, for God had made the land and called man to cultivate it.[26]

Willa Cather expressed this most clearly in her glorification of family farm life found in the final section of *My Ántonia*. Cuzak is the apotheosis of the virtuous yeoman, and his wife Ántonia, the mistress of his farm and the mother of many children, represents such a synthesis of agrarian virtues as to become almost an earth goddess. Willa Cather presents a highly idealized version of the pursuit of agriculture, stressing its attractiveness as a way of living. "No, I never get down-hearted," she has Ántonia say. "Anton's a good man, and I loved my children and always believed they would turn out well. I belong on a farm. I'm never lonesome here like I used to be in town. You remember what sad spells I used to have, when I didn't know what was the matter with me? I've never had them out here. And I don't mind work a bit, if I don't have to put up with sadness." [27]

Another characteristic quality of Willa Cather's writing is a deep nostalgia for times gone by, a nostalgia which is also characteristic of Populism. Richard Hofstadter says:

> The utopia of the Populists was in the past, not the future. According to the agrarian myth, the health of the state was

proportional to the degree to which it was dominated by the agricultural class, and this assumption pointed to the superiority of an earlier age. The Populists looked backward with longing to the lost agrarian Eden, to the republican America of the early days of the nineteenth century. . . .[28]

Time and again Willa Cather's characters evince a nostalgic mood. In *O Pioneers!* Carl Linstrum tells the heroine:

> "I even think I liked the old country better. This is all very splendid in its way, but there was something about this country when it was a wild old beast that has haunted me all these years. Now, when I come back to all this milk and honey, I feel like the old German song, 'Wo bist du, wo bist du, mein geliebtest Land?' "[29]

This remembrance of things gone by is not reserved for the farmers alone but is felt for the pioneer hunters, the railroad builders, and all the people who had a hand in making the West. Thus at the end of *A Lost Lady* Niel Herbert reflects:

> He had seen the end of an era, the sunset of the pioneer. He had come upon it when already its glory was nearly spent. . . . This was the very end of the road-making West; the men who had put plains and mountains under the iron harness were old; some were poor, and even the successful ones were hunting for rest and a brief reprieve from death. It was already gone, that age; nothing could ever bring it back.[30]

As typical of the Populist folklore as the concept of the agrarian Garden of Eden was the dualistic view of social struggles as taking place between the forces of light and the forces of darkness. To quote Richard Hofstadter again:

> Nature, as the agrarian tradition had it, was beneficent. The United States was abundantly endowed with rich land and rich resources, and the "natural" consequences of such an endowment should be the prosperity of the people. If the people failed to enjoy prosperity, it must be because of a harsh and arbitrary intrusion of human greed and error.[31]

Sockless Jerry Simpson put it more succinctly and picturesquely. "It is," he said, "a struggle between the robbers and the robbed."[32] The expropriators, as might be expected, were the gold interests, bankers, and business people in general. Especially after the defeat of William Jennings Bryan in 1896, the commercial interests were looked upon as having trampled the flower of agrarian virtue and all but destroyed civilization. The Goths had conquered Rome.

In the years during and after the First World War these people begin to appear in Willa Cather's fiction with more and more emphasis placed on them; a new set of characters is added to her repertory: the commercial villains. Not only does she regard them as the source of all that is wrong with the world; she specifically blames them for the downfall of the American West. Starting with such a comical villain as Wick Cutter (he gives everyone a trimming), she proceeds to the joyless and miserly Bayliss Wheeler and then to the malevolent Ivy Peters, who wants to destroy everyone who is not himself and every way of living which is not his own. While fighting for the arts and civilization on the fields of France, Claude Wheeler pauses to reflect that "No battlefield or shattered country he had seen was as ugly as this world would be if men like his brother Bayliss controlled it altogether. Until the war broke out, he had supposed they did control it; his boyhood had been clouded and enervated by that belief." [33]

Closely associated with the anticommercial bias of the Populists was a xenophobic and anti-Semitic strain. The *bête noire* of the movement was England and the House of Rothschild. Hofstadter points out that while this bias was found among other groups of the day, "it was chiefly Populist writers who expressed that identification of the Jew with the usurer and the 'international gold ring' which was the central theme of the American anti-Semitism of the age." [34] Anti-Semitism in Willa Cather's writing is evident only at times, but when it is there, it is there in force. Its strongest manifestations are in *The Professor's House* and the short story called "Scandal." In "Scandal" the villain is a newly rich garment manufacturer named Sigmund Stein who pretends he is having an affair with the heroine, a well-known concert singer. After a brief description of his career and rise to fortune we are informed that "The Steins now inhabit a great house on Fifth Avenue that used to belong to people of a very different sort. To old New-Yorkers, it's an historic house." [35] And at the story's conclusion we are informed that the incident described is not exceptional but typical, because "in New York so many of the circumstances are Steins." [36]

In *The Professor's House* the case is somewhat different; here the villain is the Professor's son-in-law Louie Marsellus. Far from being crude, he is represented as cultivated and charming, but somehow his good taste is unaccountably held against him as lack of taste, and his sweet reasonableness is interpreted as unreasonable. His wife and mother-in-law dote on him, but the Professor views him with extreme distaste. The anti-Semitism is not so obvious as in "Scandal" — only once in the book is he referred to as a Jew — but the novel is peppered with remarks such as, "It all comes down to this, my dear: one likes the florid style, or one doesn't," [37] and "Godfrey began to think that he understood his own wife very little. He would have said that she would feel about Louie just as he did; would have cultivated him as a stranger in the town, because he was so unusual and exotic, but without in the least wishing to adopt anyone so foreign into the family circle." [38]

The final important element of Populist folklore in Willa Cather is the idea of history as conspiracy. This notion, which has a paranoid ring to it, is not unknown in our day, and then as now seemed to appeal to uneducated people whose access to information is slight.[39] To quote Hofstadter once more:

> It was not enough to say that a conspiracy of the money power against the common people was going on. It had been going on ever since the Civil War. It was not enough to say that it stemmed from Wall Street. It was international: it stemmed from Lombard Street. In his preamble to the People's Party Platform of 1892, a succinct, official expression of Populist views, Ignatius Donnelly asserted: "A vast conspiracy against mankind has been organized on two continents, and it is rapidly taking possession of the world. If not met and overthrown at once it forebodes terrible social convulsions, the destruction of civilization, or the establishment of an absolute despotism." [40]

In Willa Cather the expression is not so crude, but the feeling is there. When one reads through her later novels written after the First World War one is struck by the waxing strength of the commercial characters; they triumph effortlessly over the creative men and women of vision, who seem altogether helpless to defend themselves. Arthur Schlesinger, Jr., may be right in asserting that one of America's continuing problems is the political aspirations of the business community, but it is hard to agree with Willa Cather's representation of humanity as divided into the good and the bad, with the commercial people intent on destroying all beauty, all art, and all the joy of living. Her disgust with the rising tide of commercialism is most explicitly stated in *A Lost Lady*. When Niel Herbert returns to Nebraska after two years in the

East, the first person he meets is Ivy Peters, who exultingly tells him of how he has drained the beautiful marshland on Captain Forrester's property and planted it with a cash crop of wheat. Then, in an editorial outburst, Willa Cather exclaims:

> The Old West had been settled by dreamers, great-hearted adventurers who were unpractical to the point of magnificence; a courteous brotherhood, strong in attack but weak in defence, who could conquer but could not hold. Now all the vast territory they had won was to be at the mercy of men like Ivy Peters, who had never dared anything, never risked anything. They would drink up the mirage, dispel the morning freshness, root out the great brooding spirit of freedom, the generous, easy life of the great landholders. The space, the colour, the princely carelessness of the pioneer they would destroy and cut up into profitable bits, as the match factory splinters the primeval forest. All the way from the Missouri to the mountains this generation of shrewd young men, trained to petty economies by hard times, would do exactly what Ivy Peters had done when he drained the Forrester marsh.[41]

However specific the Populists were in their positive proposals, their thinking often appears to have been governed by a strong impulse to reject; they were not so likely to be for something as against something.[42] As we shall see, Willa Cather shared this impulse. There is a vein of petulant negativism in her writing, especially in her later works, which may be rooted in the predominantly negative tone of Populist folklore.

SOME CONSIDERATIONS OF CHARACTER

A third influence on Willa Cather's writing is the configuration of her own personality. This has considerable literary importance in Miss Cather's case because certain idiosyncratic elements in her character are consistently reflected in her writing and shape not only the portrayal of her protagonists but the very substance and meaning of her fiction. When certain of her private predilections, finding repeated expression in her heroes and heroines, seem to form an observable obsessive pattern, some speculation about the author's personality becomes necessary to an understanding of her work. Such speculation is of course dangerous, but to shun that danger is to avoid any serious interest in literature. Consequently a brief sketch of Willa Cather's character is in order.

The personality traits which I am about to describe are drawn for the most part from a biography by her lifelong friend, Elizabeth Shepley Sergeant. This remarkable woman met Willa Cather for the first time at a turning point in the latter's career. At the age of thirty-seven, when she had been for four years a highly successful editor of a big city monthly, *McClure's Magazine,* she was contemplating leaving her position to devote all her time to the writing of fiction. Up to this point she had been a career women who for ten years had held jobs as editor, teacher, and reporter; afterwards she was to become a full-fledged author and devote the rest of her life to art.[43]

Physically, Willa Cather at this time was buoyant, energetic, and vital. Miss Sergeant describes her at their first meeting as follows:

> The only woman I could spy however coming in my direction was youngish, buoyant, not tall, rather square. No trace of the reforming feminist in this vital being who smiled at me, her face, open, direct, honest, blooming with warmth and kindness. Her eyes were sailor-blue, her cheeks were rosy, her hair was red-brown, parted in the middle like a child's. As she shook hands, I felt the freshness and brusqueness, too, of an ocean breeze. Her boyish, enthusiastic manner was disarming, and as she led me through the jostle of the outer office, I was affected by the resonance of her Western voice, and by the informality of her clothes — it was as it she rebelled against urban conformities.[44]

Miss Sergeant continues to describe "this tense dynamic person with her homespun brilliance," whose "sheer energy was alarming to a shy New Englander," [45] by commenting, "She brimmed with physical life. You could see that she was country-bred. Rapid motion was essential to her." [46] She called her ". . . a powerful masculine personality. . . . This Miss Cather filled the whole space between door and window to brimming, as a man might do." [47]

As might be expected from such a personality, she had strong opinions and was willing to fight for them. She was a side-taker, not a compromiser. Miss Sergeant says, "She was not a wily female, a diplomat, she was one to stand to her colors like a trooper, and fight her battles in the open." [48] A corollary to this was the fact that she would not spare the feelings of people she disagreed with.[49] A good example is the slashing dramatic criticism she wrote both in college and during her Pittsburgh years. Of Maggie Mitchell she could say:

> All year we have been opposed by a vague, indescribable dread. Every time we have seen the bill posters putting up posters we

have shuddered lest we should see her name, or, more still, her
picture. It has been a hard year, theatrically and otherwise, and
we have had most of the seven plagues of Egypt poured upon us,
but we have hoped the Lord would spare us Maggie, and it almost
seems that he is going to. We have seen her pictures yearly ever
since we were little, and we have grown unspeakably weary of them
and of her. Fifty years ago, when Maggie was young she had
nothing but a laugh with mirth in it and a face with a moderate
allowance of beauty. But how any actress can be so behind as
to imagine that she is beautiful after she is seventy remains un-
explained.[50]

Her pointed comment on the acting of Lillian Lewis ran as follows:

She will next year stage a magnificent spectacular production
of *Cymbeline*, in which she will play Imogen. When one knows
Lillian, her nose and her emotions, one hopes they dug Shakespeare's grave very deep.[51]

A related personal characteristic was her distaste for being reminded
that there were other views of life than her own.[52] She had a tendency
toward dogmatic narrowness in her opinions which did not improve as
her life wore on. "There was so much she did not want to see and saw
not," says Miss Sergeant. "What she did see she selected instinctively.
. . ." [53] Often when cornered in a discussion she would respond by
abruptly changing the subject.[54] These traits were to grow on her with
the years.[55]

In his biography of F. Scott Fitzgerald, Arthur Mizener says of him,
"He was thirty before experience succeeded in convincing him that
'Life was [not] something you dominated if you were any good.' " [56]
Willa Cather was near fifty before she made the same discovery. Strong
in her character was the conviction that men and women of ability
could succeed if they were only determined enough, and could force
other people to recognize their achievement.[57] She had little sympathy
for failure and no patience with excuses.[58] When she finally saw the
limitations of this viewpoint her reaction was vehement and furious.
It amounted to nothing less than the total rejection of the world in
which she lived.[59]

For all her seeming independence and self-assertiveness, something
inside her was wistful and uncertain.[60] Perhaps this lies at the root of
her worship of success, especially its material attributes.[61] In the eyes

of the uninitiated, successful people, who have achieved recognition, seem to have gained human acceptance as well. Perhaps what Willa Cather wanted more than anything else was acceptance of this kind.

One evidence that she felt the need for acceptance lies in her agonized awareness of the artist's predicament. I have already shown that she felt the need of rejecting human relations for the sake of art.[62] She was convinced that the artist suffered a fearful alienation from his fellow man and should be treated with special consideration because of his plight. She almost seems to be saying that an artist should be accepted as a human being because he is an artist. E. K. Brown says of her:

> She believed, she always had believed, that the artist is not amenable to the standards by which other folk may be rightly judged. For mastery of an art, she thought, a fearful tax is levied on the entire personality of the artist. Artistic achievement means a constant bleeding of a person's strength. Imaginative understanding of the artistic process should bring, she thought, a deep compassion for what the personality of the artist undergoes, if not homage for his acceptance of his destiny.[63]

This seems to imply a desire to substitute artistic virtues for human ones, and a belief that an individual should be accepted in one area because of his accomplishments in another. The attempt to make creativity in art take the place of creativity in human relations was probably at the root of much of the extreme unhappiness of her old age.[64]

Hand in hand with a stern, monastic dedication of self to art went a rejection of love between man and woman as a source of ultimate satisfaction. Elizabeth Sergeant returns to this subject again and again in her biography. At one point, in the midst of an impassioned discussion of art in general, Miss Sergeant demands of Willa Cather:

> Is it the fate of the creative writer, I asked (and here we were getting to the crux of our talk) to use the stuff of intense personal experience for art only? Must a novelist — especially a female — go around saying I'm only a mirror? . . . Could one let all private and personal experience be burned in the fires of *art?*
>
> Then Willa got up and wandered about the room. To be free, to work at her table — that *was* all in all. What could be more beautiful, if you had it in you, than to be the wife of a farmer and raise a big family in Nebraska? There were fates and fates but

one could not live them all. Some would call hers servitude but she called it liberation! Miss Jewett, too, had turned away from marriage.[65]

The kind of acceptance Willa Cather desired she hoped in the first half of her career to get from her artistic public.[66] Later, when she found that literary fame failed to take the place of human relations, she yearned for the kind of acceptance that came from her family and friends[67] — but from a man, apparently, never.

If up to now I have described Willa Cather as standing alone against those she considered to be her enemies, it is time I considered her in relation to her friends. Although there always were large numbers of people she despised and hated, there were a favored few to whom she gave herself completely. Her friendships were sudden and they were intense.[68] Her concept of personal relationships was based on a strong and almost unreasoning sense of loyalty: the great upheaval at *McClure's Magazine,* in which almost the entire staff walked out on the publisher because of his erratic ways, she regarded as being the next thing to treason.[69] All her life she remained and wished to remain a hero-worshipper.[70] To realize that, one need only recall her attitude toward her "Chief," S. S. McClure, the opera singer Olive Fremstad, and the Bohemian girl Anna Pavelka. She often idolized people she admired, a trait reflected in her hero Tom Outland, of whom she wrote:

> He idealized the people he loved and paid his devoir to the ideal rather than to the individual, so that his behaviour was sometimes a little too exalted for the circumstances. . . .[71]

A consequence of her hero worship was that her interest in creative people was extremely personal; she was more apt to be interested in the artist than in his art.[72] E. K. Brown says of the dramatic criticism of her Pittsburgh days: "One suspects on reading Willa Cather's metropolitan drama reviews that her emotions often ran away with her critical sense at a performance and that her interest more often lay in the players than in the play." [73] This was true even in her childhood days. Elizabeth Sergeant remarks that "Willa was given, as a little girl, an unusually good chance to learn to play the piano. But, evasively, she climbed on her teacher's lap and plied him with questions about the European background and the European languages. She wanted him to play to *her.* . . ." [74] The unhappy result of this concentration on personalities is that the artistic heroines in her novels are unconvincing as artists, however vivid they may be as characters.

All the character traits I have been describing are reflected repeatedly in the kind of protagonists around which her novels are built. These protagonists are strong-willed, aggressive, and usually female. While her most attractive heroines, such as Alexandra Bergson and Ántonia Cuzak, only partially fit this description, many of her strongest characters fit it completely, particularly Thea Kronborg, Professor St. Peter, Myra Henshawe, and Sapphira Colbert.[75] All are overly fond of having their own way and brook no interference from others. Myra Henshawe neatly summarizes their attitude in describing her uncle, upon whom she appears to have modeled herself:

> "My uncle was a very unusual man. Did they ever tell you much about him at home? Yes, he had violent prejudices; but that's rather good to remember in these days when so few people have any real passions, either of love or hate. He would help a friend, no matter what it cost him, and over and over again he risked ruining himself to crush an enemy. But he never did ruin himself. Men who hate like that usually have the fist-power to back it up, you'll notice." [76]

They are unable to take criticism and turn on everyone who disagrees with them.[77] Characteristically they reject human relations to devote themselves to whatever they think is most important in life. Thea Kronborg's response to Dr. Archie's anxious inquiry about her personal life gives the tone:

> She smiled at him with her eyes half closed. "My dear doctor, I don't have any. Your work becomes your personal life. You are not much good until it does. It's like being woven into a big web. You can't pull away, because all your little tendrils are woven into the picture. It takes you up, and uses you, and spins you out; and that is your life. Not much else can happen to you." [78]

These protagonists divide humanity into the rulers and the ruled, heroes and helots, and see life as a series of triumphs of the dominating over the subjected, rather than as a free give-and-take between equals. This attitude is found in many places in Willa Cather's fiction, perhaps most notably in Captain Forrester's after-dinner speech on his philosophy of life, in *A Lost Lady*.[79] Like their creator, her characters are given to the worship of success, especially material success and riches. Thea Kronborg reflects on one of her male admirers:

There was Fred; he was much more interesting now than he had
been at thirty. He was intelligent about music, and he must be
very intelligent in his business, or he would not be at the head of
the Brewer's Trust. She respected that kind of intelligence and
success. Any success was good.[80]

The most pungent expression of this is given by Myra Henshawe's coarse
old uncle, John Driscoll, who tells her: "I advise ye to think well. . . .
It's better to be a stray dog in this world than a man without money.
I've tried both ways, and I know. A poor man stinks, and God hates
him." [81]

In summing up the personality of Willa Cather, the most striking
thing about her is her insistence on complete self-sufficiency and self-
reliance.[82] The next most striking thing is her sense of loneliness and
alienation, her apparent necessity to reject for fear of being rejected.[83]
It is hard to avoid concluding that this is at the root of her own and
her characters' preoccupation with the struggle to triumph over ob-
stacles and quell all opposition, and led to her favorite theme of
"exceptional individuals at war with their environment." [84]

In order better to explain Willa Cather's fiction, I will advance a
hypothesis about the nature of her personality. The hypothesis is this:
that she remained all her life in a permanent emotional state of adolescent rebelliousness which was particularly apt to come to the surface
when she did not get her own way.

Much of the evidence for this has already been reviewed. Most of
the biographical sources agree that Willa Cather had a strong rejecting
nature:[85] as Robert Frost once put it, "With Carl Sandburg, it was 'the
people, yes.' With Willa Cather, it was 'the people, no.' " [86] I believe
she was able to rationalize this trait in her personality by appeal to the
strongly individualistic and diversitarian tendencies which formed part
of the romantic movement, and by adapting to her own ends some
romantic thinkers' doctrines of the glorification of the hero and the
supremacy of the will.[87] She certainly believed, as references throughout her writings show, that the differences between men are more important and more interesting than their similarities.[88]

If my view is correct, the literary consequences of her emotional bias
parallel the consequences to her own life and happiness. I believe that
her rebelliousness and rejection are not only reflected in her art but
mold it; that she was able to transcend them only occasionally and
only in her best work. On this basis I will divide her work into four
periods. During the first, when she was trying to escape from her

family and Red Cloud, she rejected her home territory of Nebraska and the family as a social unit altogether, like any rebellious adolescent. To this end she used the aesthetic movement's rejection of all that was sordid and soul-killing in one's surroundings as a lever to pry herself loose from her family. When she wrote about Nebraska, it was with a shudder of loathing; she seemed to want to demonstrate just how hostile it was to all man's finer feelings. The life she hankered after was the life of Eastern cities and the great European capitals; and roughly half of the stories she wrote in this period are about artists and the artist's life. If Nebraska was the Egypt of her bondage, the promised land that she hoped to enter was the world of art.

During her second period she had lived in the East long enough to grow dissatisfied with it. No longer did it appear to her enveloped by a romantic glow; the regions she now looked to with longing were the plains of the Great Divide. During this period she accepted her family and Nebraska; she wrote of the ordinary, not the extraordinary, and did it extremely well. Her own comment on Miss Jewett now applies to her: she "wrote of everyday people who grew out of the soil, not about exceptional individuals at war with their environment." [89] Time and distance had lent enough perspective for her to write about her native environment penetratingly and convincingly, so it is not surprising that this period saw her produce her best and most characteristic fiction, the prairie novels *O Pioneers!* and *My Ántonia*. This work was based on the Populist version of the good life as that lived by the virtuous yeoman farmers dwelling in the Middle Western Garden of Eden; in the world of nature she was able to see all the beauty that could be demanded of his surroundings by the most ardent believer in art for the sake of art.

After the First World War, when the Populist movement was unmistakably a lost cause and the agrarian dream a thing of the past, she once again turned against her surroundings and rejected them. Once again her theme became "exceptional individuals at war with their environment." During this period she produced at least one minor masterpiece, *A Lost Lady*, in which she summed up everything she had to say about the rise and fall of the West.[90] Convinced that this period was one of disintegrating values, she wrote, "The world broke in two in 1922 or thereabouts," [91] and this is the theme of the remainder of her work. The negative elements latent in both the art-for-art's-sake and Populist movements came to the fore and reinforced the negative aspects of her own personality, which by this time had risen to the surface.[92] Her rejection of her surroundings was so violent as to cause her to turn away from the present world altogether and take refuge in the world of the past.

To understand the bitterness of her later years and her almost complete withdrawal from contemporary activity one must remember the peculiar light in which she viewed the fact of human conflict and struggle. For her, struggle had to lead to the absolute triumph of the will — her will — and the putting down of all opposition. The time was to come when the opposition would refuse to be put down. When the game was no longer played according to her own rules, she simply refused to play the game at all.

CHAPTER II

THE WORLD OF ART

Art of every kind is an exacting master, more so even than Jehovah — He says only "Thou shalt have no other gods before me," Art, Science and Letters cry, "Thou shalt have no other gods at all." They accept only human sacrifices.

— *"Some Personal Characteristics of Thomas Carlyle"*

DOMINANT THEMES

As was suggested at the end of the last chapter, Willa Cather's work can be divided into four chronological epochs. A division of her work on a thematic basis will yield roughly the same four divisions, although there is a certain amount of overlapping; during each of the four periods she displayed certain preoccupations which she treated in a manner characteristic of that phase of her career. The first period extends from the fall of 1892, when as a sophomore at the University of Nebraska she first started having stories published in the campus literary magazine, through the spring of 1912, when her first novel, *Alexander's Bridge,* began appearing in serial form in *McClure's.* Thematically this period also includes a few short stories and one novel, *The Song of the Lark,* which belong chronologically to the next period.

The dominant themes of this period were two: the rejection of life as she had known it on the Divide, and the pursuit of the ideal, which for her meant the creation and enjoyment of beauty. During this period the impulse to reject was uppermost, so that her stories of Nebraska life written during this time are not only the more powerful but are artistically the more convincing. The stories she wrote of the pursuit of the ideal, which usually involved the artist's life and the life of artistic hangers-on, are not nearly so powerful or convincing.

REJECTION OF THE DIVIDE

During her first period Willa Cather wrote some nineteen short stories, excluding those produced during her college days and published in

Hesperian, the University of Nebraska literary magazine. Of these nineteen only four were reprinted in the collected edition of her work. The rest show a wide range of treatment and subject matter, and the best of them are considerably better than some of the stories she saw fit to include in her collected work. Apparently the later Willa Cather wanted to present an image of herself to the public which neither coincides with nor does justice to the actual variety and scope of her early work.[1]

Although her college writings are more juvenile than the stories which came after, their themes and subject matter are essentially the same. The best known of these are "Lou the Prophet" (1892), "Peter" (1892), and "The Clemency of the Court" (1893).[2] All three of them constitute a savage indictment of life on the Divide where Willa Cather had grown up; they deal with the starvation of mind, body, and soul undergone by the early settlers on the lonely Nebraska plains. "Lou the Prophet" tells of a young Danish boy whose solitary existence is blighted by misfortune after misfortune until finally his mind snaps after reading the Book of Revelation, so that he has an apocalyptic dream and goes about the country announcing that the end of the world is at hand. "Peter" is about a former second violinist in a Prague orchestra who is so completely defeated by the boredom and monotony of life on the plains that he commits suicide in Hemingwayesque fashion, putting a shotgun against his forehead and pulling the trigger with his great toe.[3] "The Clemency of the Court" is an ironic treatment of the justice meted out to Serge Povolitchky, who has killed a man for killing his dog, the only thing he had had on earth to love. In "Lou the Prophet" an unbearable life leads to insanity and religious mania; in "Peter," to suicide; and in "The Clemency of the Court," to murder. At this stage of her career Willa Cather sees little good in the pioneer life she was later so vastly to admire.

But the most violent story of rejection written during this period is an uncollected one called "On the Divide" (1896). Nothing she wrote afterward ever equaled in intensity the loathing here displayed toward the Nebraska land. Its hero, Canute Canuteson, is a seven-foot Norwegian giant who has led a solitary existence for ten years in a miserable shanty on the plains:

> He knew by heart every individual clump of bunch grass in the miles of red shaggy prairie that stretched before his cabin. He knew it in all the deceitful loveliness of its early summer, in all the bitter barrenness of its autumn. He had seen it smitten by all

the plagues of Egypt. He had seen it parched by drought, and sogged by rain, beaten by hail, and swept by fire, and in the grass-hopper years he had seen it eaten as bare and clean as bones that the vultures had left. After the great fires he had seen it stretch for miles and miles, black and smoking as the floor of hell.[4]

So completely are the inhabitants at the mercy of nature that their lives are shattered if she merely breathes upon them roughly. Willa Cather writes:

Insanity and suicide are very common things on the Divide. They come on like an epidemic in the hot wind season. Those scorching dusty winds that blow up over the bluffs from Kansas seem to dry up the blood in men's veins as they do the sap in the corn leaves. Whenever the yellow scorch creeps down over the tender inside leaves about the ear, then the coroners prepare for active duty; for the oil of the country is burned out and it does not take long for the flame to eat up the wick. It causes no great sen-sation there when a Dane is found swinging to his own windmill tower, and most of the Poles after they have become too careless and discouraged to shave themselves keep their razors to cut their throats with.[5]

Even more significant is the effect the Divide has on those it has not killed or driven mad. The description of Canute Canuteson's cabin tells something of the psychological impact which living close to nature has produced:

The strangest things in the shanty were the wide window-sills. At first glance they looked as though they had been ruthlessly hacked and mutilated with a hatchet, but on closer inspection all the notches and holes in the wood took form and shape. There seemed to be a series of pictures. They were, in a rough way, artistic, but the figures were heavy and laboured, as though they had been cut very slowly and with very awkward instruments. There were men plowing with little horned imps sitting on their shoulders and on their horses' heads. There were men praying with a skull hanging over their heads and little demons behind them mocking their attitudes. There were men fighting with big serpents, and skeletons dancing together. All about these pictures were blooming vines and foliage such as never grew in this world, and

coiled among the branches of the vines there was always the scaly
body of a serpent, and behind every flower there was a serpent's
head. It was a veritable Dance of Death by one who had felt its
sting. In the wood box lay some boards, and every inch of them
was cut up in the same manner. Sometimes the work was very
rude and careless, and looked as though the hand of the workman
had trembled. It would sometimes have been hard to distinguish
the men from their evil geniuses but for one fact, the men were
always grave and were either toiling or praying, while the devils
were always smiling and dancing.[6]

The underlying metaphor used to describe Nebraska is that of hell.
Rejection could hardly go further. And the action of the story also
bears out the idea that the characters are the damned living in an
inferno: maddened with ten years of hard drinking and enforced
loneliness, Canute finally kidnaps the jilt of a girl he is in love with
and forces a preacher to marry them. But this is as far as his blind
impulse toward human companionship carries him; losing his nerve, he
resolves to spend the night on the ground outside his cabin, and when
she timidly invites him in, falls prostrate on the snow in front of her
door and bursts into sobs.

Of the stories of violent rejection of the Divide, the only two which
Willa Cather thought enough of to republish in her collected works are
"The Sculptor's Funeral" and "A Wagner Matinée." For bitterness
they are the equal of anything to be found in the literature of the
revolt from the village. In "The Sculptor's Funeral" (1905) a young
pupil of a famous artist, Harvey Merrick, accompanies the sculptor's
body to the little Kansas town in which he had been born and where
the last rites are to be held for him. The disciple is revolted by the
complete lack of understanding which the town shows for its most
famous son. Merrick's father seems faintly sympathetic, but his mother,
a crude, boisterous woman, "throws herself upon the coffin shrieking:
'My boy, my boy! And this is how you've come home to me!' "[7] and
a few minutes later is abusing the maid for having forgotten to make
the dressing for the chicken salad the mourners are to eat. What the
townspeople think of him is indicated by the comments of one of the
bankers present, who says:

> "It's too bad the old man's sons didn't turn out better. . . .
> He spent money enough on Harve to stock a dozen cattle-farms,
> and he might as well have poured it into Sand Creek." [8]

"Where the old man made his mistake was in sending the boy East to school. . . . There was where he got his head full of nonsense. What Harve needed, of all people, was a course in some first-class Kansas City business college." [9]

The group is interrupted by the entrance of Jim Laird, once the town's most promising lawyer, now a shyster and a drunkard. He makes a biting speech in which he withers his fellow citizens with sarcasm about their treatment of Harvey Merrick and tells them just how small and petty and mean they are:

"Why is it that reputable young men are as scarce as millionaires in Sand City? It might almost seem to a stranger that there was some way something the matter with your progressive town. . . . I'll tell you why. Because you drummed nothing but money and knavery into their ears from the time they wore knickerbockers. . . . There was only one boy ever raised in this borderland between ruffianism and civilization who didn't come to grief, and you hated Harvey Merrick more for winning out than you hated all the other boys who got under the wheels. . . . And we? Now that we've fought and lied and sweated and stolen, and hated as only the disappointed strugglers in a bitter, dead little Western town do, what have we got to show for it? Harvey Merrick wouldn't have given one sunset over your marshes for all you've got put together, and you know it. It's not for me to say why, in the inscrutable wisdom of God, a genius should ever have been called from this place of hatred and bitter waters; but I want this Boston man to know that the drivel he's been hearing here tonight is the only tribute any truly great man could have from such a lot of sick, side-tracked, burnt-dog, land-poor sharks as the here-present financiers of Sand City — upon which town may God have mercy!" [10]

After delivering this Philippic Jim Laird becomes drunk the next day and is unable to attend the funeral. He himself lives to prove his own contention that Harvey Merrick was the only boy ever raised in the town who did not come to grief, for, as Willa Cather relates with savage irony, ". . . Jim got the cold he died of driving across the Colorado mountains to defend one of Phelps's [the banker's] sons who had got into trouble out there by cutting government timber." [11]

"A Wagner Matinée" (1904), the other story that found its way into

Willa Cather's collected works, is not so extended in treatment, being hardly more than a sketch. In it the narrator tells of his Aunt Georgiana, who had once been a music teacher in Boston but had eloped with a young farmer and spent the last thirty years of her life on the Nebraska frontier. She returns to Boston on a visit, and her nephew takes her to a Wagner concert, but soon realizes that this is a mistake. The contrast between what she has and what she has given up is too much for her. As she listens to the music tears stream down her face and when it is over she tells her nephew, "I don't want to go, Clark, I don't want to go!"

> I understood. For her, just outside the door of the concert hall, lay the black pond with the cattle-tracked bluffs; the tall, unpainted house, with weather-curled boards; naked as a tower, the crook-backed ash seedlings where the dishcloths hung to dry; the gaunt, moulting turkeys picking up refuse about the kitchen door.[12]

In both of these stories Willa Cather has managed to objectify her dislike of the Divide by relating it to an external frame of reference: there is, she seems to be saying, a better world of values than that of Sand City, and that is the world of art. Harvey Merrick can break away from a hideously uncongenial family and, going East, find the values he wants in art. (But the struggle to break with his early life has maimed him, and he pays a terrible price for his achievement (he is emotionally scarred and can have no relations with people).[13]

In "A Wagner Matinée" the case is the same, although the movement of the plot is in the other direction. The protagonist, Aunt Georgiana, is in possession of the values she deems good when she is a music teacher in Boston. But she decides to give up these values for the sake of life; she elopes with her lover to the Western frontier, and lives to regret it terribly.

In these two stories Willa Cather sets up a sharp dichotomy between everyday life and the pursuit of the ideal. This dichotomy is absolute, and remains with her for the rest of her career. In her first period the ideal to be pursued is that of artistic creation. She portrays a constant tension in her protagonists between the alternate goals of the normal life of human affections and the artistic life: one must choose between them; one cannot have both. Apparently there was something in Willa Cather's make-up which prevented her from believing that there could be any compatibility at all between the normal human life and the life of the artist; most of her heroes and heroines have to tear themselves away from the bosom of their families in order to get any work done at all.[14] But, like Harvey Merrick, her artist-protagonists are emotionally crippled by the rupture with their families and feel that they can have no other human ties. It is as if they feel guilty at breaking out of a family circle and pursuing independent artistic careers, and this sense of guilt seems to recoil upon them and makes them punish themselves by refusing to have close relations with anybody on the outside. Far from being a transient feature in Willa Cather's writing, this is found throughout her career. In *Death Comes for the Archbishop*, for instance, long after she has ceased to care about the world of art as a subject, she shows the young Father Vaillant, about to leave his home in France to do missionary work in America, torn apart by the pull between family and church. Even though he knows he is doing right, he feels he is committing a wrong. "That parting was not a parting, but an escape," she says; "a running away, a betrayal of family trust for the sake of a higher trust." [15]

Although not about the Divide, one other story of violent rejection deserves treatment here. This is "Paul's Case" (1905). It was written during Willa Cather's Pittsburgh years, and examines another environment which she considered intolerable:[16] the commercial and industrial life of a great city. Although its protagonist, Paul, is ironically treated, Willa Cather is serious in rejecting the environment which he rejects, and the story remains the clearest expression in her fiction of her kinship with the aesthetic movement.

Its hero, Paul, is an adolescent schoolboy who has been suspended from Pittsburgh High School for continual impertinence to his teachers. He shows utter contempt for them and can't bear to have anyone think that he takes them seriously. He comes from an utterly drab, depressing, middle-class section of the city where the mouthing of Sunday School platitudes is combined with the desire to make money and get ahead; the only time he feels actually alive is when he is ushering at a concert at Pittsburgh's Carnegie Hall or lingering behind the scenes of a downtown theater, where he has friends among the cast. But as a result of continuing trouble with his teachers, he is deprived of all this; his father takes him out of school and puts him to work. The manager at Carnegie Hall is told to get another usher, the doorkeeper of the theater is warned not to admit him.

With all his normal avenues of escape cut off, Paul, feeling he has no choice, steals a thousand dollars of his company's money, takes a train to New York, and spends eight days of incredible luxury. He stays in one of the city's best hotels, filling his room with flowers, drinking champagne with every meal, and dressing himself in the smartest clothes he can buy. On the eighth day he reads in the paper that his robbery has been discovered; his father has refunded the money to Paul's employers, who have no intention of prosecuting him, while his minister and Sunday School teacher express hope of reclaiming the motherless lad. Whereupon Paul goes to Newark, follows the tracks out of town, dismisses his cab, waits for an approaching train, and, when the right moment comes, jumps.

It is impossible upon reading the story not to feel that Paul did right in rejecting his environment, the dismally drab neighborhood he lives in where evangelical religion and middle-class commercial aspirations combine to make a background which is thoroughly unbeautiful. It is, in fact, exactly the kind of background against which the aesthetes were protesting:

> It was a highly respectable street, where all the houses were exactly alike, and where business men of moderate means begot and reared large families of children, all of whom went to Sabbath-school and learned the shorter catechism, and were interested in arithmetic; all of whom were as exactly alike as their homes, and of a piece with the monotony in which they lived.[17]

In spite of the humor of the passage, Willa Cather is perfectly serious in her condemnation of it. There is savagery in her description of this part of Paul's life; sometimes she shows an almost vicious hatred of it:

> Paul never went up Cordelia Street without a shudder of loathing. His home was next to the house of the Cumberland minister. He approached it tonight with the nerveless sense of defeat, the hopeless feeling of sinking that he had always had when he came home. . . . The nearer he approached the house, the more absolutely unequal Paul felt to the sight of it all; his ugly sleeping chamber, the cold bath-room with the grimy zinc tub, the cracked mirror, the dripping spigots; his father, at the top of the stairs, his hairy legs sticking out from his night-shirt, his feet thrust into carpet slippers.[18]

With this kind of background, it is obvious that Paul's revolt is a protest on behalf of the good things of life; Paul is, in fact, a devotee of Pater's life of beautiful sensations. But, unlike Pater, Paul is not interested in discovering the essence or virtue of a thing; he is content merely to enjoy self-indulgently the emotions which it arouses in him:

> When the symphony began Paul sank into one of the rear seats with a long sigh of relief, and lost himself as he had done before the Rico [a painting he had admired]. It was not that symphonies, as such, meant anything in particular to Paul, but the first sigh of the instruments seemed to free some hilarious spirit within him; something that struggled there like the Genius in the bottle found by the Arab fisherman. He felt a sudden zest of life; the lights danced before his eyes and the concert hall blazed into unimaginable splendour.[19]

> Several of Paul's teachers had a theory that his imagination had been perverted by garish fiction; but the truth was, he scarcely ever read at all. The books at home were not such as would either tempt or corrupt a youthful mind, and as for reading the novels that some of his friends urged upon him — well, he got what he wanted more quickly from music; any sort of music, from an orchestra to a barrel organ. He needed only the spark, the indescribable thrill that made his imagination master of his senses, and he could make plots and pictures enough of his own.[20]

A link with the decadence of the nineties is established by the fact that Paul continually exalts the artificial over the natural, and Willa Cather gives a hint as to why this should be so; in commenting on his passion for theaters she remarks:

> Perhaps it was because, in Paul's world, the natural always wore the guise of ugliness, that a certain element of artificiality seemed to him necessary in beauty. Perhaps it was because his experience in life elsewhere was so full of Sabbath-school picnics, petty economics, wholesome advice as to how to succeed in life, and the unescapable odors of cooking, that he found this existence so alluring, these smartly clad men and women so attractive, that he was so moved by these starry apple orchards that bloomed perennially under the lime-light.[21]

Something has happened to the gospel of Pater; Paul is much more of a decadent than an aesthete. He shares all the traits carefully cultivated by members of the decadent movement: the aristocratic pose, the personal dandyism, the love of artificiality, the desire to shock people. Paul thinks himself greatly superior to his teachers in school and lets them know it; he pays a great deal of attention to dress and always wears a red carnation; his attitude is flippant and contemptuous in the extreme, and he goes out of his way to irritate people. As if this were not enough, he also displays some of that movement's least attractive traits: the lack of any real talent, the self-indulgence, the emphasis on the abnormal and perverse.

Willa Cather's treatment of Paul is sympathetic but critical. On the one hand she compares him with "a miserable street cat set at bay by a ring of tormentors," [22] and remarks of his New York stay: "There was this to be said for him, that he wore his spoils with dignity and in no way made himself conspicuous. His chief greediness lay in his ears and eyes, and his excesses were not offensive ones." [23] But she also suggests that he is a sick boy, that he is weak and self-indulgent, and that he is evasive when facing unpleasant realities. From the very first page she gives indications of the gulf that exists between her and her creation. His pupils are described as being abnormally large, "as though he were addicted to bella-donna"; they have a glassy glitter to them; and he has "a sort of hysterically defiant manner" [24] toward his teachers, to whom he feels a physical aversion. One of them voices the opinion that he is not well.[25] More important, Paul has wildly romantic notions about the nature of the artistic life. Willa Cather suggests that he does not see artists as they really are:

> The soloist chanced to be a German woman, by no means in her first youth, and the mother of many children; but she wore a satin gown and a tiara, and she had that indefinable air of achievement, that world-shine upon her which always blinded Paul to any possible defects.[26]

> The members of the stock company were vastly amused when some of Paul's stories reached them — especially the women. They were hard-working women, most of them supporting indolent husbands or brothers, and they laughed rather bitterly at having stirred the boy to such fervid and florid inventions. They agreed with the faculty and with his father, that Paul's was a bad case.[27]

Another and still more serious objection, from Willa Cather's point of view, is Paul's utter inability to persevere in the course that would bring him the kind of life he wants. He is too eager to seize today and let tomorrow go. As he sits in the hotel dining room reflecting that his robbery has been found out and that his father is coming for him, he muses:

> He might have caught an outbound steamer and been well out of their clutches before now. But the other side of the world had seemed too far away and too uncertain then; he could not have waited for it; his need had been too sharp. If he had to choose over again, he would do the same thing tomorrow.[28]

As he throws himself under the wheels of the train, the thought occurs to him again of the folly of all that he has left undone: "There flashed through his brain, clearer than ever before, the blue of Adriatic water, the yellow of Algerian sands."[29] Instead of squandering his money in New York he might have gone abroad to some place where Cordelia Street could never catch up with him. But he is too impatient and self-indulgent for that; instead he turns his back on the one thing that might have saved him.

The reason for Paul's failure is his essential passivity. He wants to be a spectator, not an actor; when he was in New York he had no desire to meet or know the fabulous people who floated around him; "The mere stage properties were all he contended for."[30] After making up his mind to commit suicide he sits in his room for half an hour staring at the revolver. "But he told himself that was not the way,"[31] so he goes downstairs and takes a cab for the ferry. Shooting himself requires too much activity, too much effort of the will; Paul is quite right in believing that it is not for him. He is the direct opposite of Willa Cather's later protagonists who win everything they win through asserting themselves and their wills. Paul refuses to assert himself at all.

An important consideration in "Paul's Case," and one which was to play a great part in Willa Cather's subsequent fiction, is the role of money. Lionel Trilling has spoken of the fascination which the idea of money has exerted on the imagination of the Western World.[32] In Paul's case the effect is both simple and powerful: money is for him the means of gratifying all his desires. Although Paul has no use for Cordelia Street and the people at the bottom of the commercial hierarchy, he has considerable respect for those at the top; they are able to do the things he can only dream of doing. This emerges in a Sunday afternoon conversation Paul's father has with one of their neighbors:

> The young man was relating how his chief, now cruising in the Mediterranean, kept in touch with all the details of the business,

arranging his office hours on his yacht just as though he were at home, and "knocking off work enough to keep two stenographers busy." His father told, in turn, the plan his corporation was considering, of putting in an electric railway plant at Cairo. Paul snapped his teeth; he had an awful apprehension that they might spoil it all before he got there. Yet he rather liked to hear these legends of the iron kings, that were told and retold on Sundays and holidays; these stories of palaces in Venice, yachts on the Mediterranean, and high play at Monte Carlo appealed to his fancy, and he was interested in the triumphs of cash boys who had become famous, though he had no mind for the cash-boy stage.[33]

Paul shows the same fascination with the very rich, the belief that wealth is the high road to the good life, that preoccupied the early F. Scott Fitzgerald and which he portrayed in the character of Jay Gatsby. This brings up a specifically modern problem: in a commercial society one has to have money, whether one is willing to slave for it or not. It posed a special problem for the aesthetes, unless they had inherited wealth; they needed money to enjoy the beautiful things they wanted, yet were repulsed by the way in which it had to be obtained in the modern world. Many of Willa Cather's protagonists had to face this problem, particularly those she created in her third period.

As the story progresses money becomes even more important. Upon returning to his New York hotel Paul becomes aware that

. . . on every side towered the glaring affirmation of the omnipotence of wealth.

The boy set his teeth and drew his shoulders together in a spasm of realization; the plot of all his dramas, the text of all romances, the nerve-stuff of all sensations was whirling about him like the snow flakes. . . .

. . . when the roseate tinge of his champagne was added — that cold, precious, bubbling stuff that creamed and foamed in his glass — Paul wondered that there were honest men in the world at all. This was what all the world was fighting for, he reflected; this was what all the struggle was about.[34]

And when he has reached the end of his rope he reflects: "He had not a hundred dollars left; and he knew now, more than ever, that money was everything, the wall that stood between all he loathed and all he wanted." [35] Jay Gatsby's dream of the good life obtained through wealth is with Paul to the very end.

"Paul's Case" is also remarkable as the first piece of Willa Cather's fiction to show the influence of Flaubert. All her life she was an ardent admirer of the French novelist; of her college days E. K. Brown writes: "She is remembered in Lincoln as a devotee of Flaubert, and of *Madame Bovary* in particular: she often carried a copy of that novel." [36] As late as 1930, she herself wrote after a meeting with Flaubert's niece, "It was like being suddenly brought up against a mountain of memories. One could not see round it; one could only stupidly realize that in this mountain . . . lay most of one's mental past." [37] "Paul's Case" owes a double debt to Flaubert. In the first place the story is a miniature *Madame Bovary* in its structure, being based on a sustained ironic contrast between romantic aspiration and disillusioning reality. Paul is continually seeking an illusory happiness, only to find it crumble at the touch of the everyday:

> He felt a sudden zest of life; the lights danced before his eyes and the concert hall blazed into unimaginable splendour. . . . After a concert was over, Paul was often irritable and wretched. . . . He had the feeling of not being able to let down; of its being impossible to give up this delicious excitement which was the only thing that could be called living at all.[38]

In "Paul's Case" Willa Cather achieved a sustained irony similar although not equal to Flaubert's in *Madame Bovary*. The fact that it has a literary model may explain why it is the only story she ever wrote in which the ironic tone is consistently maintained. But there is another way in which she was indebted to Flaubert, that Flaubert who had despised the cautious commercialism of Louis Philippe's France as being the enemy of all the arts and in his youth had adopted as his maxim, "Hatred of the bourgeois is the beginning of virtue." [39] Flaubert's reaction to his native Rouen had been very much like Willa Cather's reaction to Red Cloud,[40] and the bourgeois of Paris bore a striking resemblance to the burghers of Pittsburgh. This gives a clue to the link between "Paul's Case" and the earlier stories of violent rejection of Nebraska. Willa Cather shared Flaubert's loathing for all that was sordid and inartistic in modern bourgeois civilization, whether found in big city or small town or barren countryside. She was able to generalize her dislike of the Divide into a condemnation of commercialism. All that she dislikes about modern life is symbolized by Cordelia Street.

PURSUIT OF THE IDEAL

In her first published volume of short stories, *The Troll Garden* (1905), Willa Cather included only three of her tales of violent rejection. These were "The Sculptor's Funeral," "A Wagner Matinée," and "Paul's Case." The other stories — "Flavia and Her Artists," "The Garden Lodge," "A Death in the Desert," and "The Marriage of Phaedra" — all have to do with that milieu of which Edith Wharton and Henry James had written, and in which Willa Cather imagined that the pursuit of her particular ideal could best be carried on: the world of the wealthy, sophisticated, cosmopolitan, upper class who were sometimes patrons of the arts, and the world of artists themselves.[41] Although in "Paul's Case" she showed an acute awareness of the danger of a passive idolization of the beautiful, she still felt that it was in the pursuit of beauty, that the good life should be found. This milieu is just the kind that would most naturally appeal to a young girl brought up in Nebraska who had gone East after graduation and was discovering the glamour of the cities of the Eastern seaboard and of Europe.

The best way to characterize these stories is to describe them as watered-down Henry James. In them Willa Cather tries to emulate James's ironic awareness of the relation between the artist and the middle class and the recoil of art's effect upon the life of the artist and those around him. But she lacks the subtlety of the Jamesian analysis of motives and is often distressingly obvious. None of these stories is particularly memorable, a fact which Willa Cather herself may have realized, for she did not include any of them in her next volume of short stories, *Youth and the Bright Medusa* (1920).

The story I will attempt to analyze as an example of Willa Cather's Jamesian phase is "The Marriage of Phaedra" (1905). In it an American painter named MacMaster makes a pilgrimage to the studio of the great Hugh Treffinger, an artist of Pre-Raphaelite cast who has died some three years earlier. MacMaster wins the confidence of Treffinger's devoted cockney servant James and from him learns something of the inner realities of the famous painter's personal life. Treffinger had risen by his own merits from the London slum in which he was born but had contracted an unfortunate marriage with a lady of high social standing who understands nothing about art and looks down upon her husband because of his origin. Shortly after MacMaster arrives on the scene, Lady Ellen Treffinger makes arrangements to sell her husband's unfinished masterpiece, *The Marriage of Phaedra,* to an art dealer from Australia in order to finance her own second marriage. This displeases MacMaster and horrifies James, who goes to the length of stealing the picture and proposes to hide it in Paris until the scandal dies down. He is only with difficulty dissuaded from doing so by the American painter, who persuades him that such an impulsive gesture of loyalty will do no good. So, at the end of the story, the priceless art treasure is ready to start for Australia, mourned alike by the dead artist's admirer and his man.

The story's theme is the predicament the artist finds himself in in a society which is suspicious of and hostile to art. In this it resembles James's "The Author of Beltraffio," whose hero also has married a cold woman of the British aristocracy who has no sympathy whatever with her husband's artistic career. Aside from the theme, the most obviously Jamesian thing about the story is the attempt at the Jamesian point of view: the drama of Treffinger's unhappy marriage is seen through MacMaster's eyes. But the Jamesian point of view, although attempted, is not consistently adhered to. Bits of dialogue such as:

> "Isn't there rather a surplus of books on that subject [Treffinger's life] already?"
>
> "Such as they are. Oh, I've read them all." Here MacMaster faced Lady Mary triumphantly. "He has quite escaped your amiable critics," he added, smiling.[42]

and

> "It's rather a fine touch of irony," he reflected, "that he [the servant James], who is so out of it, should be the one to really care. Poor Treffinger," he murmured as, with a rather spiritless smile, he turned back into his hotel. . . .[43]

alternate with intrusions of the author's opinions in the form of direct statement:

> He had always believed that the key to Treffinger's individuality lay in his singular education; in the *Roman de la Rose,* in Boccaccio, and Amadis, those works which had literally transcribed themselves upon the blank soul of the London street boy, and through which he had been born into the world of spiritual things.[44]

> When his researches led him occasionally to visit the studios of Treffinger's friends and erstwhile disciples, he found their Treffinger manner fading as the ring of Treffinger's personality died out in them. One by one they were stealing back into the fold of national British art; the hand that wound them up was still.[45]

Sometimes Willa Cather starts out in what appears to be a Jamesian manner only to have it fall disconcertingly flat:

When MacMaster walked back to High Street to take his buss [*sic*], his mind was divided between two exultant convictions. He felt that he had not only found Treffinger's greatest picture, but that, in James, he had discovered a kind of cryptic index to the painter's personality — a clue which, if tactfully followed, might lead to much.[46]

The burden of the story is Lady Ellen Treffinger's cold implacable dislike of the vocation to which her husband has given his life. Behind this lies Mark Ambient's agonized cry in "The Author of Beltraffio": "There's a hatred of art, there's a hatred of literature!"[47] In the due course of time the facts are made known to MacMaster by the faithful James:

> "You see, sir, Lydy Elling was always cruel 'ard on the *Marriage*. From the first it went wrong, an' Sir 'Ugh was out of temper pretty constant. She came into the studio one day and looked at the picture an' asked 'im why 'e didn't throw it up an' quit a-worriting 'imself. He answered sharp, an' with that she said as 'ow she didn't see w'at there was to make such a row about, no'ow. She spoke 'er mind about that picture, free; an' Sir 'Ugh swore 'ot an' let a 'andful of brushes fly at 'is study, an' Lydy Elling picks up 'er skirts careful an' chill, an' drifted out of the studio with 'er eyes calm and 'er chin 'igh. . . ."[48]

Treffinger had always had an aversion to letting any unfinished work of his come before the public eye; in this he is very much like his creator, Willa Cather.[49] Since he was convinced that *The Marriage of Phaedra* was his masterpiece, he was especially anxious about it, and on his deathbed indicated that he did not want it sold. This is why his servant goes to the length of stealing the picture after Lady Ellen disregards her husband's dying wish and sells it to a dealer who is not only Jewish (almost always a symbol of crass commercialism in Willa Cather) but also proposes to take it to Australia, which is presumably far beyond the purlieus of art.[50]

Much of the story's weakness which is not due to the inept imitation of James lies in the substitution of stereotypes for fully analyzed characters. The mawkish characterization of the faithful cockney servant is a case in point ("I'm a-going to enlist, or try the gold-fields. I've lived too long with h'artists; I'd never give satisfaction in livery now. You know 'ow it is yourself, sir; there aynt no life like it, no'ow");[51] the portrayal of the vulgar commercial Jew is another. And the story's final sentence — "To all intents and purposes the *Marriage of Phaedra* was already entombed in a vague continent in the Pacific, somewhere on the other side of the world." [52] — has an unattractive snobbery in it which sits ill on a girl who had grown up in Red Cloud. It is safe to say that in this story and in others like it Willa Cather was dealing with a milieu with which she was not entirely familiar and with characters which she had neither fully understood nor completely thought out.[53]

In summarizing Willa Cather's published fiction up to the time of the appearance of her first novel, I have described two kinds of stories: stories of violent rejection of the Divide, later broadened to include rejection of any unworthy environment; and stories of the pursuit of the ideal carried on in a society which can best be characterized as wealthy, metropolitan, and urbane. The stories of violent rejection are extremely powerful, and in one of them, "Paul's Case," the theme of rejection is handled ironically: the environment is as bad as it can be, but the boy who rejects it is self-indulgent, hysterical, and perhaps insane. The stories of the pursuit of the ideal, on the other hand, whenever they try to affirm anything, are uniformly vapid. It is for this reason that I call Willa Cather's early art an art of repudiation and denial. Moreover, even the stories of pursuit of the ideal can be read as stories of a different kind of repudiation. In "The Marriage of Phaedra" Treffinger and his wife reject each other and continue their respective careers unperturbed. In all these stories of Willa Cather's first period the rejection is based on a lack of understanding of some sort, whether on the part of the person one loves or on the part of one's environment.

A noteworthy feature of the stories of the "artistic" life is their extraordinarily static quality. The stories which describe with loathing the stunting effects of life on the frontier derive their vitality and emotional impact from a single act of rejection, such as the drunken lawyer's speech in "The Sculptor's Funeral" or Aunt Georgiana's crying, in "A Wagner Matinée," "I don't want to go, Clark, I don't want to go!" But the stories about the pursuit of the ideal in the world of art do not have even that. It is evident that at this stage of her career Willa Cather has nothing in particular to affirm, except a vague feeling that the artistic life in general is the proper subject matter for a young writer who aspires to shine.

CREATIVITY *vs.* LIFE

With the exception of "On the Divide" (which was never republished after its first appearance), all of the stories treated so far have to do with one of the basic conflicts in Willa Cather's fiction: that between normal human affections, represented by parents, husband, or wife, or lover, and the pursuit of the ideal, which at this stage usually but not always involves the creation and enjoyment of beauty in the world of art. Willa Cather's first novel, *Alexander's Bridge*, is based squarely on this conflict; it is in fact the fullest exploration of the conflict she ever made. In only one important respect does it differ from the earlier stories; its hero is not an artist but a civil engineer. But even this turns out upon examination to be not so great a difference as it might at first seem, for Bartley Alexander resembles Willa Cather's artist heroes and heroines in being essentially creative in his approach to his work.

The plot reveals much of the confusion and conflict going on in the hero's mind between the two ideals. When the book opens Alexander is forty-two years old and at the height of his career as a famous bridge builder. Besides his professional success he has a wife whom he apparently loves and a beautiful Boston home, and yet he finds himself unable to be happy. He misses his youth and the freshness of the feelings he once had had but which he has no longer. Then on a trip to London he meets Hilda Burgoyne, an actress he had known and loved a dozen years previously; and, wanting to renew his youth and make the most out of life, he renews his liaison with her. Afterwards, each time his business calls him to England, he stops off to see Hilda at her establishment in London's West End.

While this is taking place he is faced with the greatest challenge to his professional ability he has ever had when he contracts to build the great Moorlock bridge in Canada, the longest single-span cantilever in the world. An emotional crisis develops and keeps him from supervising the work as carefully as he should; he decides to give Hilda up but cannot bring himself to do it, although he goes to the length of writing her a letter of renunciation. Meanwhile the great Moorlock bridge shows signs of strain and starts to buckle. His foreman tries to telegraph him to warn him of the danger and get him to appear on the scene. But Alexander, who was already on his way, stops off at New York to be with Hilda, and so the telegram announcing the danger signals never reaches him. Construction on the bridge goes on, and Alexander reaches it the next day, too late, for just after he arrives the gigantic structure collapses under his feet, killing him and half a hundred workmen besides.

The theme is stated in the first few pages when Lucius Wilson, an old professor of his, visits him in Boston and congratulates him on his success. Lucius had always been afraid that Alexander had a weak spot in him and that some day he would buckle under some unusual strain, but now he is convinced that he was wrong. "You've changed," he says. "You have decided to leave some birds in the bushes. You used to want them all."

> Alexander's chair creaked. "I still want a good many," he said rather gloomily. "After all, life doesn't offer a man much. You work like the devil and think you're getting on, and suddenly you discover that you've only been getting yourself tied up. A million details drink you dry. Your life keeps going for things you don't want, and all the while you are being built alive into a social structure you don't care a rap about. I sometimes wonder what sort of chap I'd have been if I hadn't been this sort; I want to go and live out his potentialities, too. I haven't forgotten that there are birds in the bushes." [54]

What troubles Alexander is the incompatibility of complete self-development with the duties imposed upon him by his professional career. Apparently he regards his marriage as part of the social structure he doesn't care a rap about; Willa Cather gives no hint that emotional satisfaction might come to him through a relationship with his wife, although he seems to get along with her well enough. Alexander's flaw is that he wants to develop all facets of his personality, and he can't do this without bringing about his own ruin. He wants to have his triumphant career as bridge builder, his beautiful wife, his tasteful home in Boston, *and* his love affair with Hilda. He wants to have everything and give up nothing; in middle life he develops a renewed interest in the birds in the bushes.

Viewed in the most favorable light, Alexander is a would-be superman, a solitary hero who can only accomplish what he has to accomplish alone and who doesn't want to be built into society because he is impatient of the restraints on his creativity which would result from obligations to others. This is Alexander's view of himself, and emerges in his reverie upon meeting Hilda after an interval of ten years:

> Although Alexander often told himself he had never put more into his work than he had done in the last few years, he had to admit that he had never got so little out of it. He was paying for success, too, in the demands made on his time by boards of civic enterprise and committees of public welfare. The obligations im-

posed by his wife's fortune and position were sometimes distracting
to a man who followed his profession, and he was expected to be
interested in a great many worthy endeavors on her account as
well as on his own. His existence was becoming a network of
great and little details. He had expected that success would bring
him freedom and power; but it had brought only power that was
in itself another kind of restraint. He had always meant to keep
his personal liberty at all costs, as old MacKellar, his first chief had
done. . . . He happened to be engaged in work of public utility,
but he was not willing to become what is called a public man.
He found himself living exactly the kind of life he had determined
to escape. . . . The one thing he had really wanted all his life
was to be free; and there was still something unconquered in him,
something besides the strong work-horse that his profession had
made of him.[55]

Seen in its most unfavorable light, Alexander's wish to keep himself
free resembles the childish refusal to accept responsibility seen in the
hedonism of the twenties, for instance in the pre-1929 career of F.
Scott Fitzgerald. Willa Cather's description of her hero lays him open
to this charge:

He thought, as he sat there, about a great many things, about
his own youth and Hilda's; above all, he thought of how glorious
it had been, and how quickly it had passed, and, when it had
passed, how little worth while everything was. None of the things
he had gained in the least compensated.[56]

Here Willa Cather is strongly implying that he would very much like
to remain forever young. And when she says, ". . . he walked shoulder
to shoulder with a shadowy companion — not little Hilda Burgoyne,
by any means, but someone vastly dearer to him than she had ever
been — his own young self . . ." [57] she makes it unmistakably clear
that his real love is bestowed not upon Hilda at all but upon his own
lost youth. Seen in this light, Alexander's wish to stay perpetually
unenthralled becomes the desire to remain in a permanent state of
youth, freedom, and irresponsibility.

What one thinks of Alexander will depend in part at least on one's
judgment of the concept of the superman; whether one considers it a
heroic ideal or an adolescent one. Willa Cather inclines to the former
view. The book's main conflict lies between a high evaluation of the

superman ideal on the one hand and a healthy respect for traditional concepts of social responsibility on the other; it derives from the struggle in Alexander's mind between two warring concepts of loyalty: loyalty to the code of the society of which he is a part and loyalty to the fullest possible development of himself. The theme of the individual versus society is an ancient one and is certainly capable of tragic development. But in *Alexander's Bridge* the tragedy fails to come off.

The trouble with the book is a double one, arising in part from a failure of moral vision and in part from a structural defect. First, it seems inconceivable that a man could rise to the position and eminence that Alexander is supposed to have achieved and still believe that success could bring with it freedom, or that power does not involve restraints. Yet Willa Cather is sympathetic toward his ideal, and even suggests that MacKellar, his first chief, had been able to achieve it. If Alexander's desire not to leave any of the birds in the bushes is as immature as it seems, then the tragic conflict seen by Willa Cather is not tragic at all, for her hero is too childish to be universal. Second, there is no necessary connection between his sin and its punishment; the man's moral downfall and professional defeat are not organically related. The main symbol in the book is the collapse of the bridge, which is supposed to be the outward sign of Alexander's inner decay. But this symbol turns out to be mechanical in every sense of the word. There is no reason given in the story why Alexander should be killed or have his bridge collapse because of his love affair with Hilda. If he had made a continual practice of stopping off with Hilda on his way up to Canada the situation might be different, but as it is the telegram announcing the bridge's impending doom arrives on the one night of all nights when Alexander has not let his foreman know where he is. Thus the catastrophe upon which the whole story turns is based on mere coincidence. No doubt what Willa Cather intended to show by her manipulation of the plot was the workings of poetic justice. But what she actually demonstrated was her own fear of human emotions, since a single deviation from the path of prudence is shown as leading to death.[58]

Alexander's failure lies in his insistence on trying to be both creative and human at the same time; to carry on his art of bridge-building and simultaneously to gain emotional fulfillment from a love affair with Hilda. There is, Willa Cather is saying, a tragic split between creativity and life, particularly that part of life which constitutes human love and sexual passion. She apparently intends the crisis of the story to occur when Alexander has to make a choice between Hilda and his career, and drives home the point that, whichever one he chooses, he will lose something necessary and vital. We have met this theme before, and its persistence in Willa Cather's fiction suggests a struggle going on in her own mind. It is even possible to read *Alexander's Bridge* as an allegory of Miss Cather's divided psyche, torn between the editorial job at *McClure's*, which she was thinking of leaving at that time, and her devotion to writing, her first love. This is especially probable since we have seen that she tended to regard artistic creation as a substitute for human relations. At any rate, Alexander's fate foreshadows in some measure the fate of his creator. When he is unable to come to terms with passionate love, his creativity destroys him; something of the same sort happened in later life to Willa Cather herself, and probably accounts for her return to the past.

If my allegorical interpretation is correct and Hilda, Alexander's first love, indeed represents to Willa Cather the attractive but dangerous nature of devotion to solitary creation such as writing (as opposed to the more social but less soul-satisfying kind of creation to be found in magazine work — or, in Alexander's case, bridge-building), then *Alexander's Bridge* reveals Willa Cather as being not very comfortable about the whole art-for-art's-sake idea. Convinced that art is tremendously important, she nevertheless is uneasy about giving all to art, and is at least partially persuaded that art-for-art's-sake may be mere self-indulgence. If so, it is the last time she is willing to let us see her doubts, for it is the last time she expresses her hesitation before her readers. From now on the characters in her fiction are to reveal a marble facade to their public; henceforth her artist-protagonists are portrayed as being always above conflict and always right.[59]

THE TRIUMPH OF ART

After *Alexander's Bridge* the next book Willa Cather wrote was *O Pioneers!* (1913), the first of her prairie novels. This represents a step in a new direction and will be examined later on. But when *O Pioneers!* was completed she turned once more to the world of art, making it the subject of several short stories and of one novel, *The Song of the Lark* (1915). It is not a very good novel, and Willa Cather herself later became dissatisfied with it.[60] But it is the only full-length portrait of an artist she ever gave, so it is worth examining to see what light it throws upon her views on art.

The Song of the Lark is a success story, telling of the fierce struggle of Thea Kronborg to fight her way up from the little Colorado town in which she was born to success and fame as an opera singer in Europe and America. To do this she has to break away completely from the smug provincial world in which she grew up; consequently the story moves from Moonstone to Chicago, to Arizona, to Germany, and finally to New York, where Thea is left in a blaze of glory in front of the footlights of the Metropolitan Opera. To get where she wants she has to abandon every human tie, including her neighbors, her friends, her family, and each of the four men who loved her.[61]

The Song of the Lark is a novel about the development of an artist, but even more it is a book on conversion. Such books have been common in the history of Western thought. St. Augustine wrote about his conversion from worldly pleasure to Christianity, Rousseau wrote about his conversion to feeling; Thea Kronborg is converted to art. She is in a very real sense "born again" into a state in which art means everything and human ties nothing. The exact nature of her conversion is extremely revealing.

Thea's rebirth occurs toward the end of her first year in Chicago. She has just gone to a symphony concert — the first one she has been to since her arrival in the city — and is overwhelmed by it. The program includes Dvorak's *New World Symphony* and excerpts from *Das Rheingold,* the first operatic music she has ever heard, and Thea emerges from it rhapsodic and transfigured; a new dimension has been added to her experience. What follows is best told by Willa Cather:

> When Thea emerged from the concert hall, Mrs. Lorch's predictions had been fulfilled. A furious gale was beating over the city from Lake Michigan. The streets were full of cold, hurrying, angry people, running for street-cars and barking at each other. The sun was setting in a clear, windy sky, that flamed with red as if there were a great fire somewhere on the edge of the city. For almost the first time Thea was conscious of the city itself, of the congestion of life all about her, of the brutality and power of those streams that flowed in the streets, threatening to drive one under. People jostled her, ran into her, poked her aside with their elbows, uttering angry exclamations. She got on the wrong car and was roughly ejected by the conductor at a windy corner, in front of a saloon. She stood there dazed and shivering. The cars passed, screaming as they rounded curves, but either they were full to the doors, or were bound for places where she did not want to go. Her hands were so cold that she took off her tight kid gloves. The street lights began to gleam in the dusk. A young man came out of the saloon and stood eyeing her questioningly

while he lit a cigarette. "Looking for a friend tonight?" he asked.
Thea drew up the collar of her cape and walked on a few paces.
The young man shrugged his shoulders and drifted away.

Thea came back to the corner and stood there irresolutely. An
old man approached her. He, too, seemed to be waiting for a car.
He wore an overcoat with a black fur collar, his gray mustache was
waxed into little points, and his eyes were watery. He kept thrusting his face up near hers. Her hat blew off and he ran after it — a
stiff, pitiful skip he had — and brought it back to her. Then,
while she was pinning her hat on, her cape blew up, and he held it
down for her, looking at her intently. His face worked as if he
were going to cry or were frightened. He leaned over and whispered
something to her. It struck her as curious that he was really quite
timid, like an old beggar. "Oh, let me *alone!*" she cried miserably
between her teeth. He vanished, disappeared like the Devil in a
play. But in the meantime something had got away from her;
she could not remember how the violins came in after the horns,
just there. When her cape blew up, perhaps — Why did these men
torment her? A cloud of dust blew in her face and blinded her.
There was some power abroad in the world bent upon taking
away from her that feeling with which she had come out of the
concert hall. Everything seemed to sweep down on her to tear it
out from under her cape. If one had that, the world became one's
enemy; people, buildings, wagons, cars, rushed at one to crush
it under, to make one let go of it. Thea glared round her at the
crowds, the ugly, sprawling streets, the long lines of lights, and
she was not crying now. Her eyes were brighter than even Harsanyi had ever seen them. All these things and people were no
longer remote and negligible; they had to be met, they were lined
up against her, they were there to take something from her. Very
well; they should never have it. They might trample her to death,
but they should never have it. As long as she lived that ecstasy
was going to be hers. She would live for it, work for it, die for it;
but she was going to have it, time after time, height after height.
She could hear the crash of the orchestra again, and she rose on the
brasses. She would have it, what the trumpets were singing! She
would have it, have it, — it! Under the old cape she pressed her
hands upon her heaving bosom, that was a little girl's no longer.[62]

Here we have an experience which superficially resembles the traditional religious conversion. However it is not the kind of positive con-

version experienced by a St. Paul or a John Wesley, but a negative conversion like that undergone by Carlyle when he was "born again" on the sidewalks of Leith Walk, Edinburgh. Thea comes not so much to love good as to hate evil. Her response is like that of Carlyle's Teufelsdröckh in *Sartor Resartus* in its passionate self-assertion and defiance of the devil; like Teufelsdröckh she says in effect: "I am not thine but Free, and forever hate thee!" [63] What she hates, of course, is the sum total of all the things that tend to drag her down and keep her from becoming the great artist she wants to be. But there is an important difference between her experience and Teufelsdröckh's. As is the case with Carlyle's hero, Thea's conversion is preceded by a dark night of the soul; but, unlike his, her dark night is associated, not with doubt and unbelief, but with being accosted sexually. This fact, unimportant in itself, becomes important in view of her general treatment of the relations between the sexes in this book, and indeed in her entire career.

Consider the way in which Willa Cather has manipulated the plot. There are four men who are interested in Thea, and all four of them are placed out of bounds for her in one way or another. Ray Kennedy, who is unsuitable because he lacks education, is killed off in a railroad wreck; Dr. Archie is made considerably older than Thea and is already married to a shrewish wife; Fred Ottenburg, who is near Thea's age, has an affair with her and wants to marry her, but is bound to a wife who is hopelessly insane; and the Swedish singer Nordquist, who also wants to marry her, has a wife who will divorce him only upon presentation of a large amount of money, an offer which Thea indignantly refuses. These illustrations show Willa Cather rigging the plot against marriage for Thea and satisfactory relations between men and women in general. They serve as justification for her refusal to allow her artists to have more than abortive encounters with the opposite sex; most of the men interested in Thea do not drift out of her life, but her relations with them remain perpetually casual. This suggests not only a deep fear of emotional entanglement on Willa Cather's part but also a belief that art could and should be used as a substitute for a continued physical relationship.

To eliminate all misunderstanding about the lengths to which renunciation must go, Willa Cather even has Thea give up her mother. Mrs. Kronborg has been the only relative who had understood her or given her much encouragement,[64] but when the time comes Thea breaks with her, too, as well as with the rest. "Her mother was all right, but her mother had to be on both sides," [65] as Willa Cather says. Much later in the story Thea refuses to come home from Germany during Mrs. Kronborg's final illness because she has been given the chance to play her first big opera role and doesn't want to miss it. This defection, like that of James Joyce's Stephen Daedalus, is impressive but unattractive. Willa Cather makes her point, but only at the expense of losing a good deal of the reader's sympathy for her heroine.

Thea's strength to achieve these prodigies of renunciation arises from the ruthless force of her will, her determination to succeed at any cost. Save for Myra Henshawe, she is the most irritatingly aggressive of all Willa Cather's heroines. Her chief asset in Willa Cather's eyes is a sublime and, to the reader, often inhuman confidence in her own ability and destiny. The springs of her self-pride are fed by the men who befriend her in her youth and serve as guideposts to point the way she is to go. A prime example is Dr. Wunsch. This battered old derelict of a musician, stranded in the little Colorado town in which she lives, recognizes her ability and makes her a present of the score of a Gluck opera, the first great music she has ever seen. He tells her:

> "Nothing is far and nothing is near, if one desires. The world is little, people are little, human life is little. There is only one big thing — desire. And before it, when it is big, all is little. It brought Columbus across the sea in a little boat, *und so weiter*." [66]

Here is a character whose life is supposed to be a complete failure except for one thing: he was able to recognize musical talent in one young person of genius and help start her on her career. As an artistic creation he is superb; he is the most memorable and convincing character in the entire novel, but he just does not fit in with Willa Cather's doctrine (here put in his mouth) of the supremacy of the will. For according to this doctrine how could one of the vanquished in life give aid to one of the victors? The fact that he plays such a role in the book shows Willa Cather to have a more complex awareness of the delicate tendrils connecting success and failure than is suggested by her avowed theory. In this, as in other things, her intuitive descriptions prove better than her ability to see the implications of what she has perceived.

If Thea's negative conversion, her denial of the importance of human relations, is more convincing than her positive conversion to art, it is not for lack of trying on Willa Cather's part. The last three hundred pages of this five-hundred-page book [67] are supposed to show the dedicated artist at work. But they do not show it; they only state it.

Instead of portraying Thea dramatically in some operatic role, Willa Cather reports conversations of her admirers. Her greatness is never shown, but is talked about *ad nauseum:*

> "You see, Archie, it's all very simple, a natural development" [Fred Ottenburg tells Thea's patron]. "It's exactly what Mahler said back there in the beginning, when she sang *Woglinde.* It's the idea, the basic idea, pulsing behind every bar she sings. She simplifies a character down to the musical idea it's built on, and makes everything conform to that. The people who chatter about her being a great actress don't seem to get the notion of where *she* gets the notion. It all goes back to her original endowment, her tremendous musical talent." [68]

Much of the book's last three-fifths, written in this vein, is appallingly monotonous; the characters are either insipid or actively revolting in their abject spaniel-like devotion:

> Fred thrust his hands into his pockets and leaned back against the piano. "Of course, even a stupid woman could get effects with such machinery: such a voice and body and face. But they couldn't possibly belong to a stupid woman, could they?" Landry shook his head. "It's personality; that's as near as you can come to it. That's what constitutes the real equipment. What she does is interesting because she does it." [69]

Such a passage reveals Willa Cather at her crudest and blindest. It shows as little psychological insight as it does artistry; since the character of Thea which emerges is not that of a charmer but of an aggressive, domineering, and infuriatingly self-absorbed woman, it requires more to convince the reader of her greatness than the report of a servile male adoration which comes to seem fatuous and grotesque.

Since this is a book about an artist, we might well look at Thea's views on art. But here an inconsistency arises, for Willa Cather presents two conflicting views on the subject and does not bother to reconcile them. Sometimes she looks upon art as an expression of spontaneity, sometimes as an expression of discipline. The first of these is voiced by Dr. Wunsch, who teaches Thea to trust not only in her own will but also in her own spontaneity and passion:

> He pulled himself up from his clumsy stoop and folded his arms. "But it is necessary to know if you know somethings. Somethings

cannot be taught. If you not know in the beginning, you not know
in the end. For a singer there must be something in the inside from
the beginning. . . ."

Wunsch began to pace the arbor, rubbing his hands together.
The dark flush of his face had spread up under the iron-gray
bristles of his beard. . . . "Oh, much you can learn! *Aber nicht
die Americanischen Fräulein.* They have nothing inside them,"
striking his chest with both fists. "They are like the ones in the
Märchen, a grinning face and hollow in the insides. Something
they can learn, oh, yes, may-be! But the secret — what makes the
rose to red, the sky to blue, the man to love — *In der Brust, in der
Brust,* it is *und ohne dieses giebt es keine Kunst, giebt es keine
Kunst!* [70]

Other characters in the novel make the same theme explicit. "Her
secret? It is every artist's secret . . . — passion," [71] says Andor
Harsanyi, her Chicago piano teacher, after she has succeeded at the
Met. And Thea recognizes this in herself. Willa Cather says of her,
"She had begun to understand that — with her, at least — voice was,
first of all vitality; a lightness in the body and a driving power in the
blood." [72]

Spontaneity and passion — these are personal traits, and any aesthetic which places a premium on them is bound to look upon art as
a simple projection of the artist's personality. This rather crude
attitude, so repugnant to the generation of T. S. Eliot and his successors,
is at the core of the whole book; Thea Kronborg's entire career is
based upon it. And yet toward the end of the novel Willa Cather has
her heroine discover an aesthetic of an entirely different kind.

This happens at Panther Canyon, Arizona, where Thea is sent by
Fred Ottenburg to recuperate after her first exhausting winter in
Chicago. Here, among the relics of the ancient cliff dwellers, Thea
gets her first lesson in what tradition can mean to art. Up to this time
American art had meant for her singing at small-town funerals, evangelical hymns such as "The Ninety and Nine," and her vocal rival
Lily Fisher, the much-hated "angel-child of the Baptists." [73] Now she
finds an indigenous American civilization as culturally rich as any
Europe has to offer, and one which moreover had been old when
Europe was young. This is a tremendously exciting discovery for a
young American artist to make, particularly one who had come out of
the West. "Not only did the world seem older and richer to Thea now,
but she herself seemed older," [74] Willa Cather says. "[Formerly] she

had clung fast to whatever was left of Moonstone in her mind. No
more of that. The Cliff-Dwellers had lengthened her past." [75]
Thea's artistic insight is achieved as a result of trying to see life
through the cliff dwellers' eyes. It concerns the intimate connection they
saw between the artistic process and everyday living, between art and
life. The rancher with whom Thea is staying tells her about the civilization of the Ancient People, as Willa Cather calls them, about how they
had developed masonry and pottery far beyond all other crafts:

> He explained to her how all their customs and ceremonies and
> their religion went back to water. The men provided the food,
> but water was the care of the women. The stupid women carried
> water for most of their lives; the cleverer ones made the vessels
> to hold it. Their pottery was their most direct appeal to water,
> the envelope and sheath of the precious element itself. The
> strongest Indian need was expressed in those graceful jars, fash-
> ioned slowly by hand, without the aid of a wheel. . . .
> One morning, as she was standing upright in the pool, splashing
> water between her shoulder-blades with a big sponge, something
> flashed through her mind that made her draw herself up and stand
> still until the water had quite dried upon her flushed skin. The
> stream and the broken pottery: what was any art but an effort
> to make a sheath, a mould in which to imprison for a moment the
> shining, elusive element which is life itself, — life hurrying past us
> and running away, too strong to stop, too sweet to lose? The
> Indian women had held it in their jars. In the sculpture she had
> seen in the Art Institute, it had been caught in a flash of arrested
> motion. In singing, one made a vessel of one's throat and nostrils
> and held it on one's breath, caught the stream in a scale of natural
> intervals. [76]

This passage embodies the idea of art as order, as a pattern which is
imposed upon the chaos of human experience in an attempt to render
it meaningful. The particular form in which it is expressed suggests
the Platonic notion of the fleeting evanescence of appearances and the
desire to stop time from running away — something which was to become more and more important as Willa Cather grew older. This view
is certainly far more mature than the idea of art as spontaneity expressed earlier in the book. The only objection against it is that, in
view of the difference between the creative and interpretative arts, it
applies much more aptly to Willa Cather the novelist than it does

to Thea Kronborg the opera singer. If, after attaining such a relatively sophisticated outlook, Willa Cather was able to revert to her former simpler opinion, it is evidence of the extent to which she had been swept off her feet by her hero-worship of Thea Kronborg. And this is exactly what happens; toward the end of the book, long after the Panther Canyon episode, Thea's accompanist (male) sums up her success in a eulogy which is nowhere denied but everywhere enthusiastically assented to: "Oh, it's a question of a big personality — and all that goes with it. Brains, of course. Imagination, of course. But the important thing is that she was born full of color, with a rich personality. That's a gift of the gods, like a fine nose. You have it, or you haven't. Against it, intelligence and musicianship and habits of industry don't count at all." [77]

In *The Song of the Lark* Willa Cather definitely resolves the question of artistic creativity versus human involvement in favor of creativity, and thus announces the triumph of art, or at least the triumph of the artist. Why then does this lead to bad art and a poorly written book? The chief trouble with *The Song of the Lark* is a failure in moral vision; in it Willa Cather shows a distressing predilection for allowing her heroine to have things both ways at once. Thus in her conversion scene Thea Kronborg gives up human relations, only to get them back again in the form of all the male adulation she receives as a result of her operatic success. In the Panther Canyon episode she dedicates herself to a concept of art which is loftier and more demanding of discipline than mere self-expression, only to be allowed all the self-expression she wants by being admired for her "big personality," which is regarded as the basis of her art. Finally she is allowed a free hand to do literally anything she pleases when we are told that "what she does is interesting because she does it." This is the equivalent of giving her an emotional and artistic blank check in which any sort of conduct she may care to indulge in is approved ahead of time. Small wonder that readers balk at Willa Cather's ecstatic rhapsodizing over Thea.

From what we know of the genesis of the novel, it was written as one long love letter to Miss Cather's friend and idol Olive Fremstad, the opera singer upon whom the character of Thea is based.[78] This may account for the attitude of the book's male characters, all of whom seem to be infatuated with her. Is Willa Cather suggesting that there are only two possible attitudes an audience can take toward an artist: total acceptance or total rejection? There are only two possibilities presented in the book. Either the audience blindly worships Thea and accepts everything she does, in which case they are infatuated with her and their judgment is not to be trusted, or else they show hostility toward everything she stands for, in which case they are regarded, like the Moonstone townsfolk, as "stupid faces." This too-easy division of the world into the good and the bad is paralleled by a too-easy choice of heroines. Willa Cather nowhere attempts to soften the rough contours of Thea's character in an effort to make her more amiable; rather she seems to admire her most for those qualities which most readers find despicable. "Some others," says E. K. Brown,[79] "who knew Fremstad in her great years, and shortly afterward when her voice was ruined, found her to be unperceptive and overbearing. Undoubtedly she could be rough with those who crossed her even in trifles; and with the triflers she was habitually merciless. Like S. S. McClure she knew how to raise a rumpus, and like him she did not always have just reasons for doing so. She was often, perhaps she was usually, withdrawn and cold. To Willa Cather none of this mattered." To the reader, however, it does matter. Not being able to sympathize with such a rough and aggressive woman, and knowing that Willa Cather's partiality for termagants is not generally shared, he comes to the conclusion that her choice of heroines is at times idiosyncratic. *The Song of the Lark* is the first of her stories in which the author's personal peculiarities have a seriously adverse effect on the quality of her art.

ART AS SANCTUARY

After *The Song of the Lark* Willa Cather directed her main energies to writing about the Middle West, a subject I will take up in the next chapter. She did, however, turn out a few more short stories on artistic subjects, in which she carried the triumph of art to even greater extremes than she had in *The Song of the Lark*. She gathered the best of her new stories together with what she considered to be the best work in her previous volume, *The Troll Garden,* and published them all together as a new volume of short stories called *Youth and the Bright Medusa* (1920). Since these are the last stories about art to be found in her collected works, I will once again jump ahead in time and ignore chronological sequence in order to take up her stories thematically.

There is an interesting relation between the new stories printed in *Youth and the Bright Medusa* and the old stories which they replace. The four stories she chose to reprint from *The Troll Garden* were "Paul's Case," "A Wagner Matinée," "The Sculptor's Funeral," and "A Death in the Desert." [80] The three she omitted were "Flavia and Her Artists," "The Garden Lodge," and "The Marriage of Phaedra." The three rejected stories were all notably insipid, whereas three out of the four stories she chose to reprint were much more powerful and moving. Since these three were discussed under "Rejection of the Divide," Willa Cather's choice of stories for the new volume becomes extremely illuminating. She herself liked best the stories which showed the most violent rejection.

The new stories are four: "Coming, Aphrodite!" (ca. 1920), "The Diamond Mine" (1916), "A Gold Slipper" (1917), and "Scandal" (1919). Like the three they replace, they all deal with the world of art. The first two complement each other, one being based on the rejection of human relations and the other showing what happens to the person who doesn't reject. "Coming, Aphrodite!" is about a love affair between a budding painter and a young girl singer in Greenwich Village at the turn of the century. It is a story of two different kinds of artist: the one, contemptuous of public opinion, is experimental and *avant garde;* the other, just the opposite, uses her art primarily as a vehicle for her personality, and is interested in money, fame, and success. Together they represent the two sides of Willa Cather's artistic personality. They finally quarrel and break off because Eden Bower wants to use her influence with a highly successful but commercialized painter to help her lover, and Don Hedger makes it clear that neither his pride nor his artistic principles will stand for it. Years later, after a successful career in Paris, Eden Bower returns to New York and asks a Fifth Avenue picture dealer what kind of career Don Hedger has made for himself. She is told that he has had a great influence on modern art, but this does not impress her so much as hearing that he is much talked about and admired. Her final comment is, "One doesn't like to have been an utter fool, even at twenty." [81]

Like "The Marriage of Phaedra," "Coming, Aphrodite!" shows a couple (this time lovers instead of man and wife) rejecting each other and proceeding perfectly happily upon their respective careers. It is much too lighthearted and carefree to be convincing. Although Hedger is supposed to be "hard hit" when Eden Bower leaves him, he never once contemplates lowering his artistic standards in order to accommodate her, and Willa Cather passes over the whole incident quite lightly. Apparently at this stage of life she found it necessary to insist over and over again that superior people can't possibly be hurt by anything that has happened to them or be hindered in their careers in any way whatsoever. This is in effect a denial of human relationships and their impact; the insistence upon self-reliance is so great as to suggest that Willa Cather may have been trying to convince herself.

If "Coming, Aphrodite!" deals with the necessity of rejecting human relations, "The Diamond Mine," in contrast, shows what happens to a person who doesn't reject. Cressida Garnet, the heroine of the tale, is exploited by her family and by three of her four husbands. Because she is a highly successful opera singer, her relatives look upon her as a source of ready cash; her husbands are a drain on her in other ways. The theme of the story is that the only thing the commercially minded people about her can see in Cressida is the fact that she is a source of wealth; society exploits the artist for the sake of the money she makes and uses her as though she were a diamond mine.

This story is a good example of Willa Cather's rather rudimentary social thinking. She presents two worlds to us: the world of the commercially minded whose mission is to exploit, and the world of the artistic who try to defend themselves against exploitation. The burden of the story is that money brings misery: that it destroys all sense of value if one cares for it oneself, as the commercial people do, and lays one open to the rapacity of others if, like the artists, one doesn't. Hence Cressida's agonized cry: "Why is it? I have never cared about money, except to make people happy with it, and it has been the curse of my life. It has spoiled all my relations with people." [82]

Part of Cressida's predicament is that she is caught between the two worlds, and like Thomas Mann's Tonio Kröger is at home in neither. Her marital history rather fully illustrates this. Her first husband, Charley Wilton, is a hero straight out of a sentimental novel. He is the handsome young choirmaster in the church in the Ohio town in which she was born. They are wedded when she is nineteen, and after a blissful year he picturesquely dies of tuberculosis, leaving her no alternative but to start on an artistic career. Her second husband, whom she married in Germany, was Ransome McCord, "foreign representative of the great McCord Harvester Company." [83] He however is too bourgeois: he objects to her associating with Miletus Poppas, her accompanist and manager, because he supposes her to be having an affair with him, so they finally separate. Her third husband is Blasius Bouchalka, a young Bohemian violinist-composer whom she picks up in an Italian restaurant in New York. But he turns out not to be bourgeois enough; one night she discovers him in bed with the Bohemian maid and sends him packing in the morning. Her fourth husband, whom she is about to marry as the story begins, is named Jerry Brown, and is the worst of them all. He is after her purely for her money, since he wants to "make a mark on Wall Street."

Thus Cressida's personal life suffers because she is caught between the bourgeois and artistic worlds, here pictured as being irreconcilable. The only man who can bridge the gap between them is her accompanist and manager Miletus Poppas. He takes her money, but unlike all the rest, gives her something in return: he has trained her voice and knows how to get her to make the most out of it. Willa Cather notes the fact that he is a Greek Jew and displays an ambivalence on the subject that she is also to show in her later work; she is both anti-Semitic and admiring at the same time. Thus she notes his "lupine face," the "indescribably foreign quality in his voice," and says, "He was a vulture of the vulture race, and he had the beak of one," [84] only to add immediately, "But I always felt that if ever he had her thus at his mercy, — if ever he came upon the softness hidden under so much hardness, the warm credulity under a life so dated and scheduled and 'reported' and generally exposed, — he would hold his hand and spare." [85]

This story has to do with the artist's relations with the society in which he lives, and that society is represented as parasitic. More important, that parasitic society is personified as the family, and all Cressida's husbands except the first are pictured as being so demanding that they seriously interfere with her self-fulfillment as an artist. As in *Alexander's Bridge*, and *The Song of the Lark*, Willa Cather has rigged a plot to suit her purposes. Once again she seems to be casting about for any means to justify her rejection of human relations for art.

If "Coming, Aphrodite!" and "The Diamond Mine" show respectively the need for rejection and what happens to a person who doesn't reject, the remaining two stories show a rejection so extreme as to be unbelievable. As in *The Song of the Lark*, Willa Cather overstates her case so much that she vitiates it. "A Gold Slipper" and "Scandal" have in common the same heroine, Kitty Ayrshire, an opera singer who is a scaled-down version of Thea Kronborg. In "A Gold Slipper" Kitty has a long discussion in a Pullman car with a Presbyterian coal dealer named McKann in which she proves to him just how wrong he is in believing artists to be light people and art a frivolous and useless waste of time. His arguments are taken up one by one and demolished, and although she clearly has the right of it, she is so smugly arrogant in her manner that one can't help feeling a bit sorry for poor old McKann. Finally she leaves her gold slipper in the hammock above his Pullman berth, the idea being to haunt him with the life of beauty he has missed. In a completely incredible dénouement he is pictured as losing all interest in his work and pining away, occasionally taking her tarnished gold slipper out of his desk and looking at it.

There is something terribly strained about all this; the mere fact that Kitty needed to make such a gesture indicates that Willa Cather was not completely convinced that her values really were invulnerable. The story is studded with sentences such as: "Kitty [when facing a concert audience] sensed the chill in the air, and it amused her," "She liked the stimulus of this disapprobation," and "She had been unyielding through storms to which this was a summer breeze." [86] Behind the pose of the invulnerable artist one senses a defenseless human being trying to protect herself.

The other Kitty Ayrshire story, "Scandal," is somewhat different. This time Kitty is confined to quarters with laryngitis and is visited by the handsome and admiring Pierce Tevis. They start to talk about the legends which the public has built up around her and, after dealing with several which they consider rather romantic, finally come to one which is quite shabby. A department store millionaire named Sigmund Stein has given out the impression that Kitty is his mistress. He is able to do so because he has found a girl named Ruby Mohr who looks very much like Kitty, and, taking her out of the shirtwaist factory in which she worked, has set her up in an apartment, managing to be seen with her at the opera and at various other public places so that people will think that he and Kitty are intimate. This one action not only gains him social prestige but also serves as a business asset. Finally, when Kitty gets to be well enough known in New York so that people could see through his trick, Stein drops Ruby, marries a California heiress, and, through a ruse, gets Kitty to come and sing at a reception they hold, where she is stared at and whispered about.

The tone of the story is strongly anti-Semitic. The characters are given to making such remarks as "The Steins now inhabit a great house on Fifth Avenue that used to belong to people of a very different sort. To old New-Yorkers it's an historic house," [87] ". . . the stairway . . . was thronged with Old Testament characters," [88] "These people were all too — well, too much what they were," [89] and ". . . I don't feel compassionate about your Ruby. . . . We are both the victims of circumstances, and in New York so many of the circumstances are Steins." [90] What Willa Cather is obviously concerned with here is the increasingly commercial character of the modern big city and the victimization of human beings which is one of its results. But by making the Jew into a commercial archetype and artificially equating him with everything she dislikes in the modern world she is indulging in the same social buck-passing that T. S. Eliot displayed in "Gerontion" and "Burbank with a Baedeker, Bleistein with a Cigar." As an explanation of the world's ills this smacks of the conspiracy theory of history, the desire to blame someone else when things go wrong, which we have already seen formed an important part of the folklore of Populism. Aside from its perniciousness as a social attitude, as art this is pretty sorry stuff. Good art is based on direct observation, not pre-conceived opinions. The thinking behind "Scandal" is neither socially valid nor artistically sound, and the story suffers as a result.

In comparing these new stories with the old ones they replace, a definite change can be noted. The new ones are far from being insipid and wishy-washy; in fact they are if anything too vehemently assertive. In them Willa Cather protests a little too violently that nothing can possibly come between the artist and his work; the waves of Philistinism and commercialism can pound away at him as at a rugged granite cliff; yet no erosion occurs. Gone are her former doubts about whether certain activities of the artist might be asocial or even destructive. The artist and his public now face each other almost as enemies; if any disagreement arises between them the artist is always regarded as being completely right and the public as completely wrong.[91]

Running through all these stories on artistic subjects is a highly significant submerged metaphor. It consists of the idea that art is a kind of citadel to which the artist retreats when attacked by detractors or Philistines; once safely inside, he can shout imprecations at those outside and yet not be harmed by them. This idea is closely associated with an even more important one, that of art as sanctuary and asylum; the soul, wounded in many battles, takes refuge in the sanctuary of art; there at last one is invulnerable and immune to hurt — or so Willa Cather liked to think. The concept of art as sanctuary is an important one in the corpus of Willa Cather's writing, since it is the beginning of a whole series of images of safety and retreat which I will describe in subsequent chapters. Later in her career the concept becomes more overtly religious, since art came more and more to serve as a religion for her in arousing feelings of reverence. But early and late in her career the pattern is always the same; there is a strongly felt need to isolate the good (or the beautiful) combined with the equally strong desire to preserve it safe and inviolate from all profaning hands. Thus the mood of Willa Cather's first period, which began with rejection, ends almost in retreat.

In the novels and short stories I have dealt with in this chapter Willa Cather's theme is always "the exceptional individual at war with his environment." [92] The war begins because the protagonist is not allowed sufficient freedom for self-realization, the environment which keeps him from developing usually being the American Middle West. The problem facing the individual is that of finding a new environment which will stimulate rather than stultify him. In effect, the characters engage in a search for a civilization, for a climate of opinion which will allow them to develop their talents to the greatest possible extent. During this first period Willa Cather sees such an environment as existing in the world of art.

Willa Cather's early heroines arrive at the world of art by virtue of their search for beauty, which is their heritage from the art-for-art's-sake movement of the nineties. But the author conceives of the search as being so demanding that it comes into conflict with all other human claims. In particular it comes into conflict with responsibilities toward one's parents and passionate love for the opposite sex. The artistic life is regarded as a monastic or ascetic ideal, incompatible with the life of ordinary mortals; the artist, if he does not wish his creative energy to be drained off, must be constantly on guard against the claims of familial affection and sexual love. When a choice has to be made, as it does time after time in these stories, Willa Cather regards those who choose the way of ordinary mortals as failures; the only ones she applauds are those who follow the high lonely road of art.

But once the protagonist has reached the goal of the world of art, the struggle is still not over. There is no repose in the ideal, for the artist must constantly fight to maintain its integrity. Art is a sanctuary which must be maintained against the steady pressure of the environment, the encroachment of the real. The heavenly city which the Christian theologians had regarded as existing in an afterlife and which the eighteenth-century philosophers had placed on earth and in the future, Willa Cather very much wanted to believe existed already in the world of art.

CHAPTER III

THE WORLD OF NATURE

There seemed to be nothing to see; no fences, no creeks or trees, no hills or fields. If there was a road, I could not make it out in the faint starlight. There was nothing but land: not a country at all, but the material out of which countries are made. . . . I had the feeling that the world was left behind, that we had got over the edge of it, and were outside man's jurisdiction.

During that burning day when we were crossing Iowa, our talk kept returning to a central figure, a Bohemian girl whom we had known long ago and whom both of us admired. More than any other person we remembered, this girl seemed to mean to us the country, the conditions, the whole adventure of our childhood. To speak her name was to call up pictures of people and places, to set a quiet drama going in one's brain.

— My Ántonia

REJECTION OF THE EAST

The year 1912 was a critical one for Willa Cather; it proved to be the watershed in her career. During the course of it she did two things which were crucially important in determining the entire rest of her life. One of them was to abandon an Eastern career as a highly successful magazine editor in order to become a full-time novelist. The other was to conceive of and write *O Pioneers!*, the first affirmative story she ever wrote about Nebraska.

To realize the full import of this, it is necessary to remember that up to now her entire drive had been away from the West and toward the East. Soon after graduating from college she had left Nebraska, first for Pittsburgh and later for New York; many of the stories written at this period were, as we have seen, violent rejections of the Divide. Now she was doing a complete about-face and the result was startling. It was as if Dr. Johnson, in middle age, had suddenly sat down and written *The Deserted Village*.

Taken together, her two actions constitute a rejection of the East and all it stood for and a return to the Nebraska of her childhood. For actually she was leaving behind much more than *McClure's Maga-*

zine; she was abandoning the whole "Eastern" fashionable-cosmopoli-
tan-sophisticated point of view. Years later she set down her own
understanding of this in an article in which she contrasted her effete
"Eastern" novel *Alexander's Bridge* with *O Pioneers!,* her first novel
of the prairies:

> My first novel, *Alexander's Bridge,* was very like what painters
> call a studio picture. . . . I still find people who like that book
> because it follows the most conventional pattern, and because it
> is more or less laid in London. London is supposed to be more
> engaging than, let us say, Gopher Prairie; even if the writer
> knows Gopher Prairie very well and London very casually. Soon
> after the book was published I went for six months to Arizona
> and New Mexico. The longer I stayed in a country I really did
> care about, and among people who were a part of the country,
> the more unnecessary and superficial a book like *Alexander's
> Bridge* seemed to me. I did no writing down there, but I recovered
> from the conventional editorial point of view. . . .
>
> *O Pioneers!* interested me tremendously, because it had to do
> with a kind of country I loved, because it was about old neighbours,
> once very dear, whom I had almost forgotten in the hurry and
> excitement of growing up and finding out what the world was like
> and trying to get on in it. But I did not in the least expect that
> other people would see anything in a slow-moving story, without
> "action," without "humour," without a "hero"; a story concerned
> solely with heavy farming people, with cornfields and pasture lands
> and pig yards, — set in Nebraska, of all places! As everyone
> knows, Nebraska is distinctly déclassé as a literary background;
> its very name throws the delicately attuned critic into a clammy
> shiver of embarrassment. Kansas is almost as unpromising.
> Colorado, on the contrary, is considered quite possible. Wyoming
> really has some class, of its own kind, like well-cut riding breeches.
> But a New York critic voiced a very general opinion when he
> said: "I simply don't give a damn what happens in Nebraska, no
> matter who writes about it." [1]

This lighthearted satire on genteel taste is actually a playful rejection
of all that Willa Cather had formerly striven so hard to be. Its ban-
tering tone shows that she could now afford to be lighthearted about
Eastern standards, having values of her own to set up in their stead.
What is rather surprising is that these values turn out to be Western
agrarian ones.

At first glance this may appear to be a complete anomaly. Why should a successful woman of forty suddenly decide to accept what she had long rejected? But closer inspection will reveal that this is not so contradictory as it might seem. Willa Cather had always had a consistent emotional pattern: rejection of the environment which immediately surrounded her and pursuit of the ideal in some area which was farther afield. Formerly, when in the country, it had been the country which she rejected and the urban world of art which she pursued. Now, after she had lived in the city for a good many years, it was the city's turn to be rejected, and henceforth she was to pursue her ideal in the world of nature. But one significant change has occurred. Now, for the first time in her search for the ideal, she looks for it in the past, in memories of her childhood. This fact, seemingly unimportant in *O Pioneers!*, is to assume tremendous importance in her later career.

The chief cause of Willa Cather's change of heart about the Divide was probably Sarah Orne Jewett.[2] It was she who was instrumental in turning Miss Cather's mind away from *McClure's* and across the Missouri.[3] She wrote Miss Cather a now-famous letter of advice in which she said that what Willa Cather needed in order to develop as an artist was leisure, and that she very much doubted whether such leisure was available to a staff member on a large metropolitan magazine:

> . . . I cannot help saying what I think about your writing and its being hindered by such incessant, important, responsible work as you have in your hands now. I do think that it is impossible for you to work so hard and yet have your gifts mature as they should. . . . In the "Troll Garden" the Sculptor's Funeral stands alone a head higher than the rest, and it is to that level you must hold and take for a starting-point. You are older now than that book in general; you have been living and reading and knowing new types; but if you don't keep and guard and mature your force, and above all, have time and quiet to perfect your work, you will be writing things not much better than you did five years ago . . . I want you to be surer of your backgrounds, — you have your Nebraska life, a child's Virginia, and now an intimate knowledge of what we are pleased to call the "Bohemia" of newspaper and magazine-office life. These are uncommon equipment, but you don't see them yet quite enough from the outside, — you stand right in the middle of each of them when you write, without having the standpoint of the looker-on who takes them each in their re-

lations to letters, to the world. . . . You must find a quiet place near the best companions (not those who admire and wonder at everything one does, but those who know the good things with delight!) . . . your vivid, exciting companionship in the office must not be your audience, you must find your own quiet centre of life, and write from that to the world that holds offices, and all society, all Bohemia; the city, the country — in short, you must write to the human heart. . . .[4]

"You stand right in the middle of each of them when you write" — the basis of this criticism is a plea for more perspective. And after sixteen years away from the Divide, Willa Cather had achieved enough detachment to write with a fair degree of objectivity about the Middle West. But at least as important as this negative dissuasion was Miss Jewett's positive encouragement of Willa Cather to write about her native Nebraska. Willa Cather writes, "One of the few really helpful words I ever heard from an older writer, I had from Sarah Orne Jewett when she said to me: 'Of course, one day you will write about your own country. In the meantime, get all you can. One must know the world so well before one can know the parish.' "[5] It may seem ironic that Willa Cather's decision to write about the Nebraskan frontier should have been instigated by one of the most formidable ladies of the cultured New England literary tradition. But it is not really too surprising; Miss Jewett herself was a local colorist, one of the most sophisticated that America has produced; she had made her own reputation by writing about the seacoast of her native Maine.

The period of Willa Cather's writing we are now dealing with includes the publication of two novels which praise husbandry, *O Pioneers!* (1913) and *My Ántonia* (1918). In them, as I have said, the locus of the search for value, the pursuit of the ideal, shifts from the world of art to the world of nature. But this raises an immediate difficulty; the next novel after *O Pioneers!* is *The Song of the Lark* (1915), and that deals with an artistic subject. Willa Cather has appropriated the world of nature before letting go of the world of art. How are we to explain this? This inconsistency is not only typical but is extremely important, since it shows a genuine confusion in her mind between two completely different value systems: that found in the country and that found in the town. The conflict between the two exerted a major influence over her writing for the rest of her career. She was never able to make up her mind which she preferred, nor was she able to solve the conflict in her own life; for many years she shuttled back and forth between New York City and Red Cloud, Nebraska, spending about half her time in each. In her fiction however she had better luck; in the period with which we are dealing she temporarily solved the problem by the use of an immigrant heroine. This allowed her to combine the best features of both urban and rural life, for her immigrant heroines typically come from a European town or city to the American countryside. The importance of this solution is enormous; of all the books Willa Cather ever wrote it is the prairie novels with their European protagonists in America which are the most convincing, the most affirmative, and the most memorable.

There can be no doubt that Willa Cather's change in attitude toward prairie life reflects tremendous growth on her part, both personal and artistic. Formerly she had rejected the environment in which she had grown up. Now she accepted her background, and by accepting achieved a mastery over it which enabled her to utilize it in her novels. She came into her artistic heritage when she stopped trying to be a cosmopolite and started accepting herself for what she really was. Years later she wrote on the flyleaf of a presentation copy of *O Pioneers!*: "This is the first time I walked off on my own feet — everything before was half real and half an imitation of writers whom I admired. In this one I hit the home pasture and found that I was Yance Sorgeson and not Henry James." [6]

This realization had a profound effect on Willa Cather's conception of the form of the novel as well as its subject matter. She stopped thinking of form as something to be imposed from without and began to consider it as arising from the content itself; in short, she became converted to organic form. That she herself was aware of this can be seen in the essay she wrote contrasting *Alexander's Bridge* with *O Pioneers!*:

> When a writer once begins to work with his own material, he realizes that, no matter what his literary excursions may have been, he has been working with it from the beginning — by living it. With this material he is another writer. He has less and less power of choice about the moulding of it. It seems to be there of itself, already moulded. If he tries to meddle with its vague outline, to twist it into some categorical shape, above all if he tries to adapt or modify its mood, he destroys its value. In working with this material he finds that he need have little to do with literary devices; he comes to depend more and more on something else — the thing by which our feet find the road home on a dark

night, accounting of themselves for roots and stones which we
had never noticed by day.[7]

As for subject matter, her shift from the novel of urban society to
the novel of the soil presages a change in attitude toward content in
general. While she was dominated by Henry James, she was apparently
under the impression that there was such a thing as an intrinsically
artistic subject matter: the life of artists in high society and the world
of art. At that time she had had the extraordinarily Philistine notion
that good art consisted of writing about the right sort of people, and
the right sort consistently turned out to be like the genteel heroes and
heroines of the conventional sentimental novel. But Sarah Orne Jewett
changed all that. Under her tutelage Willa Cather learned that any
material could be artistic if it were handled in an artistic manner.
"One must know the world so well before one can know the parish," Miss
Jewett had said.[8] Willa Cather finally came to appreciate this remark;
to see that universal truths could be found in the particular experience,
that the struggles of a Swedish farm woman in Nebraska could symbolize all human endeavor everywhere, that what happened in the parish could have worldwide human significance.

These changes in Willa Cather's attitude produced a marked change
in her prose style, which in turn requires a change in critical technique
in dealing with it. Whereas her writing had hitherto consisted mostly
of direct statement and had been quite explicit, it now becomes filled
with imagery and is metaphorically dense.[9] From now on Willa Cather
is to write a kind of prose poetry; and the chief tool used to criticize
it will be imagistic analysis. Formerly she had written novels and
short stories in which, however insipid they were, there was action of
some sort. Now she abandons the dramatic for the scenic method of
presentation, which is much more static. This produces something of
a snapshot album effect. In summing up *My Ántonia* she describes it
as follows:

> Ántonia had always been one to leave images in the mind that
> did not fade — that grew stronger with time. In my memory
> there was a succession of such pictures, fixed there like the old
> woodcuts of one's first primer: Ántonia kicking her bare legs
> against the sides of my pony when we came home in triumph with
> our snake; Ántonia in her black shawl and fur cap, as she stood
> by her father's grave in the snowstorm; Ántonia coming in with
> her work-team along the evening sky-line.[10]

The books Willa Cather wrote after *Alexander's Bridge* are not so much novels as they are extended lyrics in prose. Instead of the presentation and resolution of a conflict we get the distillation of an emotion. As in the Elizabethan lyric, the form is not superimposed from without but arises from the content itself, which is subjective in the extreme and aims at producing a single unified impression. Each book is the dilation of a mood. This is what Walter Pater sought whenever he tried to discover the essence or "virtue" of an art object and thereby in effect treated it as if it were a lyric poem; it is what Willa Cather meant when she wrote, in her essay on Sarah Orne Jewett:

> Walter Pater said that every truly great drama must, in the end, linger in the reader's mind as a sort of ballad. One might say that every fine story must leave in the mind of the sensitive reader an intangible residuum of pleasure; a cadence, a quality of voice that is exclusively the writer's own. . . .[11]

THEMES OF *O Pioneers!*

A good way of approaching *O Pioneers!*, the first of Willa Cather's prairie novels, is to study in connection with it the poem "Prairie Spring" (1912), which deals with the same subject matter. The chief themes of *O Pioneers!* are presented in explicit form in this poem, which is prefixed to the later editions of the book:

> Evening and the flat land,
> Rich and sombre and always silent;
> The miles of fresh-plowed soil,
> Heavy and black, full of strength and harshness;
> The growing wheat, the growing weeds,
> The toiling horses, the tired men;
> The long empty roads,
> Sullen fires of sunset, fading,
> The eternal unresponsive sky.
>
> Against all this, Youth,
> Flaming like the wild roses,
> Singing like the larks over the plowed fields,
> Flashing like a star out of the twilight;
> Youth with its insupportable sweetness,
> Its fierce necessity,

Its sharp desire,
Singing and singing,
Out of the lips of silence,
Out of the earthy dusk.

The two themes announced in this poem are those of youth and the land. The prairie has a twofold nature for Willa Cather as is evidenced by the tension between the paired adjectives she uses to describe it. The land is both "rich and sombre," it is "full of strength and harshness," and if it contains "growing wheat" it also contains "growing weeds." This opposition between the creative and destructive aspects of the soil and the life which is based upon it is explored at considerable length in the first part of the novel. The second part is chiefly concerned with the tragic love affair between Emil and Marie and corresponds closely to the second part of the poem ("Against all this, Youth . . ."). But whereas in the poem Willa Cather gives a rather conventional picture of passionate youth with hardly a hint of the mingled attraction and repulsion which she felt to be involved in human relationships (except perhaps in the phrase "insupportable sweetness"), in the novel the ambiguous nature of human relationships is fully explored and is one of her principal themes. Willa Cather was very conscious of the fact that love, whether directed toward the land or toward people, had both a fascinating and a terrifying side, and the conflict between the two provides much of the emotional power of this novel.

One other point touched upon in the poem is important in the novel. This is the idea that the human beings who lead their lives upon the flatland receive absolutely no hint at all from their environment as to how they should act. No friendly god is hovering over them; they are the center of no cosmic drama in which their importance is assured; the universe in which they live is completely indifferent to them. The land may be rich and sombre, but it is "always silent"; the fires of sunset fade against "The eternal, unresponsive sky," and youth sings its song of desire "Out of the lips of silence,/Out of the earthy dusk." Under these conditions human emotion becomes all the more poignant, since it is the only living thing in an indifferent landscape. This unresponsive universe forms the backdrop of whatever human action and desire are to be found in *O Pioneers!*

The Frontier and the Natural Aristocrat

The first appearance of the land marks the entrance of the great theme of Willa Cather's Nebraska novels: the precariousness of the hold which civilization has on the plains of the West. This is the deepest insight she retained from childhood and comes close to summarizing her idea of the whole meaning of the frontier. It is found in the very first sentence of *O Pioneers!*

> One January day, thirty years ago, the little town of Hanover, anchored on a windy Nebraska tableland, was trying not to be blown away. . . . The dwelling-houses were set about haphazard on the tough prairie sod; some of them looked as if they had been moved in overnight, and others as if they were straying off by themselves, headed straight for the open plain. None of them had any appearance of permanence, and the howling wind blew under them as well as over them.[12]

This idea of precariousness is also expressed in the reactions of the settlers to the land they are trying to tame. In its acute form it is seen in Carl Linstrum, whose father later gives up the struggle with an inhospitable environment to return to his old factory job in St. Louis:

> But the great fact was the land itself, which seemed to overwhelm the little beginnings of human society that struggled in its sombre wastes. It was from facing this vast hardness that the boy's mouth had become so bitter; because he felt that men were too weak to make any mark here, that the land wanted to be let alone, to preserve its own fierce strength, its peculiar, savage kind of beauty, its uninterrupted mournfulness.[13]

In a somewhat less pessimistic form the same idea is held by John Bergson, who doesn't give up his homestead but who dies at the early age of forty-six, before his farm has had a chance to prove itself a success:

> In eleven long years John Bergson had made but little impression upon the wild land he had come to tame. It was still a wild thing that had its ugly moods; and no one knew when they were likely to come, or why. Mischance hung over it. Its Genius was unfriendly to man. . . .[14]

John Bergson had the Old-World belief that land, in itself, is desirable. But this land was an enigma. It was like a horse that no one knows how to break to harness, that runs wild and kicks things to pieces. He had an idea that no one understood how to farm it properly, and this he often discussed with Alexandra.[15]

In each of the three last quoted passages the expressed view of the land is a reflection of the beholder and reveals what his relations with the soil will be. But they share a common feature; they all picture the land as something living which has a stubborn will of its own. Not only is it alive, but it is endowed with personality; on more than one occasion Willa Cather actually provides it with a tutelary genius quite in keeping with the spirit of Greek and Roman mythology. This personification of the land is of great importance; it allows her to regard the land as if it were a human being, and therefore capable of arousing in the human heart all the feelings which another human being can arouse. This is most clearly seen in the passage in which Alexandra decides not to sell her farm during the hard times but to buy more land instead:

When the road began to climb the first long swells of the Divide, Alexandra hummed an old Swedish hymn, and Emil wondered why his sister looked so happy. Her face was so radiant that he felt shy about asking her. For the first time, perhaps, since that land emerged from the waters of geologic ages, a human face was set toward it with love and yearning. It seemed beautiful to her, rich and strong and glorious. Her eyes drank in the breadth of it, until her tears blinded her. Then the Genius of the Divide, the great, free spirit which breathes across it, must have bent lower than it ever bent to a human will before. The history of every country begins in the heart of a man or a woman.[16]

The land bows to the human will because it is responsive to human love, and the reason Alexandra is able to tame the land is that she is able to feel love for it. She is not merely imposing her will, but is actively giving herself to something. This marks the first great advance Willa Cather has made; for once she has written an effective story which is not based upon denial and rejection. On the contrary, *O Pioneers!* is based on affirmation, and Willa Cather has realized that love is the necessary condition for creation of any sort; it is the force which builds civilizations ("The history of every country begins in the heart of a man or a woman").

Having established the precariousness of civilized life on the plain, Willa Cather is able to differentiate between two responses to this precariousness by two different kinds of people: those who are intimidated by it and those who find it a challenge. At this point history comes to her aid; she is able to make use of the plot to point up this distinction by introducing the great drought of the year 1885-86, one of a series of natural and man-made calamities which resulted in the collapse of the Western land boom and the withdrawal of thousands of people from the trans-Mississippi region. Alexandra's best friends, the Linstrums, are disheartened by the hard times and return to the East; and Alexandra's unimaginative brothers Oscar and Lou want to do the same thing. Willa Cather has this to say about them:

> The Bergson boys, certainly, would have been happier with their uncle Otto, in the bakery shop in Chicago. Like most of their neighbors, they were meant to follow in paths already marked out for them, not to beat trails in a new country. . . . It was no fault of theirs that they had been dragged into the wilderness when they were little boys. A pioneer should have imagination, should be able to enjoy the idea of things more than the things themselves.[17]

Even at this stage of society most people are seen as followers and conformists (and it is interesting that here Willa Cather associates conformity with city life). But not all the characters are like this. Unlike her brothers, Alexandra refuses to be discouraged; instead of selling her farm she wants to buy up all the land of the neighbors who are leaving, and is willing to put another mortgage on the homestead in order to do so. She calmly insists that an increase in the value of land will make them all rich and independent within ten years, and answers the horrified questions of her brothers as to how she knows what's going to happen by saying:

> "I can't explain that, Lou. You'll have to take my word for it. I *know*, that's all. When you drive about over the country you can feel it coming." [18]

This is the pioneering imagination to which Willa Cather referred, the ability to enjoy the idea of things ten years off more than the things themselves. It turns out that Alexandra is right, and in contrasting the imaginative Alexandra with her unoriginal brothers Willa Cather makes a distinction which is crucial for the rest of her writing career. For the precariousness of civilization on the Western prairies is a symbol for the precariousness of life itself, and in distinguishing between those who are challenged and those who are cowed by it she is distinguishing between two fundamentally opposed attitudes toward life, the heroic and the unheroic. Thus she sets up the basis for a natural aristocracy. Alexandra is clearly intended to be a natural aristocrat, just as her brothers are not.

The contrast between these two attitudes is pointed up by a snatch of conversation they all have together:

> Lou held his head as if it were splitting. "Everybody will say we are crazy. It must be crazy or everybody would be doing it." "If they were, we wouldn't have much chance. No, Lou, I was talking about that with the smart young man who is raising the new kind of clover. He says the right thing is usually just what everybody don't do." [19]

Here is a fairly explicit definition of the natural aristocrat. He is the person, usually in the minority, who can size up a situation when nobody else can and come up with the right answer. The very fact of his originality requires him to be a nonconformist. That such talent has nothing to do with family is shown by the fact that Alexandra has this ability while her brothers do not. But in the very next sentence Alexandra suddenly makes an astonishing logical leap:

> "Why are we better fixed than any of our neighbors? Because father had more brains. Our people were better people than these in the old country. We *ought* to do more than they do, and see further ahead." [20]

A belief in natural aristocracy is one thing; a belief in social aristocracy is quite another. No logical connection can be made out between the two, as Alexandra's own family situation shows, and yet the connection is made. It is as if Willa Cather regards natural aristocracy, which she admires, as a helpless foundling which is liable to die of exposure unless nurtured and maintained by a social institution. At this stage of her career such an attitude is atypical, for she is usually content to let her natural aristocrats rely on their own inborn strength in their journey through the world. But later, in her old age, she came to distrust the world so much that she doubted whether even a natural aristocrat could make his way completely alone. It was at this time that she began to give up her belief in a free society of heroes in favor of a hierarchial society that was almost feudal in nature, her desire being to insure her superior people their rightful place in the world and adequate room in which to exercise their talents.

Having looked at Willa Cather's presentation of Alexandra, her father, and her two brothers, we now begin to see what qualities she thought essential to a pioneer. He must have strength, but strength alone is not enough, for Oscar and Lou have strength, and Willa Cather makes it amply evident that left to their own devices they would get nowhere. He must have imagination, but it is not sufficient for him to have imagination alone; John Bergson was imaginative enough in attempting to retrieve his fortune by coming to the New World, but he wore himself out and died, not only without becoming rich but without doing more than barely getting out of debt. A pioneer must have both imagination and strength. These are what constitute the clear superiority of Alexandra over her father and brothers, for what they possess separately, she is able to combine.

Willa Cather's natural aristocrat is not original with her; he is a familiar figure in nineteenth-century thought. He descends from the concept of the hero as outlined by such heroic vitalists as Nietzsche and Carlyle. According to them humanity is divided into two groups: the leaders and the led, heroes and ordinary people, those who are challenged by life's precariousness and those who are cowed by it; natural aristocrats and everyone else. The will of the leaders was regarded as essentially creative and no restrictions were to be placed on it lest they diminish its potency. Willa Cather's belief that the true pioneering spirit consists of a combination of imagination and strength places her squarely in the tradition of these heroic vitalists.

The distinction between great and little people worked in with another highly important nineteenth-century concept: the pointed antithesis between the real and the ideal, between appearance and reality. For manifestly some people were satisfied and complacent about the everyday world, while others were not; Carlyle (who was a great influence on Willa Cather's youth) raised his theory of the hero on just this postulation of two different kinds of psychology. According to him little people (such as Oscar and Lou, for instance) are content with the world as it is because they cannot conceive of anything better, while great people, or heroes (such as Alexandra), are able to pierce through the world of appearances or things as they are at any given moment and discern the form of things as they should be. Not only does the hero have to have insight into what should be; he must also have the ability to transform the real into the ideal; hence the tremendous emphasis on the will power and courage which are required to translate insight into action. Courage and insight are the two great qualities of the hero, and Willa Cather by taking them over simply changes their names. She calls them strength and imagination.

THE ESTABLISHMENT OF THE GARDEN

Sixteen years later Alexandra's prophecy has proved correct, and the land, once wild, has been forever tamed. Instead of the wild animal imagery Miss Cather had formerly used to describe it, she now uses geometrical imagery and emphasizes its symmetry, signifying that nature has been reduced to order by the human hand:

> It is sixteen years since John Bergson died. . . . Could he rise from beneath it, he would not know the country under which he has been asleep. The shaggy coat of the prairie, which they lifted to make him a bed, has vanished forever. From the Norwegian graveyard one looks out over a vast checker-board, marked off in squares of wheat and corn; light and dark, dark and light.[21]

But although the land has been tamed, its spirit is not broken; now that it has been subdued, it returns Alexandra's love for it. It vibrates like a gigantic Aeolian harp in the wind that is continually sweeping over the Nebraska plains. The wind for Willa Cather is a symbol of the earth spirit which breathes through a youthful land and brings it to life (and which incidentally allows her to regard the land as if it were an animate being):

> Telephone wires hum along the white roads, which always run at right angles. From the graveyard gate one can count a dozen gayly painted farmhouses; the gilded weather-vanes on the big red barns wink at each other across the green and brown and yellow fields. The light steel windmills tremble throughout their frames and tug at their moorings, as they vibrate in the wind that often blows from one week's end to another across that high, active, resolute stretch of country.[22]

The tamed land is still very much alive. The Genius of the Divide has bent to the human will, bowed to human love, and in fact even returned that love. For if we look at the exact way in which the land is described, a very interesting fact emerges. Not only does Willa Cather personify the land; she treats it as if it were a human being with a passionate sexual nature. When she comes to describe the act of spring plowing, for instance, she uses undisguised sexual imagery:

> There are few scenes more gratifying than a spring plowing in that country, where the furrows of a single field often lie a mile in length, and the brown earth, with such a strong, clean smell, and such a power of growth and fertility in it, yields itself eagerly to the plow; rolls away from the shear, not even dimming the brightness of the metal, with a soft, deep sigh of happiness. . . . There is something frank and joyous and young in the open face of the country. It gives itself ungrudgingly to the moods of the season, holding nothing back.[23]

Thus we have an implicit but unequivocal statement from Willa Cather herself that Alexandra Bergson's relation to the land is a sexual one. This raises two interesting points. In the first place, in describing the cultivation of the soil Willa Cather has, by implication at least, given to Alexandra, a woman, the aggressive or "masculine" role. This reversal of sexual roles may help explain Miss Cather's inability to portray, or perhaps even to conceive, a relation between the sexes as yielding permanent satisfaction or emotional fulfillment. Nearly all the man-woman relationships she presents are either unsatisfactory to the participants, or, if satisfactory, end disastrously. In the second place, the breaking of the soil, here described for the first time, is not only Willa Cather's greatest theme; she believes it is almost the only task her generation undertook which ended in positive achievement. Nearly every other human undertaking she describes in her novels eventually ends in failure and defeat. This can be seen even in *O Pioneers!* itself. The book's first part, dealing with Alexandra's struggle to tame the land, ends in triumph, but the second part of the book is quite a different matter. It describes the tragic love of Alexandra's brother Emil for Marie Shabata, the wife of one of his neighbors, and ends in frustration, agony, and death. Thus even in the first of Willa Cather's Middle Western novels the ending shows a falling away from the high standard of achievement set by her heroine in the book's early part; the very first of her affirmative novels ends on a note of negation and defeat.

It is evident from the previous chapter that, however sincerely

Willa Cather may have devoted herself to artistic perfection, she consistently caused her heroines to use the world of art as a substitute for human relations. Now in this second period of her writing we find her doing much the same thing, only this time it is the world of nature which is used as a substitute. If she believed that success and emotional fulfillment could only come from dealing with impersonal things such as the land, and if, as the imagery makes clear, she regarded the land itself as a sexual substitute and a fit object for passionate love, it is no wonder that she regarded every human undertaking which depended in any way upon deeply personal relations as leading inevitably to frustration and defeat. The core of this problem shows up clearly in *O Pioneers!:* her natural aristocrat is able to conquer the land, but that is all she is able to achieve. In the matter of her brother's love for Marie Shabata she is completely helpless; she does not even know there is love between the two until after they are killed by Marie's husband. The qualified nature of Alexandra's triumph, her success with the land and her failure in human relations, puts such a severe limitation on the doctrine of the great person as to call the whole theory of natural aristocracy into doubt.

In *O Pioneers!* Willa Cather introduced for the first time her great theme of taming the soil, the outcome of which endeavor is more successful than that of any other activity recorded in a Willa Cather novel. What are the results of this activity? A clue is given by the titling of the sections of the book. The first, describing actual frontier conditions, is entitled "The Wild Land." The second, which takes up the story sixteen years later, after the land has been tamed, is called "Neighboring Fields." It is in the second of these sections that Willa Cather gives the results of the taming process by describing the neatness and symmetry with which the countryside is now laid out which as I have said represent nature reduced to order by the human hand. In describing Alexandra's farm in the years of prosperity, Willa Cather writes:

> When you go out of the house into the flower garden, there you feel again the order and fine arrangement manifest all over the great farm; in the fencing and hedging; in the windbreaks and sheds, in the symmetrical pasture ponds, planted with scrub willows to give shade to the cattle in fly-time. There is even a white row of beehives in the orchard, under the walnut trees. You feel that, properly, Alexandra's house is the big out-of-doors, and that it is in the soil that she expresses herself best.[24]

This picture of an ordered landscape, which is "Nature still but Nature methodiz'd," is really a garden image; the whole purpose of taming the land is the establishment of a garden. As we shall see, the garden has not only physical but moral value; it stands for a very definite set of virtues which Willa Cather thought inherent in rural living. During her adult years it seemed to her that the best possibilities of life had in fact been realized on the Nebraska plains of the eighteen-eighties and nineties, and that for a brief period of time the myth of the Garden of Eden had come very close to being an actuality in the Middle West. The virtues of the garden, which are the same virtues the Populists saw, form the core of Willa Cather's system of social values for the rest of her life; to probe them is to probe one of the deepest levels of meaning of her entire work.

The image of the Middle West as garden was one of the dominant cultural concepts of the American nineteenth century. Professor Henry Nash Smith has pointed out in *Virgin Land* that Americans looked upon their great central valley as being the place of all places where one could lead an idyllic existence as happy as it was innocent, where food would grow in such abundance that the region could become the granary of the entire planet, in short, the garden of the world. As Professor Smith develops it the concept involves the existence of a settled agricultural society in a land so vast that everyone has the chance to become an independent landowner, so rich that labor is sure to produce a plentiful reward, and so closely associated with a beneficent nature that everyone is bound to be virtuous.[25] For Willa Cather the garden image was more sharply localized in space and time. She thought of it as having actual embodiment in the Middle West of her childhood for a few brief years. As a result her picture of early Nebraska was paradisaic in the extreme. In it the good people were indisputably good and wickedness was something which came entirely from without. Even the problem of evil seemed to lose its sting: "In the country, if you had a mean neighbor, you could keep off his land and make him keep off yours." [26]

To locate the Garden of Eden in space and time is a dangerous undertaking, especially if one attempts to locate it in the land of one's own childhood. A child's view of the world is not the same as an adult's; to equate the two is to confuse the findings of innocence with those of experience, and in order to avoid recognition of this fact one must continually push back the boundaries of Eden until they coincide with the earliest limits of one's consciousness. This is apparently what Willa Cather did in *O Pioneers!* In that book the Garden of Eden is pictured as existing in that short interval of time between the passing of the pioneers and the completion of settlement by the farmers; once the wild land had been conquered, Eden was no more. Chronologically this places the golden age in the period between 1882, when Willa Cather first arrived in Nebraska as a child of nine, and about 1887, when grasshoppers, drought, and blizzards wrought havoc with the great Western land boom and drove thousands of people out. The succeeding years saw the triumph of the settlers who, like Alexandra, were strong enough to remain, but, for the now adolescent Willa, something of the old magic had gone forever. Perhaps it was the magic of childhood and not the magic of the land. If so, she never gave any indication that she was aware of this, but frequently voiced a nostalgia for an earlier and more intoxicating time.

Thus *O Pioneers!* deals not so much with the garden itself — we have to wait for *My Ántonia* for that — as with the establishment of the garden. Once the land has been tamed there is a glory passed from the earth. When Carl Linstrum returns to the Divide after an interval of sixteen years Willa Cather has him say:

> "I think I liked the old Lou and Oscar better, and they probably feel the same about me. I even, if you can keep a secret," — Carl leaned forward and touched her arm, smiling, — "I even think I liked the old country better. This is all very splendid in its way, but there was something about this country when it was a wild old beast that has haunted me all these years. Now, when I come back to all this milk and honey, I feel like the old German song, 'Wo bist du, wo bist du, mein geliebtest Land?' " [27]

The end product of Alexandra's efforts is thus the establishment of the garden, which as I have suggested is a cross between the earthly paradise, with its connotations of rivers of milk and honey, and the Garden of Eden, with its connotations of primordial innocence and happiness. The women and men who farm the Divide are potentially like Eve and Adam, with the difference that instead of finding their Eden ready-made for them they have to make it for themselves, marking out homesteads between the Tigris and Euphrates — or, to be literal, between the Republican River and the Platte. In writing *O Pioneers!* Willa Cather was voicing a concept of the interior valley of America held by great numbers of people. There is a marked similarity between her vision of the Middle West and that held by the Populists, among whom she grew up. Both see the virtuous yeoman as the repository of all value and hold that there is no life to match the life of the soil.

HUMAN RELATIONS: THE CASE AGAINST SPONTANEITY

If the first part of the book is the story of Alexandra and the land, the second part is the story of Emil and Marie. *O Pioneers!* has been criticized for being structurally weak and breaking in two near the middle (actually, one-quarter of the way through).[28] There is some genetic evidence which would seem to bear this out; Alexandra's saga was written first and originally stood alone, ending with the description of the imaginary lover who lifts Alexandra bodily and carries her away.[29] It may be significant that Willa Cather conceived the story of Alexandra and the land before she imagined the tale of human relations which follows. But origins prove nothing about the artistic value of a work, and we must judge the novel as it exists in its completed structure and not as it was in first draft. It is possible to see a very definite relationship between Alexandra's story and that of Emil and Marie. It is this: after exploring the problems of spontaneous emotion in relation to nature and the land, Willa Cather turns to the more complicated problem of spontaneity in relation to other human beings, particularly to the relations between men and women. The results here are not nearly so satisfying, and for a brief moment Willa Cather arrives at something close to a tragic view of life. Because in it she for once admitted the validity of spontaneity in human relations, while at the same time pointing out its dangers, I regard *O Pioneers!* as being the broadest in sympathy of all Willa Cather's works and the one which has the greatest emotional depth to it.

The linkage between the two themes of the land and human love is seen in the imagery used at the point where the story of Emil and Marie begins. Miss Cather has been describing the fertility and opulence of the land which has finally been domesticated and made friendly to man. We have seen that she uses sexual imagery in describing the relation of the soil to those who till it. There is an association of the land with youth and a statement of the themes of spontaneity, of love, and giving of oneself:

> There is something frank and joyous and young in the open face of the country. It gives itself ungrudgingly to the moods of the season, holding nothing back. Like the plains of Lombardy, it seems to rise a little to meet the sun. The air and the earth are

curiously mated and intermingled, as if the one were the breath of the other.[30]

In the last sentence the submerged sexual reference of the preceding paragraph is made explicit by the mating image, so that the reader could hardly avoid concluding that all this emphasis on the land's youth and joyousness and giving itself has a familiar human connotation. Then and not till then is Emil introduced and Marie shortly thereafter: "One June morning a young man stood at the gate of the Norwegian graveyard, sharpening his scythe in strokes unconsciously timed to the tune he was whistling." [31]

The love which arises between Marie and Emil is something which is inevitable because it develops from their characters. Both of them have a talent for living and the sharing of imaginative experience, and each one recognizes this talent in the other. This is more clearly seen in the case of Marie; Willa Cather generally portrayed women better than she did men. Ántonia in *My Ántonia* is more believable than Cuzak, Alexandra in *O Pioneers!* is more believable than Carl, and Cécile Auclair in *Shadows on the Rock* is more believable than her father or Pierre Charron. Marie is pictured as someone who gives herself completely in every situation, holding nothing back, because her spontaneity is an all-or-none affair which simply cannot respond in a manner which is limited to the needs of the immediate situation·

> Marie was incapable of being lukewarm about anything that pleased her. She simply did not know how to give a half-hearted response. When she was delighted, she was as likely as not to stand on her tiptoes and clap her hands. If people laughed at her, she laughed with them.[32]

The negative connotations of the words "lukewarm" and "half-hearted" show that Willa Cather approved of all-or-none reactions. It is the ability to throw herself wholeheartedly into emotional situations that makes Marie so humanly attractive and so successful in dealing with people, just as a similar spontaneity in relation to the soil makes Alexandra successful in dealing with the land. That Marie quite naturally shows this same trait in her love relations is seen from the description of her early affection for her husband, Frank Shabata, from whom she is now estranged:

> In the first days of their love she had been his slave; she had admired him abandonedly. But the moment he began to bully

her and to be unjust, she began to draw away; at first in tearful amazement, then in quiet, unspoken disgust. . . . The spark of her life went somewhere else, and he was always watching to surprise it. He knew that somewhere she must get a feeling to live upon, for she was not a woman who could live without loving.[33]

Willa Cather considered spontaneity the trait of a great nature and gave it to all her heroines, just as she gave it to Marie. For her, spontaneity always involved extreme, total reactions, whether for good or for bad; her characters are given to violent loves and hates, and apparently one is regarded as being as good as the other. One remembers the description of Mr. Driscoll in *My Mortal Enemy* as a man who "had violent prejudices; but that's rather good to remember in these days when so few people have any real passions, either of love or hate. . . . Men who hate like that usually have the fist-power to back it up, you'll notice"[34] (as if this were any justification), and in *The Song of the Lark* Thea Kronborg can say "If you love the good thing vitally, enough to give up for it all that one must give up, then you must hate the cheap thing just as hard! I tell you there is such a thing as creative hate!"[35] Apparently Willa Cather considered spontaneity itself to be a virtue and was not particularly concerned with the direction it took. But the direction it takes becomes of overwhelming importance at the end of *O Pioneers!* when Frank Shabata murders Emil and Marie; so much so that the entire value of spontaneity itself is called into question.

Marie's instincts are those of a happy child; although she has herself suffered in her unhappy marriage she has no conception that suffering may be an inescapable part of human existence. To her, life means happiness, and the very measure of a person's vitality is the amount of joy he can draw from existence. She is like the wild duck which Alexandra and Emil have seen together and which they take to be a symbol of the beauty of spontaneous existence. And she is like her own characterization of the wild duck which she has persuaded Emil to shoot, only to be horrified when he actually drops the dead bird, dripping with blood, into her lap:

When he came back, dangling the ducks by their feet, Marie held her apron and he dropped them into it. As she stood looking down at them, her face changed. She took up one of the birds, a rumpled ball of feathers with the blood dripping slowly from its mouth, and looked at the live color that still burned on its plumage.

As she let it fall, she cried in distress, "Oh, Emil, why did you?"
"I like that!" the boy exclaimed indignantly. "Why, Marie, you asked me to come [hunting] yourself."

"Yes, yes, I know," she said tearfully, "but I didn't think. I hate to see them when they are first shot. They were having such a good time, and we've spoiled it all for them."

Emil gave a rather sore laugh. "I should say we had! I'm not going hunting with you any more. You're as bad as Ivar. Here, let me take them." He snatched the ducks out of her apron.

"Don't be cross, Emil. Only — Ivar's right about wild things. They're too happy to kill. You can just tell how they felt when they flew up. They were scared, but they didn't really think anything could hurt them. No, we won't do that any more." [36]

This is the first time in the book that Willa Cather has shown she is aware of the limitations of spontaneity. Since it is purely subjective, it takes no thought of the outside world; therefore it is unable to foresee consequences. The wild ducks had no idea they might be killed when they flew up; Marie had no idea she might make herself miserably unhappy when she asked Emil to shoot them. Spontaneity may have terrible results; however charming it may be, it can lead to the extinction of all charm, the quenching of vitality itself. Sudden death plays an important part in this book, as witness the fate of Amédée Chevalier as well as that of Emil and Marie. This scene foreshadows that other one under the white mulberry tree in which the two lovers are themselves killed. When Marie says of the wild duck that he is too happy to kill and that he didn't think anything could really hurt him, she is describing herself.

When we shift our attention from Marie to Emil, we discover that he is a rather shadowy character; we do not find out nearly so much about him as we do about Marie and pretty much have to take Carl Linstrum's word for it that "he was the best that they had." [37] The chief presumption in favor of his being the best is Marie's being drawn to him, for she is the most attractive character in the whole book. She has all the good qualities which belong to Alexandra, including the drive and the enthusiasm with which she throws herself into her work, and she also has those qualities which Alexandra knows herself to lack: an understanding of people, a keen zest for the enjoyment of living, and a vivaciousness which reflects itself on everyone. In effect she completes Alexandra by taking up where Alexandra left off; she is the new generation for which the pioneers were struggling when they came to America so that their children could have a fuller and richer life. Marie falls in love with and settles on the farm which the Linstrums had sold when they gave up their struggle; she is able to see and develop possibilities of life which they had missed. She represents the best hope of life on this continent, just as Emil does.

But there is a deeper meaning of Marie's spontaneity, one which makes her a symbol of man's emotional life in general. When she finds herself becoming involved with Emil, her very spontaneity becomes a source of worry to her. It is responsible both for her most attractive qualities and also (at least partially) for the tragedy with which the book ends. Both of the lovers regret their passionate attachment to each other; it is all the more bitter because in different circumstances it would have been so sweet a thing. Marie feels this keenly:

> Her own case was clear. When a girl had loved one man, and then loved another while that man was still alive, everybody knew what to think of her. What happened was of little consequence, so long as she did not drag other people down with her.[38]

And Emil is equally bitter when he compares his own lot with that of his happily married childhood friend and boon companion Amédée Chevalier:

> He and Amédée had ridden and wrestled and larked together since they were lads of twelve. On Sundays and holidays they were always arm in arm. It seemed strange that now he should have to hide the thing that Amédée was so proud of, that the feeling which gave one of them such happiness should bring the other such despair.[39]

Marie is a good Catholic and takes her religion seriously. She at first tries to dissuade Emil from loving her by encouraging him to pray, and, failing in this, takes comfort in religion herself. The opposition is sharp and clear-cut between his spontaneous desires and the moral imperatives of society (in this case, organized religion):

> She struck the ground with her little foot fiercely. "That won't last. It will go away, and things will be just as they used to. I wish you were Catholic. The Church helps people, indeed it does. I pray for you, but that's not the same as if you prayed for yourself."

She spoke rapidly and pleadingly, looked entreatingly into his face. Emil stood defiant, gazing down at her.

"I can't pray to have the things I want," he said slowly, "and I won't pray not to have them, not if I'm damned for it." [40]

Marie wavers between following her own spontaneous impulses and obeying the Church's commands; she would like to be able to combine the two, but of course that is just what one cannot do when one is the creature of every impulse. It is the age-old opposition between civilization and nature; one cannot have the natural virtues, at least as defined by primitivism, unless one is willing to give up some of the corresponding values of civilization. And Marie actually does veer in the direction of primitivism in the symbolic scene in which she asks Emil about the tree worship which preceded Christianity in Europe:

"Emil," she said suddenly — he was mowing quietly about under the tree so as not to disturb her — "what religion did the Swedes have away back, before they were Christians?"

Emil paused and straightened his back. "I don't know. About like the Germans', wasn't it?"

Marie went on as if she had not heard him. "The Bohemians, you know, were tree worshippers before the missionaries came. Father says the people in the mountains still do queer things, sometimes, — they believe that trees bring good or bad luck."

Emil looked superior. "Do they? Well, which are the lucky trees? I'd like to know."

"I don't know all of them, but I know lindens are. The old people in the mountains plant lindens to purify the forest, and to do away with the spells that come from the old trees they say have lasted from heathen times. I'm a good Catholic, but I think I could get along with caring for trees, if I hadn't anything else."

"That's a poor saying," said Emil, stooping over to wipe his hands in the wet grass.

"Why is it? If I feel that way, I feel that way. I like trees because they seem more resigned to the way they have to live than other things do." [41]

This illustrates Marie's belief in the natural inevitability and goodness of emotion ("If I feel that way, I feel that way"). In view of this and of her complete spontaneity it is fitting that her instincts should impel her in the direction of nature worship. It is not surprising that in the end the natural woman in her should overcome the good Catholic when she finally gives herself to Emil. The idea that trees bring either good luck or bad luck, of course, foreshadows the climax of the book, where the lovers both consummate and end their love in the shadow of the white mulberry tree.

Marie is not the only person in the novel who feels a strong kinship with the natural world. So does the holy man, Crazy Ivar, who expresses Willa Cather's views on the value of living close to nature. He is depicted as a nineteenth-century hermit who, like the mythical Leatherstocking, has fled from civilization in order to seek virtue in the wilderness, and who, through continued association with grand and noble objects, has developed a noble character. This makes him a living example of the Wordsworthian doctrine that nature, being good, can teach man to be good if he will but live close to her. Thus he dislikes guns and the killing of wild things,[42] finds contentment in solitude,[43] and makes his home in a cave hollowed out of a clay bank:

> But for the piece of rusty stovepipe sticking up through the sod, you could have walked over the roof of Ivar's dwelling without dreaming that you were near a human habitation. Ivar had lived three years in the clay bank, without defiling the face of nature any more than the coyote that had lived there before him had done.[44]

The word "defile" implies an opposition between spotless nature and sinful man; it suggests pretty strongly that human beings are impure and can contaminate the purity of nature if they do not exercise the constant vigilance of a Crazy Ivar. Thus the Wordsworthian doctrine of the redemptive power of nature is given a negative twist. Instead of ennobling man, the most nature can do is exercise a rather shaky power to prevent man from degrading himself.

Crazy Ivar has other traits which qualify him to be a seer of the wilderness. He is represented as being somewhat deranged mentally and given to cloudy spells, but, as in the case of the traditional clairvoyant fool, this is not only no drawback but actually gives him a deeper insight into fundamental mysteries than that possessed by other people. Thus he is able to understand animals and to quiet them even when they are mad with pain.[45] Living in communion with nature has also helped him to develop a highly individualistic attitude toward religion. Willa Cather says of him: "He had a peculiar religion of his own and did not get on with any of the denominations." [46] He himself points out the affinity in his mind between religion and nature, so typical of the nineteenth century and so different from the traditional orthodox Christian opposition between the two: "He best expressed his preference for his wild homestead by saying that his Bible seemed truer to him there." [47]

Willa Cather is quite explicit in pointing out Ivar's nature worship and his belief in the contaminating effect of human beings in an otherwise clean universe:

> Ivar found contentment in the solitude he had sought out for himself. He disliked the litter of human dwellings: the broken food, the bits of broken china, the old wash-boilers and tea-kettles thrown into the sunflower patch. He preferred the cleanness and tidiness of the wild sod. He always said that the badgers had cleaner houses than people, and that when he took a housekeeper her name would be Mrs. Badger. . . . If one stood in the doorway of his cave, and looked off at the rough land, the smiling sky, the curly grass white in the hot sunlight; if one listened to the rapturous song of the lark, the drumming of the quail, the burr of the locust against the vast silence, one understood what Ivar meant.[48]

Here is a man who has tried all his life to avoid evil; in fact, he puts more emphasis on the avoidance of evil than the doing of good. He thinks he can best achieve his goal by living close to nature: as he himself says, the fewer neighbors he has, the fewer temptations.[49] And what does his close association with nature get him? When Marie's husband finds and shoots Emil and Marie, it is Crazy Ivar who stumbles upon the pair of murdered lovers. Although he has tried to steer clear of human complications he unwillingly and unwittingly becomes involved in them; much as he would like to live a life of purity apart from all human beings he cannot escape the common fate of becoming involved with mankind, even if only as a spectator. Evidently the doctrine of avoiding evil by fleeing to the wilderness breaks down; as long as one deals with people at all, as long as one remains a person oneself, one has fundamental problems to contend with. This is dramatically shown when Crazy Ivar becomes the messenger of calamity who announces to Alexandra the violent action which has occurred:

> When Ivar reached the path by the hedge, he saw Shabata's rifle lying in the way. He turned and peered through the branches,

falling upon his knees as if his legs had been mowed from under him. "Merciful God!" he groaned, "merciful, merciful God!"

Alexandra, too, had risen early that morning, because of her anxiety about Emil. She was in Emil's room upstairs when, from the window, she saw Ivar coming along the path that led from the Shabatas'. He was running like a spent man, tottering and lurching from side to side. Ivar never drank, and Alexandra thought at once that one of his spells had come upon him and that he must be in a very bad way indeed. She ran downstairs and hurried out to meet him, to hide his infirmity from the eyes of her household. The old man fell in the road at her feet and caught her hand, over which he bowed his shaggy head. "Mistress, mistress!" he sobbed, "it has fallen! Sin and death for the young ones! God have mercy upon us!" [50]

This is not only a cry from the heart but also a vision of life. Ivar's baleful vision points up the whole problem we have been examining. Up to this point nature has been regarded by Ivar, by Marie, and by Alexandra as something which is decidedly benign. Now for the first time we are brought face to face with nature's ambiguity. If it can lead to the beautiful spontaneity of the love between Emil and Marie, it can also lead to the murderous rage of Frank Shabata.

Alexandra Bergson is turning over something like this in her mind three months later when she visits Frank Shabata in prison. Whether or not she makes the connection, the same spontaneity which has made her so successful in taming the wild land of a new country, when applied to human relations by Frank and Marie has been completely disastrous. What decision are we to come to then regarding spontaneity? She does not know:

Alexandra remembered the little yellow cane she had found in Frank's clothes-closet. She thought of how he had come to this country a gay young fellow, so attractive that the prettiest Bohemian girl in Omaha had run away with him. It seemed unreasonable that life should have landed him in such a place as this. She blamed Marie bitterly. And why, with her happy, affectionate nature, should she have brought destruction and sorrow to all who had loved her, even to poor old Joe Tovesky, the uncle who used to carry her about so proudly when she was a little girl? That was the strangest thing of all. Was there something wrong in being warmhearted and impulsive like that? Alexandra hated to think so. But there was Emil, in the Norwegian graveyard at home, and here was Frank Shabata.[51]

Alexandra never does solve the problem, nor does Willa Cather; the farthest she gets in grappling with it is the somewhat lame realization expressed here that it produces diverse results, some of them good, some bad. But since *O Pioneers!* contains the most sympathetic exposition of spontaneous human relations that Willa Cather ever wrote, and, since in subsequent books she gives to such spontaneity an ever diminishing place, it seems safe to assume that in this book she weighed the evidence for and against spontaneity and decided against it. She now appears to have excellent reasons for rejecting passionate human relations altogether, something we have seen her as wanting to do all along.

This unresolved problem is the real cause of her protagonists' inability to come to terms with the world as it is. Because for Willa Cather spontaneity is a total reaction, completely in favor of a thing or against it, she is unable to conceive of her characters as making the compromises necessary in everyday living. They either triumph completely or else, if balked, are powerless to adjust themselves to the new situation and try again; they are the victims of their own all-or-none emotional responses. Alexandra comes out better than most of them do, but her survival is mostly a matter of endurance and an original limitation upon her genius; she was never able to direct her spontaneity toward anything but the land in the first place, and thus avoids the dangers produced by spontaneity in human affairs.

The problem does not always produce complete ambivalence, as it does in Alexandra's mind in the passage quoted above. At its best it can lead to a tragic view of life, of the world as a place where the good is inextricably mixed up with the bad, and one's very good points can cause one's downfall. Willa Cather approaches this view two or three times in *O Pioneers!* Emil and Marie are aware of it when they talk about why Marie ran off with Frank in the first place:

> Marie drew back. "Because I was in love with him," she said firmly.
> "Really?" he asked incredulously.
> "Yes, indeed. Very much in love with him. I think I was the one who suggested our running away. From the first it was more my fault than his."
> Emil turned away his face.

"And now," Marie went on, "I've got to remember that. Frank is just the same now as he was then, only then I would see him as I wanted him to be. I would have my own way. And now I pay for it."

"You don't do all the paying."

"That's it. When one makes a mistake, there's no telling where it will stop." [52]

Marie here comes to the tragic realization that the results of our actions may far outstrip our ability to anticipate them; a man is responsible for more things than he can foresee. Marie knows this applies to her relations with Emil: when we err in judgment, other people pay for our mistakes, not just ourselves. Three months after the murder, the servant girl Signa has the same realization, although unlike Marie she is not wise enough to be able to accept it. "How awful it's been these last three months," she says to Crazy Ivar. "It doesn't seem right that we must all be so miserable. Why do we all have to be punished? Seems to me like good times would never come again." [53] Here again is the idea that human responsibility is a web in which we are all tragically caught and that we pay for other people's mistakes, as they do for ours. It is significant that in answer to this the hermit only "expressed himself in a deep sigh but said nothing." [54]

Sometime earlier in the book a tragic awareness of life is expressed by Carl Linstrum. He is talking with Alexandra about the Norwegian graveyard in which lie so many of their old neighbors:

"Isn't it queer: There are only two or three human stories, and they go on repeating themselves as fiercely as if they had never happened before; like the larks in this country, that have been singing the same five notes over for thousands of years." [55]

In the book's last pages, when Carl and Alexandra are finally united, she reminds him of this:

"You remember what you once said about the graveyard, and the old story writing itself over? Only it is we who write it, with the best we have." [56]

This is the human predicament, and Willa Cather was never able to surpass this for broadness of sympathy and realization of what it means to be alive. One thinks of her poem "Prairie Spring" with its description of agonized youth and its insupportable sweetness, its sharp desire, and fierce necessity. The problems in life may be limited in number, but they are not therefore the less intense.

And then, after achieving this tragic view, Alexandra turns away from it. The death of Emil and Marie marks the emotional climax of the book. Immediately afterwards, a reaction seems to set in, as if after long and painful suffering the only feeling that arises is a chill loathing of all feeling. This is brought out in Alexandra's interview with Frank Shabata in the state prison:

> Frank jerked a dirty blue handkerchief from his trousers pocket. He had begun to cry. He turned away from Alexandra. "I never did mean to do not'ing to dat woman," he muttered. "I never mean to do not'ing to dat boy. I ain't had not'ing ag'in dat boy. An' then I find him — " He stopped. The feeling went out of his face and eyes. He dropped into a chair and sat looking stolidly at the floor, his hands hanging loosely between his knees, the handkerchief lying across his striped leg. He seemed to have stirred up in his mind a disgust that had paralyzed his faculties.[57]

This is a metaphysical nausea, a disgust at the end results of human emotion so powerful as to cause a turning-away from emotion itself. A revulsion from feeling of this sort can be a gesture of self-defense on the part of an organism, but when maintained for more than a few moments it is self-defeating and has death in it. Alexandra feels this herself as Frank, brought up short by his nausea, stops a second time:

> Frank rubbed his head and stopped suddenly, as he had stopped before. Alexandra felt that there was something strange in the way he chilled off, as if something came up in him that extinguished his power of feeling or thinking.[58]

Her insight is a true one, for where there is no thought and no feeling there is also no life. But in spite of this realization Alexandra herself gives way to nausea on the way back home from prison:

> As the car lurched over its uneven roadbed, back toward Lincoln, Alexandra thought of how she and Frank had been wrecked by the same storm and of how, although she could come out into the sunlight, she had not much more left in her life than he. She remembered some lines from a poem she had liked in her school-days:

> Henceforth the world will only be
> A wider prison-house to me, —

and sighed. A disgust of life weighed upon her heart; some such feeling as had twice frozen Frank Shabata's features while they talked together. She wished she were back on the Divide.[59]

This is exactly the kind of thing that Crazy Ivar was trying to get away from when he fled from civilization into the wilderness; he feared human involvement because of the awful things to which it might lead. The obvious conclusion seems to be that human relations are so dangerous that the only way to avoid sin is to fly from them altogether, but this is obviously impossible. Ivar says as much to Signa in the previously mentioned conversation they have together:

> "Ivar," Signa asked suddenly, "will you tell me why you go barefoot? All the time I lived here in the house I wanted to ask you. Is it for a penance, or what?"
> "No, sister. It is for the indulgence of the body. From my youth up I have had a strong, rebellious body, and have been subject to every kind of temptation. Even in age my temptations are prolonged. It was necessary to make some allowances; and the feet, as I understand it, are free members. There is no divine prohibition for them in the Ten Commandments. The hands, the tongue, the eyes, the heart, all the bodily desires we are commanded to subdue; but the feet are free members. I indulge them without harm to anyone, even to trampling in filth when my desires are low. They are quickly cleaned again." [60]

Ivar is really not solving the problem, but avoiding it. He has managed to channelize his desires so that they do not hurt other people; by confining their expression to his feet he is not likely to get into the kind of serious trouble that Emil, Marie, or Frank Shabata got into. But if his desires cannot hurt other people, neither can they help them very much. He reaches an equilibrium, but only by turning away from life and the inevitability of human relationships. So the problem of how to control the dangerous dual nature of spontaneity is not solved by Crazy Ivar.

Maxwell Geismar has pointed out the importance to Willa Cather's thought of a remark she once made in an essay on Katherine Mansfield.[61] After speaking of the family situations which Miss Mansfield sometimes wrote about and praising her delicate understanding of them, she says:

. . . One realizes that human relations are the tragic necessity of human life; that they can never be wholly satisfactory, that every ego is half the time greedily seeking them, and half the time pulling away from them. [62]

This is a statement of paramount importance and one that throws considerable light on the second part of *O Pioneers!* The great problem there is that of achieving a satisfying and successful spontaneity in human relations. Emil and Marie seem to have achieved this; the beauty of their feeling for each other is clearly better than the unhappiness of Marie's marriage to Frank Shabata; and the natural goodness of human nature seems superior to the restraints imposed upon it by civilization. But then the whole system of moral values is suddenly inverted. Spontaneity becomes a monster; Frank Shabata shoots the two lovers, and Alexandra tells him in prison that they were more to blame than he was.[63] Alexandra, Frank, Signa, and Crazy Ivar all unite in turning from this manifestation of human emotion with loathing and disgust. The contrast between the two attitudes taken toward spontaneity would not be so striking if the love affair had not previously been represented as being so idyllic. Why does this sudden shift in values occur? Perhaps the quotation from the essay on Katherine Mansfield provides a clue. For the first part of the story the characters are greedily seeking human relations; in the last part they are desperately pulling away from them, and this accounts for the nausea and disgust at life so much in evidence there. That this is also Willa Cather's belief as well as her characters' is shown by the fact that although this is the one book in which spontaneous human relations receive extended sympathetic treatment, yet even here she has all her main characters unite in condemnation of spontaneity before the book is over.

The same adverse judgment on spontaneity is seen in Alexandra's fantasy of being "carried." This is worth quoting at length because it shows how Alexandra changes as she gets older:

There was one fancy indeed, which persisted through her girlhood. It most often came to her on Sunday mornings, the one day in the week when she lay late abed listening to the familiar morning sounds; the windmill singing in the brisk breeze, Emil whistling as he blacked his boots down by the kitchen door. Sometimes, as she lay thus luxuriously idle, her eyes closed, she used to have an illusion of being lifted up bodily and carried lightly by someone very strong. It was a man, certainly, who carried her, but he was like no man she knew; he was much larger and stronger and swifter, and he carried her as easily as if she were a sheaf of wheat. She never saw him, but, with eyes closed, she could feel that he was yellow like the sunlight, and there was the smell of ripe corn-fields about him. She could feel him approach, bend over her and lift her, and then she could feel herself being carried swiftly off across the fields. After such a reverie she would rise hastily, angry with herself, and go down to the bath-house that was partitioned off the kitchen shed. There she would stand in a tin tub and prosecute her bath with vigor, finishing it by pouring buckets of cold well-water over her gleaming white body, which no man on the Divide could have carried very far.[64]

This fantasy of desire, of wishing to be taken, is another instance of the power of spontaneity. It suggests that something is missing in Alexandra's life; this is as close as she ever comes to consciously formulated desire for human love. It is in keeping with her character that this fantasy makes her angry; the cold shower which she takes is intended to be a punishment as well as a cleansing of herself of the defiling effects which she imagines to be inherent in sexual love, and indeed in man-woman relations in general. The description continues:

As she grew older, this fancy more often came to her when she was tired than when she was fresh and strong. Sometimes, after she had been in the open all day, overseeing the branding of the cattle or the loading of the pigs, she would come in chilled, take a concoction of spices and warm home-made wine, and go to bed with her body actually aching with fatigue. Then, just before she went to sleep, she had the old sensation of being lifted and carried by a strong being who took from her all her bodily weariness.[65]

As the years pass by, the fantasy changes. It is now less erotic and becomes more of a longing to shift her burdens to somebody else and rest for a while. Desire becomes transmuted into surrender; passion gives place to a yearning for peace and for freedom from pain. The end result of this process comes three months after tragedy has struck the family. A thunderstorm has drenched Alexandra to the bone while she meditates in the Norwegian graveyard where Emil lies buried. Ivar brings her back to the house, and she goes to bed to rest:

As she lay alone in the dark, it occurred to her for the first time that perhaps she was actually tired of life. All the physical operations of life seemed difficult and painful. She longed to be free from her own body, which ached and was so heavy. And longing itself was heavy; she yearned to be free of that.

As she lay with her eyes closed, she had again, more vividly than for many years, the old illusion of her girlhood, of being lifted and carried lightly by someone very strong. He was with her for a long while this time, and carried her very far, and in his arms she felt free from pain. When he laid her down on her bed again, she opened her eyes, and for the first time in her life, she saw him, saw him clearly, though the room was dark, and his face was covered. He was standing in the doorway of her room. His white cloak was thrown over his face, and his head was bent a little forward. His shoulders seemed as strong as the foundations of the world. His right arm, bared from the elbow, was dark and gleaming, like bronze, and she knew at once that it was the arm of the mightiest of all lovers. She knew at last for whom it was she had waited, and where he would carry her. That, she told herself, was very well. Then she went to sleep.

Alexandra wakened in the morning with nothing worse than a head cold and a stiff shoulder. . . .[66]

In her physical and mental demoralization induced by Emil's murder and her drenching in the Norwegian graveyard, Alexandra has a vision of death. For of course it is Death who carries her bodily and is the mightiest of all lovers. This, as Willa Cather sees it, is the final metamorphosis of desire, the end result of emotional involvement. For her, even as a bystander, the emotional life has gotten out of hand and has become so painful that death would be a wished-for release; she is tired of her body, tired of her feelings, and tired of being tired. This change from desire to surrender and to a final longing for death is another comment of Willa Cather's on the terrible destruction that can be wrought by unbridled spontaneity, even if only by secondary involvement. The passionate response to life which she admires so much can easily become suicidal, and her greatest heroines go around clutching daggers to their bosoms. It is because Willa Cather felt this way about spontaneity that her later novels show a calculated and steadily increasing withdrawal of emotion; she feels that the results of human feelings are too horrible to contemplate, so they are at first minimized and then excluded altogether.

The shift from desire to resignation affects Alexandra's attitude toward the land as well as toward people. On the book's last pages, when the long-delayed marriage of Alexandra and Carl is about to take place, she says:

> ". . . I thought when I came out of that prison, where poor Frank is, that I should never feel free again. But I do, here." Alexandra took a deep breath and looked off into the red west.
> "You belong to the land," Carl murmured, "as you have always said. Now more than ever." [67]

Now Alexandra belongs to the land. In the early part of the book it was the land that belonged to her.

> "Lou and Oscar can't see those things," said Alexandra suddenly. "Suppose I do will my land to their children, what difference will that make? The land belongs to the future, Carl; that's the way it seems to me. How many of the names on the county clerk's plat will be there in fifty years? I might as well try to will the sunset over there to my brother's children. We come and go, but the land is always there. And the people who love it and understand it are the people who own it — for a little while." [68]

At the end of the book it is the land which endures and molds the people on it, rather than the people molding the land. This is in sharp contrast with the earlier triumphant note sounded after Alexandra has bought out dispossessed farmers and starts singing a Swedish hymn as she climbs the swells of the Divide. Thus even within the brief pages of Willa Cather's first prairie novel there is a shift from conquering to accepting, and even to being conquered. This mirrors the changing attitude man has toward life itself, as the enthusiasm of youth gradually gives way to the acceptance and resignation of old age.
Alexandra continues her reverie by telling Carl:

> "I had a dream before I went to Lincoln — But I will tell you about that afterward, after we are married. It will never come true, now, in the way I thought it might." [This refers to her dream about the greatest of all lovers. But are we really convinced of the truth of what she says?] She took Carl's arm and they walked toward the gate. "How many times we have walked this path together, Carl. How many times we will walk it again!

Does it seem to you like coming back to your own place? Do you feel at peace with the world here? I think we shall be very happy. I haven't any fears. I think when friends marry, they are safe. We don't suffer like — those young ones." Alexandra ended with a sigh.[69]

This attitude is a long way from the heroic spontaneity which tamed the soil; a life based on it will not fall very low, but neither will it soar very high. If it will avoid the kind of tragedy produced by the relation between Emil and Marie, it will also exclude all that was most beautiful in that relationship. Since Carl and Alexandra are aiming at safety, not spontaneity, the best they can achieve is a kind of Stoic calm in which passion is shunned because it is seen as leading only to suffering.[70]

Thus even the first of Willa Cather's Nebraska novels ends on a note not of triumph but of failure. Willa Cather's distrust of impulsiveness and the emotional life is apparent right down through to the last few paragraphs of the book:

> They had reached the gate. Before Carl opened it, he drew Alexandra to him and kissed her softly, on her lips and on her eyes.
> She leaned heavily on his shoulder. "I am tired," she murmured. "I have been very lonely, Carl!"
> They went into the house together, leaving the Divide behind them, under the evening star. Fortunate country, that is one day to receive hearts like Alexandra's into its bosom, to give them out again in the yellow wheat, in the rustling corn, in the shining eyes of youth! [71]

The older generation has been ground down, and is almost ready to take its place in the cyclical process of death and rebirth. Although in the book's last sentence Willa Cather explicitly puts her hope in the spontaneity of the next generation, this declaration has a tacked-on quality which is not convincing, since it contradicts so much that has gone before.

So it seems that Willa Cather was intent on making a case against spontaneity in every possible way. As we have seen her do before, she rigs her plot around mere coincidence so that spontaneous man-woman relations are presented as inevitably leading to disaster. The contrast between Emil and his lifelong friend Amédée illustrates this. Willa Cather makes an explicit contrast between legitimate and illegitimate love, between Amédée's idyllic family existence and Emil's unsatisfied longing for another man's wife:

> It seemed strange that now he should have to hide the thing that Amédée was so proud of, that the feeling which gave one of them such happiness should bring the other such despair. It was like that when Alexandra tested her seed-corn in the spring, he mused. From two ears that had grown side by side, the grains of one shot up joyfully into the light, projecting themselves into the future, and the grains from the other lay still in the earth and rotted; and nobody knew why.[72]

To Emil the universe at this juncture seems a capricious one; there is no reason behind its blind bestowal of favors on some and denial of them to others. Yet Amédée the happy husband and father whom Emil envies meets an unhappy end himself; he is stricken with abdominal pain while working in his wheatfield and is dead by three o'clock the next morning. Willa Cather has manipulated Emil's capricious universe until it has become a malignant one to him. No love is allowed to thrive at all; unsanctified love meets the same fate as sanctified; Emil meets his death by Frank Shabata's shotgun; Amédée is taken off by appendicitis.

Nothing could better illustrate the extreme danger which Willa Cather felt to result inevitably from sexual passion than the artistic use she makes of sudden death. I have shown how Bartley Alexander's bridge was made to collapse beneath him because of his affair with Hilda. Similarly in *O Pioneers!* Emil and Marie are caught and killed the one time they ever make love. The death of Amédée might superficially appear to be different, yet is part of the same general pattern apparent in Willa Cather's novels that all those who love passionately must die. Amédée's death seems all the more sinister because it leads indirectly to the snuffing out of Emil's life. Emil attends Amédée's funeral in a highly charged emotional state; he leaves it in an ecstasy of rapt adoration in which sacred and profane love are interfused. Then he goes to Marie and finds her alone in a garden transfigured by light; later Frank Shabata finds the pair together and kills them with his rifle. One coincidence is rendered all the more terrifying because of the partial effect it has in setting the stage for another. For the final murder is a coincidence, too; there is no particular reason why Frank Shabata should happen along just when he does and find the pair of lovers under the tree.

It cannot be emphasized too strongly that what Willa Cather is condemning here is spontaneity in the relation between the sexes. Any estimate of the quality of the vision of life expressed in her novels must recognize that this was always a major preoccupation with her. For instance, her stories abound with instances of frustrating and unhappy marriages. Merely confining ourselves to the novels written after *Alexander's Bridge,* in *O Pioneers!* there is the unhappy marriage between Marie and Frank Shabata; in *The Song of the Lark* there are no less than three unhappy marriages, those of Dr. Archie, Fred Ottenburg, and the Swedish singer Nordquist; in *My Ántonia* there is the debilitating liaison between Ántonia's parents, the Shimerdas; in *One of Ours* there is the ill-fated union of Claude and Enid Wheeler, with the strong suggestion that their parents are unhappily married as well; in *A Lost Lady* Marian Forrester becomes unhappy after the Captain is paralyzed; in *The Professor's House* Godfrey St. Peter becomes dissatisfied with his wife after finishing his great book; in *My Mortal Enemy* Myra Henshawe comes to hate her husband after having made a love match; in *Death Comes for the Archbishop* various minor characters have marital difficulties, for example, Magdalena, the abused wife of the murderer Buck Scales; in *Lucy Gayheart* the singer Clement Sebastian is separated from his wife; and in *Sapphira and the Slave Girl* Sapphira and Henry Colbert are estranged from each other and have separate living quarters on their plantation. This imposing array of evidence reveals Willa Cather as interested in showing that permanently satisfying relationships between men and women are impossible. Of course this is highly idiosyncratic; she seems bent on justifying her own way of life rather than portraying the world as it is. In the real world at least some marriages turn out satisfactorily. What she offers as a substitute for passionate love between man and woman is membership in a family group, usually including several generations, in which the relations between members, far from being spontaneous, are almost ritualistic in nature. But for this we must wait until *My Ántonia;* at the time she wrote *O Pioneers!* she had not yet developed her ideas that far.

THE CONFLICT BETWEEN COUNTRY AND TOWN

Another major problem in *O Pioneers!* is that of the conflict between the two opposing value systems represented by country and town. In previous stories she had set the two in clear opposition to each other and rejected the values of the country; in *O Pioneers!* she tried to maintain them both. The special contribution of her prairie novels is that in them the town is characteristically a European city or town, and the country is the American countryside. Although one has to wait for *My Ántonia* to get a detailed picture of this, even in *O Pioneers!* one gets a hint of what it is that the city, or Europe, stood for in Willa Cather's system of values. It emerges in a conversation Emil has with Alexandra:

> Emil stirred on the lounge. . . . "Father wasn't a bit like Lou or Oscar, was he?"
>
> "Oh, not at all!" Alexandra dropped her sewing on her knee. "He had better opportunities; not to make money, but to make something of himself. He was a quiet man, but he was very intelligent. You would have been proud of him, Emil."
>
> .   .   .   .
>
> Alexandra took up her sewing again. "I can remember father when he was quite a young man. He belonged to some kind of a musical society, a male chorus, in Stockholm. I can remember going with mother to hear them sing. There must have been a hundred of them, and they all wore long black coats and white neckties. I was used to seeing your father in a blue coat, a sort of jacket, and when I recognized him on the platform, I was very proud." [73]

This gives us several hints as to what Europe is meant to symbolize. It stands for a civilized society, one in which intelligence is appreciated to the extent that a man can make a career for himself by using his brain, as contrasted with the backbreaking manual labor necessary to make a career on the Divide. It is a society which provides outlets for the satisfaction of cultural needs such as the male chorus to which John Bergson belonged, and it encourages the amenities and rituals of civilized life, such as the dress suits which the singers have to wear when giving a performance. Life in Europe is seen as pleasanter and far more stimulating than in the Middle West; it is more varied and contains pleasures which Nebraska never dreamed of. In brief, the image of Europe represents civilized sensibility, a heightened enjoyment of life, and a response to art, all three of which Willa Cather sees as painfully lacking on the Divide. [74]

In spite of all its manifold virtues, however, Europe for Willa Cather lacked one thing which frontier Nebraska had, and that one thing was of the highest importance to her. She supposed that in Nebraska no restrictions were placed on the development of superior people; that America was *par excellence* the land of the creative will. On the frontier, she believed, there was freedom to develop as one pleased, to follow one's career or bent without hindrance from anybody. This accounts for her all-important choice of the immigrant as her protagonist in the prairie novels, rather than a pioneer of native American stock. For she regarded the immigrant as having, at his best, all the civilized sensibility of the European together with the freedom of action of the American. He is the cream of two continents, and combines the best features of both Old World and New.

I have said that among other things *O Pioneers!* is a celebration of the natural aristocrat. A belief in natural aristocracy agrees quite well with the belief that America is the land where natural aristocracy is freest to express itself, where the ideal of *"la carrière ouverte aux talents"* comes closer to being a reality than in any other country. This idea is the basic postulate of the rugged individualism which Willa Cather so much admired, and is several times alluded to during the course of the book. Thus Alexandra sees her brother Emil as the joint product of Old World and New, and labors that he may have the opportunity to achieve a good life here in the New World:

> "I want you to see Emil, Carl. He is so different from the rest of us!"
> "How different?"
> "Oh, you'll see! I'm sure it was to have sons like Emil, and to give them a chance, that father left the old country. It's curious, too; on the outside Emil is just like an American boy, — he graduated from the State University in June, you know, — but underneath he is more Swedish than any of us. Sometimes he is so like his father that he frightens me; he is so violent in his feelings like that."
> "Is he going to farm here with you?"
> "He shall do whatever he wants to," Alexandra declared warmly. "He is going to have a whole chance; that's what I've worked for." [75]

And the same idea is seen in a conversation between Emil and Alexandra about John Bergson:

> "Father had a hard fight here, didn't he?" he added thoughtfully.

"Yes, and he died in a dark time. Still he had hope. He believed in the land."

"And in you, I guess," Emil said to himself. . . . At last Emil said abruptly, "Lou and Oscar would be better off if they were poor, wouldn't they?"

Alexandra smiled. "Maybe. But their children wouldn't. I have great hopes for Milly." [76]

Thus it comes about that in the first of her prairie novels Willa Cather introduces what is to be the great theme of her whole career, as the theme of the natural aristocrat on the frontier becomes transmuted into the larger theme of the European in America. For the real significance of her novels lies in their probing of the meaning of the entire European experience in America, from the time of the *conquistadores* until today. This meaning, as we have seen, has to do with the unique advantages which Willa Cather saw America as offering to the adventurous European. The reason Europeans came to America in the first place is the infinite possibilities it holds for the future because it is the land where the heroic will can best operate. On the other hand the heroic will has to be European because only when it is exerted on behalf of a civilized sensibility such as that found on the continent can the objects of its endeavors be worth while.

It is highly important that for Willa Cather a European almost always meant a Continental European rather than someone from the British Isles. At this stage of her career she had a deep distrust, not so much of Englishmen as of English culture, especially as found in native-born Americans of Anglo-Saxon descent. In a factual résumé of the history of Nebraska written in 1923 she wrote:

Unfortunately, their American neighbors were seldom open-minded enough to understand the Europeans, or to profit by their older traditions. Our settlers from New England, cautious and convinced of their own superiority, kept themselves insulated as much as possible from foreign influences. The incomers from the South — from Missouri, Kentucky, the two Virginias — were provincial and utterly without curiosity. They were kind neighbors — lent a hand to help a Swede when he was sick or in trouble. But I am quite sure that Knut Hamsun might have worked a year for any one of our Southern farmers, and his employer would never have discovered that there was anything unusual about the Norwegian. A New England settler might have noticed that his

chore-boy had a kind of intelligence, but he would have distrusted
and stonily disregarded it. If the daughter of a shiftless West
Virginia mountaineer married the nephew of a professor at the
University of Upsala, the native family felt disgraced by such an
alliance.[77]

This attitude is expressed in most of her fiction. In contrast to the
greathearted Swedes, Norwegians, Bohemians, and French in her novels,
the settlers of Anglo-Saxon descent are apt to be cast as petty shop-
keepers and narrow-minded conformists, whether in country or town.[78]
In *My Ántonia* Willa Cather devotes almost the entire middle section
to a description of the imaginative and emotional shortcomings of the
townspeople of Black Hawk, most of whom are of Scotch-Irish descent
— a description that was not very kindly received in her own native
town of Red Cloud. This distrust and suspicion of Anglo-Saxons, which
the Nebraska essay shows to be especially virulent against Southerners,
is part of the larger pattern of her reaction against her family, who,
it so happens, were Scotch-Irish settlers from Virginia. It was not
until quite late in her life and career — not in fact until the publication
of "Old Mrs. Harris" (1932) and *Sapphira and the Slave Girl* (1940)
— that she was able to write with any lasting sympathy at all about
people of Anglo-Saxon descent, particularly Southerners.

Willa Cather's use of the immigrant heroine has other implications
besides the ones discussed. It allowed her to combine in very satisfying
proportions the three formative influences on her described in the first
chapter. I have already described how the choice of a protagonist of
differing racial stock from that of her parents served as a handy means
for the rejection of her family. In addition it also provided a happy
synthesis of the two other great influences on her, the Populist movement and art for the sake of art. In a sense, she herself has gone a
pilgrimage in the opposite direction from that of her literary master
Henry James. She takes James's theme of the American in Europe and
turns it around, writing instead about the European in America. In
James the American is initiated into a broader life than any he had
known by sojourning among the residents of an older civilization. In
Willa Cather it is the European who is initiated into a broader life by
coming to America. For according to Willa Cather, only in America can
he combine the aesthetic attraction of the search for beauty with the
moral virtues inherent in the idyl of the garden, the cultivated sensibility with the ethical integrity of the agrarian dream.

All of this was predicated on the assumption that the United States

was an agrarian nation, that the real America was to be found not in
quaint gabled towns but along rural lanes. In the popular mythology
of the nineteenth century, America stood for the countryside. But in
the years following the Civil War this became less and less true. America had become an urbanized culture; cities dotted the eastern seaboard
and were developing in the interior valley as well. Gone was the inter-
continental gap between "Europe" and "America"; both of them were
to be found on our own shores in the form of East and West, or, more
specifically, as "City" and "Farm." By Willa Cather's day much of
the opposition between America and Europe had resolved itself into
the opposition between country and town.

This opposition is strong in Willa Cather; and in *O Pioneers!* she is
unable to make up her mind between the two. Each one possesses
values which she is unwilling to give up and unable to reconcile. When
the nineteen-year-old Carl Linstrum tells Alexandra his family is giving
up their farm and going back to the city she says to him:

> "Yes, yes, Carl, I know. You are wasting your life here. You
> are able to do much better things. You are nearly nineteen now,
> and I wouldn't have you stay. I've always hoped you would get
> away." [79]

Here, through her spokesman Alexandra, Willa Cather seems to be
arguing for the superiority of the city. But this is not always the case.
When Carl comes back sixteen years later, he and Alexandra discuss
the relative merits of city and country life and end up pretty much in
a draw. Carl is explaining why he feels he has not accomplished much
in life:

> "You see," he went on calmly, "measured by your standards
> now, I'm a failure. I couldn't buy even one of your cornfields.
> I've enjoyed a great many things, but I've got nothing to show
> for it all."
> "But you show for it yourself, Carl. I'd rather have had your
> freedom than my land."
> Carl shook his head mournfully. "Freedom so often means that
> one isn't needed anywhere. Here you are an individual, you have
> a background of your own, you would be missed. But off there
> in the cities there are thousands of rolling stones like me. We
> are all alike; we have no ties, we know nobody, we own nothing.
> When one of us dies, they scarcely know where to bury him. Our

landlady and the delicatessen man are our mourners, and we leave nothing behind us but a frock-coat and a fiddle, or an easel, or a typewriter, or whatever tool we got our living by. All we have ever managed to do is to pay our rent, the exorbitant rent that one has to pay for a few square feet of space near the heart of things. We have no house, no place, no people of our own. We live in the streets, in the parks, in the theatres. We sit in restaurants and concert halls and look about at the hundreds of our own kind and shudder."

Alexandra was silent. She sat looking at the silver spot the moon made on the surface of the pond down in the pasture. He knew that she understood what he meant. At last she said slowly, "And yet I would rather have Emil grow up like that than like his two brothers. We pay a high rent, too, though we pay differently. We grow hard and heavy here. We don't move lightly and easily as you do and our minds get stiff. If the world were no wider than my cornfields, if there were not something beside this, I wouldn't feel that it was much worth while to work. No, I would rather have Emil like you than like them. I felt that as soon as you came." [80]

The upshot of the discussion is that each kind of life has its characteristic advantages and drawbacks, neither of which can be ignored. City life gives freedom and full play to the aesthetic sensibility, but it also gives rootlessness; you go there to make good and enjoy the finer things of life, but you have no family. Country life, because it contains your family roots, bestows status and a place in the world, but it also dulls the aesthetic instinct and imposes a heavy and even deadening burden of responsibility — and we have seen how frightened Willa Cather was of family responsibility. We are left with the confrontation of two worlds, both of which Willa Cather wants, with no suggestion of the possibility of a synthesis between them. She never was able to effect any permanent synthesis, either in her art or her life.

Perhaps Willa Cather hoped to solve this problem by joining the representatives of country and city in holy matrimony, to show how civilized sensibility and agrarian strength can mutually support and complement each other, for she arranges an engagement between Carl and Alexandra, and as the book ends they are about to be married. However, this projected marriage is not very convincing; indeed, it is hard to imagine any kind of alliance between the robust Alexandra and the ethereal Carl. The whole thing is too pat and resembles the ending of a story in a "slick" magazine. Willa Cather herself may have realized that the marriage does not quite come off; or perhaps she knew that she was unable to portray a convincing marriage of any kind; at any rate, she does not show it taking place within the confines of the book, but leaves it to occur at some later date.

One of the chief things Willa Cather finds wrong with the American countryside is the chilling disapproval with which it greets any real attempt at individualism; America may be the land of the creative will, but it is also the land of conformity. This paradox, noted long ago by Tocqueville, is a matter of great concern to Willa Cather. She makes no easy correlation between conformity and America this early in her career, since she finds both conformists and nonconformists on the Great Divide. Her great people are always nonconformists with wills of their own, while her little people (like Lou and Oscar), as might be expected, try to become as much like each other and everybody else as they possibly can. We have seen the contrast between Alexandra and her brothers. Lou and Oscar are the ones who want to pull out of the farm when times get bad; they are afraid to have Alexandra build a silo to store their feed; they object to Carl Linstrum's being seen so often at Alexandra's house because of what the neighbors might say. Further, they object to Crazy Ivar and want to have him put away in an asylum. Here, in an interchange between Ivar and Alexandra, we get the most explicit statement in the whole book on the subject of conformity vs. nonconformity:

> Ivar lifted his shaggy head and looked at her out of his little eyes. "They say that you cannot prevent it if the folk complain of me, if your brothers complain to the authorities. They say that your brothers are afraid — God forbid! — that I may do you some injury when my spells are on me. Mistress, how can anyone think that? — that I would bite the hand that fed me!" The tears trickled down the old man's beard.[81]

This demonstration of an almost feudal loyalty brings a response from Alexandra which shows her resistance to the herd instinct:

> Alexandra frowned. "Ivar, I wonder at you, that you should come bothering me with such nonsense. I am still running my own house, and other people have nothing to do with either you or me. So long as I am suited with you, there is nothing to be said." [82]

But Ivar's intuitions about the life around him stand him in good stead. He is able to read the future where his mistress is not. Brushing aside Alexandra's rugged individualism, he points out to her some of the social realities of the community in which they live:

> "Listen, mistress, it is right that you should take these things into account. You know that my spells come from God, and that I would not harm any living creature. You believe that everyone should worship God in the way revealed to him. But that is not the way of this country. The way here is for all to do alike." [83]

This is true even of life on the Divide only sixteen years after the opening of the tale. Crazy Ivar goes on to make an explicit contrast between America and Europe, where the way is apparently not for all to do alike:

> "I am despised because I do not wear shoes, because I do not cut my hair, and because I have visions. [Notice that the order in which these are arranged indicates that it is Ivar's noncon-formity rather than his insanity which is the real object of sus-picion.] At home, in the old country, there were many like me, who had been touched by God, or who had seen things in the graveyard at night and were different afterward. We thought nothing of it, and let them alone. But here, if a man is different in his feet or in his head, they put him in an asylum. . . . That is the way; they have built the asylum for people who are different, and they will not even let us live in the holes with the badgers. Only your great prosperity has protected me so far. If you had ill-fortune, they would have taken me to Hastings long ago." [84]

Crazy Ivar has a clear perception that in the society in which he lives only the possession or patronage of wealth renders nonconformity tolerable. This is an interesting idea and is probably at the root of Willa Cather's rarely mentioned but deeply held conviction that money is absolutely necessary if life is to be at all worth while. The effects of this belief dominate the plot in "Paul's Case" and *My Mortal Enemy*. Alexandra, however, does not share this point of view; she merely restates her position as an individualist and clearly doesn't care a fig for Mrs. Grundy. "Don't come to me again telling me what people say," she says. "Let people go on talking as they like, and we will go on living as we think best." [85] She speaks of other neighbors of theirs

who prefer old-country ways to new and ends up with the humorous
suggestion, "We'll have to start an asylum for old-time people, Ivar." [86]

The idea that in Europe there is more toleration of nonconformity
than exists in the New World is found in other early novels of Willa
Cather. In *The Song of the Lark* she remarks, apropos of the heroine's
addle-pated aunt Tillie:

> In older countries, where dress and opinion and manners are
> not so thoroughly standardized as in our own West, there is a
> belief that people who are foolish about the more obvious things
> of life are apt to have peculiar insight into what lies beyond the
> obvious. The old woman who can never learn not to put the
> kerosene can on the stove, may yet be able to tell fortunes, to
> persuade a backward child to grow, to cure warts, or to tell people
> what to do with a young girl who has gone melancholy. [87]

So no simple answer can be given to the question of where nonconformity is most likely to flourish. If Alexandra is able to enjoy an
almost unlimited degree of freedom on the Nebraska plains, Crazy
Ivar is not. The safest thing to do is to become wealthy, for in America
money talks, and indeed has a voice loud enough to drown out the
Mrs. Grundys of the West. This anticipates such later novels as *A
Lost Lady* and *My Mortal Enemy,* where the possession of money is
regarded as the only thing which can protect people from the vulgarity
of modern mass man.

The over-all pattern of Willa Cather's first Nebraska novel should
now be clear. In her art stories it was the professional career of an
artist which tended to divert human emotions from human contact.
In *O Pioneers!* the struggle with the land tends to divert them. If
there is any conclusion to be drawn from *O Pioneers!* it is that love of
the land is always safe, whereas love of human beings definitely is
not — one need only think of the difference in fates between an
Alexandra or a Crazy Ivar and that of Frank Shabata or Emil and
Marie to see that.

As an alternative to the warm urge to human relationships which
I have called spontaneity, which Willa Cather portrays as leading only
to destruction, she urges the Carlylean will to power directed at taming
the land. This will can be found only in an *élite,* a chosen few who by
virtue of the natural superiority of their strength and imagination are
able to bow the prairie to their will and establish on it a fruitful king-

dom of milk and honey which can serve as the garden of the world. The members of this *élite* usually come from a high culture where they have known the best there is in life; consequently they are able to carve out the fullest possible lives for themselves on the frontier. This leads to the theme of the European immigrant in America. But almost immediately a complication arises. Willa Cather is not absolutely sure that the high culture of the cities can be assimilated to the healthy life of the plains, and, when it comes to a choice between the two, she is unwilling to let either of them go. The book ends on a note of attempted resolution as Alexandra and Carl, the respective proponents of country and city, prepare to marry each other. They are going to take a wedding trip through civilized areas such as San Francisco and on up into the Klondike, which Willa Cather has indicated is the new frontier, and then return to the Divide, which she has indicated is a frontier no longer. It is not until her next prairie novel, *My Ántonia,* that she definitely resolves the city-country conflict in favor of the country.

Themes of *My Ántonia*

My Ántonia is the most famous of Willa Cather's prairie novels and is generally considered to be her best. It contains the fullest celebration ever to come from her pen of country life as opposed to the life of the cities, for the book is one long paean of praise to the joys of rural living and shows her a passionate advocate of the virtues of a settled agricultural existence. In *My Ántonia* the rural-urban conflict hardly seems to exist. The characters pass from farm to town or city and back again without feeling any incompatibility between value systems; instead they manage to extract the maximum of joy from each. But it is always the country to which they return; Ántonia permanently after a brief sojourn in Black Hawk (Red Cloud) and Denver, and the narrator Jim Burden periodically whenever he can get away from his job in a large Eastern city. Native born or immigrant, all the good characters in the book sooner or later yield to the spell of the land, and there is no doubt in the author's mind as to whether country or city is the real America.

My Ántonia thus clarifies certain values which *O Pioneers!* had left up in the air. It is as if Willa Cather had finally made up her mind that her true allegiance was to the soil. The earlier book had shown that life on the farm yielded satisfactions which were deep but narrow; certain things essential to civilized existence just were not to be found there. In the later work all that anyone could ever hope for is pictured as being found on a farm. Ántonia has managed to make her husband happy for twenty-six years in one of the loneliest regions in the world, even though he was a city man and occasionally had spells of home-sickness for the theaters and lighted cafés of the Old World.

But more important than this, the two books show different stages in the development of civilization. In *O Pioneers!* the greatest interest centers on the actual taming of the earth, the breaking of the virgin soil; only incidentally is it concerned with the attempt to found a family. The love of Emil and Marie is snuffed out and so cannot take root, and the proposed marriage of Carl and Alexandra is postponed until after the book's ending. In *My Ántonia*, on the other hand, there is much less emphasis on pioneering. What interested Willa Cather here is the quality of life on the plains, and for once in her career she focuses squarely on and affirms human relations. Much of the book deals with the attempts of the internal narrator and his heroine to come to grips with their emotional involvement with people. This finally results in Ántonia's establishing a domestic household as a going concern and the narrator's failing to do so. Ántonia's great achievement and the chief subject of the book is the founding of a family.

ÁNTONIA AND JIM: THE CONTRASTING LIFE CYCLES

My Ántonia has an interesting and rather peculiar introduction or prologue. In it Willa Cather pretends to have met Jim Burden, the fictitious narrator of the tale, on a train and has them agree that each one of them shall set down on paper his impressions of Ántonia, a mutual friend of their childhood. After months go by they meet again to find that Jim is the only one who has written anything; the rest of the book purports to be his manuscript. Thereafter Willa Cather herself drops out of the story as a separate character. The book that follows really consists of the parallel stories of Ántonia and Jim. The narrator points this out to us while explaining what he has written. "I simply wrote down what of herself and myself and other people Ántonia's name recalls to me. I suppose it hasn't any form. It hasn't any title either." [88] Then he clinches the fact that this is to be the story of a relationship rather than of an individual by changing the wording on the front of the manuscript from "Ántonia" to "My Ántonia." [89]

My Ántonia is usually called a novel with a single protagonist — the heroine — and the narrator has been considered relatively unimportant. [90] I would like to suggest a different interpretation, because the role played by Jim Burden seems to me far too important to be merely that of a first-person onlooker who is relating someone else's story. He enters into the action too much, for one thing. In the early part of the book the Burden family is continually trudging over to their neighbors the Shimerdas to see if they can help them out. Later on there is a long section in which Jim attends the University of Nebraska and flirts with Lena Lingard; here Ántonia scarcely even appears. Even in the parts of the book where Ántonia and Jim appear together, Jim's reactions to events are at least as important as hers. If Willa Cather wanted her heroine to hold the undisputed center of the stage, she should have focused less attention on her narrator. As it is, the center of interest shifts back and forth between Jim and Ántonia, and the result is best understood as the story of parallel lives.

In her later novels Willa Cather often has a double protagonist such as this, one of whom resembles herself and the other someone who is not herself but whom she admires. One of these usually stands for the contemplative life, the other for the life of action. The use of a double protagonist has certain advantages: it allows one character to be an actor and the other a spectator; one can be youth which performs and accomplishes unthinkingly, the other middle age which can interpret the significance of action in others but itself has lost the capacity to act. In *My Ántonia* this double protagonist consists of Jim Burden and Ántonia, who, true to the best traditions of the romantic movement, stand for head and heart, respectively. It is as if Ántonia actually lives life, while Jim merely records it, or at best lives vicariously through her. When he is with her, Jim is a complete personality and reaches his highest development as a human being, but his personal life falls apart when he leaves her, however successful he may be in his professional role. Later in the book when he returns to visit Nebraska after a twenty years' absence, he finds out just how far Ántonia has forged ahead of him during that time. He is generous enough to rejoice in her good fortune, but it merely underlines his own lack of progress, and even regression, during that same interval. The more she tells him about her successful present, the more his mind wanders back to thoughts of their childhood together. Together he and the friend of his youth make a complete personality, but it is Janus-faced, one of them looking forward and the other back. Ántonia has the whole future for her domain; Jim Burden has only the past.

The principle on which this parallel story is constructed is that of development by contrasts. For in spite of early childhood experiences shared together, the lives of the two protagonists are radically unlike.

Ántonia comes to Nebraska as an immigrant and in addition to other hardships of the plains has to face a language barrier; Jim Burden comes from Virginia and faces no such problem. Ántonia comes from a family wracked by internal dissensions, and her father is so unhappy that he commits suicide, largely because her mother is not a home-maker; Jim's family is a well-knit group in which order and happiness are maintained by a pair of extremely competent homemakers, his grandparents. The Shimerdas suffer from poverty for a great many years; the Burdens never have to meet this particular difficulty. As a result Jim can leave home and receive a university education, while Ántonia cannot even afford to take time off from the farm to attend grade school and learn English properly. Finally Jim leaves Nebraska for good to make his home in a large Eastern city where he enters into an unhappy and childless marriage; Ántonia stays on in Black Hawk and after a single unsuccessful effort succeeds not only in marrying but in founding a dynasty, having eleven children by the time Jim comes back to visit her twenty years later.

Although the two lives run parallel and are given almost equally extensive treatment, no doubt is left in the reader's mind that Ántonia is the one who has achieved the real success. Willa Cather loads the story in Ántonia's favor, not only by emphasizing Jim's obvious ad-miration for her, but by making all the significant action take place in Nebraska; Jim Burden's marriage and Eastern career are mentioned merely in passing. Accordingly, the early years on the plains are heavily stressed. This is not surprising, since the two main characters see relatively little of each other after childhood. But it does contribute mightily to the mood of nostalgia which is so strong an ingredient in Jim Burden's personality and which swells toward the end of the book into a hymn of praise for the past which Willa Cather aptly sums up in a line quoted from Vergil: *"Optima dies . . . prima fugit"* (*Georgics*, III, 66-67).

HUMAN RELATIONS: THE FAMILY AS RITUAL

If we consider *My Ántonia* as the story of two parallel but con-trasting lives the book reveals a threefold thematic division. The first part deals with two opposed family groups, the Shimerdas and the Burdens, and their struggles with their environment. The second, be-ginning with the Burdens' removal to Black Hawk, deals mostly with the contrasting modes of life in country and town. This forms the major part of the book. The third, which describes Jim's return to

Black Hawk after an absence of twenty years, shows Ántonia's final success in achieving her great goal in life, a family of her own. This last section fails to carry out the parallel structure of the previous parts except in briefest outline. The introduction tells us that in the intervening period Jim Burden has contracted an unfortunate and childless marriage which differentiates him from the fecund and happily married Ántonia. This would have given Willa Cather a splendid opportunity to develop the theme of the rootless city marriage versus the more stable country union, a theme which appeared later in *A Lost Lady* and *My Mortal Enemy*. But evidently Willa Cather did not care to develop the theme at this point, for she barely alludes to Jim's marriage in this final section of the book. This gives the concluding section a one-sided quality; the story here is almost entirely Ántonia's, and Jim merely stands to one side and worships her. One cannot help feeling that the ending would have been better if Jim Burden had been more dramatically implicated in it, as he had been in the previous sections. But, of course, given the nostalgic tone of the book, he couldn't have been.

As in *O Pioneers!* the first part of *My Ántonia* deals with the period of breaking the sod. Here again the precariousness of civilization on the plains is made to stand for the precariousness of life. But Willa Cather now uses different means to express this: the toughness of reality is now symbolized, not by the unwillingness of the land to be tamed, but among other things by the rigors of a continental climate. The extremes of hot and cold to be found in the Middle West stand for the best and worst life has to offer; heat is correlated with vitality and the great enemy of life is the cold. During a description of a December evening in which the Burden family is snowbound, Jim says:

> I was convinced that man's strongest antagonist is the cold. I admired the cheerful zest with which grandmother went about keeping us warm and comfortable and well-fed. . . . Our lives centered around warmth and food and the return of the men at nightfall.[91]

Here warmth obviously stands for something more than physical warmth and well-being; it represents the satisfaction of congenial family relations as well.

In other places warmth takes on a somewhat different meaning. In the introductory conversation on the train between Jim Burden and herself Willa Cather says:

We were talking about what it is like to spend one's childhood in little towns like these, buried in wheat and corn, under stimulating extremes of climate; burning summers when the world lies green and billowy beneath a brilliant sky, when one is fairly stifled in vegetation, in the color and smell of strong weeds and heavy harvests; blustery winters with little snow, when the whole country is stripped bare and gray as sheet-iron.[92]

This suggests the sequence of birth and death as outlined in the vegetation myth, that age-old interpretation of the cycle of the seasons. On the side of warmth we have life, color, fecundity, and organic material; on the side of coldness we have death, lack of color, sterility, and sheet metal, which is something mechanical with no life in it. But more is to come. An elaboration of the statement that man's worst enemy is the cold carries us further:

Winter comes down savagely over a little town on the prairie. The wind that sweeps in from the open country strips away all the leafy screens that hide one yard from another in summer, and the houses seem to draw closer together. The roads, that looked so far away across the green tree-tops, now stare you in the face, and they are much uglier than when their angles were softened by vines and shrubs.

In the morning, when I was fighting my way to school against the wind, I couldn't see anything but the road in front of me, but in the late afternoon, when I was coming home, the town looked bleak and desolate to me. The pale, cold light of the winter sunset did not beautify — it was like the light of truth itself. When the smoky clouds hung low in the west and the red sun went down behind them, leaving a pink flush on the snowy roofs and the blue drifts, then the wind sprang up afresh, with a kind of bitter song, as if it said: "This is reality, whether you like it or not. All those frivolities of summer, the light and shadow, the living mark of green that trembled over everything, they were lies, and this is what was underneath. This is the truth." It was as if we were being punished for loving the loveliness of summer.[93]

We now begin to get an idea why the cold is man's greatest enemy. It represents the light of truth, and this as Willa Cather conceives it is always unpleasant, something to be hidden. Cold fact, she feels, is mankind's greatest enemy — the fact of his mortality, his frailty, his vulnerability before the forces of nature and before himself. These insights, which other people have erected into a tragic vision, she regarded as something to be put aside. Nor was this the limit of her fear of life — that fear which later led her into so much evasion. She felt that beauty, warmth, light, and loveliness — all the things she herself loved — were somehow lies. She also felt that they were evil, and that she would be punished for loving them.

The hostility of the climate turns out to threaten something that is vitally important to Willa Cather — the family unit. It will soon be time to see just what she meant by this all-important group. We have seen how in the Burden establishment Jim's grandmother kept the family going in spite of the cold. The family there is a center of warmth and affection, against not only the coldness of nature but also the coldness of life. This affection, however, is not of the dangerous explosive spontaneous kind which we have seen Willa Cather shying away from in *O Pioneers!* In a word, it is not sexual. Instead, as we shall see, it is affection such as the members of a large closely knit family feel for each other. The ways of feeling are clearly laid down, they are socially acceptable, and they have none of the dangerous destructive aspects of passion — or of the creative ones either.

To understand Willa Cather's portrayal of the family unit it is necessary to know the kind of family in which she herself grew up. She was the eldest child of seven,[94] the daughter of a strong-willed aggressive mother[95] and a charming but ineffectual father.[96] The family came from Virginia but moved to the Nebraska frontier in the years following the Civil War. Willa Cather's father was the last of his family to move to Nebraska, leaving ten years after his brother and six years after his father had gone there. When he went, it was to live in the house of his father.[97] Previous to this remove, he and his wife lived in the house of his mother-in-law, Willa's grandmother, whom they took along to Nebraska with them. Thus when Willa Cather first came to the frontier she lived in a family consisting of several brothers and sisters, a father and mother, a grandfather, and two grandmothers. In other words, her family was a multi-generation affair, quite large and closely knit.

The importance of this becomes clear when we examine her portrayal of the family unit in her fiction. Time after time the family is represented as being the source of all civilized values; it is the only social unit which she conceives of with any degree of intensity. She was able successfully to portray human relations in a family of the kind she had known in a way in which she was not able to portray, for instance, passionate love between a man and a woman. The interesting thing about her conception of the family is that it constitutes a Platonic hierarchy. Each member is assigned his own individual role, his status being defined by his duties toward the family considered as a corporate group. There is a regular ladder of rank starting with the children and proceeding up through the parents to the grandparents, who in *My Ántonia* are regarded as the ultimate repositories of wisdom.

In *My Ántonia* such a family is presented in the Burdens, the family of the narrator. Jim is an orphan who goes west at the age of ten to grow up with his grandfather and grandmother, but the place of parents is at least partly filled by other adults of his parents' generation who live with the family. In particular their place is taken by the cowboy Otto Fuchs and the hired hand Jake Marpole, who has come to Nebraska with Jim all the way from Virginia. So, even in the Burden family, Willa Cather's three-generation pattern is maintained. It is hard not to feel that the omission of the parents in *My Ántonia* is significant in view of Willa Cather's general pattern of rejecting her immediate environment. They are dead, but their place is taken up by the goodhearted but essentially simple-minded Otto and Jake, whom Willa Cather can like but at the same time looks down on. Thus, while some of her attitudes have changed since her world-of-art period, others have persisted. However she may have changed about the Middle West, it seems likely that she still feels rebellious toward her parents.

When a Willa Cather character of this period thinks of home, however, he thinks not only of his relatives but also of the homestead. In a very real sense the universe of the prairie novels is a local, small-scale affair, embodying the family on the family farm presided over by local deities. That is why Jim Burden is so impressed when he goes to the university by his Latin professor's exposition of the beginning of the third book of Vergil's *Georgics: "Primus ego in patriam mecum . . . deducam Musas";* "for I shall be the first, if I live, to bring the Muses into my country."

> Cleric had explained to us what "patria" here meant, not a nation or even a province, but the little rural neighborhood on the Mincio where the poet was born. This was not a boast, but a hope, at once bold and devoutly humble, that he might bring the Muse (but lately come to Italy from her cloudy Grecian mountains), not to the capital, the *palatia Romana,* but to his own little "country"; to his father's fields, "sloping down to the river and to the old beech trees with broken tops." [98]

Later on Jim wonders "whether that particular rocky strip of New England coast about which he had so often told me was Cleric's *patria*" [99] because the concept of the family on the family land is so important to him. For the youthful Jim *patria* has meant his father's farm under the Blue Ridge of Virginia which he has to leave in his tenth year because of the death of his parents. This sudden uprooting and change of scene is devastating. When he is shipped out west to be reared by his grandfather it is as if he had moved to an entirely different universe where he is completely unknown. He feels he has outrun his lares and penates, and even the guardian spirits of his dead parents seem left behind. So homeless does he feel that he is not even sure that in this remote country God can hear his prayers:

> There was nothing but land; not a country at all, but the materials out of which countries are made. . . . I had never before looked up at the sky when there was not a familiar mountain ridge against it. But this was the complete dome of heaven, all there was of it. I did not believe that my dead father and mother were watching me from up there; they would still be looking for me at the sheep-fold down by the creek, or along the white road that led to the mountain pastures. I had left even their spirits behind me. The wagon jolted on, carrying me I knew not whither. I don't think I was homesick. If we never arrived anywhere, it did not matter. Between that earth and that sky I felt erased, blotted out. I did not say my prayers that night: here, I felt, what would be would be.[100]

If Jim had continued in this vein, he would have yielded to despair. Being young, however, he goes to sleep in the wagon and wakes to bright sunlight in a room in his grandparents' house. He awakens to find his grandmother looking down on him: "a tall woman with wrinkled brown skin and black hair. . . ." [101]

> "Had a good sleep, Jimmy?" she asked briskly. Then in a very different tone she said, as if to herself, "My, how you do look like your father!" I remembered that my father had been her little boy; she must often have come to wake him like this when he overslept.[102]

The family is back in the picture once more; Jim has a grandmother who is very much alive and a dead father who yet lives vividly in her memory of him. A few household details provide a reassuring contrast to the last night's experience of the wildness and strangeness of the new land, and serve as a reminder that even in this remote country civilized domestic life is possible. Jim's grandmother is able to allay his fears by using a well-recognized formula for the expressing of emotion within the family framework. The home has become a kind of sanctuary; for Willa Cather the one thing that alleviates the terrible insecurity of emigration is the emotional protection furnished by the accepted modes of thought and feeling found within the family unit.

THE BURDENS AND THE SHIMERDAS: ORDER *vs.* CHAOS

From the beginning the Shimerda family is contrasted with the Burdens. They are pictured as being much less able to cope with the soil than their American neighbors. To be sure, they are at a tremendous disadvantage because they do not know English at first, and therefore have to depend on a fellow countryman of theirs named Krajiek, who is thoroughly dishonest. He has sold them his home, which is merely a cavelike dugout in the side of a hill, and has overcharged them for it. (The Burdens, by way of contrast, live in the only wooden house west of Black Hawk, itself a sign of civilization.) He exploits them in every way he knows how, but although they realize it they do not know how to get rid of him, for he is the only one they can turn to until the Burdens start giving them neighborly advice. Krajiek is the first evil thing they come across in the wild new land. He represents an early and somewhat abbreviated Willa Cather portrait of man's cruelty to men. In the old country the Shimerdas would never have gotten into a position where he could have taken advantage of them, but in the new West he is able to make the very conditions of life serve his own wily ends:

> During those first months the Shimerdas never went to town. Krajiek encouraged them in the belief that in Black Hawk they would somehow be mysteriously separated from their money. They hated Krajiek, but they clung to him because he was the only human being with whom they could talk or from whom they could get information. He slept with the old man and the two boys in the dugout barn, along with the oxen. They kept him in their hole and fed him for the same reason that the prairie dogs and the brown owls housed the rattlesnakes — because they did not know how to get rid of him.[103]

But quite aside from the possession of such a dangling parasite, the Shimerdas are not equipped for life in the wilderness. They are improvident, for one thing, and are always giving away articles which please their friends. This characteristic, an important trait of all Willa Cather heroines, is better suited to an economy of abundance than to an economy of scarcity such as that found on the frontier. More important, they seem to lack know-how, the knowledge of how to make the most out of their scanty resources. It doesn't occur to Mrs. Shimerda to start a henhouse going in the fall so that her family will be able to have fresh eggs and poultry during the winter. For a while they are reduced to a diet of prairie-dog meat until the Burden family undertakes to revictual them with enough food to last them through the winter.

Mostly it is Mrs. Shimerda's fault that the family does so poorly. In *O Pioneers!* Willa Cather had indicated the important role she felt that women played in maintaining the usages of traditional civilization in an alien land. Of Mrs. Bergson, Alexandra's mother, she says:

> For eleven years she had worthily striven to maintain some semblance of household order amid conditions that made order very difficult. Habit was very strong with Mrs. Bergson, and her unremitting efforts to repeat the routine of her old life among new surroundings had done a great deal to keep the family from disintegrating morally and getting careless in its ways. . . . Alexandra often said that if her mother were cast upon a desert island, she would thank God for her deliverance, make a garden, and find something to preserve.[104]

Mrs. Shimerda has no such talent. She is not a homemaker; her house is a chaos, and she does nothing to bolster the morale of her gentle, mild-mannered husband, who is pining away with homesickness for his native Bohemia. It is quite understandable that Mr. Shimerda feels happiest when he is visiting with the Burdens, where everything is well regulated in a civilized manner. Willa Cather gives more than a hint that the despair which finally drives him to suicide is due at least in part to his wife's poor housekeeping:

> I suppose, in the crowded clutter of their cave, the old man had come to believe that peace and order had vanished from the earth, or existed only in the old world he had left so far behind.[105]

In marked contrast to this disorder is the well-ordered home run by the Burden family. The civilized quality of the life here is felt rather than described, although vivid little details go to build up an impression of it: the statement that the family lives in a wooden house rather than a sod hut, the fact that even in the basement the earthen walls are plastered and whitewashed; the description of the heavy copper-tipped rattlesnake cane which Grandmother used for killing rattlers she found in the garden, itself a token of the emphatic super-imposition of civilization upon the country's wildness. The key words Willa Cather uses in describing the Burdens' existence are order, tranquillity, and regularity. No wonder Mr. Shimerda, with his "fixy" ways, feels when he is with them that he is among civilized people.

The head of the whole family group is the grandfather, a wonderful fountain of common sense. A good idea of what he was like is seen in his attitude toward the Indian ring:

> Beyond the pond, on the slope that climbed to the cornfield, there was, faintly marked in the grass, a great circle where the Indians used to ride. Jake and Otto were sure that when they galloped round that ring Indians tortured pioneers, bound to a stake in the center; but grandfather thought they ran races or trained horses there.[106]

Grandfather has a realistic mind, in contrast to the romantic attitude of the cowboy Otto and the fieldhand Jake, who are child men, strong in body and in loyalty, but untutored in the ways of the world. When trouble develops between the two families over a badly used piece of farming equipment the Shimerdas had borrowed and as a consequence Jake knocks Ambrosch Shimerda down, it is Grandfather who suggests that Jake go to the town justice of the peace, tell him the story and pay the fine for the assault, thus forestalling any action that the vindictive and litigious Mrs. Shimerda might take. And it is Grandfather who finally resolves the ensuing feud between the two families by hiring Ambrosch to help harvest his wheat crop and asking Ántonia to help with the feeding of the crews in the kitchen. When the danger of religious antagonism between Catholic and Protestant seems imminent, Grandfather Burden averts it by saying, "The prayers of all good people are good," and when the Shimerdas are unable to get a priest to conduct a service over Mr. Shimerda's grave because he was a suicide, Grandfather himself undertakes to say a prayer. Grandfather's opinion on any matter is always the final court of appeal because he is such a repository of sanity and common sense.

If Grandfather is the person to whom all religious and ethical problems are referred, Grandmother is the source of all judgments on aesthetic matters. She knows instinctively what is the right thing for a woman to do. She worries about the heavy farm work that Ambrosch makes Ántonia do after their father's death. "Heavy field work'll spoil that girl. She'll lose all her nice ways and get rough ones," [107] she says, and she is right, since for a while Ántonia's hard life does make her lose all charm. Thus the Platonic hierarchy of assigned roles and qualities in the family is carried through as regards Grandfather and Grandmother Burden.

The most interesting results of the contrast between the Burden and Shimerda families are the quiet judgments that Willa Cather implicitly makes on what a family should be. The Shimerda family is not a unit. It breaks down into little groups which work at cross-purposes to one another. The grasping Mrs. Shimerda and her surly and arrogant son Ambrosch form one of these groups; Ántonia and her father form another. Old Mr. Shimerda is the most civilized person in the family and exemplifies the Old World traits that Willa Cather would most like to see carried over the seas. But unfortunately he is not strong, and we have already seen in the case of John Bergson, of *O Pioneers!*, that imagination and aesthetic sensitivity without strength are powerless to survive in a rough-and-ready new land. His wife, who might have been a prop and support to him if she had been a homemaker like Mrs. Bergson, only undermines her husband's morale. Her disorderly housekeeping, rather than emphasizing the continuity between life in Bohemia and life on the western plains, points up the disparity between the two. Her disorderly ways help contribute to her husband's despair by making his present life the exact opposite of everything he wanted his life to be, and in the end, driven beyond his endurance by misery, he commits suicide.

The Burden family, on the other hand, is a little commonwealth presided over by Grandmother and Grandfather. The latter's commands are obeyed unquestioningly since his authority comes to him straight from God — he is represented as being intensely religious — and he always uses that authority for the good of the family as a whole, not for any particular unit in it, as well as for the good of the pioneer community of which it forms a part. Grandmother Burden plays a more subdued but no less important role as maintainer of domestic routine; she succeeds in all the practical matters in which Mrs. Shimerda fails. Jake and Otto are the faithful family retainers, the men children, strong of back though weak of mind, whose devotion to

Jim's grandparents is almost feudal. Their particular province is dealing with children; they teach Jim how to ride a pony, keep him entertained with stories of the Wild West, build a sleigh for him, cut down and bring in a tree for him at Christmas and decorate it with Christmas ornaments. To a certain extent the traditional roles of parents' and grandparents' generations are reversed, since the parent surrogates Otto and Jake play with Jim all the time and it is Grandfather and Grandmother Burden who are the disciplinarians.

There is an ironic twist at the end of *My Ántonia* that heightens the contrast between the two families and tells a good deal about the novel's values. The Shimerdas are an anarchic disintegrating family group which seems bent on its own destruction, and yet it produces Ántonia, who emerges at the end of the novel as the family founder *par excellence*. All these traits she learned from the Burdens, and rightly so for they form a model family. But in spite of all its good qualities, it is the Burden family which dies out. The improvident family turns out to be the one that produces the most successful homemaker and the model family produces no one capable of carrying on its traditions. But the spirit of Grandmother and Grandfather Burden has been passed on to Ántonia. That is one reason why Jim admires her so much.

The reason for this interchange of roles between the two families has to do with one of Willa Cather's deepest feelings about the value of a family living on the family land. For after Jim Burden has been living in Nebraska for three years, his grandparents become too old for heavy farm work and decide to move into town. This produces a change of the profoundest significance in the nature of the Burden family. It makes Otto and Jake want to leave the Burdens' employ for one thing. Both men are such dyed-in-the-wool children of the wide-open spaces that they would be lost in town. Willa Cather says of them:

> Jake and Otto served us to the last. They moved us into town, put down the carpets in our new house, made shelves and cupboards for grandmother's kitchen, and seemed loath to leave us. But at last they went, without warning. Those two fellows had been faithful to us through sun and storm, had given us things that cannot be bought in any market in the world. With me they had been like older brothers; had restrained their speech and manners out of care for me, and given me so much good comradeship. Now they got on the west-bound train one morning, in their

Sunday clothes, with their oilcloth valises — and I never saw them again. Months afterward we got a card from Otto, saying that Jake had been down with mountain fever, but now they were both working in the Yankee Girl mine, and were doing well. I wrote to them at that address, but my letter was returned to me, "unclaimed." After that we never heard from them.[108]

The departure of Jake and Otto combined with the removal to Black Hawk makes the Burdens a rootless town family which no longer consists of several generations. When this happens they lose their country roots and can no longer absorb all the special virtues which Willa Cather saw as emanating from a life lived close to the land. The agrarian myth has it that the virtuous yeoman is virtuous no longer once he migrates to the city, even if the city turns out to be only a small town like Black Hawk. That is why the Burden family dwindles to nothing; Jim ends up a landless, childless failure, in marked contradistinction to Ántonia, who stays on the land.

Death in Winter and the Hardness of Life

One of the strong points of *My Ántonia* as compared with Willa Cather's other novels is that in it she comes closer than she usually does to facing the problem of evil and suffering in life. This frankness in recognizing the reality of problems which are ultimately insoluble gives the book an emotional depth which one looks for in vain in much of her work. If by evil we mean anything impairing the happiness or welfare of a person or depriving him of good, there is a good deal of evil in *My Ántonia*. Briefly, the varieties Willa Cather describes can be summed up under three headings: natural or external nonhuman evil, man-made evil inflicted by other people, and evil which is self-inflicted.

Natural evil is the simplest of the three and in a sense is no problem at all. One meets it on the frontier or elsewhere by pitting oneself against the forces of nature, and one either succeeds or fails. Sometimes one proves oneself a man by overcoming natural forces, as does the youthful Jim when he kills the great rattlesnake which attacks him in prairie-dog town. Sometimes it is the forces of nature which triumph over man.

Man-made evil inflicted by other persons is more complicated and cannot be summed up so easily. I have described how the Bohemian Krajiek exploited his fellow countrymen the Shimerdas. Another ex-

ample is Wick Cutter, the Black Hawk money lender, whom Willa
Cather treats as a comic character in spite of the ferocious reputation
she gives him. He fastens like a bloodsucker upon the poverty-stricken
farmers of the neighborhood, and Grandfather Burden has had to
rescue more than one poor devil from his clutches. He has an interestingly unhappy relation with his wife which can be summed up by
her remark to him when, in exhibiting some of her chinaware to a
caller, he accidentally drops a piece: "Mr. Cutter, you have broken all
the commandments — spare the finger-bowls!" [109] As they grow older
they quarrel continually over the disposal of his estate should she
survive him; he is afraid that it will all go to her "people," whom he
hates. He finally solves the problem melodramatically by murdering
her and then shooting himself an hour later, after firing a shot out the
window to insure the presence of witnesses to testify to the fact that
he had survived his wife and that therefore any will she might have
made would be invalid. Willa Cather's comic treatment of Wick Cutter
tends to preclude any real consideration of the moral implications of
his acts, since he is turned into a character in a grand farce. As a
comic figure of evil he lacks reality and seems to have no relation to
the world as we know it; evidently Willa Cather does not intend to
have him taken too seriously.

A more telling example of man-made evil inflicted by others can be
found in Ántonia's pregnancy. She falls in love with a railroad con-
ductor named Larry Donovan, a "train-crew aristocrat" who fancies
himself a ladies' man; he lures her to Denver with promises of marriage
and then deserts her, leaving her with a child on the way. Unlike
the love passages in *O Pioneers!* this is not presented directly to the
reader. Instead of being narrated by Jim Burden, it is told to him by
another person, the Widow Steavens, since the episode has occurred
after Jim has left the University of Nebraska for Harvard. The Widow
Steavens is a pioneer, an older woman of the same generation and
stature as Jim's grandparents, and so her comments on the tale carry
a moral authority which they would not if they had issued from the
lips of a younger person. In her mouth the story of Ántonia's seduction
assumes overtones that are almost tragic: the bad prosper, the good
come to misfortune through their very virtues, and no one knows why:

> "Jimmy, I sat right down on that bank beside her and made
> lament. I cried like a young thing. I couldn't help it. I was just
> about heart-broke. . . . My Ántonia, that had so much good in
> her, had come home disgraced. And that Lena Lingard, that was

always a bad one, say what you will, had turned out so well, and
was coming home here every summer in her silks and her satins, and
doing so much for her mother. I give credit where credit is due,
but you know well enough, Jim Burden, there is a great difference
in the principles of those two girls. And here it was the good one
that had come to grief!" [110]

For all her heartbrokenness the Widow Steavens does not turn
against Ántonia as Jim does; with the ferocity of youth he cannot
forgive her for becoming an object of pity. The Widow Steavens, on
the other hand, is able to accept the fact that there is a tragic incom-
prehensibility in the fates meted out to human beings; she can admit
that Ántonia has made a mistake and still believe in her. This makes
her superior to Jim, whose immediate reaction to Ántonia is one of
rejection as soon as the image he has of her is broken. Jim is a typical
Willa Cather character in this; he makes a hard-and-fast rule about
people and things and prefers to see the world in terms of black and
white.
But Ántonia does not remain an object of pity for long. Like Hester
Prynne, she gains from suffering a new kind of strength, and finally
is accepted even by the community:

"Folks respected her industry and tried to treat her as if nothing
had happened. They talked, to be sure; but not like they would
if she'd put on airs. She was so crushed and quiet that nobody
seemed to want to humble her." [111]

Her bitter experience has given her more self-knowledge than Marie
Shabata ever had a chance to learn; she now knows the dangers as
well as the delights of unbridled spontaneity and of absolute commitment to the objects of one's affection. As she tells Jim when he comes
back to visit her twenty years after, "The trouble with me was, Jim, I
never could believe harm of anybody I loved." [112]
One would expect the birth of Ántonia's illegitimate child to form the
climax of the book, but no. The whole episode is only thirty pages
long and is related to Jim Burden by a third person, the Widow
Steavens. In other words, the reader is not once removed from the
action but twice removed from it. This in itself is the most significant
thing about the whole event. It shows a trait highly characteristic of
Willa Cather's fiction — that in it she did not really want to present
directly any sort of serious human conflict. The really emotional situa-

tions, the scenes in which it was necessary to face up to the hard facts
about human nature and passions, she avoided if she could. Of *My
Ántonia* she said:

> There was material in that book for a lurid melodrama. But I
> decided that in writing it, I would dwell very lightly on those
> things that a novelist would ordinarily emphasize, and make up
> my story of the little, every-day happenings and occurrences that
> form the greatest part of everyone's life and happiness.[113]

If this was her attitude one may ask why she bothered including
the story of the birth of the baby at all. For she was not bound to
follow in every detail the life of the person upon which the character
of Ántonia was based. The fact that she chose both to include the
episode and to treat it in the precise way that she did indicates that
she was bent on devaluing some of the devastating conflicts that occur
in life, particularly those relating to sex. And if this is so she is being
dishonest and evasive, and her representation of the human scene
suffers from distortion in consequence.

From what has gone before it seems clear that Willa Cather tended
to make light of the difficulties raised by man-made evil inflicted by
other persons. It is natural for her to do so, since this sort of evil
runs directly counter to her belief in the overriding power of the heroic
will, and to admit its potency to hurt us is to admit the inadequacy of
that will. For this reason the real interdependence of men and women
is minimized in her novels; she is more interested in making them
appear independent.

But there is one other kind of man-made evil in *My Ántonia,* and
one to which a person who aspires to be independent is particularly
prone. This is self-inflicted evil or despair, and its logical result is
suicide. Two acts of despair and self-destruction are described in the
book, one minor one which is mentioned as an anecdote in passing
and an important one which forms a major part of the book. The important one is the suicide of Ántonia's father, Mr. Shimerda.

The minor one has to do with a tramp who arrives at Black Hawk
during harvest time. He comes up to a crew running a threshing machine and remarks to Ántonia, who is one of them: "The ponds in this
country is done got so low a man couldn't drownd himself in one of
'em." Ántonia objects:

> "I told him nobody wanted to drownd themselves, but if we
> didn't have rain soon we'd have to pump water for the cattle.

" 'Oh, cattle,' he says, 'you'll all take care of your cattle! Ain't you got no beer here?' " [114]

The tramp offers to help run the threshing machine, and after cutting bands for a few minutes, jumps into the hopper. By the time they get the machine stopped, he is cut to pieces. The incident itself is not so important as the way Willa Cather treats it. This is what she supplies by way of comment:

"Now wasn't that strange, Miss Frances?" Tony asked thoughtfully. "What would anybody want to kill themselves in summer for? In thrashing time, too! It's nice everywhere then."

"So it is, Ántonia," said Mrs. Harling heartily. "Maybe I'll go home and help you thresh next summer. Isn't that taffy nearly ready to eat? I've been smelling it for a long while." [115]

The discussion then shifts to another field. Here in a nutshell is one of Willa Cather's most glaring weaknesses: when her mind is presented with something unpleasant, it shies away from it. The problem of evil is posed, but not commented on. Instead she is evasive and changes the subject.[116]

The best example in the book of self-inflicted evil resulting from despair is the suicide of Mr. Shimerda. Willa Cather treats this differently from the death of the tramp; for once she faces the problem of evil squarely and gives a satisfactory artistic presentation of it. For there is no flinching from the reality of death in the description of Mr. Shimerda's suicide and its consequences. When he can stand things no longer, he washes with hot water, dresses up in clean clothes, and goes out to the barn where he puts the barrel of a gun in his mouth and pulls the trigger. What happens to the people around him after that, the Shimerdas and the Burden family and the community at large, Willa Cather describes at length and deals with not in terms of what death means to the individual but of what it means to the people who survive him.

The reason Mr. Shimerda kills himself is that he cannot stand life on the Divide. Like John Bergson in *O Pioneers!* he is a prime example of a man who has imagination enough to be a pioneer, but not the strength. Except his death, every single important event in his life had been determined for him by others. He need not have married Mrs. Shimerda in the first place — as Ántonia tells Jim, he could have paid her some money instead.[117] He had not wanted to come to America at all, but was browbeaten into coming by his ambitious wife. As her daughter puts it, "All the time she say: 'America big country; much money, much land for my boys, much husband for my girls.' " [118] When he is exposed to the chaos and squalor of the Shimerda farm it apparently never occurs to him to pick up and leave — to go back to an Eastern city, or even to Europe. He is not a man of action, and any other kind of man is lost on the frontier. Unable to use force against the external world, he finally raises his hand against himself.

This causes consternation among his family, since aside from the abdication of responsibility involved he is a Catholic and suicide is not allowed to him. But through her narrator Jim Burden Willa Cather makes clear that she is sympathetic with Mr. Shimerda's act:

> "As I understand it," Jake concluded, "it will be a matter of years to pray his soul out of Purgatory, and right now he's in torment."
> "I don't believe it," I said stoutly. "I almost know it isn't true."
> . . . Nevertheless, after I went to bed, this idea of punishment and Purgatory came back to me crushingly. I remembered the account of Dives in torment, and shuddered. But Mr. Shimerda had not been rich and selfish; he had only been so unhappy that he could not live any longer. [119]

The details of the suicide itself are handled very briefly, in the space of a couple of pages. The rest of the episode describes the effect of Mr. Shimerda's death on his family, his friends, and the pioneer community. Willa Cather does not dwell on the emotional reactions of the Shimerda family except to say that the oldest son Ambrosch was "deeply, even slavishly, devout," [120] sitting with a rosary in his hands and praying all morning while the Burdens make arrangements for his father's burial. Significantly enough Ántonia's responses are hardly mentioned. [121] What Willa Cather does describe is the emotional impact of the calamity on the Burden family. The Burdens rise to the occasion to fill their friends' needs. It is they who do most of the work in preparation for Mr. Shimerda's burial, and it is their emotional reactions which Willa Cather seems to find most interesting. Grandfather is the usual fountain of good sense, the grandmother, in the maternal role once again, gives food and comfort to the younger Shimerdas, who now have nobody to look after them. But it is Otto Fuchs, the Austrian cowboy, upon whom the burden of meeting the crisis devolves. It is he who relates the circumstances of Mr. Shimerda's death to Grandmother Burden and young Jim. He volunteers to make the long ride through the snow into Black Hawk in order to fetch the priest and coroner. And it is he who volunteers to make a coffin, and by his cheerful matter-of-fact awareness and acceptance of death helps the people around him to realize that in spite of disaster life can and does go on:

> "The last time I made one of these, Mrs. Burden," he continued as he sorted and tried his chisels, "was for a fellow in the Black Tiger mine up above Silverton, Colorado. . . . It's a handy thing to know, when you knock about like I've done."
> "We'd be hard put to it now, if you didn't know, Otto," grandmother said.
> "Yes, 'm," Fuchs admitted with honest pride. "So few folks know how to make a good tight box that'll turn water. I sometimes wonder if there'll be anybody about to do it for me. However, I'm not at all particular that way." [122]

The pleasure he gets from handling his carpenter's tools shows that, far from being squeamish or afraid of death, he readily accepts it. He is able actively to enjoy the job at hand, since he realizes its constructive and even religious nature; his intellectual simplicity does not prevent him from recognizing death as one of the great facts of existence.

> All afternoon, wherever one went in the house, one could hear the panting wheeze of the saw or the pleasant purring of the plane. They were cheerful noises, seeming to promise new things for living people: it was a pity that the freshly planed pine boards were to be put underground so soon. The lumber was hard to work because it was full of frost, and the boards gave off a sweet smell of pine woods, as the heap of yellow shavings grew higher and higher. I wondered why Fuchs had not stuck to cabinet work, he settled down to it with such ease and content. He handled the tools as if he liked the feel of them; and when he planed, his hands went back and forth over the boards in an eager, beneficent way as if he were blessing them. He broke out now and then into German hymns, as if this occupation brought back old times to him.[123]

Another effect of Mr. Shimerda's suicide is that it makes the pioneers much more talkative than they usually are. It releases speech in the people who hear about it, and thus unites the living into a closer-knit group than they had formed before. Since their talk is mostly about the deaths of others they have known of or heard about, it serves to tighten the organic bonds of the little frontier community in much the same way as a funeral service is supposed to do:

> One pleasant thing about this time was that everybody talked more than usual. I had never heard the postmaster say anything but "Only the papers, to-day," or "I've got a sackful of mail for ye," until this afternoon. Grandmother always talked, dear woman; to herself or to the Lord, if there was no one else to listen; but grandfather was naturally taciturn, and Jake and Otto were often so tired after supper that I used to feel as if I were surrounded by a wall of silence. Now everyone seemed eager to talk. That afternoon Fuchs told me story after story; about the Black Tiger mine, and about violent deaths and casual buryings, and the queer fancies of dying men. You never really knew a man, he said, until you saw him die. Most men were game, and went without a grudge.[124]

The rallying together of the community's forces enables the people better to face up to the unpleasant reality of the hardness of life. To express that hardness Willa Cather refers to the already mentioned rigors of the continental climate in a submerged metaphor based on her statement that "man's greatest enemy is the cold." The submerged metaphor is that of frozen blood. It is hard in both the literal and figurative senses; the very stuff of life itself has been reduced to immobility by nature's indifference:

> The dead man was frozen through, "just as stiff as a dressed turkey you hang out to freeze," Jake said. The horses and oxen would not go into the barn until he was frozen so hard that there was no longer any smell of blood. They were stabled there now, with the dead man, because there was no other place to keep them.[125]

> Mr. Shimerda lay dead in the barn four days, and on the fifth day they buried him. All day Friday Jelinek was off with Ambrosch digging the grave, chopping out the frozen earth with old axes. On Saturday we breakfasted before daylight and got into the wagon with the coffin. Jake and Jelinek went ahead on horse-

back to cut the body loose from the pool of blood in which it was
frozen fast to the ground.[126]

The fact that the pioneers are willing to chop Mr. Shimerda's body
loose from the pool of frozen blood shows that they are facing un-
flinchingly the toughness of reality, the hardness of life. It is no
accident that the body is frozen, or that the death occurs in the midst
of winter. According to the old vegetation myth winter is the death
of the year, because all crops have died down in the fall, and are not
to be reborn until spring. The meaning of the myth is that death is
not final; one year's crop dies, but next year's crop takes its place;
in human terms, the individual dies but the community lives on. This
is just what happens in *My Ántonia;* the chapter following the one
describing the burial of Mr. Shimerda, and dealing with the further
fortunes of his family, begins with a description of the coming spring.[127]

COUNTRY *vs.* TOWN: THE SUPERIORITY
OF THE COUNTRYSIDE

The middle portion of the book, which is largely the story of Jim's
school and college days, deals with a problem which we have seen
was left unsolved at the end of *O Pioneers!* and which is unresolved
in Willa Cather's work as a whole. It is the problem of the relative
advantages between country and town. Although the book ends with
a glorification of the life of the country, it turns out to be a qualified
glorification. Ántonia may become an earth-goddess, but she gets many
of her good qualities from her father, who was a town dweller. Thus
Willa Cather's idea of the good country life really turns out to be that
of one in which urban and rural traits which she considers desirable
are combined.

My Ántonia's middle section opens with the removal of the Burdens
from farm to town. Just as in the book's first part the edge is taken
off the strangeness of Jim's arrival in the West by a description of the
cozy life led by Jim's grandparents, so the town is rendered more
friendly to him by the description of another family whom he admires,
the Harlings. These nextdoor neighbors are as much paragons of town
life as the Burdens were of life in the country. The father and eldest
daughter are in business — a calling which the later Willa Cather comes
to detest; yet she has nothing but approval for them. The father is
quite authoritarian: when he is at home no one is allowed to make any
noise, and he insists on having all his wife's attention to the exclusion

even of his children. He is much more authoritarian than the bearded patriarch who was his country counterpart, for Mr. Harling is not shown as having a saving sense of humor; but, far from resenting this, Jim seems to find it interesting and rather grand. There is no doubt that Willa Cather enjoyed the portrayal of authoritarian personalities. The oldest daughter, Frances Harling, is her father's business associate and takes care of his transactions for him while he is away on trips. Jim admires her, too, and finds her quite as satisfactory a human being as if she were a man.

Into this ménage Willa Cather introduces Ántonia, who, tiring of the rough life she knows on the farm, comes into town to "go into service," thus hoping to earn money for the folks back home and at the same time see a little more of life than had hitherto come her way. Through the agency of the Burden family she goes to work for the Harlings. She immediately becomes popular with her employers, and they carry on the process of education which had been begun by her father but which would never have gotten very far if it had been left in the tender hands of the grabby Mrs. Shimerda and the sullen Ambrosch. Jim, too, finds himself drawn to the brightly lighted Harling home, from which seem to emanate all the most desirable things in civilization:

> Frances taught us to dance that winter, and she said, from the first lesson, that Ántonia would make the best dancer among us. On Saturday nights, Mrs. Harling used to play the old operas for us, — "Martha," "Norma," "Rigoletto," — telling us the story while she played. Every Saturday night was like a party. The parlor, the back parlor, and the dining room were warm and brightly lighted, with comfortable chairs and sofas, and gay pictures on the walls. One always felt at ease there. Ántonia brought her sewing and sat with us — she was already beginning to make pretty clothes for herself. After the long winter evenings on the prairie, with Ambrosch's sullen silences and her mother's complaints, the Harling home seemed, as she said, "like Heaven" to her.[128]

Part of the reason Mrs. Harling is able to educate Ántonia is that, town-bred or not, she is essentially the same kind of person that Ántonia is. Both have a deep instinctive response to life:

> There was a basic harmony between Ántonia and her mistress. They had strong, independent natures, both of them. They knew

what they liked; and were not always trying to imitate other people. They loved children and animals and music, and rough play and digging in the earth. They liked to prepare rich, hearty food and to see people eat it; to make up soft white beds and to see youngsters asleep in them. They ridiculed conceited people and were quick to help unfortunate ones. Deep down in each of them there was a kind of hearty joviality, a relish of life, not over-delicate, but very invigorating. I never tried to define it, but I was distinctly conscious of it. I could not imagine Ántonia's living for a week in any other home in Black Hawk than in the Harlings'.[129]

In spite of her great fondness for her employers, Ántonia finally leaves them. One night a young man who has escorted Ántonia home from a dance tries to kiss her, and when she protests — because he is going to be married the following Monday — he uses strong-arm tactics and she slaps him. The autocratic Mr. Harling has heard all this and puts his foot down: she will have to stay away from Saturday night dances or else find a new place. Ántonia utterly refuses: nothing is going to make her give up her good times, and so she and the Harlings part.

Ántonia's revolt against the Harlings is only one extension of the rebellion she had already begun against her own family. It is a rebellion in favor of the good things of life; years of drudgery on a remote farm with only an unpleasant mother and brother for company had begotten in her a fierce desire to enjoy life's sweets. To us the rebellion seems mild, since it consists chiefly of having a good time and going out with young men to dances, although it culminates in her being "fooled" by Larry Donovan's promise of marriage and having a baby by him after he had abandoned her. The significance of her rebellion is that it shows Ántonia's asserting her independence from her family as well as from the Harlings. This is a vitally important step for Willa Cather's early heroines, since they seem to feel that without completely rejecting parental authority they cannot be individuals in their own right.

My Ántonia is unique in Willa Cather's early writing in that in it she for once represents a happy marriage and a family at its best; that is, she is able to feel more attraction for the family than revulsion against it. Later on, Ántonia, this nonconformist and rebel against the family, lives to marry and found a family of her own; having experienced many sides of life, she now knows a good deal of what life is about, and is all the better a mother for it. To achieve this effect, Willa Cather has manipulated the plot so that Ambrosch and Mrs. Shimerda are as unattractive as possible; thus a revolt from them is a revolt toward life itself. Ántonia must rebel against a bad family before she can set up a good family. Thus she is able both to be a rugged individualist and later on to enjoy the advantages of group membership too.

If the youthful Ántonia is spirited enough to be rebellious, the same cannot be said of the town girls. One of the most explicit contrasts between town and country which Willa Cather makes in the book is that between the farm-bred females and the girls of Black Hawk. Other girls besides Ántonia get tired of the country and go into service in Black Hawk in order to make the most of town life. When Jim Burden is growing toward manhood he becomes their great admirer. Here is what he has to say about them:

> There was a curious social situation in Black Hawk. All the young men felt the attraction of the fine, well-set-up country girls who had come to town to earn a living, and, in nearly every case, to help the father struggle out of debt, or to make it possible for the younger children of the family to go to school.
>
> Those girls had grown up in the first bitter-hard times, and had got little schooling themselves. But the younger brothers and sisters, for whom they made such sacrifices and who have had "advantages," never seem to me, when I meet them now, half as interesting or as well educated. The older girls, who helped to break up the wild sod, learned so much from life, from poverty, from their mothers and grandmothers; they had all, like Ántonia, been early awakened and made observant by coming at a tender age from an old country to a new. [It is a matter of interest to note that Willa Cather herself came from Virginia to Nebraska at the tender age of nine.] I can remember a score of these country girls who were in service in Black Hawk during the few years I lived there, and I can remember something unusual about each one of them. Physically they were almost a race apart, and out-of-door work had given them a vigor which, when they got over their first shyness about coming to town, developed into a positive carriage and freedom of movement, and made them conspicuous among Black Hawk women.[130]

Unlike the town girls, they had had the hard jolt of coming from one civilization into another of an entirely different kind; they were not able to take for granted habits and customs which were after all only peculiar to one time and place, but were less likely to be conformist and more likely in a given situation to think things out for themselves. This is Jim Burden's analysis of the "strong, independent natures" which he admires so much.

For the town girls he has nothing but a qualified contempt. "Girls who had to walk more than half a mile to school were pitied," he says:

> There was not a tennis court in the town; physical exercise was thought rather inelegant for the daughters of well-to-do families. Some of the High School girls were jolly and pretty, but they stayed indoors in winter because of the cold, and in summer because of the heat. When one danced with them their bodies never moved inside their clothes; their muscles seemed to ask but one thing — not to be disturbed. I remember those girls merely as faces in the schoolroom, gay and rosy, or listless and dull, cut off below the shoulders, like cherubs, by the ink-smeared tops of the high desks that were surely put there to make us round-shouldered and hollow chested.[131]

Such is Jim Burden's attack on the genteel tradition whose ideal of feminine refinement is an anemic passivity which regards any form of physical activity as vulgar. The contrast between the hired girls and their mistresses is the opposition between country and town life, between vitality and listlessness. The townspeople, blissfully unaware of their own shortcomings, looked down on the prairie-bred girls because they earned their living, because they were "foreigners," and (so Willa Cather hints) because they were so attractive. As Jim Burden tells us:

> The country girls were considered a menace to the social order. Their beauty shone out too boldly against a conventional background. But anxious mothers need have no alarm. They mistook the mettle of their sons. The respect for respectability was stronger than any desire in Black Hawk.[132]

And he goes on to tell the story of Sylvester Lovett, the halfhearted swain who becomes so infatuated with Lena Lingard that he is unable to make his bankbooks balance, but who manages to cure himself by running away with a widow six years older than himself, "who owned a half-section." [133] Jim Burden is perfectly furious with him when this cure takes: he had "hoped that Sylvester would marry Lena, and thus give all the country girls a better position in the town." [134] In this incident we have Willa Cather's commentary on the social history of Black Hawk: All the young men of good families were afraid to marry the immigrant girls. If they hadn't been the old New England stock might have been rejuvenated by mating with a more vital breed — vital because it was able to profit from being transplanted into new surroundings — and might not have gone on to produce a generation of Wick Cutters.

This failure of town and country to mingle spells the death of the town. In her next novel, *One of Ours,* Willa Cather gives her view of what happened to communities like Black Hawk when the descendants of the original settlers lost whatever vitality their progenitors possessed. They became completely immersed in a conventional commercial existence in which they learn a great deal about how to make money but nothing at all about how to spend it wisely. Willa Cather here shows striking similarities to Sherwood Anderson, Sinclair Lewis, and others who figured in the post–World War I revolt from the village. This attitude is present in *My Ántonia* also:

> On starlight nights I used to pace up and down those long, cold streets, scowling at the little, sleeping houses on either side, with their storm-windows and covered back porches. They were flimsy shelters, most of them poorly built of light wood, with spindle porch-posts horribly mutilated by the turning-lathe. Yet for all their frailness, how much jealousy and envy and unhappiness some of them seemed to contain! The life that went on in them seemed to me made up of evasions and negations; shifts to save cooking, to save washing and cleaning, devices to propitiate the tongue of gossip. This guarded mode of existence was like living under a tyranny. People's speech, their voices, their very glances, became furtive and repressed. Every individual taste, every natural appetite was bridled by caution. The people asleep in their houses, I thought, tried to live like the mice in their own kitchens; to make no noise, to leave no trace, to slip over the surface of things in the dark.[135]

This last simile is a good example of the "do I dare to eat a peach" attitude; the townspeople feel that they are intruders in a universe in which they have no business to be. Usually, however, the narrator's impatience with Black Hawk is treated in a lighter vein. As the adolescent Jim Burden tramps the streets looking for things to do, he finds that most of the people around him are as bored as he is. There is for example this fine description of small-town ennui:

> One could hang about the drug-store, and listen to the old men who sat there every evening, talking politics and telling new stories. One could go to the cigar factory and chat with the old German who raised canaries for sale, and look at his stuffed birds. But whatever you began with him, the talk went back to taxidermy. There was the depot, of course; I often went down to see the night train come in, and afterward sat awhile with the disconsolate telegrapher who was always hoping to be transferred to Omaha or Denver, "where there was some life." He was sure to bring out his pictures of actresses and dancers. He got them with cigarette coupons, and nearly smoked himself to death to possess these desired forms and faces. For a change one could talk to the station agent; but he was another malcontent; spent all his spare time writing letters to officials requesting a transfer. He wanted to get back to Wyoming where he could go trout-fishing on Sundays.[136]

From the stifling confinement of small-town life Jim turns with relief to the open air. The gay country girls come to signify for him the joyful expansiveness of country life as opposed to the contraction of the circle of living which oppresses him so much in town. The highest point of the book's middle section occurs when he goes with Ántonia and the hired girls on a picnic. They spend an idyllic day by the shores of the river, and in a long passage meant to celebrate the joys of country living the girls point out their fathers' farms to him, talk about them, and boast of the things they are going to get for their families. Then comes the passage which is meant to be the climax:

> "Jim," Ántonia said dreamily, "I want you to tell the girls about how the Spanish first came here, like you and Charley Harling used to talk about. I've tried to tell them, but I leave out so much."
> They sat under a little oak, Tony resting against the trunk and the other girls leaning against her and each other, and listened to the little I was able to tell them about Coronado and his search for the Seven Golden Cities. At school we were taught that he had given up his quest and turned back somewhere in Kansas.

But Charley Harling and I had a strong belief that he had been along this very river. A farmer in the county north of ours, when he was breaking sod, had turned up a metal stirrup of fine workmanship, and a sword with a Spanish inscription on the blade. He lent these relics to Mr. Harling, who brought them home with him. Charley and I scoured them, and they were on exhibition in the Harling office all summer. Father Kelly, the priest, had found the name of the Spanish maker on the sword, and an abbreviation that stood for the city of Cordova.

"And that I saw with my own eyes," Ántonia put in triumphantly. "So Jim and Charley were right, and the teachers were wrong!"

The girls began to wonder among themselves. Why had the Spaniards come so far? What must this country have been like, then? Why had Coronado never gone back to Spain, to his riches and his castles and his king? I couldn't tell them. I only knew the school books said he "died in the wilderness, of a broken heart."

"More than him has done that," said Ántonia sadly, and the girls murmured assent.

We sat looking off across the country, watching the sun go down. The curly grass about us was on fire now. The bark of the oaks turned red as copper. There was a shimmer of gold on the brown river. Out in the stream the sandbars glittered like glass, and the light trembled in the willow thickets as if little flames were leaping among them. The breeze sank to stillness. In the ravine a ringdove mourned plaintively, and somewhere off in the bushes an owl hooted. The girls sat listless, leaning against each other. The long fingers of the sun touched their foreheads.

Presently we saw a curious thing: There were no clouds, and the sun was going down in a limpid, gold-washed sky. Just as the lower edge of the red disc rested on the high fields against the horizon, a great black figure suddenly appeared on the face of the sun. We sprang to our feet, straining our eyes toward it. In a moment we realized what it was. On some upland farm, a plough had been left standing in the field. The sun was sinking just behind it. Magnified across the distance by the horizontal light, it stood out against the sun, was exactly contained within the circle of the disc; the handles, the tongue, the share — black against the molten red. There it was, heroic in size, a picture writing on the sun.

Even while we whispered about it, our vision disappeared; the ball dropped and dropped until the red tip went beneath the earth. The fields below us were forgotten, the sky was growing pale, and that forgotten plough had sunk back to its own littleness somewhere on the prairie.[137]

Coronado stands for the spirit of adventure and romance, and the kind of life young people dream about. The pedantic mind, which is the enemy of Coronado and all his kind, denied that that Spanish *conquistador* had ever set foot between the Republican River and the river Platte; Nebraska, it holds, is too mundane ever to have been part of the realms of romance. But the young people's own experience gives this the lie; they are sure Coronado has been along this very river, and sure enough, a Spanish sword is plowed up, with an inscription and an abbreviation of Cordova on the blade. So the spirit of romance has been to this dry, flat country; but the spirit of romance is not enough. It can see things, but it cannot persevere. Coronado never did find what he was looking for, but died in the wilderness of a broken heart. But if the spirit of romance had been to this country, so has the spirit of civilization. This is symbolized by the plough against the sun. The agricultural implement is made the symbol of a whole way of life; as it stands with its tongue and shares contained within the circle of the sun it becomes representative of everything Willa Cather has been glorifying. Willa Cather prepares for this symbol, as she does for others, by the use of light as a transfiguring agent. The world as seen under ordinary light, the common light of day, looks as ordinary and commonplace as the pedantic mind can conceive of it as being, but when illuminated by some special kind of light, such as sunset, it becomes transfigured and the real glory that lies latent in everyday things is brought out. In this manner a perfectly ordinary, homely farming tool is made the symbol of a settled agricultural civilization, which is thereby given a kind of cosmic approval.

Coronado and the plough against the sun are two opposites which, taken together, are meant to embrace the whole of life; neither one is sufficient alone, but together they suffice. Coronado had his heart broken by the plains country, but the plough conquered it. In her choice of the plough as a symbol, Willa Cather shows that the people she is most interested in are not the nomadic pioneers but the tillers of the soil who come after them; her symbol stands in marked contrast to the hunting dog and musket grouped around the dying Leatherstocking at the end of Cooper's novel, *The Prairie*.

Jim Burden now fully realizes the superiority of country life to life
in a small town, but so far he has little acquaintance with the world
outside the rural areas: his vision is still bounded by the horizon of
his neighbors' cornfields. Desperately wanting to get into the great
world outside, he looks forward to going off to Lincoln to attend the
university. Once there, he finds out what an important part the countryside has played in the history of civilization itself. He falls under the
influence of Gaston Cleric, a brilliant young scholar newly made head of
the Latin department. Cleric introduces him to the great artistic tradition of the Western world, the tradition of ornate dignity and the
grand style stemming ultimately from Vergil. It is from him that Jim
learns that the word "patria" has a purely local meaning, and that
Vergil had loved the little rural neighborhood as much as he himself
loved his grandparents' farm. He begins to get some faint glimmering
of the way in which human existence is the same in all times and at all
places, but he does not yet know how to correlate art and life:

> Although I admired scholarship so much in Cleric, I was not
> deceived about myself; I knew that I should never be a scholar.
> I never could lose myself for long among impersonal things. Mental
> excitement was apt to send me with a rush back to my own naked
> land and the figures scattered upon it. While I was in the very
> act of yearning toward the new forms that Cleric brought up
> before me, my mind plunged away from me, and I suddenly
> found myself thinking of the places and people of my own in-
> finitesimal past. They stood out, strengthened and simplified now,
> like the image of the plough against the sun. They were all I had
> for an answer to the new appeal. I begrudged the room that Jake
> and Otto and Russian Peter took up in my memory, which I
> wanted to crowd with other things. But whenever my conscious-
> ness was quickened, all those early friends were quickened within
> it, and in some strange way they accompanied me through all my
> new experiences. They were so much alive in me that I scarcely
> stopped to wonder whether they were alive anywhere else, or
> how.[138]

Like many another young person going off to college, Jim Burden
considers the things he knows about to be supremely unimportant, and
the things he doesn't know about to be of crucial importance. He
underrates his own past and is irate when the people in it keep
bobbing up in his consciousness. What do Otto Fuchs and Russian

Peter have to do with Vergil? It is too early for him to know that his little world is part of the great world; he hasn't yet seen that his life is not unique but that he is part of humanity. He still doesn't understand his background, but he is beginning to realize that it is important.

In his second year at Lincoln, Jim has an experience which helps to clarify for him the relation between life and art. Lena Lingard, one of the country girls he admires so much, comes to Lincoln and they strike up a friendship. On the evening of her first visit he is already in the mood to see new relations between things:

> One March evening in my Sophomore year I was sitting alone in my room after supper. . . . On the edge of the prairie, where the sun had gone down, the sky was turquoise blue, like a lake, with gold light throbbing in it. Higher up, in the utter clarity of the western slope, the evening star hung like a lamp suspended by silver chains — like the lamp engraved upon the title page of old Latin texts, which is always appearing in new heavens, and awakening new desires in men.

By the very act of thinking of such a comparison, he is beginning to see how his life fits in with the classic past.

> I propped my book open and stared listlessly at the page of the Georgics where tomorrow's lesson began. It opened with the melancholy reflection that, in the lives of mortals, the best days are the first to flee. "Optima dies . . . prima fugit." [139]

Then Lena Lingard knocks at the door, and for a time Jim is dragged back very pleasantly into the present. He has had recurrent dreams about Lena, and now the dreams seem about to translate themselves into reality. He and she have some kind of love experience together, but Willa Cather gingerly avoids telling us of what it consists. After Lena leaves, he realizes for the first time that the things he has experienced are the kind of things people write about, that literature is a reflection of the experience of real people, and that life and art coincide:

> When I turned back to my room the place seemed much pleasanter than before. Lena had left something warm and friendly in the lamplight. How I loved to hear her laugh again! . . . When I closed my eyes I could hear them all laughing — the Danish laundry girls and the three Bohemian Marys. Lena had brought them all back to me. It came over me, as it had never

done before, the relation between girls like those and the poetry of Vergil. If there were no girls like them in the world, there would be no poetry. I understood that clearly, for the first time.[140]

Jim Burden has a great insight as he stands in his room after Lena has gone. In seeing the relation between girls like her and Vergil's *Georgics* he has made a discovery important enough to rank as a creative act: he has succeeded in bringing Nebraska in line with the great tradition. And the great tradition — as Willa Cather sees it, at least — is a rural tradition; one need only think of the importance which the Vergil of the *Georgics* and the Horace of the *Odes* gave to the countryside. No longer does Jim have to feel like a young man from the provinces who comes up to the metropolis and is looked down upon, nor does he have to accept the inferiority of America to Europe; he has seen the unity of all life and all art everywhere; he has seen the ultimate unity of human experience.

The Fruition of the Soil: The Garden of the World

If one of the main themes of *My Ántonia* is the superiority of the countryside and the excellence of rural life, the chief image that Willa Cather uses to express that excellence is one we have already come across in discussing *O Pioneers!*: that of the garden of the world. It is in fact the basic metaphor of the whole book; everything in the novel leads up to the final section in which Ántonia has become the mistress of a large and fertile farm.

The garden image is present in the minds of both Willa Cather and some of her characters. Not the least of Grandfather Burden's insights is his ability to understand the larger meaning of the enterprise in which he and his neighbors are engaged. To the hundreds of thousands of toiling individuals who settled the West it must have seemed that each of them was seeking solely to improve his own lot, but according to the thinking of the time they were actually fulfilling a much larger destiny. The settlement of America was considered to be a part of a divine plan. When the great basin of the Mississippi Valley was completely populated, it was to become not only an earthly paradise for the inhabitants, who would thus live in a latter-day Garden of Eden, but also the whole earth's granary; by means of its immense fertility it would feed the people of Europe and Asia as well. Willa Cather had hinted at this in *O Pioneers!;* in *My Ántonia* she makes it quite explicit:

July came on with the breathless, brilliant heat which makes the plains of Kansas and Nebraska the best corn country in the world. It seemed as if we could hear the corn growing in the night; under the stars one caught a faint crackling in the dewy, heavy-odored cornfields where the feathered stalks stood so juicy and green. If all the great plain from the Missouri to the Rocky Mountains had been under glass, and the heat regulated by a thermometer, it could not have been better for the yellow tassels that were ripening and fertilizing each other day by day. The cornfields were far apart in those times, with miles of wild grazing land between. It took a clear, meditative eye like my grandfather's to foresee that they would enlarge and multiply until they would be, not the Shimerdas' cornfields, or Mr. Bushy's but the world's cornfields; that their yield would be one of the great economic facts, like the wheat crop of Russia, which underlie all the activities of men, in peace or war.[141]

This is one way in which Willa Cather adjusts Nebraska to the macrocosm and gives local happenings a cosmic importance.

But it is not merely the garden that Willa Cather is celebrating in *My Ántonia;* it is a garden with people living in it, and the people form one of those tightly knit Willa Cather families. The ultimate achievement of Willa Cather's heroine in *My Antonia* is the setting up of a family. The whole drive of her nature is toward this; we could have guessed it from the description of the basic likeness between Ántonia and her town employer, Mrs. Harling:

They loved children and animals and music, and rough play and digging in the earth. They liked to prepare rich, hearty food and to see people eat it; to make up soft white beds and to see youngsters asleep in them.[142]

Ántonia makes two attempts at marriage and the founding of a family: the first is unsuccessful but the second succeeds. The unsuccessful attempt with Larry Donovan has already been discussed. Ántonia's second attempt comes to a better fruition. Jim Burden does not witness the events leading up to it, since after graduation from college he has moved east permanently, but he does hear that another Bohemian has married her, that they are poor, and that they have a large family. He does not come back to visit his home town for nearly twenty years, and when he does he is afraid to visit Ántonia. "In the course of twenty crowded years one parts with many illusions," he says. "I did not wish to lose the early ones. Some memories are realities, and are better than anything that can ever happen to one again." [143] In such brief passages as this he lets the reader know that he has become disappointed in life, that he has been beaten in the things that really count. But his dread turns out to be needless, for Ántonia when he sees her is not a disappointment to him; she has become old and battered, but her vitality is undiminished. She is surrounded by a large happy brood of eleven children, all of whom either come tumbling around him in curiosity to see the man their mother has talked so much about, or else are attractively shy. Ántonia's fecundity is a sign of vitality and success, and the nicest compliment she can pay to some friends of their youth, the three Bohemian Marys, is that they are now married and have large families of their own. The lack of offspring, on the other hand, she regards as a sign of failure. Significantly enough, when she hears that Jim Burden has no children she becomes embarrassed, and tries to shift the conversation to a more neutral subject.

The relation between the various members of this large and happy family are of intense interest to Jim, who feels that he himself has failed at human relations. He observes that there is a kind of physical harmony between them, and that they are not afraid to touch each other.[144] They take great pride in each other, and particularly in their wonderful mother.[145] He describes the attitude of husband and wife toward each other as being "easy friendliness touched with humor." [146] Father Cuzak in particular seems to express his affection for his family by finding them highly amusing: "He thought they were nice, and he thought they were funny, evidently." [147] It is clear that love is the tie that binds them all together, and that they are very happy in one another's affection. And yet there is some slight suggestion of tension between Cuzak, the city-bred man, and Ántonia, the country girl. In the struggle between the sexes envisaged by Willa Cather, Ántonia seems to have gotten the upper hand:

> I could see the little chap, sitting here every evening by the windmill, nursing his pipe and listening to the silence; the wheeze of the pump, the grunting of the pigs, an occasional squeaking when the hens were disturbed by a rat. It did rather seem to me that Cuzak had been made the instrument of Ántonia's special mission. This was a fine life, certainly, but it wasn't the kind of life he had wanted to live. I wondered whether the life that was right for one was ever right for two! [148]

This last comment brings into question the entire feasibility of a city-country union. Willa Cather seems to have doubts as to whether the two modes of life can ever be rendered compatible. In addition, it also recalls her distrust of marriage in general. The marriage of the Cuzaks is as idyllic a union as she was ever to portray in any of her novels, and yet even here there is the suggestion not only of female dominance but of marriage as being inevitably frustrating.

The human fertility of the Cuzak homestead is matched by the fertility of the soil. The years of backbreaking labor spent tending the crops has at last yielded a rich fruit. Ántonia is especially proud of her orchard, which has been planted in the painstaking way that orchards are in Willa Cather's novels: every tree had to be watered by hand after a hard day's labor in the fields. The result is a yearly apple crop that far surpasses that of any of their neighbors. At the center of all this fertility is a symbol of civilization. Years before, Ántonia had told Jim she was homesick for the garden behind her father's house in Bohemia which had had a table and green benches in it where they could entertain their friends and talk about such things as music and woods and God and when they were young.[149] This garden image seems to stand in her mind for exactly the right relation between human beings and the nature in which they are placed, a nature modified and well stocked with benches so that civilized people need not get their clothes dirty when they discuss philosophical problems and wish to sit down. Now Ántonia leads Jim to the center of her orchard, and there he finds a grape arbor with seats along the sides and a warped plank table.[150] She has reproduced in the middle of her ideal farm her own idea of the civilized garden. Jim's detailed description of it enhances its importance:

We sat down and watched them. Ántonia leaned her elbows on the table. There was the deepest peace in the orchard. It was surrounded by a triple enclosure; the wire fence, then the hedge of thorny locusts, then the mulberry hedge which kept out the hot winds of summer and held fast to the protecting snows of winter. The hedges were so tall that we could see nothing but the blue sky above them, neither the barn roof nor the windmill. The afternoon sun poured down on us through the drying grape leaves. The orchard seemed full of sun, like a cup, and we could smell the ripe apples on the trees. The crabs hung on the branches as thick as beads on a string, purple-red, with a thin silvery glaze over them. Some hens and ducks had crept through the hedge and

were pecking at the fallen apples. The drakes were handsome
fellows, with pinkish gray bodies, their heads and necks covered
with iridescent green feathers which grew close and full, changing
to blue like a peacock's neck. Ántonia said they always reminded
her of soldiers — some uniform she had seen in the old country,
when she was a child.[151]

This passage contains a cluster of images, all of which contribute to
the agricultural image used also in *O Pioneers!*, that of the garden of
the world. Several ideas are at work here. First, there is the idea that
at the center of all this fertility of farm and family is a place of quietness, a place which contains the deepest peace which human beings can
know. The still center is protected from the outside world by a triple
barrier which excludes not only strangers (the wire fence) but also
extremes of heat and cold, with their connotation of everything else
which man finds unpleasant. But aside from shutting out, it also shuts
in; it confines the inhabitants of the garden so they cannot tell what
is going on in the outside world; they can't even see their farm or
windmill, the symbols of the way in which they earn their living.
Thus the garden becomes another of those images of sanctuary and
retreat which we have seen as giving so important a clue to Willa
Cather's attitude toward life. The orchard resembles a cornucopia; it
is full like a cup, and the fragrance of its fruit hangs over it. The
concept of plenitude finds further development in the idea of round-
ness, when the crab apples on the trees are compared with beads on a
string. Finally Ántonia's comparison between the iridescent shimmer-
ingness on the necks of her ducks and the uniforms of soldiers she had
seen as a child in Bohemia suggest that the aesthetic response to life
has been carried from Europe to America, but instead of being aroused
by an artificial and destructive product of civilization, it is now tamed
and rendered beneficent by being brought closer to nature, and is
simulated by such a harmless and thoroughly natural creature as a
barnyard fowl.

In the middle of this earthly paradise stands its Eve, the now
victorious Ántonia. She has triumphed over adversity and over nature;
she has wrestled with life and imposed an order on it, her order, just
as she has imposed order on the wilderness of Nebraska by converting
part of it into a fruitful farm with a garden at its center. In her double
role as founder of a prosperous farm and progenitor of a thriving
family she becomes the very symbol of fertility, and reminds us of
Demeter or Ceres of old, the ancients' goddess of agriculture. Willa

Cather herself points up the comparison, and it is of value to her to do this, for she makes an earth-goddess of Ántonia; the mortal who struggles with the adverse powers of nature and conquers them becomes the type of all successful human endeavor and passes over into the realm of myth. That Willa Cather quite deliberately makes an earth-goddess of Ántonia is seen in the following passage:

> She lent herself to immemorial human attitudes which we recognize by instinct as universal and true. I had not been mistaken. She was a battered woman now, not a lovely girl; but she still had that something which fires the imagination, could still stop one's breath for a moment by a look or gesture that somehow revealed the meaning in common things. She had only to stand in the orchard, to put her hand on a little crab tree and look up at the apples, to make you feel the goodness of planting and tending and harvesting at last. All the strong things of her heart came out of her body, that had been so tireless in serving generous emotions.
>
> It was no wonder that her sons stood tall and straight. She was a rich mine of life, like the founders of early races.[152]

And what becomes of the other protagonist in the story, Jim Burden? When he revisits his past by returning to Black Hawk, it gives him no clue to his identity or to the meaning of life such as he has found in the Cuzak farm. He is not able to build on his past as Ántonia is on hers:

> My day in Black Hawk was disappointing. Most of my old friends were dead or had moved away. Strange children, who meant nothing to me, were playing in the Harlings' big yard when I passed; the mountain ash had been cut down, and only a sprouting stump was left of the tall Lombardy poplar that used to guard the gate. I hurried on.[153]

The town no longer means anything to him, although the country still does. It has changed too much; the children and the trees are gone. The town families he had known had had no roots, since the community in which they lived had given them none, and so they had passed on to other places. But there are parts of the country that haven't changed at all. Jim takes a long walk out of town and stumbles upon an old road, the first road built from Black Hawk to the north, in fact the very same road over which Ántonia and he had traveled on the first night of their arrival in the Midwest. The road becomes a symbol of the unchanging quality of the countryside, and carries him back to the region of childhood memories:

> I had only to close my eyes to hear the rumbling of the wagons in the dark, and to be again overcome by that obliterating strangeness. The feelings of that night were so near that I could reach out and touch them with my hand. I had the sense of coming home to myself, and of having found out what a little circle man's experience is.[154]

The wheel has come full circle, and the same road which had first brought him to Black Hawk now carries him away from an unsatisfying present and into a nostalgically remembered past. Nothing could illustrate better than this final contrast between the Cuzak farm and Black Hawk the difference between country and town, Ántonia and Jim, the yea-saying and nay-saying attitudes toward life. Both had been set down in the Middle West without any previous training which would help them, both had once literally traveled down the same road, but their circumstances and temperaments were different. Ántonia now prefers the country because it gives her a greater chance to fulfill herself; Jim because it has changed less than the city and because it is linked with the past, to which he turns because it is all he has:

> For Ántonia and for me, this had been the road of Destiny; had taken us to those early accidents of fortune which predetermined for us all that we can ever be. Now I understood that the same road was to bring us together again. Whatever we had missed, we possessed together the precious, the incommunicable past.[155]

Perhaps the best way of summing up the meaning of *My Ántonia* is to recapitulate the story of each of the three sections in terms of the dominant imagery. The first part, concerning the struggle of the Burdens and the Shimerdas with the wild land, is described in terms of animal imagery; as in *O Pioneers!* the central symbol is the unbroken colt. This represents inchoate material waiting to have form imposed upon it, vitality ready to be harnessed by order. Ántonia too is waiting to have form imposed upon her; by her father, by the Burden family, and by the Harlings, form being in this context the stamp of civilization itself. The imposition of form on wild nature is a difficult thing, as those who do not have the strength to achieve it find out; Mr. Shimerda fails at the task and kills himself, while even Ántonia barely survives. But she does survive.

In the book's second part the dominant image is the plough. Both Ántonia and the land are now ready to be creative and fertile; to produce children and crops. This section contains the struggle between town and country traditions, with Ántonia absorbing both: she first learns from and then emancipates herself from the Harlings. Unlike her father, she is able to triumph over adversity — in her case, an unfortunate love affair.

In the third section of the book the dominant image is the earth-goddess in the garden of the world. This section shows the final fruition of both woman and land, which comes about because Ántonia is able to combine the vitality of nature with the order of civilization, both in her own life and in the life of the land. In this section Jim Burden meets adversity and is inspired by Ántonia.

The importance to her career of Willa Cather's two prairie novels can hardly be overestimated. In them she gives the fullest expression she ever gave to one of her major themes, the meaning of the European experience in America. The exact significance of America differs in the two prairie novels. In *O Pioneers!* America functions as pure raw material; it is the land where the creative will best can operate. *My Ántonia* does not contradict this, but the emphasis has shifted; America is now the land in which "Europe" can reach its finest flower. For Willa Cather as for many other nineteenth-century people Europe and America stood for pairs of opposites: Europe was tangibly the past, America tangibly the present; Europe stood for order, America for chaos. The two are connected, since the present is always visibly chaotic and needs to have order imposed upon it by applying the lessons learned in the past. The most important antithesis of all, however, was that America stood for nature whereas Europe represented civilization. The difference between the two novels is that in *O Pioneers!*, even while Alexandra is struggling to conquer it, it is the wildness of nature which is being celebrated, the untamed vitality of the frontier, whereas in *My Ántonia* the vitality and the discipline of civilization are combined to form a new synthesis, which provides the basis for a settled agricultural society like that eulogized by Horace and Vergil.

I have shown that at a certain point in her career Willa Cather gradually ceased looking to the world of art for subject matter and began seeking it in the world of nature. But this did not mean that she gave up her belief in the world of art as a source of value. Because she did not her former cultural ideal came into conflict with her present one, for the world of urban sophistication has little in common with the world of simple homely virtues associated with the countryside. This conflict between cultural ideals was by no means peculiar to Willa Cather but was part of a much more general conflict present in the minds of nineteenth-century Americans concerning their ideas about themselves; it revolved around the question of whether they owed their allegiance to the concept of primitivism or the concept of civilization and the stages of society. According to primitivism, since nature is seen as the source of all value, the closer a man lives to nature the better off he is, physically, mentally, and morally. According to the concept of the stages of society, all men progressed through certain stages of development proceeding from the most primitive to the most civilized, starting with the nomadic and proceeding upward through the pastoral and agricultural until finally they reached the industrial and commercial stages. These last two — the agricultural and industrial-commercial — correspond to the rural and urban stages, which I have discussed under the headings of country and town. In the nineteenth century the two turn up over and over again as contrasting ideals as to how life should be lived, the best literary expression of this being in the novels of James Fenimore Cooper.[156] As we have seen, Willa Cather herself vacillated between the two, as indeed Americans traditionally have done. In *O Pioneers!*, she merely states the case for both sides, without making any choice between the two. But in *My Ántonia* she resolves the conflict in the direction of a highly civilized and sophisticated rural civilization, and this remains her ideal for the rest of her career, although in her later books (starting with her very next novel) she believes it to be an ideal impossible of achievement.

But this highly civilized and sophisticated rural way of living which she celebrates is actually a little too good to be true. It is doubtful whether anybody could achieve that particular combination of urban-bred sensibility and rural rootedness and strength which she envisaged. When this is seen as combined with a hierarchal three-generation family unit in which the roles are assigned and the whole is sustained by ritual, ironically enough the place where it is most likely to be found is not in the country at all but in the city. Such a pattern is common among orthodox Jewish families who (like the Cuzaks) are not too far removed from their immigrant ancestors. But this is hardly where Willa Cather looked for her heroines.[157]

The concepts of primitivism and civilization have an all-pervasive influence on Willa Cather's fiction. They affect, for instance, her presentation of her heroines. In *O Pioneers!* she emphasizes the heroine as a solitary individual; in *My Ántonia* she emphasizes the heroine as part of a group, first as a member of a family and then as its head. Similarly the differing treatment of the prairie in the two books likewise shows the influence of the two concepts. In *O Pioneers!* the land being eulogized is the entire Great Divide; Willa Cather tells us, "Alexandra's house is the big out-of-doors." [158] In *My Ántonia* the center of attention has been narrowed down to the family living on the family farm; in other words, the homestead. This shows Willa Cather dealing in literary terms with a vitally important historical reality. The entire trans-Mississippi region was settled in the post–Civil War period by farmers called homesteaders; in fact, the Homestead Act of 1862 was conceptually based on just such a family unit as the Cuzaks.

O Pioneers! forms a sharp contrast to *My Ántonia* in structure as well as subject matter. In structure the earlier book has a superimposed form while the form of the latter is largely organic and arises from the cycle of the seasons. The organizing principle of *O Pioneers!* is the theme of the creative will directed, first toward the world of nature, then toward the world of man; the organizing principle of *My Ántonia*, as we shall see later, is the vegetation myth. Of the two *O Pioneers!* has the tighter structure, popular opinion to the contrary. [159] In *My Ántonia* the part tends to be greater than the whole: one remembers fine but isolated passages such as Jim Burden's killing of the rattlesnake or the description of the plough against the sun.

To study the spirit behind the form of an artistic work is a fascinating albeit highly speculative occupation. In the case of the two prairie novels some light is shed on structure by what we know of Willa Cather's biography and temperament. What she was trying to do in *O Pioneers!* was evidently to show that the power of love, although it can succeed with the land, must fail when it comes to people. But this is highly idiosyncratic, and reflects her own inner fears rather than any universal human truth. What she was trying to do in *My Ántonia* was somewhat different. Leaving the vegetation myth aside for a moment, a part of the book's form is still superimposed. Willa Cather has constructed the novel as a series of snapshots or vignettes, each of them commemorating some important event. Since we know that she tended to omit struggle and conflict from both books, as well as the direct presentation of evil, it seems that her vignettes are meant to present only life's happy and successful moments, and such as

showed the triumph of the will. If this is true, she was willfully failing
to see life steadily and see it whole, or to give an artistically convincing
representation of the entire human scene as she knew it.

In spite of its flaws, *O Pioneers!* on the whole is a successful portrait
of an important American historical era. In the larger sense, it can
be regarded as a kind of allegory on Western man and his entire history.
It shows him — as he has historically been — as much more successful
in dealing with his physical environment than with his fellow man:
Alexandra's saga follows a success-failure pattern as she moves away
from relatively simple problems and toward the more complex. I find
it necessary to make separate judgments on the two parts of the book.
In the main I believe Willa Cather is aesthetically and historically
right when she takes the wild frontier as a symbol of the challenge
offered to heroic souls by the precariousness of human existence, and
sees the westward expansion in nineteenth-century America as a working out of the romantic aspiration toward a better life. But I believe she
is dangerously idiosyncratic in seeing spontaneous relations between
the sexes as being as uniformly dangerous and unrewarding as she
makes them out to be. This view reflects her own particular upbringing
and temperament — particularly the latter — and it severely limits her
art. Nevertheless, in spite of its limitations, *O Pioneers!* is a convincing
novel; in it Willa Cather comes as close as she ever does to a frank and
square confrontation of the conflicts inherent in human life. But this
is all she does; she faces them but is unable to resolve or transcend
them. And even in *O Pioneers!* she turns her face away from the
conflict before the book is over.

My Ántonia, in some ways more successful than *O Pioneers!,* in
other ways is less successful; it is more affirmative but less honest.
If in the first book Willa Cather gives a frank portrayal of her gloomy
and one-sided view of human relations, in the second she is willing to
falsify the material she has at hand in order to make the final triumph
of the heroine appear almost effortless. *O Pioneers!* is the more original
in form, with its brilliant linking of plots to project the success-failure
motif; *My Ántonia* is more conventional in theme, if not in content,
since it comes at the end of a long tradition of literary works written
in praise of husbandry. It is an agrarian idyl, and its real subject is
man's right relation to nature. The right relation turns out to be, not
that defined by primitivism, but that of the agrarian tradition, a version
of the concept of civilization which held that the stages of society
culminate in the settled agricultural level, and that any further development in the direction of the city is a step downward.

In the largest sense the structure of *My Ántonia* is based on the vegetation myth. The core of this age-old mystery, as we have said, is the taking of the cycle of the seasons as the pattern for all recurrent rhythmical processes in nature, including human death and birth. It regards birth as rebirth and holds that, although death is inevitable, every person is "born again" through his children; the individual dies but the community lives on. *My Ántonia* is about this mystery of death and birth. Mr. Shimerda dies in the dead of winter, and when Ántonia is reborn as the head of a group of her own she is described in terms of the sensuous summer imagery of the garden of the world. In a sense when Mr. Shimerda dies, a good part of his daughter dies too; all her more civilized attributes wither away. She gives up her fine manners and becomes coarse and crude like her brother Ambrosch. She is reborn to civilization when she goes to town to live and relearns nice ways of doing things from the Harlings. Finally, after learning all she has to learn, she is ready to take her place in society by starting a family of her own and is reborn once again into the human community.

If we compare the two prairie novels in terms of their use of vegetation myth, we find that *O Pioneers!* deals with the death of nature and *My Ántonia* with its rebirth. *O Pioneers!* presents fertility of the soil and sterility in human beings; *My Ántonia* shows fertility of both the soil and human beings. Thus, in a profound sense *My Ántonia* is the most affirmative book Willa Cather ever wrote. Perhaps that is why it was her favorite.

But we have seen that as an author Willa Cather could not face certain facts of human experience — as, in *My Ántonia,* the problem of apparently motiveless evil involved in Larry Donovan's seduction and abandonment of Ántonia. It is also true that in her work as a whole she could not accept the emotional profundity of the vegetation myth as for the most part she did in this novel. In brief, she could accept fertility in crops more easily than in human beings, the reason being her fear of physical passion and the dependence upon others which it entails. This is evident even in *My Ántonia,* which of all her novels most celebrates fecundity. As far as the reader is concerned, Ántonia's family is produced ready-made. Never once is a pregnancy or birth directly presented in Willa Cather's novels; what we do see is the corn growing. This implies that she only half understood the vegetation myth; she understood the cycle of the seasons but did not understand its application to the life of human beings and to their recurrent crises of birth, love, and death. She substituted in its stead, as we shall see in her later novels, an almost Platonic belief in essences, and the desire to freeze the world in the grip of form once the ideal is achieved.

CHAPTER IV

THE WORLD DISSOLVED

In Nebraska, as in so many other States, we must face the fact that the splendid story of the pioneers is finished, and that no new story worthy to take its place has yet begun. The generation that subdued the wild land and broke up the virgin prairie is passing, but it is still there, a group of rugged figures in the background which inspire respect, compel admiration. With these old men and women the attainment of material prosperity was a moral victory, because it was wrung from hard conditions, was the result of a struggle that tested character. They can look out over those broad stretches of fertility and say: "We made this, with our backs and hands." The sons, the generation now in middle life, were reared amid hardships, and it is perhaps natural that they should be very much interested in material comfort, in buying whatever is expensive and ugly. Their fathers came into a wilderness and had to make everything, had to be as ingenious as shipwrecked sailors. The generation now in the driver's seat hates to make anything, wants to live and die in an automobile, scudding past those acres where the old men used to follow the long corn-rows up and down. They want to buy everything ready-made: clothes, food, education, music, pleasure. Will the third generation—the full-blooded, joyous one just coming over the hill — will it be fooled? Will it believe that to live easily is to live happily?

— WILLA CATHER, *"Nebraska: the End of the First Cycle"*

From then on — though at first it was spoken below her breath — she was to utter a sad little refrain which her friends dreaded to hear her repeat: "Our present is ruined — but we had a beautiful past." She said it in letters and she said it in conversation, mournfully.

— ELIZABETH SARGEANT, *Willa Cather: A Memoir*

REJECTION OF THE CASH NEXUS

After the First World War a marked change appears in the writing of Willa Cather, both in subject and in tone. Hitherto, her two great subjects had been the interpretative artist and the pioneer farmer, the natural aristocrat in the world of art and the natural aristocrat in the world of nature. Now something quite unexpected happens. The world of art as a subject for fiction drops out altogether; after a collection of short stories entitled *Youth and the Bright Medusa* (1920) she never again goes back to it. The world of nature she does treat in *One of Ours* (1922), but it is a nature strangely changed. Its antithesis, the city, is no longer the source of the arts and graces; it is instead the center of a commercial and industrial colossus which in order to survive must take the whole country for its market. The result is the gradual spread of the new urban ways over the countryside and the destruction of traditional modes of living associated with the soil.

The new dispensation of commercialism and industrialism was inimical to Willa Cather's most deeply cherished feelings; it struck squarely at the root of her belief in the hero and in natural aristocracy. The most obvious social effects of the factory system have been the standardization of product and producer and the interdependence of men. Both of these are hostile to the idea of the hero as a solitary individual performing tremendous feats. A world in which conformity was valued as an adjunct to industrialism and often for its own sake seemed to leave no place for the exceptional individual, or indeed for excellence of any kind, and the interdependence of man in modern society made the chances for individual heroic action vanishingly slight. An individual simply couldn't have enough power to become a hero. Thus Claude Wheeler, the protagonist of *One of Ours*, looks all around his native Midwest in an attempt to find some course of action which would be at the same time socially useful and individually satisfying. He fails to find it, since the commercial minded society in which he lives frustrates every attempt he makes to lead the comely life. Eventually he finds his role, not, however, in America but in France, fighting for what he believes to be European civilization in the First World War. Even here the only way in which he can fulfill himself is to die.

Another result of the Industrial Revolution was that the economic side of life, the necessity for making a living, made increasingly heavy demands on the energy and attention of the individual. Whereas formerly money, in theory at least, had been a reward for services rendered to the community, and, in the case of the natural aristocrat, had been an incidental by-product of heroic action, it now of necessity became an end in itself, one of the goals of all human struggling, and absorbed energies which could better have gone into more directly creative activities. Willa Cather became painfully aware of this, and all the books of her middle years are directly concerned with money. The theme was not new to her, but now it becomes a central preoccupation. Lack of money makes civilized life impossible; it is a necessity for gracious living, but unfortunately there is no gracious way of getting it; one must have it, preferably by inheritance. Thus in *My Mortal Enemy* (1926) Myra Henshaw, who gives up her inheritance to marry for love, becomes embittered with her husband when he lapses into poverty and cannot give her the life she wants. The disintegration of Marian Forrester in *A Lost Lady* (1923) is hastened when her husband refuses to salvage something for her after a bank failure but insists on paying off his creditors in full, thus leaving himself penniless. In *The Professor's House* (1925) the problem is not the obtaining of money but the proper use of it once it has been obtained. The professor's family is living comfortably on the proceeds of an invention of his dead protégé, who would have become his son-in-law had he lived; and the professor himself has honorably come by a large sum received as a prize for a scholarly work in history. But he is shocked and pained by what he regards as the vulgar and ostentatious way in which his family contrives to spend it. Here the possession of money entails an added problem; it vulgarizes the possessor. In all of these novels money, or the specter of it, is never absent from Willa Cather's pages for very long; always it is treated gingerly and with extreme distaste, as if it were one of the less pleasant bodily functions which could not be discussed in polite society.

FAILURE OF THE HERO

This emphasis on money and the acquiring of it also made it exceedingly difficult for the artist to affirm the social values held by the group in which he lived. These social values themselves had, in Willa Cather's eyes, dwindled down to almost nothing. In the last analysis the only thing that people had in common was their separateness and their feeling of being set against one another in the economic race. There was no longer a basis for that common agreement upon what is valuable which is necessary before any artistic creation can have general significance. The fragmentation of modern society poses, in addition to the overriding social problem, an artistic one.

Willa Cather's natural aristocrats simply could not express themselves through modern society. They also could not express themselves through a different institution, the modern unrooted family, and therefore were balked in another outlet for their energies. The kind of family which Willa Cather regarded as ideal is the kind she presented in *My Ántonia,* first in the Burdens, then in the Cuzaks. It was a multigeneration affair, containing children and parents and sometimes grandparents; in this it resembled the tribal organization on the tribal land, and stressed the continuity of traditional modes of living from generation to generation. In all respects save that of having come from elsewhere, it was the same kind of family unit which had existed for centuries and continued to exist right up to the time of the Industrial Revolution. But with the coming of that event, the multigeneration family unit was doomed to destruction; instead of supplying the basis for society, it became the exception. An increased social mobility led the children of such families to drift to the cities in search of employment, and this Willa Cather was emphatically against, since it ran directly counter to the agrarian dream. In all her middle novels she presents modern marriage as a single-generation affair, not related to a clan organization at all, but a tenuous union between husband and wife. All of these marriages reveal varying degrees of rootlessness, and, with the exception of Professor St. Peter's family, they are all childless. Significantly enough, Willa Cather shows each one of these marriages in the process of disintegration. Claude Wheeler's ill-fated union with the cold and rejecting Enid Royce is terminated when she leaves him to go to China and nurse a sick missionary sister; Marian Forrester's marriage begins to break up when she is unable to satisfy herself with a husband twenty-five years her senior and must take lovers; Professor St. Peter has what appears to be an excellent family but after years of contentment suddenly finds himself out of sympathy with them and with their ideas about what they want from life; and Myra Henshawe suddenly decides in her old age that she regrets ever having left the family religion and family fortune in order to marry, however loving and kind her husband may be.

What happens to the natural aristocrat who is unable to express himself through either society or the family? He has nothing to expend his energies on; lacking the conventions through which to express himself, he goes to pieces. This is the fate of Willa Cather's protagonists in her middle period. True, in *One of Ours* Claude Wheeler seems to be an exception to this, since he is shown as having found himself before dying on the battlefield, but Willa Cather makes it very clear that, had he lived, the modern world would have given him nothing he could care about, and that the only way he could express himself was to die. In other books the record is perfectly consistent. Marian Forrester's personality starts to disintegrate once the powerful protective force of her husband is shattered through illness. Godfrey St. Peter withdraws not only from the modern world but also from his own family and from all human relationships whatever to the extent that while he does not actively court death, neither does he seek to avoid it when the chance presents itself. Myra Henshawe, like the Professor, turns completely from all human ties, and turning her back on the world and on her husband alike, chooses to die alone, with the crucifix, the symbol of the childhood religion which she had renounced, pressed against her lips. In all of these novels the same harsh judgment is passed on the modern age. As the microcosm reflects the macrocosm, so chaos on one level is mirrored by chaos on all other levels. The fragmentation of society has its counterpart in the breakdown of the family and the disintegration of the individual.

THE MODERN WASTE LAND

What caused this change in Willa Cather's outlook from excessive optimism to excessive pessimism? Why, after the affirmation of her golden period, the prairie novels, should she suddenly become so negative? The answers to such questions are necessarily speculative, but certain biographical facts suggest a clue. One of the chief things Willa Cather objected to in the modern world was its ugliness — the lack of beauty inherent in cheap, shoddy articles mass-produced for a commercial market. This ran completely counter to her belief that life at its best should be a search for beautiful sensations which was her heritage from Walter Pater. Since this was one of her most deeply cherished beliefs, anything which opposed it was not likely to go down very well with her. Connected with this was her growing conviction that the agrarian dream, however desirable, was rapidly becoming a thing of the past — as indeed it was — for mass-produced consumers' goods together with Hollywood culture habits had spread over rural hamlets as well as crowded cities and left little to choose between country and town. But there was an even more important aspect of the modern world which Willa Cather loathed with all her being. Up till now, she had held that men and women who were any good at all dominated life, and she had believed in the omnipotence of the will. But in the nineteen-twenties belief in the will seemed all but impossible. The events of the First World War made her realize that there were impersonal forces abroad in the world which were bigger than any individual will, even that of heroes. This was a crushing discovery, and one from which she never did recover. Since her protagonists were accustomed to depending almost entirely upon will power to make their way in the world, it is no wonder that they found themselves helpless once their chief source of strength is rendered inoperative or cut off.

"She saw or divined more clearly than I," says Elizabeth Sergeant, "how finally the Victorian age had, when the peace was signed, retreated into the past." [1] The values which Willa Cather believed in most wholeheartedly were going down the drain; she felt that she was looking on at the dissolution of all values, and indeed at the world's dissolution. Her agonized awareness of the spiritual dismemberment of the Victorian age can be traced in a rising arc through the books she wrote during this period, from *One of Ours* (1922) through *A Lost Lady* (1923) and rising to a climax in *The Professor's House* (1925). Between this book and the publication of her next work something must have happened in her spiritual life, for in *My Mortal Enemy* (1926) she returns to the habit of basing a book upon rejection which we have seen was characteristic of the first period of her career. In *My Mortal Enemy* she wrote a hymn of hate against the present, so violent that it is not too surprising that in subsequent works she turned entirely to the past.

The literary effect of her agonized awareness can be traced in the imagery in her novels, particularly in the dominant imagery which she uses to unify their structure. As she passes from her second period to her third, the image of the garden is replaced by that of the waste land.[2] Thus she moves from one phase of the vegetation myth to another, from that dealing with creation to that dealing with destruction. Sterility replaces fruitfulness as the vitality and fertility of the soil celebrated in the prairie novels gives place to the emotional and spiritual drought of the later books. It is not that the land is suffering from any physical blight, for the Middle West is as blooming as ever; the land is fruitful but the people are parched. The crops renew themselves, but they are no longer given their old moral significance; the products of the soil are traded off for inanimate, mass-made products which have no real relation to man or nature; the machine-made replaces the homemade; inanimate objects replace animate; the automobile replaces the horse. The basic metaphor she uses to describe the waste land is one of drying up. Sometimes there is a literal evaporation, as when the commercial villain Ivy Peters drains Captain Forrester's beautiful marshland in *A Lost Lady;* usually however the drying up is figurative only, and stands for the disappearance of the aesthetic and imaginative qualities which Willa Cather associated with the Old West.

In the original waste-land myth the land scorched with drought is finally saved by a questing knight who comes from without and is instrumental in bringing the waters back. However agonized the present, the myth implies, there is always hope of deliverance in the future. But no such knight comes riding in these Willa Cather novels; she sees no hope in the future; instead she looks longingly at the past. Something of the nostalgic melancholy with which she viewed former times comes out in her description of the vanished lagoons of her childhood, the grass-lined lagoons which used to dot the prairie but which have long since passed with the passing of the frontier:

> The buffalo trails still ran north and south then; deep, dusty paths the bison wore when, single file, they came north in the spring for the summer grass, and went south again in the autumn. Along these trails were the buffalo "wallows" — shallow depressions where the rain water gathered when it ran off the tough prairie sod. These wallows the big beasts wore deeper and packed hard when they rolled about and bathed in the pools, so that they held water like a cement bottom. The freighters lived on game and shot the buffalo for their hides. The grass was full of quail and prairie chickens, and flocks of wild ducks swam about on the lagoons. These lagoons have long since disappeared, but they were beautiful things in their time; long stretches where the rain water gathered and lay clear on a grassy bottom without mud. From the lagoons the first settlers hauled water to their homesteads, before they had dug their wells. The freighters could recognize the lagoons from afar by the clouds of golden coreopsis which grew up out of the water and waved delicately above its surface. Among the pioneers the coreopsis was known simply as "the lagoon flower." [3]

In explanation of her attitude Willa Cather was prone to argue that the deprivation of beauty in modern life would lead to an impoverishment of art. E. K. Brown relates:

> In a lecture at Omaha, in October 1921, she pointed to the tendencies in Nebraska that were contrary to life itself and would surely suffocate art. Democracy was more and more applied as a regime of sameness, in which the Bohemian housewife must be encouraged to give up her ancestral recipes for roast goose and draw food from an array of tins, and her children were to be denied instruction in their rich and beautiful tongue so that they might speak English like all the rest of Nebraska, and nothing else. The new god was the short cut, dependent on the machine. "We have music by machines, we travel by machines — the American

people are so submerged in them that sometimes I think they can only be made to laugh and cry by machines." In art there were no short cuts and, besides, a dead level of sameness would be the end of art.[4]

As criticism of modern American life this viewpoint is not without its validity. But certain of Willa Cather's emotional reactions during these years make one wonder whether her change in attitude did not have a more personal basis. "By the time she had finished *One of Ours*," says E. K. Brown, "she was beginning to feel that estrangement from modern American life that was to grow more acute as she got older. . . . Her friends noticed the pessimism that was so strangely unlike the exuberance of her youth and her first years in New York."[5] Elizabeth Sergeant is more pointed:

> Willa did not seem to enjoy talk as *difference;* as argument and ferment. When she had made her mind up, she wanted to prevail. . . .
> Her intolerance began to trouble me. She was truly skeptical about the post-war world. Take this Viennese Freud: why was everybody reading him? Tolstoy knew as much about psychology — with no isms attached — as any fiction writer needed. I didn't agree. Freud was here; I had to try to read him, because I lived in today's world. But Willa, like the Pueblo Indians who — I had been told in New Mexico — had no word for "future," looked backward with regret. Our present lay about us in ruins but we had, she wistfully remarked, a beautiful past.[6]

However good the past may have looked to her, the present seemed to be falling to pieces. To Willa Cather this meant a new outbreak of an old conflict, one which she thought she had solved permanently in the first period of her career. This was the conflict between life and art. With her it was a personal problem as well as a professional one; apparently she could not enjoy even her writing if she thought that the quality of the life around her was declining. This seems reasonable enough, since the acclaim which she wanted as an author depended in large measure on the maintenance of a certain kind of society which shared her values. In the twenties the only kind of society in which she felt at home seemed on the verge of vanishing. She could no longer feel at one with her contemporaries through their complete acceptance of her art; new writers were arising in profusion with entirely different interests and preoccupations from those which Willa Cather felt to be important. Consequently there is an increasing tension in this period between the active and the aesthetic life, the life of human involvement and the monastic ideal of art for art's sake. At this time Willa Cather became terribly concerned lest she may have made the wrong choice by sacrificing all close human relations to a career; she felt that instead of leading to victory it may only have led to defeat. One remembers Thea Kronborg's impassioned cry to Dr. Archie: "It's easy to fail, and if I fail, you'd better forget about me, for I'll be one of the worst women that ever lived. I'll be an awful woman!" [7] In her third period Willa Cather wondered whether she herself might not have failed. But she finally decided that she had not. There was the emotional investment of a lifetime at stake, and she didn't want to throw it away. And so Professor St. Peter and Myra Henshawe, the last two protagonists of her crisis period, decide that it is human relations which are a mistake, and not the terms of their dedication to the comely life or the life of art.

But if the renewed conflict between the aesthetic and the active life ends in another triumph for the aesthetic ideal, it is a triumph won at terrible cost. The ultimate price is the almost complete destruction of Willa Cather as an artist. Certain tendencies inherent in her personality all along now come to the surface and reveal themselves in ways which will threaten the validity and even the sincerity of her own view of life expressed in her work. Two of the most prominent of these tendencies are the unwillingness to see that which she does not want to see, a disinclination to recognize the existence of points of view other than her own; and her apparent inability to compromise in any way in the face of life's vicissitudes, her belief that the only honorable alternative to the triumph of one's will is the complete rejection of all that prevents one's will from prevailing. In the novels of her third period these traits, occasionally overpowering her judgment, will carry her into an oscillation between pessimism and escapism which culminates in a virtual rejection of life itself. In *One of Ours* and *A Lost Lady* they lead up to nothing less than a complete and unqualified repudiation of the present and all its works — a repudiation which, in the case of the latter book, mars the ending of an otherwise fine novel. In *The Professor's House* and *My Mortal Enemy,* as her agony reaches its climax, the protagonists not only reject the present; they turn against life itself. For the first time she makes her characters reject their immediate environment without suggesting any alternative mode of life to put in its stead; even in her early hate stories about Nebraska she had been reacting in favor of an artistic ideal. But now she seems to be blindly reacting. Apparently her emotions have gone out of control and impaired her artistic vision. For an artist, to be successful, must have at least some idea of what he considers to be the essence of the good life.

Another sign of artistic weakening makes its appearance about this time: the main characters, when the stress becomes too acute, beat a mental retreat to an earlier and less frustrating phase of their existence; in other words, they regress. Willa Cather treats this as if it were an adequate and permanently satisfactory way for an adult to respond to problems that have become too pressing. Thus Professor St. Peter and Myra Henshawe both indulge in daydreams and reveries about their childhood and early youth, not so much because it brings them solace as because their present life seems to them to be so unbearable that they don't even want to think about it. This evasion of difficulties is a form of escapism to which Willa Cather was peculiarly liable at this time and is symptomatic of the slump into self-indulgence which characterized her fiction at its worst and which became even more marked as the years wore on.

The emotional crisis which Willa Cather underwent in the twenties and which led her to completely reject the world about her is reflected in her fiction, but she is not always able to find an objective correlative for what she feels. Consequently the later novels of her crisis period are apt to prove more than a little mystifying; they build up a tremendous amount of emotional tension, but the reader, unless he is acquainted with the author's personal situation, is not always sure precisely what the emotion is about. It is hard to understand or sympathize with Professor St. Peter's total rejection of his family; they have their faults, to be sure, but no more than they had had during all the years when he had loved them, and as for Myra Henshawe, the heroine of *My Mortal Enemy,* she is such a thoroughly unpleasant woman that it is hard to sympathize with her about anything at all. Without biographical knowledge about Miss Cather, the reader can hardly avoid feeling that there is something mysterious about these characters' emphatic repudiation of the present; when the facts of her life are known, however, the actions of her later protagonists seem merely to be projections of some unfortunate personal traits of her own.

This biographical insight, while explaining what might otherwise prove obscure, does not of course make up for these books' artistic deficiencies; a work of literature should not require any special knowledge of the author's life in order to be readily intelligible, but should stand on its own. Furthermore, the books' gain in intelligibility is achieved only at the expense of the reader's recognizing their lack of universality. The kindest thing which can be said of the later crisis novels is that they present a world-view at once idiosyncratic and bizarre. I am inclined to make the severer judgment that they embody an outlook on life so distorted and falsified as to be practically worthless as an interpretation of human experience. If this is true, the beauty of parts cannot compensate for the deficiency in structure of the whole; no amount of charm in the writing can make a novel convincing if the author's moral vision has failed.

THE TRIUMPH OF GREED

The next novel Willa Cather wrote after *My Ántonia* was *One of Ours*. Although it won the 1922 Pulitzer Prize (probably a reward for its author's previous work) it is one of the least interesting books she ever wrote. Nevertheless it is important on several counts. It gives her idea of what finally happened to the Middle West in the generation following that of Ántonia and Alexandra. It also has the distinction of being the only book in which she deals directly with the First World War and its impact on America, and so provides a clue as to why she later wrote: "The world broke in two in 1922 or thereabouts," [8] and then turned to the past. So it is worth at least a cursory examination because of its historical importance, despite its artistic defects.

One of Ours splits into two parts. The first concerns itself with Claude Wheeler's growth to manhood in the prewar Middle West and the second with his finding himself through fighting in France in the First World War. The first part is by far the better. It gives Willa Cather a chance to probe deep into the anatomy of Middlewestern decay, and portrays in convincing fashion the groping, bewildered efforts of a farm boy to transcend the limitations of his environment and discover the comely life. Claude, like Leopold Bloom, is modern man in search of a soul. In the first part of the book he is searching in vain for the springs of life and culture. If they ever existed in the Middle West, they have dried up; and he doesn't know where to find them. Consequently his whole life is a frustrated search for value. Eventually, through the accident of the Great War and his enlistment in the American Expeditionary Force, he seeks them at their source in the Old World and finds them in France before he dies.

Whereas Ántonia and Alexandra had grown up in the late eighteen-eighties and nineties, Claude Wheeler belongs to the generation that came to maturity just before 1914. He has a New England school-

teacher for a mother, religious, dreamy, and given to reading the Bible
and *Paradise Lost,* and a hard-headed Yankee farmer for a father who
is outgoing, cheerful, and given to practical jokes, of which Claude is
more often than not the butt. Needless to say, it is his mother whom
Claude takes after. His life is one long series of frustrations, with everything that conceivably could going wrong, as if Willa Cather were determined to show just how bad life could be on the Great Plains. Claude
dislikes farming, the dull, backbreaking labor that leaves him so exhausted at night that he is too tired to think; but he knows of no other
occupation that he feels he could do better at. He loves the idea of
learning and longs for the new vistas he feels would open up for him if
only he could attend the state university, but, obedient to parental pressure, he continues to attend the small denominational college which he
entered at his mother's request. Eventually he ceases to attend even
that because he is needed at the farm. This necessitates his giving up
the only stimulating contact he had made during his college days, his
friendship with the cultivated and artistic Ehrlich family of Lincoln.
Finally he tries to fulfill his unsatisfied longings for some vague splendor
in life by marrying Enid Royce, the daughter of a neighboring miller.
But this turns out to be a disastrous mistake. Enid pushes Claude out
of their train compartment on their wedding night because, she says,
she has eaten too much cold chicken salad and is indisposed. Later she
spends most of her time traveling around the countryside attending
meetings of the Anti-Saloon League, leaving her husband to get his own
meals and neglecting him generally. Claude is not at all sorry when
she finally leaves him for an indefinite period to nurse a sick missionary
sister in China.

There is a marked difference in tone between this and the previous
prairie novels. Where *O Pioneers!* and *My Ántonia* are often breath-
taking and ecstatic, *One of Ours* seems tired. Gone are the golden days
when everything about life on the plains seemed challenging; now that
life appears only dull, dreary, and monotonous. Not only does nothing
happen, but the chief character, Claude, is not of the sort to make things
happen; he is at a far remove from those whirling dynamos of energy,
Alexandra and Ántonia. What kind of person he is emerges in his conversation with his Bohemian friend Ernest Havel:

> "I don't believe I can ever settle down to anything. Don't you
> feel that at this rate there isn't much in it?"
> "In what?"
> "In living at all, going on as we do. What do we get out of it?

Take a day like this: you waken up in the morning and you're glad to be alive; it's a good enough day for anything, and you feel sure something will happen. Well, whether it's a workday or a holiday, it's all the same in the end. At night you go to bed — nothing has happened."

"But what do you expect? What can happen to you, except in your own mind? If I get through my work, and get an afternoon off to see my friends like this, it's enough for me."

"Is it? Well, if we've only got once to live, it seems like there ought to be something — well, something splendid about life, sometimes." [9]

Unlike the earlier prairie protagonists, Claude Wheeler is not of the heroic breed; he "feels sure something will happen" and expects stimulation from the outside; Alexandra or Ántonia would have made things happen themselves.[10] The reason is that there has been nothing in Claude's environment to stimulate heroism; he has neither had the immigrant's experience of crossing the water and passing from one kind of culture to an entirely different kind, nor has he had to face the precarious struggle for existence on the frontier. When he gets to France and has a chance to prove himself in battle, the result is different.

If latter-day Nebraska fails to encourage heroism, it also fails to encourage imaginative and aesthetic growth. Claude has the sensitivity to realize that something in his life is missing but is too ignorant to know what it is. When he says there ought to be "something splendid about life, sometimes," what he really wants, if he only knew it, is the comely life.

The general tone of Middle Western society in Claude's day is given in the portrait of his brother Bayliss Wheeler. Willa Cather evidently considers this older brother to be typical of the new generation that is taking over from the pioneer settlers of the previous novels. Too small for heavy farm work, Bayliss has moved into town and opened a business there, devoting his life to buying and selling rather than to producing — a direct step away from the virtues of rural living inculcated by the agrarian dream. The one absorbing interest of his life is the making of money. There is no moral passion in him of any sort; if he is a pacifist during the early part of the First World War, it is merely because it is more profitable for him to be so. His attitude toward learning and art and all the finer things of life toward which Claude yearns is shown by his response when Claude tells him about a friend, one of the Ehrlich family, who wants to go to Europe to do graduate work:

"Julius is going abroad to study this fall. He intends to be a professor."

"What's the matter with him? Does he have poor health?" [11]

Bayliss Wheeler is the successor of Wick Cutter in *My Ántonia* and the forerunner of Ivy Peters in *A Lost Lady*. Apparently Willa Cather meant him to stand for everything she had come to dislike in the modern commercial generation: the single-minded greed, the contempt for all human interests other than money-making.

It is a far cry from the heroic life of the pioneers to the humdrum business existence of Bayliss Wheeler, in which generosity is replaced by stinginess as an ideal. But Willa Cather does not see commerce as the sole villain; she also sees the Middle West as succumbing to the slowly advancing blight of the machine. More than any other single thing, she considered the machine and its products to blame for the shattering of the agrarian dream. They took men's minds away from the primary agrarian virtues and were, she believed, the only things people spent money on any more. Sometimes she objected to machinery because it superseded what she considered to be a desirable social ritual:

> In the Wheeler family a new thrasher or a new automobile was ordered without a question, but it was considered extravagant to go to a hotel for dinner.[12]

Sometimes she regards machinery as a will-o'-the-wisp which distracts men's minds from the really important things such as education and culture:

> Nearly every time Claude went into the cellar [which was filled with machinery junked by the Wheeler household], he made a desperate resolve to clear the place out some day, reflecting bitterly that the money this wreckage cost would have put a boy through college decently.[13]

Sometimes she objects to the falling-off in quality as well as aesthetic attractiveness that seemed to her to result when the homemade is replaced by the machine-made:

> The farmer raised and took to market things with an intrinsic value; wheat and corn as good as could be grown anywhere in the world, hogs and cattle that were the best of their kind. In

return he got manufactured articles of poor quality: showy furniture that went to pieces, carpets and draperies that faded, clothes that made a handsome man look like a clown. Most of his money was paid out for machinery, — and that, too, went to pieces. A steam thrasher didn't last long; a horse outlived three automobiles.[14]

This is really a political and economic protest, a plea for the maintenance of the old "close household economy" in which the family farm produced nearly everything it needed. It is an extremely conservative ideal, one which could be held in the nineteen-twenties only by a stand-patter, if not a downright reactionary. Sometimes she objects not only to the disappearance of the old household economy of the self-sufficient farmstead but also to the belief that change itself is desirable for its own sake and that the old is necessarily inferior to the new. This idea is repeated over and over again in the novels of her third and fourth periods:

> Claude felt sure that when he was a little boy and all the neighbors were poor, they and their houses and farms had more individuality. The farmers took time then to plant fine cottonwood groves on their places, and to set osage orange hedges along the borders of their fields. Now these trees were all being cut down and grubbed up. Just why, nobody knew; they impoverished the land . . . they made the snow drift . . . nobody had them any more. With prosperity came a kind of callousness; everybody wanted to destroy the old things they used to take pride in. The orchards, which had been nursed and tended so carefully twenty years ago, were now left to die of neglect. It was less trouble to run into town in an automobile and buy fruit than it was to raise it.[15]

More often than not she sees commerce and the machine as a source of social discord, as the cause of the replacement of harmony among the people by disunity:

> The people themselves had changed. He could remember when all the farmers in this community were friendly toward each other; now they were continually having law suits. Their sons were either stingy and grasping, or extravagant and lazy, and they were always stirring up trouble. Evidently it took more intelligence to spend money than to make it.[16]

Needless to say, this does not square with the picture she gave of life on the plains in her prairie novels, in which there were always plenty of people willing to oppose the protagonists. But the Oscars and Lous and Kronborgs and Krajieks seem to have receded from her memory. In her disgust with the present, she is willing to overidealize the past.

What has happened is that the small people have organized and triumphed. Now it is the little people rather than the heroes who are the molders of society. In place of the heroic life one finds the commercial life; the pursuit of beauty is replaced by the pursuit of the machine, or gadgets, as Willa Cather considers them; instead of a yea-saying religion like the Catholic church of Amédée Chevalier there is the nay-saying religion of the pietistic Enid Royce.

This is Willa Cather's picture of the changed Middle West in which her new protagonist finds himself. She sees it as a country in which heroism is impossible, because people like Claude's father and brother stand in the way and match their wills against his. It is a country in which the achievement of the comely life is impossible, because machinery stands in the way and debases taste by substituting quantity for quality. It is a country in which the agrarian dream has been shattered because man deliberately chose to destroy his right relation to nature; instead he values the artificial products of the machine above the natural products of the soil. All these changes, which Willa Cather regards as bad, her countrymen persist in seeing as good; moreover, they regard change itself as being valuable, and so sacrifice beauty to novelty.

Such is Willa Cather's anatomy of Middle Western decay, and her description of it forms the most convincing part of the novel. The rest of the book is concerned with Claude's quest for value which leads him to Europe by way of the army. There he finds an introduction to the comely life through association with the talented and sensitive violinist David Gerhardt, whom he never would have met had he spent all his days on a Nebraska farm. He is stimulated to heroism by being given a chance for leadership in the AEF, where he is made an officer; there can now be no matching of wills against his since the men under him have to obey him. Finally the agrarian dream is given a new lease on life by his discovery of the French countryside, where, unlike their Nebraska counterparts, people like Mlle. Olive de Courcy still maintain the right relation to nature and yet are civilized. In attempting to portray all this Willa Cather is conspicuously unsuccessful. But her lack of artistic success is less important for us here than is the drift of her ideas, for the failure of solution in this novel leads directly to the crisis of the next. In *One of Ours* she still believed that the comely life could be achieved in the present, even if only in wartime France. In *A Lost Lady* she became convinced that it could not be achieved in the present at all.

THE AEF AND THE LAST CRUSADE

Claude's initiation into the realms of broader experience comes about in an interesting way. One of the best things in the book is Willa Cather's description of the Middle West's gradually growing awareness of the European war and its impact on the lives of people in America. The first time a character in the book mentions the war it is to comment casually on its effect on the price of wheat in the Chicago market, but there is a slow growth in awareness until the prairie farmers come to believe that not only their economic welfare but civilization itself is at stake. But this increased awareness of the life of the world beyond the horizon has its unpleasant side. It is paralleled by a change in attitude toward the German people. The Wheelers cannot reconcile the atrocity stories they have heard about the rape of Belgium with what they know about their peace-loving and industrious German neighbors. Claude reflects:

> He had always been taught that the German people were preeminent in the virtues Americans most admire; a month ago he would have said they had all the ideals a decent American boy could fight for. The invasion of Belgium was contradictory to the German character as he knew it in his friends and neighbors. He still cherished the hope that there had been some great mistake; that this splendid people would apologize and right itself with the world.[17]

In view of Claude's relations with the Yoeders and Oberlieses and other admirable neighbors of his this attitude is very sympathetic and understandable. But a shift occurs and he comes around to the view of the First World War held by the street-corner speakers or Five Minute Men. This attitude is typified by the remark of his friend Leonard Dawson, who is about to enlist in the Marines, and who replies to Claude's surprised expostulation:

> "Good Lord, Claude, you ain't the only fellow around here that wears pants! What for? Well, I'll tell you what for," he held up

three large red fingers threateningly; "Belgium, the Lusitania, Edith Cavell. That dirt's got under my skin. I'll get my corn planted, and then Father'll look after Susie till I come back." [18]

Willa Cather apparently shared the general Allied indignation at the alleged German atrocities, since there is nothing in the rest of the book to contradict Leonard Dawson's stand. But in addition to moral indignation Willa Cather introduces another element into her story. During the war there emerged one phenomenon which filled her with ominous foreboding. This was the mechanization of the military, which promptly changed the entire nature of battle and rendered obsolete forever the old heroic conceptions about war. The war of 1914-18 was the first modern war; that is, it was the first war which was so thoroughly mechanized that in it individual human strength and courage counted for little or nothing. To Claude this was just another instance of the triumph of the machine, of the impoverishment of value attendant upon letting mechanism take the place of human endeavor. The particular symbol of mechanization which impressed itself on his mind was that of the siege gun:

> About the middle of the month came the story of the fall of the forts at Liège, battered at for nine days and finally reduced in a few hours by siege guns brought up from the rear, — guns which evidently could destroy any fortifications that had ever been, or ever could be constructed. Even to these quiet wheat-growing people, the siege guns before Liège were a menace; not to their safety or their goods, but to their comfortable established way of thinking. They introduced the greater-than-man force which afterward repeatedly brought into this war the effect of unforeseeable natural disaster, like tidal waves, earthquakes, or the eruption of volcanoes.
>
> On the twenty-third came the news of the fall of the fort at Namur; again giving warning that an unprecedented power of destruction had broken loose in the world. A few days later the story of the wiping out of the ancient and peaceful seat of learning at Louvain made it clear that this force was being directed toward incredible ends. By this time, too, the papers were full of accounts of the destruction of civilian populations. Something new, and certainly evil, was at work among mankind. Nobody was ready with a name for it. None of the well-worn words descriptive of human behaviour seemed adequate. The epithets grouped about

the name of "Attila" were too personal, too dramatic, too full of old, familiar human passion.[19]

Just as Claude, and with him Willa Cather, believes the beauties of the Middle West are being destroyed by the machine, so he sees the heroic values associated with the old-fashioned conception of war as undergoing the same fate. In each case the frightening thing is that the process, once started, is self-perpetuating; it is beyond anyone's power to control. It destroys comfortable old ways of thinking because, being something completely new, it defies classification and doesn't fit into the old neat categories. But the chief reason Willa Cather is so frightened of it is that it attacks the very roots of everything which she has held dear. Before it both the heroic life and the comely life go down to defeat. The real danger she sees in the impersonal power of mechanization is that it spells death to her all-important concept of the heroic will.

But if German atrocities and the mechanization of warfare have distorted and falsified the values which Willa Cather held dearest, how is she able to show Claude as finding fulfillment in the AEF? The answer is that it was in the army that Claude, for the first time in his life, feels united with other men in pursuit of a common goal; in other words, he finds a community in which he feels able to perform a significant action. The army consists of men drawn from every walk of life; it is able to bring together people as different as the artist-intellectual David Gerhardt and the nonartistic Claude. The significant action which Claude performs may not be very convincing to us since it consists of fighting and dying in a war now considered to have been useless and a cause which has since been exploded, but it was almost universally considered to be an act of praiseworthy heroism at the time: Willa Cather accurately records the emotional temperature of the age and circumstances in which she lived.

When Claude is billeted with the handsome young lieutenant from New York, a change comes into his life. Except for his sporadic contact with the Ehrlich family of Lincoln, he had never been thrown together with young men who were cultivated and refined, certainly not in the course of day-to-day living. But this is one of the values that Willa Cather sees in army life; in it, she thinks, a simple farm boy and an urban intellectual can meet and become friends. What Claude gets from David Gerhardt is easy enough to discuss; through him Claude becomes acquainted for the first time with music, French culture, and the beauties of French provincial life. What David gets from Claude and indeed from the army in general is of course different. He no longer feels that he is isolated from his countrymen or that as an artist and intellectual he is alienated from the mass public; instead he finds appreciation from such men as Claude and, as well, a companionship and sense of belonging which he had previously lacked.[20] David and Claude together, with their sharing of knowledge proceeding from separate specialized skills, represent in miniature what Willa Cather considered the army to be: an organic community which supplies them with roles to fill; in fact, an organization not very different in structure from that of the Middle Western family which she had celebrated in *My Ántonia*.

In sharp contrast the society of the Middle West, as she sees it, is not a community at all; it is a crowd, not a group. According to her the only thing its members share in common is a feeling of alienation from each other and of being set against each other in the competition for the material goods of life. What she is aiming at in this book is to show the clear superiority of the group over the crowd. Of course it may be argued that the AEF was not all she thought it to be, but what is important here is the use she makes of it and the part it plays in her ideas. The idea of a perfect society is to become increasingly strong with her as she no longer believes that solitary heroic individuals can make a satisfactory life for themselves alone. There are certain kinds of fulfillment which her protagonists now find only if the society of which they are a part happens to be satisfactory, and, since this turns out to be less and less often the case, her next few protagonists are doomed to frustration by the very nature of the civilization in which they live.

This is why the picture which she painted of army life and war in general is so outrageously idealistic that it brought forth a chorus of protests from veterans and votaries alike. This did not, however, prevent the book from receiving a Pulitzer Prize for the year 1922; sentimentality and idealization seldom do. But the gap between the army Willa Cather described and that of the returned veterans is so great that Claude's victory must be accounted a bogus triumph. The AEF in which he found himself was not the real AEF. Instead, it was another romanticized version of military life of the type satirized by George Bernard Shaw a quarter of a century earlier in *Arms and the Man*.

The artistic result of her attitude is that after Claude's enlistment in the army the book rapidly deteriorates. Willa Cather was no longer dealing with familiar subject matter and had to use second- and third-hand reports about army life with which she never did feel very comfortable.[21] She correctly grasped the fact that induction into the army

was for many people a sought-for and welcome release from a monotonous or intolerable personal existence, but she accepted in toto the army's
own glorified evaluation of itself. After the long, drawn-out business
about the voyage of the troop-ship *Anchises* and the influenza epidemic
abroad — episodes not necessary to the plot — Claude and his company
land in France, and the sentimentalizing begins in earnest. There is an
overidealization of French culture, for one thing:

> He wished he could talk to her [Mme. Joubert] as Gerhardt
> did. He admired the way she roused herself and tried to interest
> them, speaking her difficult language with such spirit and precision.
> It was a language that couldn't be mumbled; that had to be
> spoken with energy and fire, or not spoken at all. Merely speaking
> that exacting tongue would help to rally a broken spirit, he
> thought.[22]

There is an overidealization of the American doughboy. Mlle.
Olive de Courcy, whom Claude visits, has this to say about the AEF:

> "But you do come, — so many, and from so far! It is the last
> miracle of this war. I was in Paris on the fourth day of July, when
> your Marines, just from Belleau Wood, marched for your national
> fête, and I said to myself as they came on, *'That is a new man!'*
> Such heads they had, so fine there, behind the ears. Such discipline
> and purpose. Our people laughed and called to them and threw
> them flowers, but they never turned to look . . . eyes straight
> before. They passed like men of destiny." [23]

Finally there is overidealization of the war itself:

> They were bound for the big show, and on every hand were
> reassuring signs; long lines of gaunt, dead trees, charred and torn;
> big holes gashed out in fields and hillsides, already half concealed
> by new undergrowth; winding depressions in the earth, bodies of
> wrecked motor-trucks and automobiles lying along the road. . . .[24]

And again in the description of the death of Victor Morse, the American airman who had enlisted in the RAF and had been shot down in
flames:

> That was one of the things about this war; it took a little fellow

from a little town, gave him an air and a swagger, a life like a movie-film, — and then a death like the rebel angels.[25]

All this sounds pretty overblown to a reader who has lived into the nineteen-fifties. Claude's character seems hopelessly romantic and his role in the second part of the book wholly out of keeping with what we know about modern war. The very phrases which he lives by, once mouthed by millions, now seem curiously unreal. A fight to save Western civilization, to avenge the rape of Belgium, to preserve the fair name of France — what could be better calculated to appeal to the chivalrous instinct? To be sure, there are certain facts which don't seem to fit the argument: the cultivated Ehrlichs, who first introduce Claude to the artistic life while he is at college, are from the wrong side of the Rhine; and the violinist friend who teaches him to love music also appears to be a German. Life is more complex than Claude Wheeler seems to realize. The music which David Gerhardt so extravagantly admires is just as much a product of German civilization as is the army that invaded Belgium.[26] But nowhere is Claude ever made to take account of all this. By the end of the book he is firmly convinced that the French are good and the Germans are evil, and that is that.

Willa Cather's only explanation for this seeming anomaly is that Germany too has become mechanized like the American Middle West, and that consequently the artistic culture of the older Germany of the Ehrlichs has been replaced by an industrial order based on an acquisitive society. This is implied by the following reverie of Claude's:

No battlefield or shattered country he had seen was as ugly as this world would be if men like his brother Bayliss controlled it altogether. Until the war broke out, he had supposed they did control it; his boyhood had been clouded and enervated by that belief. The Prussians had believed it, too, apparently.[27]

In such a struggle as this the only place for one of Willa Cather's creative heroes is fighting against the new commercial-industrial dispensation; thus she is able to justify American participation in the First World War as a defense of an agricultural France against a mechanized Germany. (Although much is made in the early part of the book about Paris being the capital city of France and of civilization, it is the rural part of France which Willa Cather celebrates when Claude finally arrives overseas.) Willa Cather considers France to be much the same kind of agricultural civilization that Nebraska had been, with the addition that culture and urbanity are to be found in every farmhouse; the cultural ideal of rural France replaces that of the Divide. This kind of civilization must be protected against its would-be destroyers, and the struggle turns out to be very much like the struggle of the pioneers against the wild elements. The No-Man's-Land between the trenches becomes the new frontier, and the First World War becomes the last manifestation of the pioneer spirit.

But if we are intended to accept Claude as a latter-day manifestation of the old-time pioneer spirit, Willa Cather has grievously erred in giving us a protagonist so notably nonheroic. Claude cannot by any stretch of the imagination be considered a pioneer. He lacks the strength of the typical Cather pioneer-creative spirit, and even the presence of imagination in him is dubious, since it needs stimulation from the outside in order to achieve any unified vision of life. Claude's character, although amiable, is weak throughout the book; he never does undergo the transformation necessary for us to believe that he became an efficient and respected officer who died fighting gloriously on the Western front. Claude is much too passive to be credible as the romantic hero Willa Cather makes him out to be. Most of the time he is presented as a mere spectator who seems powerless to perform any significant action at all, and as such he resembles nothing so much as the observer heroes who serve as protagonists in the novels of Norman Mailer, Irwin Shaw, and other writers of the Second World War.

The very choice of the nonheroic Claude as a protagonist in this novel is a fact of supreme importance in Willa Cather's development. It shows that she is beginning to doubt her most heartfelt convictions; she is no longer at all sure that superior men and women can succeed in life through the mere exercise of their wills. What weaned her from her belief in the will's omnipotence was the triumph of the machine, which she described so thoroughly in the book's early part dealing with the twentieth-century Middle West. Mechanization involves the development of strong impersonal forces greater than any individual can withstand, and thus renders individual courage such as Claude is supposed to display in battle meaningless as well as fruitless. It is small wonder that the novel's final pages are steeped in the blackest pessimism. The book ends with a mood of Claude's mother, nowhere denied by Willa Cather, in which she sees the postwar world as completely buried by an avalanche in which mechanization, commercialization, and the triumph of ugliness and greed make a waste land of the present by obliterating all the values of the past:

In the dark months that followed, when human nature looked to her [Mrs. Wheeler] uglier than it had ever done before, those letters were Mrs. Wheeler's comfort. As she read the newspapers, she used to think about the passage of the Red Sea, in the Bible; it seemed as if the flood of meanness and greed had been held back just long enough for the boys to go over, and then swept down and engulfed everything that was left at home. When she can see nothing that has come out of it all but evil, she reads Claude's letters over again and reassures herself; for him the call was clear, the cause was glorious. Never a doubt stained his bright faith. . . . He died believing his own country better than it is, and France better than any country can ever be. And those were beautiful beliefs to die with. Perhaps it was as well to see that vision, and then to see no more. She would have dreaded the awakening, — she sometimes even doubts whether he could have borne at all that last, desolating disappointment. One by one the heroes of that war, the men of dazzling soldiership, leave prematurely the world they have come back to. Airmen whose deeds were tales of wonder, officers whose names made the blood of youth beat faster, survivors of incredible dangers, — one by one they quietly die by their own hand. Some do it in obscure lodging houses, some in their office, where they seemed to be carrying on their business like other men. Some slip over a vessel's side and disappear into the sea. When Claude's mother hears of these things, she shudders and presses her hands tight over her breast, as if she had him there. She feels as if God had saved him from some horrible suffering, some horrible end. For as she reads, she thinks those slayers of themselves were all so like him; they were the ones who had hoped extravagantly, — who in order to do what they did had to hope extravagantly, and to believe passionately. And they found they had hoped and believed too much. But one she knew, who could ill bear disillusion . . . safe, safe.[28]

Willa Cather gives her implicit approval of Mrs. Wheeler's belief that the present is hopeless, that Claude died full of illusions about the nature of reality, and that it was better for him to have had beautiful illusions than to face life as it actually is. Here belief in the superiority of the will to the external world is replaced by a concept of the will in which it is apparently regarded as necessary to lie to oneself in order to succeed. Whatever the nature of this will may be, it is certainly not omnipotent. This dreary and muted picture of the present, following so closely on the heels of an unconvincing affirmation of the AEF, suggests that Willa Cather was not really convinced that her ideal society could be found in the present at all but was whistling in the dark to keep her spirits up. Not many of the men of dazzling soldiership may have actually committed suicide, as Willa Cather suggests they did, but Professor St. Peter comes close to doing so in her next novel but one. Clearly she has now reached a state of mind in which the present is regarded as being no place for an intelligent and sensitive person to remain.

In some ways *One of Ours* represents a reversion to the emotional pattern of the stories of Willa Cather's first period, of which "The Sculptor's Funeral" can be taken as the prototype. There the hero's family is his enemy and stands in his way in such a manner as to block the road to the outside world of accomplishment and self-fulfillment. The hero flies from his family and makes good his escape into the realm of some ideal, an ideal which the reader usually finds vague, shadowy, and not very convincing. In *One of Ours* the pattern is somewhat transformed; the family which Claude must fight or evade has become the whole society in which he lives, and the world of art, which had been the goal in Willa Cather's first period, has become the world of war, or more specifically, that little band of heroes, the officers of the AEF. As in the earlier stories, the rejection is stronger than the affirmation. Two other changes show the movement of Willa Cather's mind toward increasing pessimism. First, Claude's chance to become a hero has to come from the outside ("History had condescended to such as he; this whole brilliant adventure had become the day's work.");[29] an earlier Willa Cather protagonist would have made his own chance. Second, Willa Cather portrays the First World War as being the last chance for heroism anybody of his generation would ever have. She implies in the long reverie of Claude's mother that, had he come back from France, he too would have been defeated by the society which was but a larger projection of his own unsympathetic family.

A Lost Lady: THE DECLINE OF THE WEST

From *One of Ours* through *My Mortal Enemy* Willa Cather's protagonists become increasingly preoccupied with one problem: how to lead the comely life in the modern world. They endeavor to engage in the search for the comely life and become more and more frustrated in this by the very nature of modern times; in particular by the triumph of commerce, which she sees as identical with institutionalized greed.

In a society grounded upon organized hoggishness, she seems to be saying, there is no place for the cult of beauty. And since she holds beauty to be the highest good there is, once she becomes convinced that the comely life cannot be lived in the modern world, she turns against that world. Rejection of the present becomes for her an act of virtue.

This is clearly seen in her next novel, *A Lost Lady* (1923). It has for its heroine a lovely woman who can exert her charms only in a society which recognizes her worth. That society is represented as passing away with the death of her husband and the approaching old age and helplessness of his friends. Marian Forrester does not herself turn against the present — this is why she is lost — but Willa Cather makes it perfectly clear that it would have been much better if she had. Thus the revulsion against the modern world which was implicit in the ending of the previous novel becomes explicit in this one.

A Lost Lady is one of Willa Cather's best novels and is central to her thought. In compact prose and in the brief space of 174 pages she manages to present as much as she ever could of what she felt to be the nature of life and the meaning of civilization, as well as give her interpretation of the history of an epoch. The book is an excellent example of that kind of writing which is at the same time realistic and highly symbolic; the story runs along perfectly credibly on the literal level and yet every incident and almost every spoken word stands for more than itself and tells another tale. What Willa Cather has done is to present the story on two different levels, and much of the artistic beauty of the work comes from the fact that in large measure the two are united, that action and significance, symbol and meaning, are one.

On the literal level the story is about the decay of Marian Forrester, a charming lady, after a crippling accident has made an invalid of her once powerful husband, the Captain. On the symbolic level Willa Cather was writing social allegory expressing her view on the significance of the history of the West. To her mind this history was no less than that of the creation and destruction of a civilization. *O Pioneers!* and *My Ántonia* had centered on the problems of founding and consolidating a civilization. In *A Lost Lady* the cycle is completed. It shows the decay of the pioneer spirit and its replacement by the spirit of commerce, the decline of the broad imaginative vision that created the West and the substitution for it of the narrow goal of petty self-aggrandizement. The two opposing principles are identified with successive generations and are embodied in the contrasting figures of Captain Forrester, the aging and crippled railroad builder, and the shrewd young shyster lawyer, Ivy Peters.

The fact that she is writing social allegory does not detract in the slightest from Willa Cather's fascination with her heroine. Mrs. Forrester was based on a real person, the wife of an ex-governor of Nebraska whom Willa Cather had known as a child.[30] The disintegration of her personality under the influence of Ivy Peters and his generation is but another fictional portrayal of the suffering inflicted on the creative spirit at the hands of a petty commercial Philistinism which has been presented to us so often in the European and American literature of the last one hundred and twenty years. Marian Forrester, pining for the fashionable life of the winter hotels at Denver and Colorado Springs but forced by the Captain's infirmity to spend the remaining years of her youth in a small Nebraska town, first takes lovers, then alcohol, and finally bogs down in a mass of debt which involves her with the town's most unsavory character, Ivy Peters. On this level Mrs. Forrester is a Middle Western Madame Bovary, although her troubles do not drive her to suicide. (After the Captain's death she manages to escape to Argentina.) Willa Cather and Flaubert present the same picture of a soul thirsting for beauty set down in a bourgeois world filled with ugliness and incapable of coping with it; she lavishes the same meticulous care on Marian that Flaubert did on Emma. Both authors manage to make their characters very appealing while still maintaining a certain aesthetic distance from them (something of Keats's negative capability applies here since both heroines are treated sympathetically but without sentimentality). After reading *A Lost Lady* one is not at all surprised to find that one of Willa Cather's favorite novels was *Madame Bovary*.

The social allegory in the novel is deliberately made apparent from the very first page. Briefly, the Lost Lady represents civilization in the West, for all the amenities of gracious living which can make life the agreeable and charming thing which at best it can be. Her husband, the Captain, is a pioneer railroad builder, "a contractor, who had built hundreds of miles of road for the Burlington, — over the sage brush and cattle country, and on up into the Black Hills."[31] He embodies all the virtues which Willa Cather has led us to expect in a pioneer: the imagination to see, the strength to achieve, and an absolutely incorruptible moral integrity. Willa Cather is saying that only when civilization is wedded to moral values can it amount to anything more than a beautiful parasitic growth. But Marian Forrester's union with the Captain is threatened by forces from without and within. Not only does the change in civilization threaten the moral values on which the marriage is based, but the deterioration of Mrs. Forrester's character imperils the union and also reflects the social disintegration brought about by the rising tides of commerce.

It is usual for Willa Cather to begin her novels with some symbolic incident which seems unimportant in itself but which imaginatively foreshadows all the action in the book and also its meaning. These incidents function as signposts which point the way to future action, which in turn illuminates and makes clear the meaning of the symbol. An example of such a symbol, we recall, is found on the opening page of *O Pioneers!*, in which the little Nebraska town of Hanover, near which the characters live, is trying hard not to be blown away.[32] *A Lost Lady* opens in like manner, but since it tells a twofold story about both the creation of a civilization and its destruction, it uses two symbolic incidents at its beginning. These are the locating by Captain Forrester of his house and garden on the Sweet Water and the blinding of the woodpecker by Ivy Peters.

The opening page of *A Lost Lady* begins with a description of the house that Captain and Mrs. Forrester live in: "a house well known from Omaha to Denver for its hospitality and for a certain charm of atmosphere." [33] This house was a rendezvous for what Willa Cather calls the railroad aristocracy — "the directors, general managers, vice-presidents, superintendents whose names we all knew; and their younger brothers or nephews [who] were auditors, freight agents, departmental assistants." [34] In other words, "the railroad aristocracy" consisted of the natural aristocrats who had built the railroads and their relatives who helped to run them, and who, chosen through nepotism, formed the beginnings of a social aristocracy. Unlike earlier books, this one is about people whose contemporaries actually recognized them as aristocrats; all others do not count. Again Willa Cather has divided the world she writes about into heroes and helots, and makes no bones about the fact that it is the heroes she is interested in:

> There were then two distinct social strata in the prairie states; the homesteaders and hand-workers who were there to make a living, and the bankers and gentlemen ranchers who came from the Atlantic seaboard to invest money and to "develop our great West," as they used to tell us.[35]

All of the railroad men frequently broke their journeys to stop at the house of Captain Daniel Forrester at Sweet Water. This house was of a very special kind, for it stood for the kind of life that Willa Cather thought could and should be lived on the western plains, a life which was both civilized and generous. The couple who presided over it managed to bestow on it some of their charm: "The Forrester place, as everyone called it, was not at all remarkable; the people who lived there made it seem much larger and finer than it was." [36] Located on a hill just a mile outside the town, it seemed to the weary railroad men an oasis of civilization set down in the midst of the wilderness:

> Thus placed on the hill, against its bristling grove, it was the first thing one saw on coming into Sweet Water by rail, and the last thing one saw on departing.[37]

Years before, just after the Civil War, while driving for a freight company, the Captain had come across an Indian encampment near the Sweet Water and, becoming convinced that this was the ideal location for a house, had decided to return some day and build. It was years before he did:

> "There were those that were dependent on me," he said. "I had sickness to contend with, and responsibilities. But in all those years I expect there was hardly a day passed that I did not remember the Sweet Water and this hill. When I came here a young man, I had planned it in my mind, pretty much as it is today; where I would dig my well, and where I would plant my grove and orchard. I planned a house that my friends could come to, with a wife like Mrs. Forrester to make it attractive to them. I used to promise myself that some day I would manage it." [38]

The Captain finally returned and built his house, setting it in the midst of a garden which, although not nearly so carefully ordered as that in *My Ántonia,* is just as much an image of the earthly paradise:

> To approach Captain Forrester's property, you had first to get over a wide, sandy creek which flowed along the eastern edge of the town. Crossing this by the foot-bridge or the ford, you entered the Captain's private lane, bordered by Lombardy poplars, with wide meadows lying on either side. Just at the foot of the hill on which the house sat, one crossed a second creek by the stout wooden road-bridge. This stream traced artless loops and curves through the broad meadows that were half pasture land, half marsh. Any one but Captain Forrester would have drained the bottom land and made it into highly productive fields. But he had selected

this place long ago because it looked beautiful to him, and he happened to like the way the creek wound through his pasture, with mint and joint-grass and twinkling willows along its banks.[39]

This immediately tells the reader a good deal about what the Captain was like. To him, beauty was much more important than utility. The silvery meadows, half pasture land, half marsh, are later to be drained by Ivy Peters and made into wheat fields, but under the Captain they remain unproductive, serving as a reminder that beauty was an essential ingredient of the pioneer's vision of the West.

The Captain had built his house largely as a tribute to and a setting for his second wife, Marian Forrester. She is pictured as a great and gracious lady, who not only transmits the values of civilization but also herself embodies them. Willa Cather gives a charming picture of her manner of receiving unexpected visitors. If she heard the rumble of wheels on the bridge, she would run out of the kitchen with a buttery spoon in her hand or wave cherry-stained fingers at the visitor. "She never stopped to pin up a lock; she was attractive in dishabille, and she knew it." [40] She would even rush out in her dressing gown, with her long black hair rippling over her shoulders, to welcome that highest nabob of the plains, Cyrus Dalzell, president of the Colorado and Utah. Then follows a passage highly revealing of the values held in the book:

> In his eyes, and in the eyes of the admiring middle-aged men who visited there, whatever Mrs. Forrester chose to do was "lady-like" because she did it. They could not imagine her in any dress or situation in which she would not be charming.[41]

This reflects the nineteenth-century view of women as cultural conservators and transmitters of civilization: they were the source of civilized values, and men took their cue from them. According to this view women also set the moral tone of society and were the transmitters of all morality, the implication being that when they went wrong, everything went wrong. The typical symbol of woman's going wrong was, of course, sexual indiscretion. Women — that is, good women — were considered fragile vessels, the slightest flaw in whose chastity was fraught with dire peril for the social order. Willa Cather deliberately uses this stereotype from the genteel tradition in order to make her point about Marian Forrester. On the literal level she becomes a lost lady because she is sexually promiscuous; Niel Herbert says of her, "Lilies that fester smell far worse than weeds." [42] On the level of social allegory a lost lady stands for a lost civilization; promiscuity becomes a symbol of social degeneration. This equating of the chastity of women with the moral integrity of a civilization provides the fundamental metaphor upon which the book is based.

Mrs. Forrester's character is not sharply sketched but is hinted at with a kind of romantic suggestiveness. As Willa Cather was later to say, "Whatever is felt upon the page without being specifically named there — that, we might say, is created." [43] The following passage is an example:

> There could be no negative encounter, however slight, with Mrs. Forrester. If she merely bowed to you, merely looked at you, it constituted a personal relation. Something about her took hold of one in a flash; one became acutely conscious of her, of her fragility and grace, of her mouth which could say so much without words; of her eyes, lively, laughing, intimate, nearly always a little mocking. [44]

Like a true child of Walter Pater, Willa Cather is here trying to get at the essence of a thing — in this case, the essence of Mrs. Forrester's charm. What she suggests is Mrs. Forrester's ability to make herself understood, the grace with which she manages to endow every action, her vitality, her gift for communicating warmth, and her ironic awareness of the complexities of life. And this method works, for, without being told anything very definite about Marian Forrester, we are convinced that she is a very charming lady indeed.

One other anecdote about our heroine throws some light on her nature and on Willa Cather's attitude toward her:

> Captain Forrester himself, a man of few words, told Judge Pommeroy that he had never seen her look more captivating than on the day when she was chased by the new bull in the pasture. She had forgotten about the bull and gone into the meadow to gather wild flowers. He heard her scream, and as he ran puffing down the hill, she was scudding along the edge of the marshes like a hare, beside herself with laughter, and stubbornly clinging to the crimson parasol that had made all the trouble. [45]

This shows her charming as ever but not fully grasping the nature of the situation in which she finds herself and holding on to beauty in the form of her personal possessions no matter what danger threatens —

an attitude fundamentally frivolous. It puts her, and through her, all women in a rather ambiguous relation to reality: she screams, and yet she holds on to the parasol. The incident is emblematic of a complete lack of knowledge of human limitations — a lack which later leads to her downfall.

All that I have been describing so far — the part played by Captain Forrester in the building of railroads across the plains, his locating of a house on the Sweet Water and establishing of a garden which is an earthly paradise, and finally his bringing there to live with him a wife who is young and beautiful, and who makes life pleasing for his friends — all this Willa Cather compresses into a short chapter which gives her idea of how life and culture came to the plains; it is the story of the creation of a civilization. As in *O Pioneers!* and *My Ántonia,* the plains life is described as paradisiacal; the early Middle West is a Garden of Eden. But every Garden of Eden must have its serpent: Sweet Water has Ivy Peters. He is an embodiment of evil, a personification of pure malicious destructive will.

Here we arrive at the second of Miss Cather's initial symbolic incidents, which counterbalances Captain Forrester's locating his house on the Sweet Water. The way the serpent in the garden reveals himself is this: several of the town boys, including the young Niel Herbert, ask Mrs. Forrester's permission to fish and wade in the Captain's beautiful marsh and have lunch there, wanting to disport themselves in the earthly paradise; and she, being Lady of the manor, grants them that favor. While laughing and playing there they are suddenly approached by a sinister figure:

> A well-grown boy of eighteen or nineteen, dressed in a shabby corduroy hunting suit, with a gun and gamebag, had climbed up from the marsh and was coming down the grove between the rows of trees. He walked with a rude, arrogant stride, kicking at the twigs, and carried himself with unnatural erectness, as if he had a steel rod down his back. There was something defiant and suspicious about the way he held his head. He came up to the group and addressed them in a superior, patronizing tone.
>
> "Hullo, kids. What are *you* doing here?"
>
> "Picnic," said Ed Elliott.
>
> "I thought girls went on picnics. Did you bring teacher along? Ain't you kids old enough to hunt yet?"
>
> George Adams looked at him scornfully. "Of course we are. I got a 22 Remington for my last birthday. But we know better

than to bring guns over here. You better hide yours, Mr. Ivy, or
Mrs. Forrester will come down here and tell you to get out."
    "She can't see us from the house. And anyhow, she can't say
anything to me. I'm just as good as she is." [46]

Two things are significant here. First, the fact that the Forresters'
garden is a wildlife sanctuary where destruction of birds and game is
forbidden. This fits in with the larger concept already noted, that it
is a sanctuary of another sort, where beauty of all kinds is preserved
against the encroachments of the world. Ivy Peters' refusal to recognize
it as a sanctuary makes him a barbarian who has no respect for
aesthetic or moral authority. Second, Willa Cather links this barbarism
with his refusal to recognize Mrs. Forrester as a superior being ("I'm
just as good as she is!"). This is extremely important, coming as it
does right after a chapter in which she has described Mrs. Forrester
as being the epitome of all civilization. Civilized values are shown to
form a hierarchy which is completely at odds with Ivy Peters' rude
egalitarianism. That Willa Cather was fully conscious of this is seen
in the very next paragraph:

> To this the boys made no reply. Such an assertion was absurd
> even to fish-mouthed Thad; his father's business depended upon
> some people being better than others, and ordering better cuts of
> meat in consequence. If everybody ate round steak like Ivy
> Peters's family, there would be nothing in the butcher's trade.[47]

Behind this paragraph lies the old Federalist assertion that inequality
is the proper basis of society and that wealth is a good index to ability.
This strain, fundamental to conservative thought, was always present in
Willa Cather and grew stronger as the years wore on.
    Presently Ivy notices a bird in the branches above his head, and there
follows a passage which illuminates his whole character and future course
of action:

> "See that woodpecker tapping; don't mind us a bit. That's
> nerve!"
> "They are protected here, so they're not afraid," said precise
> George.
> "Hump! They'll spoil the old man's grove for him. That tree's
> full of holes already. Wouldn't he come down easy, now!" . . .
> He drew from his pocket a metal sling-shot and some round
> bits of gravel. "I won't kill it. I'll just surprise it, so we can
> have a look at it."

"Bet you won't hit it!"

"Bet I will!" He fitted the stone to the leather, squinted, and let fly. Sure enough, the woodpecker dropped at his feet. He threw his heavy black felt hat over it. Ivy never wore a straw hat, even in the hottest weather. "Now wait. He'll come to. You'll hear him flutter in a minute."

"It ain't a he, anyhow. It's a female. Anybody would know that," said Niel contemptuously, annoyed that this unpopular boy should come along and spoil their afternoon. . . .

"All right, Miss Female," said Ivy carelessly, intent upon a project of his own. He took from his pocket a little red leather box, and when he opened it the boys saw that it contained curious little instruments: tiny sharp knife blades, hooks, curved needles, a saw, a blow-pipe, and scissors. "Some of these I got with a taxidermy outfit from the *Youth's Companion,* and some I made myself." He got stiffly down on his knees, — his joints seemed disinclined to bend at all, — and listened beside his hat. "She's as lively as a cricket," he announced. Thrusting his hand suddenly under the brim, he brought out the startled bird. It was not bleeding, and did not seem to be crippled.

"Now, you watch, and I'll show you something," said Ivy. He held the woodpecker's head in a vice made of his thumb and fore finger, enclosed its panting body with his palm. Quick as a flash, as if it were a practiced trick, with one of those tiny blades he slit both the eyes that glared in the bird's stupid little head, and instantly released it.

The woodpecker rose in the air with a whirling, corkscrew motion, darted to the right, struck a tree-trunk, — to the left, and struck another. Up and down, backward and forward among the tangle of branches it flew, raking its feathers, falling and recovering itself. The boys stood watching it, indignant and uncomfortable, not knowing what to do. They were not especially sensitive; Thad was always on hand when there was anything doing at the slaughter house, and the Blum boys lived by killing things. They wouldn't have believed they could be so upset by a hurt woodpecker. There was something wild and desperate about the way the darkened creature beat its wings in the branches, whirling in the sunlight and never seeing it, always thrusting its head up and shaking it, as a bird does when it is drinking. Presently it managed to get its feet on the same limb where it had been struck, and seemed to recognize that perch. As if it had learned something by its bruises, it pecked and crept its way along the branch and disappeared into its own hole.[48]

As an exemplar of extraordinary and gratuitous cruelty Ivy Peters is unsurpassed. He uses his dissecting instruments, not for any humane purpose but for a destructive one, slitting the eyes of the bird, the organs of perception of sunlight, of beauty, of life itself. Incidentally, it is not improbable that here Willa Cather is showing a typical romantic revulsion against science and the uses to which it has been put. But more to the point, the woodpecker symbolizes the Lost Lady, as she will come to be: the slow, wheeling flight of the bird after Ivy releases her is similar to Marian Forrester's hectic fluttering after the death of the Captain. She, too, batters her head against familiar objects in an attempt to regain her former elevation, and feels the presence of the sunlight but never sees the sun.

Ivy Peters, in his wanton destructiveness, is an embodiment of pure evil and represents everything in the modern world which Willa Cather hated, for as we shall see again and again, she thought of the modern world as essentially destructive. All of the book develops from the single image of Ivy Peters's blinding the bird, and it is a symbol of everything in the book that he is responsible for: the draining of the marshes — the despoiling of the garden — the debauching of Marian Forrester; in short, the attempted destruction of all beauty by the commercialization of life. His career involves the undoing of everything which Captain Forrester has managed with such pains to accomplish; that is why the real subject of the book is the story of the destruction of civilization itself.

As we have seen, Willa Cather was never able to arrive at a really satisfying solution to the problem of the relative merits of city and country. The best she could manage was a rather uneasy compromise: Ántonia stays in the country, but Jim Burden returns to the city. This compromise appears in the lives of Mr. and Mrs. Forrester, too, who spent their winters in Denver and Colorado Springs and their summers in Sweet Water — leaving Sweet Water soon after Thanksgiving and returning about the first of May. But then comes the Captain's fall from his horse which puts an end to his career as a road builder. After recuperating all winter in Colorado Springs, he returns to his house in a semi-invalid condition and is able to putter around in his garden but can't do much else. His accident tends to isolate him in the country and destroys the city-country balance: "He and his wife still went away for the winter, but each year the period of their absence grew shorter." [49] It is when she is entirely deprived of city delights and driven into an enforced rustication that the real disintegration of Marian Forrester begins.

Her first love affair is with Frank Ellinger. He is a pattern of the physically attractive male: "Frank Ellinger was a bachelor of forty, six feet two, with long straight legs, fine shoulders, and a figure that still permitted his white waistcoat to button without a wrinkle under his conspicuously well-cut dinner coat." [50] Niel Herbert, the observer of the story, is conscious of Frank's tremendous vitality, yet finds something sinister about him; he is too exaggeratedly the male animal for Niel to feel completely comfortable when he is about.

> His whole figure seemed very much alive under his clothes, with a restless, muscular energy that had something of the cruelty of wild animals in it. Niel was very much interested in this man, the hero of many ambiguous stories. He didn't know whether he liked him or not. He knew nothing bad about him, but he felt something evil.[51]

Niel is, of course, idealistic as only a very young man can be about Marian Forrester and can't stand the thought of there being an overtly sexual side to her nature. But it is not too hard for the reader to see what Mrs. Forrester sees in Frank Ellinger. The Captain, whatever his virtues, is twenty-five years older than his wife, and during most of the course of the novel is a semi-invalid. Marian is able to give the Captain everything he wants and needs, but he is not able to give her everything she needs, and she must turn elsewhere if she is to fulfill her passionate nature. Moreover, the Captain is perfectly aware of this, and accepts the situation. In the scene in which he intercepts his wife's letter to Frank Ellinger and, without even opening it, comments to Niel on the beauty of her penmanship, he indirectly indicates that he knows all there is to know about Mrs. Forrester's private life.

In her treatment of this relationship Willa Cather maintains a sympathetically detached attitude; she is neither indignant nor maudlin about the affair, but presents it in a manner that presumes neither to take sides nor to make judgments. There is one scene in which Mrs. Forrester and Frank take a sleigh ride into the woods, ostensibly to cut cedar boughs for Christmas. As they emerge from the forest, carrying buffalo robes over their arms, they are observed by the little German boy, Adolph Blum, who happens to be there hunting rabbits.

If anyone else had chanced along at that particular time, Marian Forrester's reputation would have been in dire peril, but Adolph comes from a family which through background and training recognizes the prerogatives of aristocracy: "They realized, more than their companions, that such a fortunate and privileged class was an axiomatic fact in the social order." [52] The outcome of this intrusion would have been quite different had it been, for instance, Ivy Peters who had observed the couple after their tryst.

> But with Adolph Blum her secrets were safe. His mind was feudal: the rich and fortunate were also the privileged. These warm-blooded, quick-breathing people took chances, — followed impulses only dimly understandable to a boy who was wet and weather-chapped all year, who waded in the mud fishing for cat, or lay in the marsh waiting for wild duck. Mrs. Forrester had never been too haughty to smile at him when he came to the back door with his fish. She never haggled about the price. She treated him like a human being.[53]

There is no particular mystery about why Adolph Blum never thinks of betraying Mrs. Forrester's secret. In his eyes she is a privileged and likable being who had been kind to him; social habit and personal bias combine to make him a partisan of hers. But Willa Cather refuses to be partisan herself. We feel that she has devoted herself to rendering the scene without making any moral judgment on it; this is life, we feel, this is the way people act.

It is about this time that the growing Niel Herbert begins to realize that he values the Captain more than the Captain's wife.

> Curiously enough, it was as Captain Forrester's wife that she most interested Niel, and it was in relation to her husband that he most admired her. Given her other charming attributes, her comprehension of a man like the railroad-builder, her loyalty to him, stamped her more than anything else. . . . His admiration of Mrs. Forrester went back to that, just as, he felt, she herself went back to it.[54]

Apparently, then, the aesthetic life is valuable and interesting not so much in itself but in relation to pioneer virtues. The cardinal point in Mrs. Forrester's character as Niel sees it is her absolute loyalty to moral integrity. This is ironic, since we know and Niel is soon to find out that she is not loyal to the Captain physically and she is later to be disloyal in other and more serious ways. But Niel's whole attitude toward Mrs. Forrester's attraction for men has a rather ambivalent ring to it:

> He rather liked the stories, even the spiteful ones, about the gay life she led in Colorado, and the young men she kept dangling about her every winter. He sometimes thought of the life she might have been living ever since he had known her, — and the one she had chosen to live. From that disparity, he believed, came the subtlest thrill of her fascination. She mocked outrageously at the proprieties she observed, and inherited the magic of contradictions.[55]

Here we have that ambiguous attitude toward the city which is found so often in the works of Willa Cather. On the one hand she pictures the life of cities as an endless round of delights, so that Marian Forrester, in marrying the Captain, has had to make a considerable sacrifice. On the other hand she has the notion that the urban life is morally inferior to the rural, so that she makes Niel Herbert share the puritanical suspicion of the country-bred that cities are sinks of sin and iniquity.[56] He tends to regard the good things of life as being both fascinating and spiced with evil, showing a *fin de siècle* tendency to associate beauty with wickedness. But Marian Forrester he regards as both naughty and good; that is the reason he is fascinated by her and believes she inherits "the magic of contradictions."

The Captain, as we have previously said, is pictured as one of the great ones of the earth. He has achieved absolute mastery over life, at least until his crippling accident; and the symbol of his mastery is his ability to impose order upon his environment: upon the American West, upon his house on the Sweet Water, upon the people around him. This last emerges from the description of his ability to calm people whom hysteria has touched:

> His repose was like that of a mountain. When he laid his fleshy, thick-fingered hand upon a frantic horse, an hysterical woman, an Irish workman out for blood, he brought them peace, — something they could not resist. That had been the secret of his management of men. His sanity asked nothing, claimed nothing; it was so simple that it brought a hush over the disturbed creatures. In the old days, when he was building road in the Black Hills, trouble sometimes broke out in camp when he was absent, staying with

Mrs. Forrester at Colorado Springs. He would put down the
telegram that announced an insurrection and say to his wife,
"Maidy, I must go to the men." And that was all he did, — he
went to them.[57]

The kind of order which he brought with him had nothing repressive
about it; rather, it consisted of peace, repose, sanity. This is the kind
of order that Willa Cather delighted in and regarded as the essence of
civilization.

Niel Herbert, who has slowly been taking shape during the course
of the novel, now begins to grow up. He has his twentieth birthday
during the very first year that Marian and her husband were forced to
spend entirely at Sweet Water, and under their influence and that of
his uncle, Judge Pommeroy, begins his initiation into the mysteries of
literature and life. He comes upon a set of the Bohn classics in his
uncle's back office and becomes absorbed in reading them: *Don Juan,
Tom Jones,* Montaigne, and Ovid. There follows a good expression of
the influence of the classics on an imaginative young man from the
hinterland:

> He was eavesdropping upon the past, being let into the great
> world that had plunged and glittered and sumptuously sinned long
> before little Western towns were dreamed of. Those rapt evenings
> beside the lamp gave him a long perspective, influenced his con-
> ception of the people about him, made him know just what he
> wished his own relations with these people to be.[58]

Niel Herbert is learning about life from literature much as Jim
Burden had; part of the process of growing up consists in realizing
the connection between the two. But Niel never learns to correlate
Mrs. Forrester with Ovid as Jim had Lena Lingard with Vergil, for he
can accept certain things in literature which he will not accept in life.
Willa Cather reveals this through a significant juxtaposition of incidents.
Immediately after the passage on his rapt discovery of the classics,
Willa Cather contrives to have a Denver savings bank, of which the
Captain was president, fail. He and Judge Pommeroy have to take
the evening express to the West the same day. While they are gone
Niel decides to pay his respects to a gracious lady by getting up early
in the morning and gathering for her a bouquet of roses:

> Under the bluffs that overhung the marsh he came upon thickets
> of wild roses, with flaming buds, just beginning to open. Where

they had opened, their petals were stained with that burning rose-colour which is always gone by noon, — a dye made of sunlight and morning and moisture, so intense that it cannot possibly last . . . must fade, like ecstasy. Niel took out his knife and began to cut the stiff stems, crowded with red thorns.

He would make a bouquet for a lovely lady; a bouquet gathered off the cheeks of morning . . . those roses, only half awake, in the defencelessness of utter beauty. He would leave them just outside one of the French windows of her bedroom. When she opened her shutters to let in the light, she would find them, — and they would perhaps give her a sudden distaste for coarse worldlings like Frank Ellinger.

After tying his flowers with a twist of meadow grass, he went up the hill through the grove and softly round the still house to the north side of Mrs. Forrester's own room, where the door-like green shutters were closed. As he bent to place the flowers on the sill, he heard from within a woman's soft laughter; impatient, indulgent, teasing, eager. Then another laugh, very different, a man's. And it was fat and lazy, — ended in something like a yawn.

Niel found himself at the foot of the hill on the wooden bridge, his face hot, his temples beating, his eyes blind with anger. In his hand he still carried the prickly bunch of wild roses. He threw them over the wire fence into a mudhole the cattle had trampled under the bank of the creek. He did not know whether he had left the house by the driveway or had come down through the shrubbery. In that instant between stooping to the window-sill and rising, he had lost one of the most beautiful things in his life. Before the dew dried, the morning had been wrecked for him; and all subsequent mornings, he told himself bitterly. This day saw the end of that admiration and loyalty that had been like a bloom on his existence. He could never recapture it. It was gone, like the morning freshness of the flowers.

"Lilies that fester," he muttered, *"lilies that fester smell far worse than weeds."*

Grace, variety, the lovely voice, the sparkle of fun and fancy in those dark eyes; all this was nothing. It was not a moral scruple she had outraged, but an aesthetic ideal. Beautiful women, whose beauty meant more than it said . . . was their brilliancy always fed by something coarse and concealed? Was that their secret? [59]

The symbolic gift of the roses, the sad Cyrenaicism with its poignant

awareness that any kind of intense beauty is too fragile to last, provide
the setting for Niel's first direct contact with experience and his initiation into adulthood. For him that loyalty which Marian Forrester had
shown toward her husband was gone forever. He did not realize that
the particular kind of loyalty which he had envisaged was largely a
product of his own imagination; that the Captain envisages a different
and subtler kind of loyalty which did not have to include sexual faith-
fulness, and which in part at least was based on a more realistic sense
of human limitations than he was prepared to admit. For it is certainly
true that Niel Herbert, idealistic and adolescent as he is, will not recognize that human life has a sexual basis. Overhearing Marian Forrester
in her bedroom is far different to him from imagining her leading a gay
life in Colorado, flirting with young men and keeping them dangling
from her string. It is even appropriate that Niel's excessive disillusionment is a product of his own idolatry. It is naïve of him to come
offering her flowers at a moment when she had every reason to expect to
be alone and undisturbed, and it is precisely his visiting her at an hour
normally proscribed by etiquette which is responsible for his disillusion.

The center of attention now shifts to the Captain, who has been
engaged in trying to make amends for the failure of his savings bank.
Once again Willa Cather manages to make her point by a significant
juxtaposition of events: while Marian Forrester is having her affair
with Frank Ellinger, her husband is in Denver paying off his creditors
one hundred cents on the dollar. Mrs. Forrester may represent gracious
living, but her attractiveness dims when compared with the absolute
moral probity of her husband. The aesthetic aspect of life, we gather,
must be rooted in the moral virtues and is not nearly so agreeable when
presented unattached to them.

From here on the novel focuses on the irruption of the modern world
into the primitive Arcadian simplicity of life on the Sweet Water. The
failure of the savings bank at Denver brings up the whole problem of
the importance of money in modern life, and the Captain meets it in a
way which has been characteristic of his whole career:

> "Maidy," he said, not looking at her, "I've come home a poor
> man. It took about everything there was to square up. You'll have
> this place, unencumbered, and my pension; that will be about all.
> The livestock will bring in something."
>
> Niel saw that Mrs. Forrester grew very pale, but she smiled and
> brought her husband his cigar stand. "Oh, well! I expect we can
> manage, can't we?"

"We can just manage. Not much more. I'm afraid Judge Pommeroy considers I acted foolishly."

"Not at all, Mrs. Forrester," the Judge exclaimed. "He acted just as I hope I would have done in his place. But I am an unmarried man. There were certain securities, government bonds, which Captain Forrester could have turned over to you, but it would have been at the expense of the depositors."

"I've known men to do that," said the Captain heavily, "but I never considered they paid their wives a compliment. If Mrs. Forrester is satisfied, I shall never regret my decision." For the first time his tired, swollen eyes sought his wife's.

"I never question your decisions in business, Mr. Forrester. I know nothing about such things."

.   .   .   .

Judge Pommeroy began to explain to Mrs. Forrester the situation they had faced in Denver. The bank, about which Mrs. Forrester knew nothing but its name, was one which paid good interest on small deposits. The depositors were wage-earners; railroad employes, mechanics, and day labourers, many of whom had at some time worked for Captain Forrester. His was the only well-known name among the bank officers, it was the name which promised security and fair treatment to his old workmen and their friends. The other directors were promising young business men with many irons in the fire. But, the Judge said with evident chagrin, they had refused to come up to the scratch and pay their losses like gentlemen. They claimed that the bank was insolvent, not through unwise investments or mismanagement, but because of a nation-wide financial panic, a shrinking in values that no one could have foreseen. They argued that the fair thing was to share the loss with the depositors; to pay them fifty cents on the dollar, giving long-term notes for twenty-five per cent, settling on a basis of seventy-five per cent.

Captain Forrester had stood firm that not one of the depositors should lose a dollar. The promising young business men had listened to him respectfully, but finally told him they would settle only on their own terms; any additional refunding must be his affair. He sent to the vault for his private steel box, opened it in their presence, and sorted the contents on the table. The government bonds he turned in at once. Judge Pommeroy was sent out to sell the mining stocks and other securities in the open market.

At this part of his narrative the Judge rose and began to pace the floor, twisting the seals of his watch-chain. "That was what a man of honour was bound to do, Mrs. Forrester. With five of the directors backing down, he had either to lose his name or save it. The depositors had put their savings into that bank because Captain Forrester was president. To those men with no capital but their back and their two hands, his name meant safety. As he tried to explain to the directors, those deposits were above price; money saved to buy a home, or to take care of a man in sickness, or to send a boy to school. And those young men, bright fellows, well thought of in the community, sat there and looked down their noses and let your husband strip himself down to pledging his life insurance! There was a crowd in the street outside the bank all day, every day; Poles and Swedes and Mexicans, looking scared to death. A lot of them couldn't speak English — seemed like the only English word they knew was 'Forrester.' As we went in and out we'd hear the Mexicans saying, 'Forrester, Forrester.' It was a torment for me, on your account, Ma'am, to see the Captain strip himself. But, 'pon my honour, I couldn't forbid him. As for those white-livered rascals that sat there, — " the Judge stopped before Mrs. Forrester and ruffled his bushy white hair with both hands, "By God, Madam, I think I've lived too long! In my day the difference between a business man and a scoundrel was bigger than the difference between a white man and a nigger. I wasn't the right one to go out there as the Captain's counsel. One of these smooth members of the bar, like Ivy Peters is getting ready to be, might have saved something for you out of the wreck. But I couldn't use my influence with your husband. To that crowd outside the bank doors his name meant a hundred cents on the dollar, and by God, they got it! I'm proud of him, Ma'am; proud of his acquaintance!"

It was the first time Niel had ever seen Mrs. Forrester flush. A quick pink swept over her face. Her eyes glistened with moisture. "You were quite right, Judge. I wouldn't for the world have had him do otherwise for me. He would never hold up his head again. You see, I know him." As she said this she looked at Niel, on the other side of the room, and her glance was like a delicate and very dignified rebuke to some discourtesy, — though he was not conscious of having shown her any.[60]

The financial panic referred to here is probably the Panic of 1893, and the whole episode raises an interesting moral issue. When the other directors claim that "the bank was insolvent, not through unwise management, but because of a nation-wide financial panic, a shrinking of values that no one could have foreseen," they have a good point. They realize, as the Captain does not, the importance of finance in modern America and know that post–Civil War capitalism operates on a nation-wide scale. It has become immensely bigger than any individual. But to Captain Forrester the whole thing is a matter of personal responsibility. He feels financially liable for those who have trusted him, and recognizes no limits to this liability, although the extreme interdependence of men in a commercial-industrial society makes such a responsibility impossible to live up to. The old-fashioned, Kentucky-born judge sees the incident as a dramatization of the conflict between the old and new business ethics: "By God, Madam, I think I've lived too long! In my day the difference between a business man and a scoundrel was bigger than the difference between a white man and a nigger." To him the Captain is an honest man among knaves who is defeated by his own honesty; his ruin shows the incompatibility of the pioneer virtues with the modern commercial world.

Marian's attitude in the above scene tells us a great deal about her. She flushes at Judge Pommeroy's mention of her husband's integrity, feeling her own to be of an inferior caliber. But here it is important to remember that she is her husband's junior by at least twenty-five years; she is halfway between his generation and that of Ivy Peters. Thus she finds herself caught in an intolerable dilemma; brought up to believe that women were supposed to be looked after by men, she lives on into an age in which they must fend for themselves. The generation to which her husband belongs has for the most part lost its wealth in the hard times following the collapse of the Western land boom, so the Captain's friends are unable to help her much; the new generation represented by the rising young bank directors drives a hard bargain and feels little responsibility to its elders. Marian Forrester is caught halfway between the old and the new modes of life; she wants the graces of the old generation with the money of the new. For an instant, while listening to the narrative, she has a flash of insight; she realizes that the things she wants are incompatible, that the old is superior to the new and that it is doomed to destruction. This is a tragic realization, and as she rises to the occasion it gives her a moment of greatness. But it rapidly slips away from her, and she returns to her old and charming habit of cheerful irresponsibility.

If one reason stands out above the rest as to why the Lost Lady is lost, it is that she is utterly unable to accept for more than an instant the tragic view of life. She cannot live with it. We have seen this inability hinted at in a lighter vein in her flight from the bull in the pasture, screaming and laughing at the same time and refusing to let go of the crimson parasol which had caused all the trouble. Now it appears in earnest as a refusal to face grim realities such as change, old age, and death. After the Captain's ruin there occurs a scene in which Mrs. Forrester and Niel are out walking and she urges him up the lane faster and faster, talking to him of her plans to return to California and begin living again. " 'Perhaps people think I've settled down to grow old gracefully, but I've not. I feel such power to live in me, Niel.' Her slender fingers gripped his wrist." [61] She tells him of a recent vacation she has spent in Colorado where she rode horseback all day, danced all night, and outshone women far younger than she:

> "I accepted the Dalzells' invitation with a purpose; I wanted to see whether I had anything worth saving. And I have, I tell you! You would hardly believe it, I could hardly believe it, but I still have." [62]

All this is in marked contrast to her husband. The Captain, shortly after his return from Denver, has a stroke, the physical symbol of his financial ruin. Soon he is almost completely helpless, and his wife has to take care of him in everything. Accepting the fact that his life is finished, he can live with the tragic vision: he spends long periods of time in his garden with his eyes fixed on a red block of Colorado sandstone which he has had made into a sundial, marking the passage of the hours. His wife cannot understand this. "How can anybody like to see time visibly devoured?" she asks Niel. "We are all used to seeing clocks go round, but why does he want to see that shadow creep on that stone?" [63] Usually in Willa Cather's system of values individuals either transcend themselves or die. But Marian does neither; she prefers life at any cost.

The rest of the story deals almost entirely with the rise of commercialism in the Midwest and the ineffectual attempts made by the Captain's generation to forestall it. Niel Herbert goes east to become an architect, and when he returns to Sweet Water two years later Ivy Peters is the first person he meets on the train. Ivy, with some smugness, tells of how he has drained the Forresters' marsh, which meant destroying the Captain's earthly paradise:

"I rent that meadow-land on the Forrester place. I've drained the old marsh and put it into wheat. My brother John does the work, and I boss the job. It's quite profitable. I pay them a good rent, and they need it. I doubt if they could get along without. Their influential friends don't seem to help them out much. Remember all those chesty old boys the Captain used to drive about in his democrat wagon, and ship in barrels of Bourbon for? Good deal of bluff about all those old-timers. The panic put them out of the game. The Forresters have come down in the world like the rest. You remember how the old man used to put it over us kids and not let us carry a gun in there? I'm just mean enough to like to shoot along that creek a little better than anywhere else, now. There wasn't any harm in the old Captain, but he had the delusion of grandeur. He's happier now that he's like the rest of us, and don't have to change his shirt every day." [64]

Ivy shows the urge to degrade everything which is not himself and bring it down to his own level which Willa Cather always associated with commercial characters in her novels. The same spirit which had blinded the woodpecker is now blighting the West. Niel reflects on this as he listens to his fellow townsman:

He felt that Ivy had drained the marsh quite as much to spite him and Mrs. Forrester as to reclaim the land. Moreover, he seemed to know that until this moment Ivy himself had not realized how much that consideration weighed upon him. . . . By draining the marsh Ivy had obliterated a few acres of something he hated, though he could not name it, and had asserted his power over the people who had loved those unproductive meadows for their idleness and silvery beauty.[65]

Then comes one of the few notable flaws in an otherwise well-constructed novel. Not content with letting Ivy Peters speak and act for himself, Willa Cather steps forward to point the moral by telling the reader exactly what he stands for and how unspeakably bad it is. She has set up a straw man, an image of all that she dislikes in the modern world, and now proceeds to rail at it:

After Ivy had gone on into the smoker, Niel sat looking out at the windings of the Sweet Water and playing with his idea. The Old West had been settled by dreamers, great-hearted adventurers, who were unpractical to the point of magnificence; a courteous

brotherhood, strong in attack but weak in defence, who could conquer but could not hold. Now all the vast territory they had won
was to be at the mercy of men like Ivy Peters, who had never dared
anything, never risked anything. They would drink up the mirage,
dispel the morning freshness, root out the great brooding spirit of
freedom, the generous, easy life of the great land-holders. The
space, the colour, the princely carelessness of the pioneer they
would destroy and cut up into profitable bits, as the match factory
splinters the primeval forest. All the way from Missouri to the
mountains this generation of shrewd young men, trained to petty
economies by hard times, would do exactly what Ivy Peters had
done when he drained the Forrester marsh.[66]

Here we catch a glimpse of what the later Willa Cather was to become:
querulous, opinionated, given to stating her position with increasing
dogmatism as the years passed by, sure that the good times were over
and would never come again. The emotional fervor with which she
writes expresses the strength of her blanket condemnation of the present
which was to result so soon in a retreat to the past.

To continue the story, Marian Forrester continues rapidly on her
downhill course. The first real sign of her cracking morale comes when
she learns that her old lover, Frank Ellinger, has succumbed to the
new commercial generation by marrying the unattractive daughter of a
successful businessman. The news maddens her. Leaving the crippled
Captain alone in the house on a wild stormy night, she comes to the
Judge's office to put through a long-distance phone call to Denver, where
Ellinger and his bride are staying, and after some pretense of light conversation, spews forth a stream of abuse which Niel is able to halt only
by cutting the telephone wires with a pair of tin shears. Soon after
this the Captain has another stroke and becomes completely helpless.
While attempting to care for him, Mrs. Forrester goes to pieces. She
tries to keep herself going on coffee and brandy, but can no longer
keep the townspeople at arm's length; the house is inundated by a host
of female Ivy Peterses who have always wanted to see what the Forrester place was like. They chatter like magpies and go over the house
like ants, rummaging among her most cherished possessions. A little
later she puts herself beyond the bounds of decency by taking her legal
affairs away from Judge Pommeroy and placing them in the hands of
Ivy Peters, a twofold defection which involves both the desertion of
an old and faithful family friend and the abandonment of moral standards as well.

After the Captain dies, it becomes painfully evident that without him Marian is completely lost:

> Since her husband's death she seemed to have become another woman. For years Niel and his uncle, the Dalzells, and all her friends, had thought of the Captain as a drag upon his wife; a care that drained her and dimmed her and kept her from being all that she might be. But without him, she was like a ship without ballast, driven hither and thither by every wind. She was flighty and perverse. She seemed to have lost her faculty of discrimination; her power of easily and graciously keeping everyone in his proper place.[67]

This merely restates what we have been told before: that the Captain was more real than Mrs. Forrester, that civilized graces require moral virtue for their perfection, and that the former cannot exist without the latter. From here on Miss Cather's social allegory becomes increasingly overt. Looking in at Marian Forrester's house one day, Niel Herbert sees Ivy Peters come up behind her and put both arms around her, his hands meeting over her breast. When she fails to object, Niel realizes that she has become Ivy's mistress. The symbolic debauching of the civilization of the West by commercialism is complete.

Niel reacts to this with all the prideful self-righteous indignation of inexperienced youth. "For the last time," he says, as he crosses the bridge away from her place, "for the last time":

> He had given her a year of his life, and she had thrown it away. . . . All those years he had thought it was Mrs. Forrester who made that house so different from any other. But ever since the Captain's death it was a house where old friends, like his uncle, were betrayed and cast off, where common fellows behaved after their kind and knew a common woman when they saw her.[68]

In the height of his boyish disillusion, Niel cannot wait to get away from the Midwest and leave behind him everything which reminded him of his boyhood. He leaves Sweet Water and never sees Mrs. Forrester again, although he later hears that she has been deserted by Ivy Peters and has returned to California. But when he is older, he comes around to a more balanced view and realizes again what a charming woman she was. He is glad that he had known her and "that she had had a hand in breaking him in to life." [69] His view of her has become more

mature; she has become for him a human being with all the good and
bad that that implies; as he had said of her earlier, "she inherited the
magic of contradictions." Years later, in a Chicago hotel lobby, he
meets an old acquaintance of his from Sweet Water, now a mining
engineer, who has seen Mrs. Forrester in Argentina. There she has
married a rich, cranky, eccentric Englishman and lives with him on a
big stock ranch outside Buenos Aires. When he saw her, he says, she
was a good deal made up, with plenty of powder, a little rouge, and
dyed hair. Everything is artificial about her now except her laugh;
that was the one thing which hadn't changed a particle. He remarks
that it was amazing how she had come up again, since she had pretty
well gone to pieces before leaving Sweet Water. This is a deceptively
hopeful note, but one with the most ironic overtones, for Willa Cather
gives us a number of negative indications about the quality of the life
Mrs. Forrester is leading. Hers is a rootless international marriage,
and although she has managed to extricate herself from a seemingly
impossible predicament, the man who has rescued her is described as
being eccentric and stingy. He has no real relation to the land on
which he lives; as a successor to Captain Forrester he is unprepossessing
in the extreme. Mrs. Forrester's own natural grace has been replaced
by a complete artificiality; just as she covers her face with paint to
hide the fact that she is getting old, so she tells the mining engineer
that the Englishman is the kindest of husbands when we have already
found out that he is not. She is still unable to accept reality; the Lost
Lady still is lost. But in spite of this Niel and his friend feel grateful
that she has been able to save even the little she has from the general
ruin, and we learn that she has helped to pass on the amenities to at
least these two young men:

> "So we may feel sure that she was well cared for, to the very
> end," said Niel. "Thank God for that!"
> "I knew you'd feel that way," said Ed Elliott, as a warm wave
> of feeling passed over his face. "I did!" [70]

In spite of her spiritual estrangement from post–World War I
America, Willa Cather found herself in agreement with the new
literary generation on at least one important point. This was in her
sense of malaise and dislocation, the feeling that modern man had
somehow lost his bearings and must try desperately to find them again.
Like many of her younger contemporaries, she felt that the pursuit of
value was all but impossible in a commercial world and could be en-

gaged in only by flying in the face of that world. In *A Lost Lady* the corrupting factor is money. Money, although seldom mentioned, presides over the entire action and makes its power felt upon almost every page. It is the Captain's old-fashioned notions about financial integrity that lead not only to his own downfall but to his wife's as well. His determination to remain heroically solvent and pay off all his creditors after the Denver bank failure results in Mrs. Forrester's being left destitute after he dies, and where else can she turn to for money if not to the Ivy Peterses? Willa Cather does not deal with this problem, but it is of crucial importance. If in the modern world money can be obtained — or kept — only by means of chicanery or pettifogging, what is the honorable man or woman to do?

This problem, which is also the problem of Myra Henshawe in *My Mortal Enemy*, is left unsolved by Willa Cather, probably because no satisfactory solution presented itself to her. True, in *The Professor's House* Godfrey St. Peter lives on the salary he draws from his university. This stipend is the reward for honorable work and presumably is not tainted with commercial greed. But it is hardly satisfactory to suggest that all the members of society become professors. And even St. Peter has his financial troubles; he feels that the preoccupation with money-spending has ruined his family's taste. Although he has a comfortable income honorably come by he is not at all happy about the things upon which his family contrives to spend it. By and large, the protagonists of Willa Cather's third period find it increasingly difficult merely to survive in the modern world without engaging in the hectic pursuit for wealth which their society demands of them. And the pursuit of wealth runs counter to everything they hold to be most valuable and to constitute life's highest good.

Here Willa Cather joins company once more with her master, Flaubert. Like Flaubert, she instinctively recoils from the modern world of the bourgeoisie because of the inherent split it contains between what ought to be and what is, between noble aspiration and self-seeking greed. In a world devoted mainly to self-aggrandizement, the idealistic person is at a distinct disadvantage. We have seen this split in earlier stories of Willa Cather's such as "A Sculptor's Funeral" and "A Wagner Matinée." In each case the spectator through whose eyes the story is observed would like to do something for the main character but is powerless to do so: his hands are tied and he is in no position to perform a significant action of any kind. This is equally true of Niel Herbert in *A Lost Lady;* he is unable to help the heroine in any way whatsoever or to act in accordance with the values he holds. And Marian Forrester, caught halfway between the pioneer and the commercial generations, is herself unable to act according to the values she holds. She is unable to remain faithful to her husband while he is alive or live the kind of life he stood for after he is dead.

Because Willa Cather felt frustrated and unable to express herself in the present, it was easy for her to think that the era she had grown up in was ethically superior. This attitude comes out clearly in her description of Niel Herbert's farewell to Sweet Water. Here a panegyric on the passing heroic age is combined with criticism of Mrs. Forrester for refusing to die with that age. Although the thoughts and reflections start out as Niel Herbert's they seem gradually to pass over into comments and generalizations by the author in a way which is quite characteristic of Willa Cather's endorsements of the point of view of her major characters, especially in her later novels:

> With the summer months Judge Pommeroy's health improved, and as soon as he was able to be back in his office, Niel began to plan to return to Boston. . . . It was a melancholy time for him. He was in a fever of impatience to be gone, and yet he felt that he was going away forever, and was making the final break with everything that had been dear to him in his boyhood. The people, the very country itself, were changing so fast that there would be nothing to come back to.
>
> He had seen the end of an era, the sunset of the pioneer. He had come upon it when already its glory was nearly spent. So in the buffalo times a traveller used to come upon the embers of a hunter's fire on the prairie, after the hunter was up and gone; the coals would be trampled out, but the ground was warm, and the flattened grass where he had slept and where his pony had grazed, told the story.
>
> This was the very end of the road-making West; the men who had put plains and mountains under the iron harness were old; some were poor, and even the successful ones were hunting for rest and a brief reprieve from death. It was already gone, that age; nothing could ever bring it back. The taste and smell and song of it, the visions those men had seen in the air and followed, — these he had caught in a kind of afterglow in their own faces, — and this would always be his.
>
> It was what he most held against Mrs. Forrester; that she was not willing to immolate herself, like the widow of all these great men, and die with the pioneer period to which she belonged; that

she preferred life on any terms. In the end, Niel went away without bidding her good-bye. He went away with weary contempt
for her in his heart.[71]

It is clear that the past is being glorified in this passage and the
present rejected. In this novel Willa Cather everywhere acquiesces in
this mood and nowhere contradicts it. On the contrary, Marian Forrester is condemned precisely because she declined to reject the present.
She refused to commit suttee on her husband's funeral pyre; as Willa
Cather puts it, "she preferred life on any terms."

If we make the experiment of viewing Willa Cather's novels of this
period in the light of the vegetation myth so important to her prairie
period, we find that they are based on that part of the myth which has
to do with failure of the crops to renew themselves; that is to say, on
the theme of the waste land. In all of the novels with which we are
dealing in this section, modern life is represented as a barren desert of
materialism.[72] In *One of Ours,* for instance, the culture of the original
settlers of the Alexandra and Ántonia stamp is shown as having died out
among their descendents. Claude has to go to Europe to imbibe that
culture at its source; even though it had once been present in the
Middle West, it had dried up, much as the grass-bottomed lagoons which
studded the prairies in Willa Cather's childhood had dried up and
vanished. In *A Lost Lady,* the theme of the waste land becomes even
more explicit than in *One of Ours.* In the original versions of the
waste-land myth the land is under a blight because its king is aged, or
impotent, or sick, or all three. This ailment is reflected throughout his
kingdom by failure of the crops through drought and sterility in cattle
and women. The blight is finally lifted when a young knight comes
questing into the land, undergoes great dangers at the Castle Perilous,
and as a result of triumphing over them restores the king to health,
the restoration being symbolized in some versions at least by the
knight's sexual union with the king's young wife. If we compare this
story with *A Lost Lady,* Captain Forrester becomes a type of the
Fisher-King, aged and impotent. If this is so, Marian Forrester's
sexual encounters take on something of the nature of fertility rites,
attempts to re-establish the bases of life. But a bitter irony has twisted
the fable. Willa Cather, herself, actually shows a mingled acceptance
and rejection of Marian Forrester's sexuality; she pictures it as being
the source of her vitality, yet finds it degrading.[73] In terms of the
myth she is both attracted and repelled by the fertility rite, showing a
mixture of affirmation of the cult of life with Christian (and perhaps

spinsterish) ascetism. Mrs. Forrester is quite different in one respect from the young wife of the Fisher-King, however. No chaste questing knight comes riding to her aid; only passionless vulgarians. For Willa Cather, evidently, this is all that the modern world can provide.

The Professor's House: FAILURE OF THE WILL

The next novel that Willa Cather wrote marks the turning point in her career. Although by no means her best work, it is highly interesting because of the light it sheds on her later intellectual and artistic development; the conclusions she comes to in this novel help determine and define the rest of her literary career. In *The Professor's House* she raises once again an old problem of hers, that of the conflicting claims of creative effort and human relations. But this time she raises it with so great an intensity, so agonized an awareness of the unsatisfactory nature of the choices involved, as to make this book utterly unlike any of her earlier work.

The Professor's House is unique among Willa Cather's novels in that it contains almost no external action, since most of what action there is takes place within the mind of the chief protagonist. The Professor, at the age of fifty-two, suddenly realizes that he will not live forever, that he cannot count on the future to bring him more happiness than he has in the present, and that whatever satisfaction is to be obtained from life he must get in the here and now. But he no longer can find satisfaction in the quarters where he had formerly sought it. Whereas in the past he had derived immense enjoyment from both his work and his family, now neither human relations nor creative endeavor have any power to charm him. He seems to be suffering from the emotional confusion attendant on the male climacteric, since most of the things that he had formerly cared for greatly he now finds himself caring for not at all. Above all he does not want to have any demands made on him. But both the creative life and the life of the family are demanding in the extreme; both involve serious limitations on the individual's right to do just as he pleases. The Professor does not want to realize this and fights recognition of it as long as he can; he has always believed that the superior individual need recognize no bounds and is utterly unwilling to admit that there are any limitations on the human will whatsoever. When finally driven to admit that limitations are an inescapable part of human existence, his revulsion is extreme. Not only does he lose all belief in the omnipotence of the will; he also loses his faith in life.

On passing from *A Lost Lady* to *The Professor's House,* we go from a work which leaves us with a considerable feeling of completeness and fulfillment to one which is at best puzzling. There is good reason to think that Willa Cather did not herself understand all the implications of what she says in the book. We have her own word for it that much of even her best writing was composed spontaneously with little or no conscious control exerted by the author;[74] this impression is borne out by other observers as well.[75] It should not be surprising then that in an agonized novel written at her life's most critical period she should express some attitudes of whose consequences she herself was not fully aware.

In order to elucidate the meaning of this bizarre book we must look at the plot, to understand the events which lead the Professor to his crisis and which, in Willa Cather's eyes at least, justify him in turning against his entire past. Briefly, the story is this: Godfrey St. Peter, a professor of history in a small middle-western college, has had two great loves in his life — his wife and his work. He has also had a great friendship with a brilliant student of his, Tom Outland, who had made an astounding archeological discovery before coming up out of the American Southwest to go to Hamilton College. Tom had inspired St. Peter to write his great historical work, *The Spanish Adventurers in North America,* which won him an Oxford prize in history as well as an international reputation as a scholar. But by the time the story opens Tom has died in the First World War; the Professor feels let down and is suffering from a depression of spirits consequent to having finished his great work, and he feels himself spiritually estranged from his wife. He has filled his life with the creation of a monumental work in scholarship, and when it is finished finds that life has gone on beyond him. While he has been living in another world, his family has been living in this one. His daughters have grown up and married and have lives of their own, while his wife has worldly wants which he finds it hard to satisfy. These personal frustrations added to an increasing disgust with the materialistic money-grubbing of the America of the twenties produce in him a kind of boredom with life which eventually causes him to lose all will to live. He does not go out and actively seek death, but when the chance of death comes to him, he does not turn away from it. A leaky gas stove in the study of the house in which he is working nearly asphyxiates him, and he is saved only at the last moment by a pious German Catholic seamstress, who teaches him that it is possible to live without delight and that it is necessary to face the ultimate realities alone.

The book has frequently been criticized as being structurally weak because its middle section, which takes the form of a flashback, apparently has little relation to the rest of the story. Actually, as we shall see, it is largely by means of this structure that Willa Cather manages to communicate her theme. The novel is divided into three parts, each one being shorter than the previous section but also more intense. The first of the three is about the Professor's squabbles with his family over such everyday things as houses, clothes, and jewels. The second, in the form of a diary which the Professor is editing, tells of Tom Outland's discovery of the cliff dwellings of the Southwest on the mysterious Blue Mesa. The third records the Professor's growing disillusionment with his personal life and that of his community, its climax being his near-annihilation by the leaky gas stove and his rescue and rehabilitation by the seamstress Augusta. Although the novel's middle section is a story in itself and at first glance doesn't seem to have much to do with the other two sections, we soon find that this very incongruity is vital to the central meaning of the book.

Willa Cather once said of this book that in it she had meant to get an effect similar to that seen in Dutch pictures of an interior where a square window offers a contrasting vista of a gray sea or the masts of ships.[76] In other words, by using an inset she is able to give a new dimension to her work. Just as a Vermeer is able to contrast the little private world of his domestic interiors with the great world of ships and trade and exploration, so Willa Cather is able to contrast the narrow concerns and petty anxieties of Professor St. Peter's private life with the spacious life of the Pueblo Indians who dwelt long centuries ago on the Blue Mesa. In short, Willa Cather is trying to make the same point that T. S. Eliot made in *The Waste Land;* she is contrasting a sordid present with a heroic past.

Tom Outland's Southwest: Tradition and the Comely Life

Since "Tom Outland's Story" contains the core of the book's meaning, it is necessary to examine it in some detail. This section tells how Tom falls in with another young Westerner, Roddy Blake, and how the two of them get jobs as cowpunchers in a lonely winter camp near a remarkable outcropping of rock known as the Blue Mesa. This mesa has a fascination for them, as no one has ever explored it, since its sides are too steep to climb and the only entrance is through a winding canyon at one end of the mesa which can be reached only by crossing a river too swift to swim. Not only does it keep changing its appearance and personality under the play of constantly changing light at different hours of the day; it also manages to lure a good many of their cattle away from the winter camp; they sniff the wild herds that run loose on the summit, swim the river at its base, bolt into the mesa, and are never seen again. Finally Tom Outland, overcome by curiosity, summons up enough daring to swim the river, follows the winding canyon up into the mesa, and discovers in a shallow cavern set in the canyon's side a whole city of cliff dwellings. Looking up a branch canyon he sees another arch, and another group of buildings. He tells Roddy that night that he has discovered the remains of a vanished civilization, and, after saving up enough money for food and supplies, the two of them return to the mesa and spend the next summer digging up the archeological remains of the cliff dwellers. They are overwhelmed by the beauty of the pueblo and the high level of culture evinced by the fragments they have uncovered. That winter Tom goes to Washington to try to interest the government in his findings, but is disappointed when the officials of the Smithsonian Institution show no interest at all in American antiquities, since their minds are completely preoccupied with the chances of being sent abroad to various European expositions. Meanwhile a German archeologist Fechtig has come along and for four thousand dollars has managed to persuade Roddy Blake to sell all the remains of the cliff city to him, and Roddy has deposited the money in Tom's name at the local bank. When Tom returns from Washington he is furious with Roddy for thinking that he had dug up all those relics merely in order to sell them. They have a bitter quarrel which terminates their friendship and ends with Roddy's leaving the Blue Mesa forever. Tom, who won't touch the money in the bank, works until he has enough saved up to enter Hamilton College, where he becomes a student in one of Professor St. Peter's classes in history.

This in brief is the story of Roddy and Tom's discovery. The Blue Mesa is really Mesa Verde, Colorado, which Willa Cather visited in 1915 and fell in love with; and her story closely parallels the actual events of the discovery of the cliff dwellings in Mesa Verde by Dick Wetherill and Charlie Mason, who were the originals of Roddy and Tom.[77] What no plot summary can possibly manage to convey is the strange luminosity and evocativeness of language with which Willa Cather describes the American Southwest, colorful enough even to the unromantic eye.

I have said that "Tom Outland's Story" is the core of the book and is the source of value against which the shoddy ideals of the present are contrasted. What is the meaning of the story? What values does Tom see in the Blue Mesa? His description of the first time he ever saw the cliff city gives us a clue:

It was such a rough scrambling that I was soon in a warm sweat under my damp clothes. In stopping to take breath, I happened to glance up at the canyon wall. I wish I could tell you what I saw there, just *as* I saw it, on that first morning, through a veil of lightly falling snow. Far up above me, a thousand feet or so, set in a great cavern in the face of the cliff, I saw a little city of stone, asleep. It was as still as sculpture — and something like that. It all hung together, seemed to have a kind of composition: pale little houses of stone nestling close to one another, perched on top of each other, with flat roofs, narrow windows, straight walls, and in the middle of the group, a round tower.

It was beautifully proportioned, that tower, swelling out to a larger girth a little above the base, then growing slender again. There was something symmetrical and powerful about the swell of the masonry. The tower was the fine thing that held all the jumble of houses together and made them mean something. It was red in colour, even on that grey day. In sunlight it was the colour of winter oak-leaves. A fringe of cedars grew along the edge of the cavern, like a garden. They were the only living things. Such silence and stillness and repose — immortal repose. That village sat looking down into the canyon with the calmness of eternity. The falling snow-flakes, sprinkling the piñons, gave it a special kind of solemnity. I can't describe it. It was more like sculpture than anything else. I knew at once that I had come upon the city of some extinct civilization, hidden away in this inaccessible mesa for centuries, preserved in the dry air and almost perpetual sunlight like a fly in amber, guarded by the cliffs and the river and the desert.[78]

The key words here are "composition" and "repose." Tom likes the cliff dwellings because they form a symmetrical pattern which is held together by the centrally located round tower. They remind him of sculpture because of the feeling they give of rest, of ordered tranquillity. But that is not all he gets from observing the ruins. A little later in his account he observes:

But the really splendid thing about our city, the thing that made it delightful to work there, and must have made it delightful to live there, was the setting. The town hung like a bird's nest in the cliff, looking off into the box canyon below, and beyond into the wide valley we called Cow Canyon, facing an ocean of clear air. A people who had the hardihood to build there, and who lived day after day looking down upon such grandeur, who came and went by those hazardous trails, must have been, as we often told each other, a fine people.[79]

This recalls Frank Lloyd Wright's idea of organic architecture, in which the best style of building is regarded as that which is best adapted to its surroundings and seems to grow out of the landscape. Willa Cather describes the town as hanging on the edge of the cliff like a bird's nest, perhaps like the nests of the eagles which soared above Panther Canyon in *The Song of the Lark*. The description of the organic union between city and canyon is particularly vivid; just as a fishing village lies facing a sea of water, so the cliff city faces an ocean of air; the ocean floor lies far below the level of human settlement in the one case; the bottom of Cedar Canyon stretches hundreds of feet below the cliff dwellings in the other. The word "ocean" also suggests a three-dimensional quality which is characteristic of the atmosphere of clear dry places, especially of the air of Mesa Verde.

Tom finds that the ancient cliff dwellers applied the principle of organicism to many other fields besides architecture. The same feeling for design guided them in the making of everyday household utensils. Father Duchene, Tom's clerical friend, declares that the shape and decoration of their water jars and food bowls is better than that in any of the existing pueblos he knows and reminds him of the geometric designs on the early pottery of Crete.[80] Every artifact Tom and Roddy pick up indicates that the people who produced it had managed to an extraordinary degree to combine the beautiful with the useful; they had made of their everyday lives something which approached the order and harmony of a work of art. The comely life, then, had been practiced by these ancient Indian cliff dwellers. The composition, symmetry, and organic form of the cliff city symbolizes for Tom the balanced and orderly lives of the people who had once inhabited it. Living in houses closely packed together, they must have had a tightly knit clan organization; in fact, they very probably formed an organic community resembling Willa Cather's idea of the larger or multigeneration family unit.

But the possibility of beauty in everyday life is not the only value which Tom Outland derives from his archeological labors; there is also the sense of tradition. The feeling of being united with all the past generations who have worked and died on the land you press with the soles of your feet, the sense of continuity in the history of all mankind, is not one that would easily be attained by a young cowpuncher who was orphaned at an early age and brought up by strangers. And yet Tom Outland manages to develop just such a sense of tradition. When he is in winter cattle camp and happens to notice the ancient irrigation mains which first suggest to him that there might be relics of an Indian civilization in the neighborhood, he remarks:

> To people off alone, as we were, there is something stirring about finding evidences of human labour and care in the soil of an empty country. It comes to you as a sort of message, makes you feel differently about the ground you walk over every day. I liked the winter range better than any place I'd ever been in.[81]

Later, when he castigates Roddy Blake for having sold the relics, he says:

> "I'm not so poor that I have to sell the pots and pans that belonged to my poor grandmothers a thousand years ago." [82]

> "There was never any question of money with me, where this mesa and its people were concerned. They were something that had been preserved through the ages by a miracle, and handed on to you and me, two poor cowpunchers, rough and ignorant, but I thought we were men enough to keep a trust. I'd as soon have sold my own grandmother as Mother Eve [a mummy from Blue Mesa] — I'd have sold any living woman first." [83]

After Roddy has left him and Tom is all alone on the mesa, he says:

> For me the mesa was no longer an adventure, but a religious emotion. I had read of filial piety in the Latin poets, and I knew that was what I felt for this place. It had formerly been mixed up with other motives, but now that they were gone, I had my happiness unalloyed.[84]

By responding to the Blue Mesa in the way he did, by having it waken in him a sense of tradition and the possibility of beauty in day-to-day existence, Tom, untutored though he is, shows an appreciation of the values of civilization; he is a natural aristocrat in his feeling for culture. However ignorant he may be he has native good taste; it is because he realizes this that he eventually goes to Hamilton College to get an education.

THE PROFESSOR'S VISION: THE MEANING OF THE AMERICAN PAST

I have already mentioned that *The Professor's House* has been criticized as being structurally weak because of the apparent lack of relevance of its middle section "Tom Outland's Story." Actually the only justification for the presence of Tom Outland in the novel is the effect he has on the Professor. But this effect is tremendous: "Just when the morning brightness of the world was wearing off for him," Willa Cather says, "along came Outland and brought him a kind of second youth." [85] Tom not only serves as St. Peter's personal friend; he also helps him in his work. Tom, by his intelligent understanding of the relics he has found and his ability to reconstruct from them what the life of the cliff dwellers must have been like, shows himself adept at the Professor's specialty, the interpretation of the past, and inspires the Professor in his own interpretation of the past, his eight-volume history of *The Spanish Adventurers in North America.* Tom and St. Peter are not only able to re-create the past and make it come alive, they also believe in history as inspiration, for they see in it certain values which they find admirable and think should be carried over into the present. This is the clue to the significance of Professor St. Peter's name. Since he regards history as the source of all value, it becomes for him a kind of heaven. As a historian, he is like the original St. Peter who holds the keys to the kingdom of heaven much as his namesake holds the key to history.

Presumably, Tom has a direct effect on the Professor's vision of the American past, so to understand his influence we must know what that vision is. It is embodied in *The Spanish Adventurers in North America,* but nowhere in the novel does Willa Cather tell us what this historical landmark is supposed to be like.

However, we can gather some idea of its nature from her description of how the Professor came to write the book in the first place; it deals with an old subject of hers, the naturally aristocratic European in America. Very early in the novel St. Peter is trying to determine the high point in his life after which everything has seemed anticlimactic. Finally he decides upon a date in his extreme youth, so long ago in fact that his wife was not even in it:

Indeed, nobody was in it but himself, and a weather-dried little
sea captain from the Hautes-Pyrénées, half a dozen spry seamen,
and a line of gleaming snow peaks, agonizingly high and sharp,
along the southern coast of Spain.[86]

One day stood out above the others. All day long they were
skirting the south coast of Spain; from the rose of dawn to the
gold of sunset the ranges of the Sierra Nevadas towered on their
right, snow peak after snow peak, high beyond the flight of fancy,
gleaming like crystal and topaz. St. Peter lay looking up at them
from a little boat riding low in the purple water and the design
of his book unfolded in the air above him, just as definitely as the
mountain ranges themselves. And the design was sound. He had
accepted it as inevitable, had never meddled with it, and it had
seen him through.[87]

The snowy peaks signify a romantic desire for the infinite, the longing
to aspire and achieve, as well as being a symbol of the imagination in
general. On a lower level the mountain symbol serves as a link between
two continents. The Sierra Nevada mountains in Spain gave their
name to the Sierra Nevada of North America, which were named by
the Spanish explorers about whom the Professor was to write. In this
way they represent Europe in America. Moreover, each range is part
of a cordillera, the main mountain axis and backbone of a continent.
The book which begins to take shape in the Professor's mind has a
form just as definite and just as natural as the mountains themselves.
It too represents the backbone of a continent; it will describe the
meaning of the European experience in America.

Seen in this light, *The Spanish Adventurers in North America* is
another treatment of the pioneer theme, in which the conquest of
America is a symbol of the conquest of life itself. This, it will be
remembered, was a part of the great theme of Willa Cather's prairie
novels, where Europe was represented as the world of tradition, America
the world of innovation, and the naturally aristocratic European in
America the hero who achieved an ideal balance between the two. In
The Professor's House the roles are reversed. Here an indigenous
American tradition is presented, that of the cliff dwellers, so that Tom
Outland doesn't have to borrow from European tradition; he discovers
a native one on the Blue Mesa. Conversely, in this novel the land of
innovation is represented by Europe, which stands for infinite aspiration
and brave endeavor. This characteristic Willa Cather sums up in the

symbol of the Spanish *conquistadores,* who form the subject of Professor St. Peter's eight-volume history. Thus the Professor gets from the Sierra Nevada the quality which is opposite and complementary to that which Tom Outland derives from the cliff palace; civilization and the spirit of adventure, having changed places, are once again united, and the image of their union is once again a naturally aristocratic European in America.

It is true that the conventional roles of "Europe" and "America" also have a place in this book, although relegated to inferior status. Europe also stands for tradition in the conventional sense, and the new. as opposed to aboriginal, America for innovation. Both continents have their traditionalists as well as their innovators, and Tom knows the civilization which the Professor is ignorant of — that of the ancient Southwest — just as the Professor knows the culture and monastery libraries of Spain. Each knows the world which is a mystery to the other; that is why they can have such a creative friendship, and Tom can help the Professor to write his book.

We are now ready to look at Tom's contribution to St. Peter's understanding of the uses of history. Because of the youthful enthusiasm he brings to his historical reconstruction, he is able to make the past come alive for St. Peter, to show him that the European conquest was the last great adventure of the human imagination, and thus enable the Professor to put life and fire into the last four volumes of his work. Moreover, Tom's sympathetic understanding of the inhabitants of the Blue Mesa, whose mode of living was utterly unlike his own, shows him able to synthesize very diverse elements and combine the best qualities of value systems usually thought incompatible. Thus he can combine the highly individualistic life of the cowpuncher with an appreciation of the highly organized life of the cliff dwellers and, in this way, achieve a satisfactory balance between individuality and communality, innovation and tradition, spontaneity and ritual. His ability to use history to supply values which have been missing in his own life shows him striving to be a complete man who is superior to the fragmented men of his time. This is what makes him so interesting to St. Peter. He symbolizes what the Professor thinks modern man should be, a person who through his sense of belonging to an entire cultural tradition is able to make up for some of the deficiencies of the present; in a word, one who is able to achieve wholeness through correct use of the past.

In sharp contrast to the Professor's vision of the past stands his vision of the American present. The almost mystical experience he has had, when the idea of his book came to him in a flash of insight, is a vision of the ideal, of the true meaning of what America could be. But, implies Willa Cather, even that part of modern America which respects tradition at all has forgotten the meaning of this ideal. Of the two competing traditions at its disposal, it thinks only the Old World one is good. The young Tom Outland is bitter when Mrs. St. Peter suggests that he give his Indian pottery to a museum: " 'Museums,' " he says, " 'they don't care about our things. They want something that came from Crete or Egypt.' " [88] Likewise when Tom is staying in Washington and trying to interest the director of the Smithsonian Institution and his staff in the Blue Mesa, he finds the only thing they are really interested in is getting enough Congressional appropriations to be sent abroad to represent America at international expositions. If the small minority of Americans who respect the past spurn their own antiquities, the case is even worse with the vast majority which is not at all tradition-minded. Modern commercial America has forgotten all tradition, all adventure, and thinks only of money. Professor St. Peter muses over Tom's departure for the First World War in this manner:

> And suppose Tom had been more prudent, and had not gone away with his old teacher? St. Peter sometimes wondered what would have happened to him, once the trap of worldly success had been sprung on him. He couldn't see Tom building "Outland," or becoming a public-spirited citizen of Hamilton. What change would have come in his blue eye, in his fine long hand with the back-springing thumb, which had never handled things that were not the symbols of ideas? A hand like that, had he lived, must have been put to other uses. His fellow scientists, his wife, the town and State, would have required many duties of it. It would have had to write thousands of useless letters, frame thousands of false excuses. It would have had to "manage" a great deal of money, to be the instrument of a woman who would grow always more exacting. He had escaped all that. He had made something new in the world — and the rewards, the meaningless conventional gestures, he had left to others.[89]

This elegiac oration on what might have happened to Tom had he lived through the First World War is a sermon on the text, "Nothing fails like success." Tom is a leftover from the earlier, more hopeful America of the transcendentalists; "his fine long hand which had never handled things that were not the symbols of ideas" is reminiscent of

Emerson with his saying "Every natural fact is a symbol of a spiritual fact." Had Tom lived on, says Willa Cather, group responsibilities would have stifled the creativity of the heroic individual. Especially deadening would be the getting and managing of money, since Emerson had long since been replaced by Rockefeller as a cultural hero.

FATHER DUCHENE'S THEORY OF HISTORY: THE DECLINE OF CIVILIZATIONS

Willa Cather parallels present-day America's lack of appreciation of the finer things of life with an earlier lack of appreciation shown by hostile Indians to the high civilization of the cliff dwellers. Tom Outland learns about this from his friend Father Duchene. The priest speculates on the development of the culture of the Blue Mesa from the time of its inception through its downfall; in a long speech he interprets Tom's discovery to him, emphasizing the cliff dwellers' strong desire to raise themselves above the level of barbarism and become civilized, and the probable course of the history of such a people:

". . . I am inclined to think that your tribe were a superior people. Perhaps they were not so when they first came upon this mesa, but in an orderly and secure life they developed considerably the arts of peace. There is evidence on every hand that they lived for something more than food and shelter. They had an appreciation of comfort, and went even further than that. Their life, compared to that of our roving Navajos, must have been quite complex. There is unquestionably a distinct feeling for design in what you call the Cliff City. Buildings are not grouped like that by pure accident, though convenience probably had much to do with it. Convenience often dictates very sound design. . . .

"I see your tribe as a provident, rather thoughtful people, who made their livelihood secure by raising crops and fowl — the great number of turkey bones and feathers are evidence that they had domesticated the wild turkey. With grain in their store-rooms, and mountain sheep and deer for their quarry, they rose gradually from the condition of savagery. With the proper variation of meat and vegetable diet, they developed physically and improved in the primitive arts. They had looms and mills, and experimented with dyes. At the same time, they possibly declined in the arts of war, in brute strength and ferocity.

"I see them here, isolated, cut off from other tribes, working out their destiny, making their mesa more and more worthy to be a home for man, purifying life by religious observances, caring respectfully for their dead, protecting the children, doubtless entertaining some feelings of affection and sentiment for this stronghold where they were at once so safe and so comfortable, where they had practically overcome the worst hardships that primitive man had to fear. They were, perhaps, too far advanced for their time and environment.

"They were probably wiped out, utterly exterminated, by some roving Indian tribe without culture or domestic virtues, some horde that fell upon them in their summer camp, and destroyed them for their hides and clothing and weapons, or from mere love of slaughter. I feel sure that these brutal invaders never even learned of the existence of this mesa, honeycombed with habitations. If they had come here, they would have destroyed. They killed and went their way. . . .

"Like you, I feel a reverence for this place. Wherever humanity has made that hardest of all starts and lifted itself out of mere brutality, is a sacred spot. Your people were cut off here without the influence of example or emulation, with no incentive but some natural yearning for order and security. They built themselves into this mesa and humanized it." [90]

The central premise of this speech is that civilization is sacred, and the desire to produce civilization is worthy of the reverence accorded life itself. Father Duchene describes this desire almost as if it were a cosmic force which would operate even on people existing on a desert island. "Your people were cut off here without the influence of example or emulation, with no incentive but some natural yearning for order and security." In actuality, the Mesa Verde Indians upon whom the story is based borrowed some of their most characteristic skills from outside tribes: the use of the bow and arrow, for instance, and the very art of pottery-making which Father Duchene so much admired. It is doubtful whether any people could be as culturally self-sufficient as Willa Cather makes the cliff dwellers out to be. But the way in which she deviated from the actual facts is revealing. She apparently believed, with Emerson, that "imitation is suicide";[91] yet there is a paradox here. She wants us to believe that the originators of culture among the Indians of Blue Mesa were natural aristocrats, great innovators who were able to make their discoveries with no help at all from the outside. Yet the generations that came after them are praised for being extreme traditionalists who make no innovations whatsoever. Here no balance is struck between tradition and innovation, for the statements are cast in such an extreme form as to be incompatible. This lack of balance is at the heart of much that is unsatisfactory in Willa Cather's thinking; it explains her rather contradictory attitude toward nature on the one hand and civilization on the other.

Father Duchene's speech is remarkable in revealing another of Willa Cather's attitudes: namely, her theory of history. This theory is really an elaboration on her own statement that her theme was always that of "exceptional individuals at war with their environment." [92] Briefly, it holds that superior groups or nations, as well as individuals, are disliked by their inferior neighbors; that the more time they spend on developing the arts of civilization the less they have to spend on self-defense, that they consequently become more vulnerable as time goes by, are eventually exterminated by their more brutal neighbors. Father Duchene, who introduces Tom to the cultural heritage of the West, is Willa Cather's spokesman, and, in the paragraph beginning, "They were probably wiped out, utterly exterminated, by some roving Indian tribe without culture or domestic virtues," he gives her highly subjective theory of history in a nutshell. It will be seen that this part of his speech is unduly speculative, intemperate, and illogical; it contains at least five assumptions, all of them unfavorable to the supposed enemies of the cliff dwellers, most of them unverifiable. Here again the way in which Willa Cather has deviated from her sources is interesting. Although the exact fate of the real cliff dwellers is something of a mystery, it is known that they left Mesa Verde during a period of twenty-four years' drought. While there is some evidence that they were under attack by hostile Indians before they left the mesa, there is no reason for thinking that they were slaughtered by their enemies on the plains below; it is now thought likely that they migrated to the southeast and became the ancestors of the present-day cliff dwellers on the Rio Grande. [93] What Willa Cather means to say in Father Duchene's speech is that civilized and artistic peoples eventually are destroyed by their more warlike neighbors: natural aristocrats are always victimized by the epigones. She makes the hypothetical hostile Indian tribe into a symbol of the destroying present wreaking havoc on the civilized past. This one instance is not treated as being a specialized case; we have seen that in *One of Ours* she thought of the same fate as overtaking Western European civilization itself in the First World War.

Father Duchene's view of history should be easily recognized by

anyone familiar with the Populist literature of the nineties. It is a
new version of the conspiracy theory of history, which we have seen
Willa Cather absorb in her youth along with other elements of the
Populist folklore. The warlike Indians who slaughter the inhabitants
of Blue Mesa are not commercial, being predatory in other ways, but
they are pictured as destroying the peaceful agricultural community of
cliff dwellers just as surely as, according to Willa Cather, a commercial
generation was destroying the older agrarian America at the beginning
of the twentieth century. *The Professor's House,* together with *One of
Ours* and *A Lost Lady*, embodies a dualistic version of the social struggle
as taking place between the forces of light and the forces of darkness,
and, like the Populists after the defeat of Bryan in 1896, Willa Cather
saw the forces of darkness as winning.

Against the story of Tom Outland, of splendid creative achievement
in the past, Willa Cather sets the Professor's story, which tells of chaos,
frustration, and sterility in the present. For the Professor at the age
of fifty-two is no longer satisfied with any part of his life. He can no
longer enjoy his writing, for his great work, *The Spanish Adventurers
in North America,* has been completed, leaving an aching void in his
life. He can no longer enjoy his teaching, because year after year the
young men and women who come into his classes seem to him to be
less and less interested in the things of the mind. He can no longer
enjoy friendship, for his one great friend, Tom Outland, had been
futilely killed in the First World War. He can no longer enjoy his
family, for he feels that his wife has become too worldly, too anxious
to get the most out of occasions and people,[94] and one of his daughters
is married to a man he finds obnoxious because he has made the family
wealthy by exploiting an aeronautical invention of Tom Outland's. He
can no longer enjoy the society in which he lives because it is mostly
interested in cheap material gewgaws, and even the university is in
danger of being farmed out to the agricultural and commercial schools.[95]
Most of all, he can no longer enjoy himself. The things that once moved
him deeply move him no longer; he is as indifferent to his life as if
it were that of another person, and he finds, not with surprise but with
a feeling that it was inevitable, that he no longer has the wish to live.

In company with many others, Willa Cather felt that the thing
which is corrosive of value in modern life is the belief that the acquisition
of money is the principal object of human endeavor. I have shown how
she makes the acquisitive instinct one of her principal objects of attack
in *One of Ours* and *A Lost Lady* in the persons of Bayliss Wheeler and
Ivy Peters. In *The Professor's House,* however, the getting of money

is not so much of a problem; the real problem is the proper disposal of it once it is obtained. The Professor has no objection to money itself as long as it is used in the service of beauty, but in the modern world the things upon which money is spent lead very often not to beauty but to ugliness. In his own life he has seen what he considered the misapplication of money in two cases: his wife has used the five thousand pounds of the Oxford history prize money to build a new house, when he was perfectly satisfied with the old, and his family has used most of the fortune which Louie Marsellus made out of Tom Outland's aeronautical invention for material things, such as houses, clothes, furs, and jewelry. Neither of these strikes him as leading to any enrichment of the human spirit. His family has other ideas about the matter, and this seems to him to be good enough reason to dislike his family.

The only other person in Professor St. Peter's acquaintance who seems even remotely interested in things of the mind is Dr. Crane of the physics department. He is the only other member of the faculty who is doing research of a noncommercial nature, and he happens to be the man under whom Tom Outland was working when he developed his bulkheaded vacuum [*sic*]. But Dr. Crane had been brought up in a Baptist community and retains all its prejudices; the Professor feels he could not invite him over for dinner because he would be made uncomfortable if a bottle of claret were on the table.[96] Furthermore, the physicist is cursed with a nagging wife who feels that her husband ought to be getting the royalties from Tom Outland's invention, and threatens to have her shyster brother sue the St. Peter family if they will not disgorge. So the proper disposal of money becomes an issue which threatens to break up even the one intellectual friendship St. Peter is now able to have.

We now have enough of the pieces to understand how by contrasting the story of the Professor's life with the story of Tom Outland's Willa Cather meant to contrast the unity of the past with the fragmentation of the present. What Willa Cather means to imply is this: there was a time, long before the Industrial Revolution, when life was still whole, before existence had become compartmentalized, and the split between the useful and the beautiful, between fact and value, had occurred. Tom Outland, with his knowledge and appreciation of the civilization of the cliff dwellers, has an intuitive understanding of this long-vanished time. He has the right attitude toward the past and knows how to use it; thus he is able to live in the compartmentalized present and yet be a whole man. He is able to combine scientific discovery with archeo-

logical research; he has worked with the professor of physics as well
as with St. Peter, and has been able to make a brilliant success in
both fields. But most modern men are unable to do this. After Tom's
death the divorce between fact and value affected even his own works;
both his scientific and historical studies were seized upon and exploited
by different figures representing commercial civilization. The bulkheaded vacuum yielded its profit to Louie Marsellus, and the end
result of his archeological labors, the Oxford prize money obtained by
the book he had inspired the Professor to write, is seized upon by the
Professor's wife. Tom himself, had he lived long enough, would have
been an alien figure in his own civilization, an outlander, as his name
implies.

Bearing in mind the contrast Willa Cather makes between past and
present, we can see how she develops her theory of history. In her
eyes, the same thing is happening to European and American civilization
that happened to the civilization of the cliff dwellers; both were fated
to be destroyed by barbarian hordes. She believes that the peaceful and
creative peoples of the earth are invariably annihilated by the brutal
vulgarity of the destructive, and the way in which she manipulates the
plot is deliberately calculated to substantiate such a theory. First she
has the First World War destroy Tom Outland, the only real friend
the Professor had; then she makes material values almost succeed in
destroying his university by turning it into a trade school under pressure
from the state legislature. She next pictures these same values as
warping the Professor's family so that he no longer has anything in
common with them, and finally she pictures his life as becoming so
unbearable that he begins to crack under the strain and loses his will
to live. This is a picture of a waste land indeed. It can hardly be
denied that Willa Cather is more than meticulous in her working out of
the effects as she saw them of a commercial-industrial civilization on
all phases of human life, individual, familial, and social. She is determined that no one and nothing shall escape her waste land.

Her theory of history buttresses a view that Willa Cather already had,
one which we have seen finding expression in her early stories about art
and the artist's life. This is what I have called the idea of sanctuary,
a firm belief in the necessity of isolating the good in order to protect
it from a hostile environment. Formerly Willa Cather had believed
that the good could be preserved permanently by enshrining it in the
timeless and eternal world of art. Now this idea is given a pessimistic
and even desperate twist. Willa Cather no longer believes that the
good can somehow be indefinitely preserved; her theory of history is

erected on the belief that it is bound to be destroyed by a hostile and vulgar world. Her problem will soon become one of trying to freeze the social order exactly as it is in order to slow down and put off as long as possible the destruction which inevitably attends on beauty. Western civilization is interpreted as being in its death throes and breathing its last gasp; the immediate problem is to postpone as long as possible the approach of the undertaker.

THE HUMAN CRISIS: THE PROBLEM OF THE AGING ARTIST

The development of a generalized theory of history is not the only important thing found in *The Professor's House,* revealing as that is in terms of Willa Cather's later exclusive preoccupation with the past. There is also, owing to the consciousness of approaching old age, the old conflict between the aesthetic life and the life of human relations. It is as if at the age of fifty-two Willa Cather felt called on again to make a choice she already had made before. She still chooses the same way, but this time the decision is a far more painful one than it ever had been in her early days. She is no longer so sure of herself as she had been when she still had the confidence of youth.

The problem of art versus human relations, which is central to the novel, is posed in the conflict between Roddy Blake and Tom Outland, as well as in that between Lillian and Godfrey St. Peter. For Roddy and Tom, who have hitherto been inseparable, quarrel and dissolve their friendship over the disposal of the Blue Mesa relics. When Tom attacks Roddy Blake for selling them to a German archeologist who has taken them out of the country, Roddy retorts that he had had the chance of a lifetime, and that he had only wanted the money for Tom to go to college on. The two of them have a painful interview which drags on for hours, in which each one misunderstands the other's position. Roddy has made the mistake of assuming that Tom valued the relics only for the money they would bring. But he acted from the kindest of motives, out of consideration for his friend. Tom will not admit this even for an instant.

Here is something new in Willa Cather: a character in disagreement with one of her protagonists is nevertheless shown in a favorable light. Although she obviously wants the reader to sympathize with Tom, Willa Cather makes the struggle between the two points of view sufficiently complex so that the reader is aware that it is a real struggle between two reasonable positions. Tom's point of view is simple: he

regards the relics as part of a national heritage, and therefore not his
or Roddy's to dispose of.

> I admitted I'd hoped we'd be paid for our work [he says], and
> maybe get a bonus of some kind, for our discovery. "But I never
> thought of selling them, because they weren't mine to sell — nor
> yours! They belonged to this country, to the State, and to all the
> people. They belonged to boys like you and me, that have no
> other ancestors to inherit from. You've gone and sold them to a
> country that's got plenty of relics of its own." [97]

When Roddy protests that the money had been banked in Tom's name
in order to put him through college, he is greeted with cold scorn.
"You think I'd touch that money?" Tom says. "No more than if you'd
stolen it. You made the sale. Get what you can out of it." [98] Roddy
eventually replies, "Motives don't count, eh?" [99] — a perfectly just
reproach; and finally, just before he leaves Tom for good, ". . . I'm
glad it's you that's doing this to me, Tom; not me that's doing it to
you." [100]

The issue involved is the incompatibility between art, or Willa
Cather's conception of it, and life, or the tug and pull of human relationships and responsibilities. In Tom's eyes Roddy Blake has laid
hands on the untouchable and violated sanctuary by daring to sell the
relics, even though for a good purpose. Tom upholds the primacy of
aesthetic over human values; as he so clearly puts it, "I'd as soon
have sold my own grandmother as Mother Eve [the mummy] — I'd
have sold any living woman first." [101] But he cannot make this assertion
with a clear conscience. Willa Cather is evidently deeply disturbed
by the tension between the value systems of the two men. We know
this not only from the lines she gives Roddy Blake, but also from the
fact that Tom himself is very far from convinced that he is right:

> I didn't for a minute believe he'd meant to sell me out, but I
> cussed his stupidity and presumption. I had never told him just
> how I felt about those things we'd dug out together, it was the
> kind of thing one doesn't talk about directly. But he must have
> known; he couldn't have lived with me all summer and fall with-
> out knowing. And yet, until that night, I had never known myself
> that I cared more about them than almost anything else in the
> world.[102]

This passage is quite significant, in that here Tom acknowledges that
Roddy had had good intentions, and admits that he had never even

told his friend how he felt about the relics. He is unreasonable enough to expect Roddy to understand him without Tom's having opened his heart to him; yet the next minute confesses that he himself had not understood his own feelings until that very night. Evidently he is quite confused in his attitude toward Roddy; he feels both sympathy and antipathy for him at the same time. This ambivalence can be found throughout the whole episode. When Blake finally gets ready to leave, Tom says of himself, "I wanted to protest, but only succeeded in finding fault. . . . There was an ache in my arms to reach out and detain him, but there was something else that made me absolutely powerless to do so." [103] He lets him go, but adds, "I went to sleep that night hoping I would never waken." [104]

To recapitulate, Tom Outland, in choosing artistic over human values, makes the same choice that Thea Kronborg and Willa Cather's other artist-protagonists had made, but unlike them he has a bad conscience about his decision. He is deeply disturbed by the failure of artistic and human worlds to articulate with each other. Having once chosen the artistic world he receives his rewards; he has his supreme aesthetic experience with the mesa only after Roddy leaves.

> . . . in a sense, that was the first night I was ever really on the mesa at all — the first night that all of me was there. This was the first time I ever saw it as a whole. . . . Something had happened in me that made it possible for me to co-ordinate and simplify. . . . It was possession. The excitement of my first discovery was a very pale feeling compared to this one. For me the mesa was no longer an adventure, but a religious emotion. I had read of filial piety in the Latin poets, and I knew that this was what I felt for this place. . . . I wakened with the feeling that I had found everything, instead of having lost everything.[105]

For a while he forgets about Roddy, feeling sure he will eventually turn up. When he doesn't, Tom starts an all-out search for him enlisting the aid of the police, the Catholic missionaries, and the Santa Fe operatives, inserting advertisements in the local papers and offering a thousand dollars reward for whoever finds him. But all to no avail. Blake has disappeared completely. Then all Tom's doubts as to the rightness of what he has done begin to crowd back on him. His diary ends on a foreboding note, with the joy of possession of the Blue Mesa almost completely obscured by a sense of guilt at having betrayed a friend:

But the older I grow, the more I understand what it was I did that night on the mesa. Anyone who requites faith and friendship as I did will have to pay for it. I'm not very sanguine about good fortune for myself. I'll be called to account when I least expect it.[106]

The Professor is in many ways a good deal like Tom. He too thinks art is superior to life and that any conflict between the two should be resolved in favor of the former. He has ranked historical writing ahead of his relations with his wife (the supreme moment of his life did not even have Lillian in it), and now that he has finished his work nothing his family does seems to satisfy him. He has occupied himself exclusively for several years with the writing of *The Spanish Adventurers in North America,* but cannot understand why his family should have grown away from him during that time and turned elsewhere for the attention he was too busy to give them. In particular he cannot forgive his wife for her friendship with Louie Marsellus, their effusive and outgoing son-in-law. Marsellus is enthusiastic about St. Peter's work, but the interest is not reciprocated; St. Peter, like Tom, doesn't want anyone to impinge on his own particular version of the past. As his wife says, "You won't let him discuss your affairs, and you are annoyed when he talks about his own." [107] Although Marsellus is charming and kindhearted and very generous with his wife and in-laws, the Professor resents him because he is a Jew (St. Peter is an anti-Semite) and a commercial success, and is, he feels, an embodiment of the kind of materialism that is subtly destroying America. This sets him at cross purposes with his wife, who is devoted to Louie. "You grow better-looking and more intolerant all the time," she tells him.

"Intolerant?" He put down his shoe and looked up at her. The thing that stuck in his mind constantly was that she was growing more and more intolerant, about everything except her sons-in-law; that she would probably continue to do so, and that he must school himself to bear it.[108]

Throughout the book there is an ever widening rift between St. Peter and his wife; Lillian accuses the Professor of pulling away from his family, while the Professor accuses his family of pulling away from him. The conflict between husband and wife comes out in the open when Marsellus offers to take his parents-in-law to France for the summer with all expenses paid. Everyone is delighted with this arrangement except the Professor, and although "he hated himself for the ungracious drawing-back that he felt in the region of his diaphragm," [109] nevertheless he declines. Lillian St. Peter then faces the issue squarely:

> "Godfrey," she said slowly and sadly, "I wonder what it is that makes you draw away from your family. Or who it is."
>
> "My dear, are you going to be jealous?"
>
> "I wish I were going to be. I'd much rather see you foolish about some woman than becoming lonely and inhuman."
>
> "Well, the habit of living with ideas grows on one, I suppose, just as inevitably as the more cheerful habit of living with various ladies. There's something to be said for both."
>
> "I think your ideas were best when you were your most human self."
>
> St. Peter sighed. "I can't contradict you there. But I must go on as I can. It is not always May." [110]

Lillian's criticism is remarkably apt and applies not only to Professor St. Peter but also to Willa Cather herself. When she remarks, "I think your ideas were best when you were your most human self," she implies that ideas have their roots in human experience and do not form an airtight little world of their own. This denies the whole concept of art as sanctuary and questions some basic assumptions of the art-for-art's-sake movement. The very fact that Willa Cather was willing to give Lillian such a line shows the qualms she had about the rightness of the Professor's position.

It should be apparent that the conflict between the characters is also a conflict between two different world views, one materialist and the other nonmaterialist. Lillian St. Peter and Roddy Blake hold the first view, the Professor and Tom Outland the second. Materialism as presented in the persons of Mrs. St. Peter and Roddy Blake is not unattractive; it includes warmth and generosity and an appreciation of beauty and most of the good things of life. Yet it has its limitations; Lillian does not understand her husband's state of mind and Roddy sells the Indian relics. The besetting sin of both is a blindness to certain aspects of human experience. Since Godfrey St. Peter and Tom are nonmaterialistic, they are free from this particular kind of vice, but they too are far less than perfect. Godfrey is so offended by the doings of his supposedly worldly family that he tries to withdraw from them completely, and Tom values his cliff city more than his friendship with Roddy. In each case an abstract aesthetic value is placed before human relations, which are consequently sacrificed to it.

Now the excesses of materialism are gross and easily detectible; it is hard for anyone to be fooled about their essential nature. But the excesses of the opposing view are subtler and far more apt to be mistaken for virtues; it is easy for a fanatic to pass as a saint. Tom and St. Peter run this other and more insidious danger, which is that of spiritual pride. For what has the Professor to offer that is better than the goodhearted materialism of his wife and Louie Marsellus? Mere aloof coldness, emptyhearted aestheticism, art for the sake of art rather than for the sake of life — and of course, an irreplaceable work of scholarship.

In the passages quoted Willa Cather shows herself deeply concerned with the issues involved. Tom is obsessed with guilt at his rejection of Roddy Blake, and the Professor regrets his alienation from his wife. Yet for all their guilt and regret, when faced with the same issues, Willa Cather still has them choose the same way; even though they feel it may be a weakness they still choose art over life. Although they have some sort of intellectual realization that compromise and acceptance of human limitations is in order, temperamentally they are incapable of doing anything except what they had done before. This can be seen in the continuation of the previously quoted conversation between Lillian and Godfrey St. Peter:

"You are not old enough for the pose you take. That's what puzzles me. For so many years you never seemed to grow at all older, though I did. Two years ago you were an impetuous young man. Now you save yourself in everything. You're naturally warm and affectionate; all at once you begin shutting yourself away from everybody. I don't think you'll be happier for it." . . . "Why is it, Godfrey? I can't see any change in your face, though I watch you so closely. It's in your mind, in your mood. Something has come over you. Is it merely that you know too much, I wonder. Too much to be happy? You were always the wisest person in the world. What is it, can't you tell me?"

"I can't altogether tell myself, Lillian. It's not wholly a matter of the calendar. It's the feeling that I've put a great deal behind me, where I can't go back to it again — and I don't really wish to go back. The way would be too long and too fatiguing. Perhaps, for a home-staying man, I've lived pretty hard. I wasn't willing to slight anything — you, or my desk, or my students. And now I seem to be tremendously tired. One pays, coming or going. A man has got only just so much in him; when it's gone he slumps. Even the first Napoleon did." [111]

Here we have the real reason for the Professor's (and perhaps Willa Cather's) withdrawal from human intercourse. The feeling that a man has only just so much in him results in a failure to give oneself because of a fear of being used up. This fear, a neurotic one, is usually caused by the existence of severe repressions; it is the same fear which plagued the mind of F. Scott Fitzgerald, who conceptualized the feeling in the term "emotional bankruptcy."

The Professor, then, feels that his wife may be right, but he is powerless to reach out and touch her, just as Tom Outland feels that Roddy Blake is at least partially right, but is unable to meet him halfway. Because of an inability to give in human relations, Willa Cather's later protagonists make the same choice that had been made by her earlier artist heroines, but the mood now is entirely different. Then she had felt that, faced with the alternate goals of art and human ties, any right-minded aesthete would choose the former. Now she becomes excruciatingly aware that neither goal is perfect, and that since some elements of both are necessary for human happiness, any choice made would lead to frustration. This marks a new stage in her thinking. At this point one would think she might drop her belief in the omnipotent will, accept the necessity of compromise, and come to a real aesthetic and emotional maturity. But Willa Cather was temperamentally incapable of compromising. Instead of accepting the inevitable, she tried her best to ignore it, and lapsed into the bitter negativism that was to last the rest of her life.

THE WAY OUT: SANCTUARY, RITUAL, AND RETREAT

Even before the crisis of his near-suicide St. Peter shows symptoms of withdrawal, and, since these symptoms form the pattern of Willa Cather's fourth and final period, they are worth examining. Conceptually stated, they include the desire for sanctuary, the reliance on ritual, and the retreat from human relationships.

The desire for sanctuary is nothing new in Willa Cather; we have seen that it formed the basis of her interest in the world of art. Now however it becomes embodied in far more concrete symbols, one of which provides the title for this novel, the house of one's own or, more specifically, the room of one's own. At the beginning of the book St. Peter's family moves out of the old house in which he has spent his entire married life, but the Professor decides to stay behind; as he puts it, he will work in the old house and board at the new. He is especially attached to his study — a bare, uncomfortable room at the top of the house in which he had written *The Spanish Adventurers in North*

America. The house is not beautiful at all; Willa Cather says of it: "It was almost as ugly as it is possible for a house to be; square, three stories in height, painted the colour of ashes — the front porch just too narrow for comfort, with a slanting floor and sagging steps." [112] The workroom is equally unattractive: "Walls and ceiling alike were covered with a yellow paper which had once been very ugly, but had faded into inoffensive neutrality. The matting on the floor was worn and scratchy. . . . This dark den had for many years been the Professor's study." [113]

The Professor likes the house and room, not because they are beautiful but because they are old. The new house may be perfectly satisfactory, but St. Peter dislikes change of any kind, and prefers old things even when they are not the best. The room of one's own has turned up before in Willa Cather's fiction and will turn up again; Thea Kronborg had her own room in *The Song of the Lark;* so will Cécile Auclair in *Shadows on the Rock.* Ultimately these are based on Willa Cather's own childhood memories of her room in her parents' house.[114] It is not hard to imagine why this particular kind of sanctuary appealed to her. For somebody as afraid of struggle as she was, it was comforting to have a place of one's own in which one could do as one wished with nobody to interfere.

But the room of one's own is not the only image of sanctuary to be found in *The Professor's House.* The basic figure in Tom Outland's story, the inaccessible mesa cradling a civilization which it manages to preserve inviolate from marauding tribes below, is a sanctuary of a similar sort. It will be remembered that as long as the Indians remained on their high outcropping of rock they were safe; it was only when they descended to the plain that they were slaughtered. This image of security and repose I will refer to as the symbol of the enchanted mesa. It had already formed the subject of an early Willa Cather short story,[115] and is to appear again in her most famous treatment of the Southwest, *Death Comes for the Archbishop.*

A second sign of the Professor's withdrawal is his increasing interest in ritual. Certain kinds of personalities find it soothing to do the same things over and over again in the same way; ritual can help bring the emotions under control by offering a standardized pattern for behavior which affords some protection against fear of the uncertainties of life. Ritual is to play an important part in the fiction of Willa Cather's fourth period, particularly in her Catholic novels; *Death Comes for the Archbishop* deals at considerable length with the aesthetic aspects of religious ritual, while the ritual of domestic routine lies at the heart of

Shadows on the Rock. Both types are anticipated in the present work. The Professor's insistence on ritual in daily living helps produce that rigidity of character which alienates him from his family, while his interest in Catholic ritual can be seen in the "art-religion" speech which he gives to his class at the university:

"No, Miller, I don't myself think much of science as a phase of human development. It has given us a lot of ingenious toys; they take our attention away from the real problems, of course, and since the problems are insoluble, I suppose we ought to be grateful for distraction. But the fact is, the human mind, the individual mind, has always been made more interesting by dwelling on the old riddles, even if it makes nothing of them. Science hasn't given us any new amazements, except for the superficial kind we get from witnessing dexterity and sleight-of-hand. It hasn't given us any richer pleasures, as the Renaissance did, nor any new sins — not one! Indeed, it takes our old ones away. It's the laboratory, not the Lamb of God, that taketh away the sins of the world. You'll agree that there is not much thrill about a physiological sin. We were better off when even the prosaic matter of taking nourishment could have the magnificence of a sin. I don't think you help people by making their conduct of no importance — you impoverish them. As long as every man and woman who crowded into the cathedrals on Easter Sunday was a principal in a gorgeous drama with God, glittering angels on one side and the shadows of evil coming and going on the other, life was a rich thing. The king and the beggar had the same chance at miracles and great temptations and revelations. And that's what makes men happy, believing in the mystery and importance of their own little individual lives. It makes us happy to surround our creature needs and bodily instincts with as much pomp and circumstance as possible. Art and religion (they are the same thing, in the end, of course) have given man the only happiness he has ever had.

"Moses learned the importance of that in the Egyptian court, and when he wanted to make a population of slaves into an independent people in the shortest possible time, he invented elaborate ceremonials to give them a feeling of dignity and purpose. Every act had some imaginative end. The cutting of the finger nails was a religious observance. The Christian theologians went over the books of the Law, like great artists, getting splendid effects by excision. They reset the stage with more space and mystery, throwing all the light upon a few sins of great dramatic value — only seven, you remember, and of those only three that are perpetually enthralling. With the theologians came the cathedral-builders; the sculptors and glass-workers and painters. They might, without sacrilege, have changed the prayer a little and said, *Thy will be done in art, as it is in heaven.* How can it be done anywhere else *as* it is in heaven? But I think the hour is up. You might tell me next week, Miller, what you think science has done for us, besides making us very comfortable." [116]

Several of the values in this speech show the direction of the Professor's development. There is, for instance, the outright identification of science with technology. Willa Cather never saw science as a way of understanding human experience in abstract terms; to her it is no more than a bundle of gadgets. The Professor has just suggested to one of his students that science hasn't made any important contributions to human life; in doing so he disadvantageously compares the present with the Middle Ages, thus implying Willa Cather's whole theory of history. He holds that the great advantage of the medieval view of life was that it gave man a place of importance in the scheme of things, as modern world views do not; he opposes the laboratory to the Lamb of God, saying, "You'll agree there is not much thrill about a physiological sin." This suggests that the present is so thoroughly mechanized and uninteresting that any expression of vitality, even sin, would be desirable — shades of Baudelaire and the early T. S. Eliot — but a scientific age doesn't even believe in sin. The Professor seems to feel that it is more important for men to have their egos soothed than to admit that they are not all-important. When he says, ". . . that's what makes men happy, believing in the mystery and importance of their own little individual lives. It makes us happy to surround our creature needs and bodily instincts with as much pomp and circumstance as possible," he sounds almost as if he were deliberately advocating self-deception.

The Professor then proceeds to a description of Judaism and Christianity, the essence of which he conceives of as ritual. Ritual, he feels, is important because it gives to human beings a sense of dignity and purpose. Apparently it is the aesthetic aspect of ritual which appeals to him most, judging from statements like, "The Christian theologians went over the books of the Law, like great artists, getting splendid effects by excision," and "With the theologians came the cathedral-builders; the sculptors and glass-workers and painters. They might, without sacrilege, have changed the prayer a little and said, *Thy will be done in art, as it is in heaven.*"

These passages reveal once again the long continuing influence on Willa Cather of the aesthetic movement. The Professor states that art and religion are the same thing in the end; Walter Pater had said that art *is* religion. The Professor's whole speech reads like a commentary on Pater's famous "Conclusion" to *The Renaissance;* at the bottom of it is the ideal of the comely life. This constant emphasis on the aesthetic element in even sacred human experience becomes very important to Willa Cather for a time. It set the tone for the Catholic novels for her next period.

The third symptom of the Professor's withdrawal is his precipitate retreat from human relations. Lillian St. Peter has already suggested this in a previously quoted passage when she says: "Two years ago you were an impetuous young man. Now you save yourself in everything. You're naturally warm and affectionate; all at once you begin shutting yourself away from everybody." [117] But the retreat goes considerably farther than this. The Professor actually begins to have daydreams about his childhood:

> St. Peter had always laughed at people who talked about "daydreams," just as he laughed at people who naively confessed that they had "an imagination." All his life his mind had behaved in a positive fashion. When he was not at work, or being actively amused, he went to sleep. He had no twilight stage. But now he enjoyed this half-awake loafing with his brain as if it were a new sense, arriving late, like wisdom teeth. He found he could lie on his sand-spit by the lake for hours and watch the seven motionless pines drink up the sun. In the evening, after dinner, he could sit idle and watch the stars, with the same immobility. He was cultivating a novel dissipation — and enjoying a new friendship. Tom Outland had not come back again through the garden door (as he had so often done in dreams!) but another boy had; the boy the Professor had long ago left behind him in Kansas, in the Solomon Valley — the original, unmodified Godfrey St. Peter.

. . . . .

> . . . now that the vivid consciousness of an earlier state had come back to him, the Professor felt that life with this Kansas boy, little as there had been of it, was the realest of his lives, and that all the years between had been accidental and ordered from the outside. His career, his wife, his family, were not his life at all, but a chain of events which had happened to him. All these things had nothing to do with the person he was in the beginning.[118]

The Professor rejects both his family and career, thus repudiating everything in adult life which he had formerly cared for:

> The man he was now, the personality his friends knew, had begun to grow strong during adolescence, during the years when he was always consciously or unconsciously conjugating the verb "to love" — in society and solitude, with people, with books, with the sky and open country, in the lonesomeness of crowded city streets. When he met Lillian, it reached its maturity. From that time to this, existence had been a catching at handholds. One thing led to another and one development brought on another, and the design of his life had been the work of this secondary social man, the lover. It had been shaped by all the penalties and responsibilities of being and having been a lover. Because there was Lillian, there must be marriage and a salary. Because there was marriage, there were children. Because there were children, and fervour in the blood and brain, books were born as well as daughters. His histories, he was convinced, had no more to do with his original ego than his daughters had; they were a result of the high pressure of young manhood.[119]

It is not surprising to find here a repudiation of physical love — there are many such in the works of Willa Cather — but it is surprising that the Professor should repudiate his whole career. This is the first time a Willa Cather protagonist has turned against his own works; never before has she carried negativism so far as this. For what the Professor turns against is his entire adult life:

> The Professor knew, of course, that adolescence grafted a new creature into the original one, and that the complexion of a man's life was largely determined by how well or ill his original self and his nature as modified by sex rubbed on together.
>
> What he had not known was that, at a given time, that first nature could return to a man, unchanged by all the pursuits and passions and experiences of his life; untouched even by the tastes and intellectual activities which have been strong enough to give him distinction among his fellows and to have made for him, as they say, a name in the world. Perhaps this reversion did not often occur, but he knew it had happened to him. . . . He did not regret his life, but he was indifferent to it. It seemed to him like the life of another person.[120]

Once he has given up the struggle of adult life, the Professor becomes passive and docile. He is quite content to bask quietly in the sunshine, enjoying the feeling of being completely absorbed in nature:

> The Kansas boy who had come back to St. Peter this summer was not a scholar. He was a primitive. He was only interested in earth and woods and water. Wherever sun sunned and rain rained and snow snowed, wherever life sprouted and decayed, places were alike to him. He was not nearly so cultivated as Tom's old cliff-dwellers must have been — and yet he was terribly wise. He seemed to be at the root of the matter; Desire under all desires, Truth under all truths. He seemed to know, among other things, that he was solitary and must always be so; he had never married, never been a father. He was earth, and would return to earth. When white clouds blew over the lake like bellying sails, when the seven pine-trees turned red in the declining sun, he felt satisfaction and said to himself merely: "That is right." Coming upon a curly root that thrust itself across his path, he said: "That is it." When the maple leaves along the street began to turn yellow and waxy, and were soft to the touch, — like the skin on old faces, — he said: "That is true; it is time." All these recognitions gave him a kind of sad pleasure.[121]

After all the images of death presented in the last paragraph, it comes as no surprise that the Professor does not believe he will live to see his classes in the fall term, and that he feels he is ready to die.

The crisis comes when the Professor, alone in the old house, takes a nap in his study one stormy night and is nearly asphyxiated by escaping gas. When he awakes in a cold and numbed condition in the gas-filled room, he makes a passive attempt at suicide, if not an active one:

> . . . The storm had blown the stove out and the window shut. The thing to do was to get up and open the window. But suppose he did not get up — ? How far was a man required to exert himself against accident? How would such a case be decided under English law? He hadn't lifted his hand against himself — was he required to lift it for himself? [122]

But he is rescued from this lethal atmosphere of his study by Augusta, the pious German Catholic sewing woman, much as in *The Faerie Queene* the Red Cross Knight is rescued by Una from the knife offered

him by the giant Despair. For the first time in his life he looks at
Augusta as someone whose ideas and attitudes might be worthy of
respect, since they enable her to meet crises much more effectively than
he had been able to:

> . . . Augusta was like the taste of bitter herbs; she was the
> bloomless side of life that he had always run away from, — yet
> when he had to face it, he found that it wasn't altogether re-
> pugnant.[123]

Augusta is not afraid to face the hard facts of life, but on the other
hand, neither does she dwell on them:

> Sometimes she used to telephone Mrs. St. Peter that she would
> be a day late, because there had been a death in the family where
> she was sewing just then, and she was "needed." . . . she would
> reply to [the Professor's] polite questions about the illness or
> funeral with befitting solemnity, and then go readily to another
> topic, not holding the dolorous note.[124]

She neither fears death nor is romantically in love with it, as is the
Professor. Rather, she regards it as a fact:

> She hadn't any of the sentimentality that comes from a fear of
> dying. She talked about death as she spoke of a hard winter or a
> rainy March, or any of the sadnesses of nature.[125]

Because of the comfort she gives him the Professor comes to feel that
he has more in common with Augusta than he does with any member
of his family, and that he would do well to emulate her:

> It occurred to St. Peter . . . that he would rather have Augusta
> with him now than anyone he could think of. . . . He even felt a
> sense of obligation toward her. . . .
> He didn't, on being quite honest with himself, feel any obliga-
> tions toward his family. Lillian had had the best years of his
> life. . . . But they were gone. His daughters had outgrown any
> great need of him. . . . There was still Augusta, however; a world
> full of Augustas with whom one was outward bound.[126]

The Professor is finally converted away from the nineteenth-century belief in the supremacy of the will. Early in the book Willa Cather had written:

> A man can do anything if he wishes to enough, St. Peter believed. Desire is creation, is the magical element in that process. If there were an instrument by which to measure desire, one could foretell achievement.[127]

Just before his near-suicide, when the Professor is courting death, Willa Cather writes: "But now he thought of eternal solitude with gratefulness; as a release from any obligation, from every form of effort." [128] When the crucial moment comes, even his instinct of self-preservation fails him; the man who had formerly believed that desire is all cannot even make up his mind whether or not to save his own life. "When he was confronted by accidental extinction, he had felt no will to resist," writes Willa Cather, "but had let chance take its way, as it had done with him so often." [129] This invocation of chance as the arbiter of destinies represents a complete abdication of reason in the face of human suffering. It is a sign of intellectual and artistic bankruptcy on Willa Cather's part that she can think of no other way to bring her hero off than to have him rescued by the *deus ex machina* of Augusta the seamstress.

After his near-suicide, the Professor comes to reject all human endeavor as vanity. It has been suggested that this rejection is a preparation for death and that *The Professor's House* is a religious novel.[130] Actually it is more Stoic than Christian. "He had never learned to live without delight," says Willa Cather. "And he would have to learn to, just as, in a Prohibition country, he supposed he would have to learn to live without sherry." [131] But stoicism cannot account for the Professor's final attitude. When we recall the tremendous struggle that had taken place in his mind between the claims of human ties and those of art, and remember his agonized awareness that neither was in itself complete, it is evident that his final calm is not that of victory but of defeat. By ceasing to care about anything at all in life, he has not solved his problems but given up on them. The Professor has not come to an acceptance of life as it is; instead he has committed spiritual suicide.

We have now reached a new stage in Willa Cather's artistic development. The doubts she expressed in *One of Ours* about the possibility of heroism in the modern world by the choice of the unheroic Claude Wheeler as protagonist have now come to a head. The protagonists of *The Professor's House* and *My Mortal Enemy*, her next work, are desperately unhappy people, and the author identifies with them by giving their actions her approval. Why should they come after a long line of protagonists with whom the author also identifies, who felt they could achieve everything through their will? Apparently Willa Cather has come to a point where it is evident to her that her will is not omnipotent. She has reached the stage where she sees that the world is fundamentally indifferent to her; that it includes countless other people besides herself who have desires and wishes that they will try to follow despite her own desires and wishes. She realizes, in other words, that she cannot have her way with the world or control it. At this point she rejects the world. She shows St. Peter changing from a man who believed that desire was all to one who is convinced that desire is nothing. As a balanced view of life, this does not seem to be much of an improvement. A wiser head than Willa Cather's, Jonathan Swift, made a comment relevant to her work when he said that "The Stoical scheme of supplying our wants, by lopping off our desires, is like cutting off our feet when we want shoes." [132]

My Mortal Enemy: PRIMER OF NEGATION

After the despair of *The Professor's House,* any further exercises in negativism might well seem anticlimactic. Yet Willa Cather wrote two more works which can be considered as postscripts to the above novel. The first, a novel published the year after *The Professor's House,* is *My Mortal Enemy*. The second, a medium-length story written a dozen years later, is "The Old Beauty."

The story of *My Mortal Enemy* is simple enough. Myra Driscoll, an Irish-American beauty, falls in love and runs off with a young freethinker, Oswald Henshawe, and is disinherited by her uncle, a rich, capricious, arbitrary, and tyrannical old man. She and Oswald lead a worldly life at first, associating with artists, musicians, and cultured German businessmen. But eventually they fall on evil days; Oswald loses all his money, and Myra loses her health. In the last part of the book they are seen leading a wretched, squalid existence in a rooming house. Myra, who is dying, has assumed all the arbitrary high-handed ways of her uncle, and, although her husband is abject in his devotion to her, she makes his life miserable. She becomes convinced that it was a mistake for her to disobey her uncle and marry for love, since it entailed giving up her childhood home, her religion, and, most important of all, her inheritance. She finally dies as she had wished, alone on a headland by the sea, and with a crucifix in her hand, but not before she has said aloud in her husband's presence, "Why must I die like this, alone with my mortal enemy?" [133]

This book is like the previous one in that the protagonist turns against the values of his entire adult life. But Myra Henshawe's rejection is much more violent than St. Peter's. Willa Cather writes of the Professor, "He did not regret his life, but he was indifferent to it," [134] while she has Myra say, "We've destroyed each other. I should have stayed with my uncle. It was money I needed. We've thrown our lives away." [135] Both protagonists become increasingly estranged from their marriage partners. Even in her best days Myra Henshawe had been an aggressive woman who trampled on her husband. But now she turns on Oswald with a positive ferocity and blames him for decisions she herself has made, even to the point of calling him her mortal enemy. Like the Professor she seeks relief in sanctuary, ritual, and retreat. However, her attempts to find sanctuary are hampered by her lack of money. "Oh, that's the cruelty of being poor," she says, "it leaves you at the mercy of such pigs! [noisy tenants in the rooming house she and Oswald are living in]. Money is a protection, a cloak; it can buy one quiet, and some sort of dignity." [136] It is evident that money is important to her because it enables one to buy sanctuary. Her interest in ritual goes even beyond the Professor's, since unlike him she returns to the Catholicism of her childhood and dies with a crucifix in her hand. Again, like the Professor, she engages in a retreat into nature. "Light and silence," she says, "they heal all one's wounds — all but one, and that's healed by dark and silence. I find I don't miss clever talk, the kind I always used to have about me, when I can have silence. It's like cold water poured over fever." [137]

To sum up, both the Professor and Myra Henshawe are searching for escape. The Professor, who can find no way out of his problems, ultimately searches for it by passively seeking death. Myra, who is also unable to solve her problems, attempts to escape by refusing to accept the consequences of her actions and by blaming everyone but herself for the way her life has turned out. In particular, she thinks that if she had money she could buy the peace of mind she needs. She does not realize that, however much money might soften the blows of fate, it is her own emotional inadequacies which are making her miserable.

In this novel, as in the previous one, Willa Cather realizes that there are grounds for criticizing the protagonists' actions and includes a character who serves as critic. In *The Professor's House* this part is given to the Professor's wife; in *My Mortal Enemy* to the aunt of the narrator. The latter occasionally delivers herself of some caustic comments about the relative merits of Oswald and Myra. "Everything is always for Myra," she complains. "He never gets anything for himself. And all the admiration is for her; why shouldn't he have a little? He has been devoted to a fault. And she's often most unreasonable with him — most unreasonable." [138] Later, in a moment of acute exasperation, she declares:

> "I'm sick of Myra's dramatics . . . I've done with them. A man never *is* justified, but if ever a man was . . ." [139]

But in spite of these flashes of criticism, Myra is allowed to proceed imperiously on her own way, riding roughshod over all those who have been kindest to her. Typical of her tone is the curt note she leaves for her husband just before going off to die:

> "Dear Oswald: My hour has come. Don't follow me. I wish to be alone. Nellie [the narrator] knows where there is money for masses." That was all. There was no signature. [140]

It is possible that Willa Cather considered *My Mortal Enemy* to be another of her attacks on the materialism of modern-day America. Myra Henshawe considers herself to have been a grasping, worldly woman, [141] and her return to the religion of her childhood may have been intended to show a developing interest in spiritual things. However, an examination of the text fails to bear this out. When Nellie, in straightening up Myra's bed, removes her crucifix, Myra quickly says, "Give it to me. It means nothing to people who haven't suffered." [142] And when she is closeted with a priest, Nellie overhears her say, "Ah, Father Fay, that isn't the reason! Religion is different from everything else; *because in religion seeking is finding.*" [143] This is surely a strange description of Catholicism, and it also shows her telling the priest his own business. The hardest thing to square with a religious interpretation of the book is the description of old John Driscoll's funeral. Nellie says:

> . . . I myself could remember his funeral — remember it very vividly — though I was not more than six years old when it happened. I sat with my parents in the front of the gallery, at the back of the church that the old man had enlarged and enriched during the latter days of his life. The high altar blazed with

hundreds of candles, the choir was entirely filled by the masses of flowers. The bishop was there, and a flock of priests in gorgeous vestments. When the pall-bearers arrived, Driscoll did not come to the church; the church went to him. The bishop and clergy went down the nave and met that great black coffin at the door, preceded by the cross and boys swinging cloudy censers, followed by the choir chanting to the organ. They surrounded, they received, they seemed to assimilate into the body of the church, the body of old John Driscoll. They bore it up to the high altar on a river of colour and incense and organ-tone; they claimed it and enclosed it.

In after years, when I went to other funerals, stark and grim enough, I thought of John Driscoll as having escaped the end of all flesh; it was as if he had been translated, with no dark conclusion to the pageant, no "night of the grave" about which our Protestant preachers talked. From the freshness of roses and lilies, from the glory of the high altar, he had gone straight to the greater glory, through smoking censers and candles and stars.[144]

This passage abounds with the tinsel vulgarity of the Gilded Age in which Willa Cather grew up. It is a fantasy about extreme wealth corrupting the church itself and envisages a projection of a moneyed aristocracy into eternity. Compared with this picture of the stiff-necked old Irishman buying his way into heaven, Myra's death with a crucifix in her hand seems a poor second best. It seems clear that the book has no religious overtones whatsoever, but is a brute glorification of the power of money. And Oswald's real crime in his wife's eyes is, not taking her away from her family, but daring to become poor. In view of the increasingly important role which money plays from *One of Ours* through *A Lost Lady* and *The Professor's House,* it appears that the only way Willa Cather saw of effectuating one's will in the modern world was through the possession of great wealth. Hence the glorification of John Driscoll, "a coarse old codger, so unlettered that he made a poor showing with a pen," [145] but a successful self-made man. Unfortunately, money is almost the only value stressed in the book. It is a dismal picture Willa Cather paints when she has Myra say, "I should have stayed with my uncle. It was money I needed. We've thrown our lives away." [146]

As is the case with Professor St. Peter, Myra Henshawe's rejection of her husband is followed by a return to the values of childhood. All her life she has had a tyrannical streak in her personality, but it becomes much more marked now. This, as she recalls in her old age, was one of the distinguishing characteristics of her uncle:

> ". . . Yes, he had violent prejudices; but that's rather good to remember in these days when so few people have any real passions, either of love or hate. He would help a friend, no matter what it cost him, and over and over again he risked ruining himself to crush an enemy. . . ." [147]

Myra's fondness for money also seems to be an avuncular inheritance. Just before disinheriting his niece old Driscoll tells her, "I advise ye to think well. . . . It's better to be a stray dog in this world than a man without money. I've tried both ways, and I know. A poor man stinks, and God hates him." [148] In turning against her husband Myra seems to be acting the same role John Driscoll had in disowning her; both involve the cold, selfish rejection of a human tie for reasons which are purely personal. Willa Cather seems aware of this similarity in character; she has Myra say, "As we grow old we become more and more the stuff our forbears put into us. I can feel his savagery strengthen in me. We think we are so individual and so misunderstood when we are young; but the nature our strain of blood carries is inside there, waiting, like our skeleton." [149]

The climax of the book comes when Myra, on her sickbed, asks her husband, "Why must I die like this, alone with my mortal enemy?" [150] The narrator, Nellie, who overhears this, is horrified. But: "As I sat on through the night, after Oswald had gone to catch a few hours of sleep, I grew calmer. I began to understand a little what she meant, to sense how it was with her. Violent natures like hers sometimes turn against themselves . . . against themselves and all their idolatries." [151] This states that Myra is turning, not so much against Oswald, although she is nasty enough to him, as against her own idolatrous love for him. Like the Professor, she is finally forced to give up her belief in the omnipotence of the will. But again like the Professor, she relinquishes her old illusions only to embrace new ones. It is not her selfishness but her love for Oswald which she comes to hate, although both are included in the passions, and it is the passions which she comes to distrust. In turning from worldly satisfactions to religious ritual she shows no real understanding of either. She has no idea that her passions have hurt other people who have deserved better of her (witness the tone of her farewell note); she is only concerned because they have hurt her. In dying she is as self-centered and selfish as she was in living; she leaves life without having begun to understand it.

It can be argued that the fate of Myra is treated as if it were the punishment of a wayward child whose naughtiness consisted of daring to marry against her uncle's wishes. The instrument by which he tried to control her is money, as it has been for many another irate parent figure. As long as Oswald has money of his own her uncle's actions cannot hurt her, but after Oswald loses his wealth, Myra comes to feel the full weight of her uncle's punishing hand. Thus the story is, among other things, a sermon against love and marriage. Myra is given to making such statements as "Love itself draws on a woman nearly all the bad luck in the world. . . ."[152] and "See the moon coming out, Nellie — behind the tower. It wakens the guilt in me. No playing with love; and I'd sworn a great oath never to meddle again. You send a handsome fellow like Ewan Gray to a fine girl like Esther, and it's Christmas eve, and they rise above us and the white world around us, and there isn't anybody, not a tramp on the park benches, that wouldn't wish them well — and very likely hell will come of it."[153] Significantly enough the book's last words, uttered not by Myra but the narrator, reveal the same attitude.

> Sometimes, when I have watched the bright beginning of a love story, when I have seen a common feeling exalted into beauty by imagination, generosity, and the flaming courage of youth, I have heard again that strange complaint breathed by a dying woman into the stillness of night, like a confession of the soul: "Why must I die like this, alone with my mortal enemy!"[154]

This is the same warning against physical passion that has sounded so often in the writings of Willa Cather, but *My Mortal Enemy* is the only book in which the punishment for transgression proceeds directly from a parental figure. We are now entering the second stage of Willa Cather's development in relation to her own family situation. Formerly, when she had been moving away from her family, her protagonists were strong individualists who had done their best to break away from their own families and make their way in the world alone. Now, when she is moving back to the family, her protagonists are people who admit the fundamental rightness of their parents and submit to their yoke.

My Mortal Enemy is in many ways the most bizarre of Willa Cather's books. Not since *The Song of the Lark* have we been asked to admire so thoroughly unpleasant a heroine. The values of the book seem to be entirely perverse, since they consist chiefly of the exaltation of money and brute power. Above all, the lesson driven home is that of the sanctity of success and the blasphemy of failure. However, the novel, once read, is unforgettable. It is the most fascinating and least likable of Willa Cather's works.

"THE OLD BEAUTY": BATHOS AT AIX-LES-BAINS

The other story of negation, "The Old Beauty," was written considerably later in Willa Cather's life, being composed in 1936, although not published until 1948. By this time the emotional crisis which had produced *My Mortal Enemy* and *The Professor's House* was past, and Willa Cather had entered a period of relative calm. Perhaps for this reason "The Old Beauty," although extremely negative, is not so violently so as is the previous novel. If *My Mortal Enemy* is comparable to *The Professor's House* because both involve a revulsion against life itself, "The Old Beauty" is comparable to *A Lost Lady*, in which it is not life but the present which is rejected.

The plot is simple. In the year 1922 Henry Seabury returns to Europe after having spent the greater part of his life in China. At Aix-les-Bains he meets Gabrielle Longstreet, a superannuated beauty whom he had known thirty years before. The high point of their previous acquaintance had been when he had rescued her from rape in a New York drawing room. This time, however, they merely talk quietly about famous personages they had known, now long since dead, and the general inferiority of the present to the past. They go on an excursion together to the Grande-Chartreuse, and, on the way back, have a slight motor accident when their way is blocked by a car containing two young American girls wearing dirty white knickers. Gabrielle is shaken up a bit, but as she puts it: "After one has been *exaltée*, there usually comes a shock. Oh, I don't mean the bruises we got! I mean the white breeches." [155] The next morning she is dead.

The tone of the story is one of utter dislike for the present and nostalgia for the good old days. The text is studded with such references as: "He was hunting for something, some spot that was still more or less as it used to be." [156] " 'You are always dissatisfied when we go to the Casino. There are more of the kind you hate there.' " [157] " 'And how are things [in China]?' 'Not so good now, Lady Longstreet. . . . China is rather falling to pieces.' " [158] " 'My friends mean more to me now than when they were alive. I was too ignorant then to realize what remarkable men they were. I supposed the world was always full of great men.' " [159] " 'What an astonishing lot they are [photographs of the "great men"]. . . . How can a world manage to get on without them?' 'It hasn't managed very well, has it?' " [160]

Both characters agree that the world was a better place when they were young. It is hard to see in these remarks anything more than the maunderings of a garrulous old couple who refuse to accept the passage of time. Both of them identify themselves with the *ancien régime:*

> "We have lived through a storm to which the French Revolution, which used to be our standard of horrors, was merely a breeze. A rather gentlemanly affair, as one looks back on it. . . . As for me, I am grateful to be alive, sitting here with you in a comfortable hotel (I might be in a prison full of rats), in a France still undestroyed."
>
> The old lady looked into his eyes with the calm, level gaze so rare with her now. "Are you grateful? I am not. I think one should go out with one's time." [161]

And Willa Cather treats with evident approval Gabrielle Longstreet's willingness to do what Marian Forrester would not do — go out with one's time.[162]

But the story is not completely one-sided. Lady Longstreet has a companion named Cherry Beamish (Mrs. Allison), a former music-hall actress, who is a little more willing to accept things than she is. Cherry says at one point, "We have the past, and the present — which is really very interesting, if only you will let yourself think so." [163] The difference in their attitudes becomes clear when they dine at a hotel and watch the young people dancing a tango. Cherry says:

> "There must be something in all this new manner, if only one could get it. That couple down by the bar now, the girl with the *very* low back: they are doing it beautifully; she dips and rises like a bird in the air . . . a tired bird, though. That's the disconcerting thing. It all seems so tired."
>
> Seabury agreed with her cheerfully that it was charming, though tired. He felt a gathering chill in the lady on his right. Presently she said impatiently: "Haven't you had enough of this, Chetty?"
>
> Mrs. Allison sighed. "You never see anything in it, do you, dear?"
>
> "I see wriggling. They look to me like lizards dancing — or reptiles coupling."
>
> "Oh, no, dear! No! They are such sweet young things. But they are dancing in a dream. I want to go and wake them up.

They are missing so much fun. Dancing ought to be open and free, with the lungs full; not mysterious and breathless. I wish I could see a *spirited* waltz again." [164]

If Cherry's defense of the present seems rather halfhearted, it at least shows that Willa Cather had some awareness of the limitations of Gabrielle's attitude. But this does not keep her from letting Lady Longstreet carry the day. As is the case with *The Professor's House* and *My Mortal Enemy,* although the protagonist is criticized, it is his view that prevails in the end. Throughout the story one hears echoes of that famous outburst of Edmund Burke's: "The age of chivalry is gone. That of sophisters, economists, and calculators has succeeded, and the glory of Europe is extinguished forever." [165]

"The Old Beauty" is a reworking of the story of *A Lost Lady* in a different setting, although it is handled with considerably less skill. Like Marian Forrester, Gabrielle is a symbol of a civilization which has almost vanished:

> Lord H—— would recognize that this death [Gabrielle's] was more than the death of an individual. To him her name would recall a society whose manners, dress, conventions, loyalties, codes of honour, were different from anything existing in the world today.[166]

The modern world rejects the civilization of which Madame Longstreet was a part, and Willa Cather symbolizes this rejection by showing its changed attitude toward women. The references to this are both direct and indirect. At one point Henry Seabury muses:

> Perhaps the few very beautiful women he remembered in the past had been illusions, had benefited by a romantic tradition which played upon them like a kindly light . . . and by an attitude in men which no longer existed.[167]

This is the same attitude Marian Forrester had revealed in a conversation with Niel Herbert in *A Lost Lady:*

> "And tell me, Niel, do women really smoke after dinner now with the men, nice women? . . . It's all very well for actresses, but women can't be attractive if they do everything that men do."
> "I think just now it's the fashion for women to make themselves comfortable, before anything else."

Mrs. Forrester glanced at him as if he had said something shocking. "Ah, that's just it! The two things don't go together. Athletics and going to college and smoking after dinner — Do you like it? Don't men like women to be different from themselves? They used to."

Niel laughed. Yes, that was certainly the idea of Mrs. Forrester's generation.[168]

But more important than the direct references are the indirect ones. Two assaults are made on Lady Longstreet's femininity thirty years apart, the one on her physical person, the other on her sensibilities. In both cases she is rescued by Henry Seabury, who does the right thing at the right time. The distinction Willa Cather makes between the two incidents is the contrast she draws between two ages: in the first case the attack is made by a person outside Gabrielle's society who does not respect the dignity of women, in the second by two girls within that society who do not (according to Willa Cather) respect their own dignity. In the first case the assault is regarded as an exception to the norm; in the second it is the norm itself.

Upon looking at the rape episode, one notices that a very interesting fact emerges. The man who offers violence to Gabrielle, although not identified as a Jew, has most of the characteristics of the anti-Semitic stereotype which Willa Cather has used elsewhere. Thus he is a dark, stout banker, of whom Gabrielle says: "Of course his personality was repulsive to me. One knew at once that under his smoothness he was a vulgar person";[169] and Seabury comments, "That fellow had a very clever way of pushing himself,"[170] and "The man's accent must have told you that he belonged to a country you did not admire."[171] When Seabury leaves at midnight after spending the evening consoling Gabrielle, the following conversation takes place:

"At some other time I shall explain what you saw here tonight. How could such a thing happen in one's own house, in an English-speaking city . . . ?"

"But that was not an English-speaking man who went out from here. He is an immigrant who has made a lot of money. He does not belong."

"Yes, that is true. I wish you weren't going out to China. Not for long, I hope. It's a bad thing to be away from one's own people."[172]

The Willa Cather who writes, "It's a bad thing to be away from one's own people," is not the same Willa Cather who took so much delight in riding around to the homes of her French and Scandinavian and Bohemian neighbors in Nebraska and observing all that went on there. It is not the Willa Cather who created Alexandra Bergson or Marie Shabata or Ántonia Cuzak. Instead, it is an older, sadder, but not wiser Willa Cather who has forgotten how to read her own books.

But the anti-Semitic stereotype has an importance in Willa Cather's thinking that goes beyond her acceptance of it as part of the old Populist explanation of what was wrong with the modern world. In her fiction the figure of the Jew is made to symbolize not only commercial success but all the brutal vulgarity which she associates with the present day. For her the Jew is the present, and her fear and hatred of Jews is actually her fear and hatred of life.[173] In this connection it is interesting to note how often she casts the Jew in the role of sexual aggressor. Sigmund Stein in "Scandal" had sexual pretensions to the singer Kitty Ayrshire; Louie Marsellus in *The Professor's House* had dared to marry the dead Tom Outland's fiancée, and the dark, pushing banker in "The Old Beauty" is on the verge of violating the heroine when he is stopped in the nick of time by the appearance of Henry Seabury murmuring, "Am I too early, Madame Longstreet?"[174] In view of Willa Cather's constant distrust of physical passion as expressed in her fiction it seems probable that sexual assault was for her a symbol of the ever present dangerousness of life. One thinks of Thea Kronborg's outcry upon being accosted, "Oh, let me *alone!*" and her subsequent retreat from the violence of human relations into the sanctuary of the world of art.

The second assault, the motor accident which serves as climax to the story, is so trivial as to appear ridiculous, for Willa Cather's choice of the knicker-clad girls as a symbol of what is wrong with the present is both inappropriate and superficial. The aftermath of the accident is described as follows:

> Immediately the two women from the other car sprang out and ran up to Seabury with shrill protestations; they were very careful drivers, had run this car twelve thousand miles and never had an accident, etc. They were Americans; bobbed, hatless, clad in dirty white knickers and sweaters. They addressed each other as "Marge" and "Jim." Seabury's forehead was bleeding: they repeatedly offered to plaster it up for him. . . .
>
> The two girls who had caused all the trouble had lit cigarettes and were swaggering about with their hands in their trousers

pockets, giving advice to the driver about his wheel. The Savoyard never lifted his eyes. He had not spoken since he ran his car into the wall. The sharp voices, knowingly ordering him to *"regardez, attendez,"* did not pierce his silence or his contempt.[175]

Gabrielle whispers to Seabury: "I think I am not hurt . . . faintness, a little palpitation. If you could get those creatures away . . ."[176] and, after this has been accomplished, Willa Cather comments, "Three elderly people had been badly shaken up and bruised, but the brief submersion in frightfulness was over."[177] This response is out of all proportion to the provocation and shows a complete lack of sense of humor. When Willa Cather writes, "'After one has been *exaltée,* there usually comes a shock. Oh, I don't mean the bruises we got! I mean the white breeches,'"[178] one would like to suspect her of displaying the flippancy of the Decadence; of implying, "Accidents can happen any time, but the white breeches — well, they really are uncivilized!" But the whole tone of "The Old Beauty" contradicts this interpretation, for the story is deadly serious. And this incident, slight as it is, is what finishes Gabrielle, for she is dead the next day.

These things being so, it is not surprising to hear that when the story was offered to the *Woman's Home Companion* in 1937 the editor, Gertrude Lane, said that although she would publish it, she did not feel any enthusiasm for it. Whereupon Willa Cather asked for her manuscript back. The story remained unpublished until it came out as the title piece of a posthumous volume issued the year after Miss Cather's death.[179]

So ended the third period of Willa Cather's development. As we have seen, it closed with her completely rejecting what she regarded as the sordidness of the present for what she considered to be the beauties of former times. This is not the first time we have seen her reject what was immediately around her in favor of what was more remote. From now on, and with ever increasing frequency, that for which she rejects her immediate surroundings is going to be the world of the past. This is not too hard to understand, although it may be hard to sympathize with. Willa Cather had spent forty-five years of her life trying to find herself, personally and artistically, and by the time she did so, in *My Ántonia,* the world in which she had just gained her bearings had all but disappeared. Small wonder that she saw the gap between the ideal and the real, the comely life and life as it actually is, as becoming painfully wide; it seemed too great for even the hero to bridge. Since the present departed widely from everything which she held dear, and since she felt that the past had allowed her to bring at least some of her ideals to fruition, she gradually came to identify all value with the past. Another way of putting it would be to say that after the First World War she felt she had lost the thread of continuity between present and past, and went to the past in search of it. Becoming convinced that this continuity could not be found, she finally gave up on the twentieth century entirely and tried to prolong the last lingering remnants of the Victorian age as long as possible.

To put the matter bluntly, in her third period Willa Cather's belief in the omnipotence of the will collided head-on with the plain hard fact of human limitations. This conflict may have been heightened by the radically changed environment of the twenties, which seemed less conducive than earlier decades of the century to the optimistic belief that desire is all, but some sort of clash was inevitable as the natural aristocrat neared fifty and the possibility of death came into view. At one point, in *The Professor's House,* Willa Cather almost rose to a tragic vision, when for a brief moment she seemed to realize that even the comely life, when achieved, may be a hollow conquest, that such triumphs as the will can have do not insure happiness or even freedom from pain. But instead of transcending herself and accepting the human lot as a limited thing — which would have brought her to aesthetic and emotional maturity — she turned away from it, and never afterward dealt with the ultimate problems. Her subsequent work, although often brilliant stylistically, would seldom contain the same head-on confrontation of human problems which her work had hitherto displayed.

CHAPTER V

THE WORLD OF THE PAST

They sat talking about people who were no longer in this world. She knew much more about them than he. Knew so much that her talk brought back not only the men, but their period; its security, the solid exterior, the exotic contradictions behind the screen; the deep, claret-coloured closing years of Victoria's reign. Nobody ever recognizes a period until it has gone by, he reflected: until it lies behind one it is merely everyday life.
— *"The Old Beauty"*

The feeling of being at home was complete, absolute: it made her sleepy. And that feeling was not so much the sense of being protected by her father and mother as of being with, and being one with, her brothers. It was the clan feeling, which meant life or death for the blood, not for the individual.
— *"The Best Years"*

Art is a concrete and personal and rather childish thing after all. . . . Art is too terribly human to be very "great," perhaps. Some very great artists have outgrown art, the men were bigger than the game. Tolstoi did, and Leonardo did. When I hear the last opuses, I think Beethoven did. Shakespeare died at fifty-three, but there is an awful veiled threat in The Tempest *that he too felt he had outgrown his toys, was about to put them away and free that spirit of Comedy and Lyrical Poetry and all the rest he held captive — quit play-making and verse-making for ever and turn his attention — to what, he did not hint, but it was probably merely to enjoy with all his senses that Warwickshire country which he loved to weakness — with a warm physical appetite. But he died before he had tried to grow old, never became a bitter old man wrangling with abstractions or creeds. . . .*
— *"Light on Adobe Walls"*

REJECTION OF THE PRESENT

The last few years of Willa Cather's career were by no means her happiest. As I have tried to show in the previous chapter, her discontent was not sudden but had been developing for some time. Part of its cause lay in the rigidity of her own character, part in the direction that modern-day America was taking, which seemed to contravene all the values of the America in which she had grown up. As F. Scott Fitzgerald said, in the twenties America went on the greatest, gaudiest spree in history; in the thirties the boom was followed by a bust, and in both decades the virtues Willa Cather cared for most seemed to the majority of Americans to be totally inapplicable to their time, mere relics of the horse-and-buggy days.[1] Willa Cather bitterly resented this turn of events. Never one to compromise, she turned her back on her contemporaries[2] and rejected the present as much as she felt the present rejecting her.

One sign of her revulsion against the times into which she had lived can be seen in her essay "148 Charles Street," which is a description of the Boston home of Mrs. James T. Fields, the publisher's widow to whom she had been introduced by Sarah Orne Jewett in 1908. Mrs. Fields had been extremely helpful in introducing her to the culture of the East and of New England; Willa Cather wrote: "At 148 Charles Street an American of the Apache period and territory could come to inherit a Colonial past." [3] While recalling all the good talk she had heard in that household, and all the stories of famous men who had been Mrs. Fields's guests, Willa Cather wistfully remarks:

> Today, in 1936, a garage stands on the site of 148 Charles Street. Only in memory exists the long, green-carpeted, softly lighted drawing-room, and the dining-table where Learning and Talent met, enjoying good food and good wit and rare vintages, looking confidently forward to the growth of their country in the finer amenities of life. Perhaps the garage and all it stands for represent the only real development, and have altogether taken the place of things formerly cherished on that spot. If we try to imagine those dinner-parties which Mrs. Fields describes, the scene is certainly not to us what it was to her: the lighting has changed, and the guests seem hundreds of years away from us. Their portraits no longer hang on the walls of our academies, nor are their "works" much discussed there. The English classes, we are told, can be "interested" only in contemporary writers, the newer the better. A letter from a prep-school boy puts it tersely: "D. H. Lawrence is rather rated a back-number here, but Faulkner keeps his end up."

Not the prep-school boys only are blithe to leave the past untroubled: their instructors pretty generally agree with them. And the retired professors who taught these instructors do not see

Shelley plain as they once did. The faith of the elders has been shaken.

Just how did this change come about, one wonders. When and where were the Arnolds overthrown and the Brownings devaluated? Was it at the Marne? At Versailles, when a new geography was being made on paper? Certainly the literary world which emerged from the war used the new coinage. In England and America the "masters" of the last century diminished in stature and pertinence, became remote and shadowy.[4]

This passage reveals one of the fundamental limitations of Willa Cather's mind. It apparently never occurred to her that the nineteenth-century writers to whom she looked up had been just as revolutionary in their day as twentieth-century authors were in her own, that Shelley, for example, had once been just as upsetting to oldsters as D. H. Lawrence now was to her.[5] She overlooks the fact that the past had once been the present. And, with all her love for the past, she lacked a sense of the continuity of history. She had no idea of history as movement or flow, as something which could be re-examined and reinterpreted; instead, she saw it as something static, accomplished, and not to be argued about.[6] For her the past was an achievement, much as a work of art is an achievement. Consequently, in her fourth period she turns to the past as sanctuary, much as she had formerly turned to the world of art.

When Willa Cather glanced backward, she was apt to be nostalgic. But when she looked at the world about her, her voice often became angry and shrill. Her later writings contain outbursts such as the following, which appeared in an essay on Sarah Orne Jewett, published in *Not Under Forty* (1936):

It is easy to understand why some of the young students who have turned back from the present to glance at Miss Jewett find very little on her pages. Imagine a young man, or woman, born in New York City, educated at a New York university, violently inoculated with Freud, hurried into journalism, knowing no more about New England country people (or country folk anywhere) than he has caught from motor trips or observed from summer hotels: what is there for him in *The Country of the Pointed Firs?*

This hypothetical young man is perhaps of foreign descent: German, Jewish, Scandinavian. To him English is merely a means of making himself understood, of communicating his ideas. He may write and speak American English correctly, but only as an

American may learn to speak French correctly. It is a surface
speech: he clicks the words out as a bank clerk clicks out silver
when you ask for change. For him the language has no emotional
roots. How could he find the talk of the Maine country people
anything but "dialect"? Moreover, the temper of the people which
lies behind the language is incomprehensible to him. He can see
what these Yankees *have not* (hence an epidemic of "suppressed
desire" plays and novels), what they *have,* their actual preferences
and their fixed scale of values, are absolutely dark to him. When
he tries to put himself in the Yankee's place, he attempts an impossible substitution.[7]

This essay, like the story called "The Old Beauty," which was written
at about the same time, shows the tremendous narrowing of her sympathies which has occurred since the days when she wrote her Nebraska
novels. One detects behind the peevishness of approaching old age
a yielding to attitudes which must have formed Willa Cather's prairie
background: the lack of desire to understand ways of life other than
her own, the rural-evangelical suspicion of big cities, and the angry
xenophobia of the Populist movement.[8]

In the last twenty years or so of her life the present seemed so odious
to Willa Cather that she did her best to insulate herself from it in every
way possible. She seemed to be withdrawing into a shell of her own.[9]
E. K. Brown says:

> . . . One cannot help but feel that in the years after 1931 Willa
> Cather was erecting walls behind which she carried on a life that
> was essentially inward — retrospective, creative, and speculative.
> One main reason for her withdrawal was undoubtedly a decline
> in physical energy. Edith Lewis believes that the physical and
> emotional exertion in the years of her mother's [last] illness
> [1928-1931] was so great and sustained for so long a period that
> Willa Cather never overcame altogether its effects. . . . Besides
> the failure in energy, her withdrawal was induced by what Harvey
> Newbranch, her friend from college times, describes as a slow
> spreading of the virus of pessimism. She was out of sympathy
> with the world about her.[10]

Elizabeth Sergeant writes:

> My happiest moments with Willa were still those when her own
> spring, now often frozen over in talk by fame, or busyness, or just

taciturnity, broke through and I found, gushing up in her, that old sense of intimacy between herself and her material, that freshness of heart and intense enthusiasm that I had first known in her. In her maturity, these elements were often buried deep below the surface.[11]

One of the signs of Willa Cather's withdrawal was her almost complete lack of interest in contemporary artistic movements. Earlier in life she had been interested in cubism and the school which called itself the Fauves,[12] but now nothing resembling a literary or artistic *avant garde* interested her in the slightest. Miss Sergeant writes:

. . . At heart, she was deeply aware of post-war life and literary currents, bewildering and new; and did not conceal from her friends her round aversion for the strong, disillusioned young talents that rushed along the literary seas, as if they alone possessed the rights of navigation.[13]

In art, as in life, she glanced backward rather than forward, and was very apt to think that old ways were the best ways:

If I spoke of Eugene O'Neill, my new enthusiasm, Willa looked at me sadly. But you're interested in experimentation, I said. You like Virginia Woolf, for instance, who deals with the inner side of things. *The Great God Brown, Desire Under the Elms* are dramatic discoveries. And that little Sheridan Street Theatre is just a stone's throw from Bank Street [Willa Cather's home in Greenwich Village from 1913 to 1927].

She wouldn't consider going there, not for a moment.

O'Neill's stark revelations of lust, fear, weakness, cruelty, even poignant goodness, on the stage, offended her taste. Why spend an evening in Hades when there were still good comedies of manners — even of morals, say Galsworthy's, on Broadway? [14]

UNCERTAINTY AND PERSONAL LOSSES

In the midst of this growing withdrawal from the life of the present, two things happened to Willa Cather which increased the precipitancy of her retreat. These were the loss of her home and the deaths of her parents. First the house on Bank Street in which she had lived for fourteen years was torn down and she was forced to move out. Miss Sergeant writes:

Though the city and its traffic had encroached on her quiet;
though intrusive feet overhead had forced her to rent — and keep
empty — a second apartment over her own, all that counted for
nothing when she faced a move. She felt like a turtle that was
losing its shell. The psychic pain of stripping off this protective
integument was unbearable; she was exposed and miserable.[15]

When thus deprived of the sanctuary of her home, Willa Cather could
not make up her mind about where to establish a new one. Her old
vacillation between city and country came to the fore:

In the enforced move from Bank Street in the autumn of 1927
with Miss Lewis [the friend with whom she shared an apartment
from 1909 until her death], Willa had chosen the Grosvenor as a
haven. This discreet small hotel on lower Fifth Avenue was to be
a temporary refuge only. But, in fact, four years elapsed before
they left it. Both Willa's and Miss Edith Lewis' mothers were
taken ill and must be visited in distant places. . . . But there
was another reason for the delay in finding a satisfactory home,
which Willa frankly stated to me: she could not decide what to
do next.

She was half inclined to live in the country: why endure these
urban restrictions and complications? But Miss Lewis was still
working in the city and wanted to go on doing so. So, obviously,
it must be an apartment. But where? Any decision that she almost
reached was followed by a recoil.[16]

Even more upsetting was the death of her father in March 1928.
"His death . . . was shattering to Willa," [17] writes Miss Sergeant, and
E. K. Brown remarks: "The death of Charles Cather was not only the
loss of a father; it meant the breakup of what Willa Cather had always
continued to think of as her home, the household in Red Cloud." [18]
Even more illuminating is an incident reported by Mildred Bennett:

The death of her father was a blow that Willa Cather could
scarcely accept. She paced frantically back and forth between the
house and the little Episcopal church where his body lay, wringing
her hands, apparently unable to conquer the grief and panic which
overwhelmed her. Acquaintances felt that her grief was not un-
mixed with still another emotion — fury — and resentment that
time, her greatest enemy, could effect such changes. She knew
that her home would never be the same again. Her close friends,

trying to help her regain some of her lost control, talked with her for hours to convince her if they could that the beauty and fullness of his eighty years was all that one could expect from a well-spent life. At length she calmed down, but the episode serves well to illustrate her flat refusal to accept the dictatorship of time.[19]

The reader of Willa Cather's biography finds it easy to sympathize with her early struggle to break away from her environment and make something of herself. A spunky refusal to be passively molded by life is always admirable. But to refuse to face or acknowledge advancing old age is something else again. Evidently Willa Cather was reluctant to surrender her already discredited faith in the omnipotence of the will; she would still like to believe that desire is all.

THE RETREAT TO THE FAMILY

As an accompaniment to the calamity and personal loss of the late twenties, a marked change took place in Willa Cather's outlook. This can be only imperfectly documented from her life, owing to an intense desire for privacy and seclusion which became almost overwhelming at this time.[20] Nevertheless, anyone examining the stories and novels which she wrote in her fourth period cannot help seeing that the values they express differ significantly from those found in her earlier work. Briefly, there is a shift in interest from the values inherent in extreme individualism to the values held by a group, particularly the family group. One can sum up her entire lifetime search for values by describing it as a movement first away from the family as an institution and then toward the family. In the early part of her career, when she was breaking away from her own family, her heroes and heroines are doing exactly the same thing; hence her protagonists at this time are heroic individualists such as Harvey Merrick, Thea Kronborg, Ántonia, and Alexandra. But after more than fifty years of battling with life Willa Cather seems to have decided that the heroic individual was not monarch of all he surveyed, and that there were limits to his will. Thereupon she began moving mentally back toward the very institution she had formerly struggled so hard to escape, and sought the source of all value in the family unit. The true secret of life she now held to reside not in the self-confidence of talented youth, but in the traditional wisdom of the elders of the tribe. On more than one occasion, these turned out to be members of her own parents' generation.

Whatever the cause, it is an indisputable fact that the protagonists she now chooses to create are most spiritually at home when in the bosom of their families. That this was hastened by the deaths of both of her parents within three years of each other seems highly likely. This attitude has its beginnings in the final pages of *My Mortal Enemy*, where Myra Henshawe declares her spiritual affinity with her uncle, but it grows rapidly until in the writings of Willa Cather's fourth period it sets the dominant tone. Gone almost completely from her pages is the exaltation of the heroic individual, either as a romantic or artistic rebel or as the dynamic moving force behind a family. The heroic individual is now rarely considered as having any importance; even personality tends to become merely an attribute of group life. Each step taken away from the family is a step into danger (*Lucy Gayheart, Sapphira and the Slave Girl,* and "The Best Years"), and the only significant action which can be undertaken is that which furthers the family purposes ("Old Mrs. Harris" and *Shadows on the Rock*).

But once the safety of solidarity within the family unit had been achieved, Willa Cather evidently found that she could not rest in it. She apparently was unable to forget her own early triumphs, all of which had involved the depiction of protagonists who were heroic individualists. Consequently, whenever she became something less than desperate about the uncertainties of the modern age, she would revert to the habit of writing about individualists, but always with the conviction that such characters would be doomed to defeat. The result is that the stories of her fourth period turn out to be of two kinds: those which emphasize the group and especially the family (*Shadows on the Rock,* "Old Mrs. Harris," and *Sapphira and the Slave Girl*) and those which contain a sentimental exaltation of the individual, who nevertheless pathetically perishes (*Lucy Gayheart* and "The Best Years").

The Elimination of Conflict: The Past as Safe Harbor

Another way in which these stories can be divided is as follows: those which deal in a very sentimental way with the world as it was at the turn of the century (most of these take place in the Middle West of her childhood), and those which take place in a past so remote as to be untroubled by the problems of a commercial or industrial era, usually in a period long before Willa Cather was born. This last group comprises her two "Catholic" novels, *Death Comes for the Archbishop* (1927), set in nineteenth-century New Mexico, and *Shadows on the Rock* (1931), set in seventeenth-century Quebec. The Middle Western group includes the three stories published in *Obscure Destinies* (1932) and one novel, *Lucy Gayheart* (1935). Her last novel, *Sapphira and the Slave Girl* (1940), takes place in the pre–Civil War South and is a Protestant affair, having to do with the abolitionist movement in the flight of a slave on the Underground Railroad. For several reasons, it deserves treatment by itself. Consequently, I will treat the writings of Willa Cather's final years under three headings: the Catholic Past, the Middle West Revisited, and the Protestant Past.

The most noteworthy feature of the writing of Willa Cather's later years is the lengths to which she goes in order to eliminate conflict from her stories. I have tried to show that even in her early work she was unable to resolve the struggles which arose as a result of the interaction of her characters. In *My Ántonia* the relations between Ántonia and Larry Donovan which result in his abandoning her with a child on the way are not presented but described, and described at third hand, at that; in *Alexander's Bridge* and *O Pioneers!* the moral problems presented are not resolved at all but eliminated by the adventitious deaths of the principals, and in *The Professor's House* the moral problem is shuffled off when the protagonist is accidentally rescued from death. All these devices show the writer to have been extremely uneasy in the presence of major conflict between her characters, and ready to adopt all sorts of expedients in order to cope with the problem. Now that she has reached her fourth period she deliberately sets out to write stories in which conflict will not occur. She explicitly states this in a letter to *The Commonweal* Magazine describing the genesis of *Death Comes for the Archbishop:*

> I had all my life wanted to do something in the *style of legend,* which is *absolutely the reverse of dramatic treatment.* Since I first saw the Puvis de Chavannes frescoes of the life of Saint Geneviève in my student days, I have wished that I could try something a little like that in prose; *something without accent,* with none of the artificial elements of composition. In the Golden Legend the martyrdoms of the saints are no more dwelt upon than are the trivial incidents of their lives; it is as though all human experiences, measured against one supreme spiritual experience, were of about the same importance. *The essence of such writing is not to hold the note, not to use an incident for all there is in it — but to touch and pass on.* [The italics are mine.] [21]

"Absolutely the reverse of dramatic treatment" applies equally well to her next book, *Shadows on the Rock* (1931). Even the appreciative

Wilbur Cross states in his review that in it "Action is reduced to a minimum. . . . Quarrels are indicated, not described";[22] whereas the more critical John Chamberlain, writing for the *New York Times,* says: "The lack of conflict in the method is almost fatal to continued enjoyment of 'Shadows on the Rock'; once one has got the flavor — and it is the flavor of wine of a good vintage — there is little excuse for going on. . . . One can only wish that Willa Cather had chosen a more dramatic method."[23] This tendency toward the elimination of all conflict from her fiction is equally marked in her later writings, with the single exception of her last novel, *Sapphira and the Slave Girl.* But even this exception is more apparent than real, for the conflict which is developed in the book's first part is completely undercut before the book is finished, as will be described later. The elimination of conflict in a novel must have been to Willa Cather a tempting ideal. How it worked out in practice we will see later on.

The absence of conflict and the choice of the more or less remote past as setting have significant consequences. By having the action of her stories take place at a safe remove from the present, she is able to write about what she wants to without having her characters face up to the major problems of either their day or ours; as Archibald MacLeish has put it, "The dead are excellent hosts; they have no objections."[24] Even in her earlier work she was not above manipulating her material in order to avoid all conflict, and from now on this becomes a standard practice of hers. It is hard to escape the impression that her use of historical material is self-indulgently escapist, and the world of the past becomes no more for her than just another kind of sanctuary. This is a serious charge, but one which I believe to be justified.

THE CATHOLIC PAST

Death Comes for the Archbishop and *Shadows on the Rock* resemble each other in so many ways that they inevitably invite comparison. Both stand in sharpest contrast to the novels Willa Cather had written immediately before them. In place of the agonized tension of that group one finds instead a flat calm, a fact which bodes ill for the artist's future development. There is a shift in setting from the America of the present day to the America of the more remote past; from Calvinist and capitalist society to one that is Catholic; there is a change in the values affirmed from the democratic and individualistic to the hierarchal and feudal. It is evident that Willa Cather is shifting her interest from the individual to the group; this can be seen not only by comparing these two books with her previous ones, but also by examining the structure of the novels themselves. Both show an orderly, methodical, even ritualistic generation of men working within a rigidly hierarchal social framework, taking over from an earlier pioneering generation which had lived a life of heroic adventure. In *Death Comes for the Archbishop* Willa Cather presents this shift as being a good thing, but in *Shadows on the Rock* she begins to have her doubts and feels the necessity of reintroducing the individualistic hero once more.

Death Comes for the Archbishop: THE RECOVERY OF THE PAST AND THE TRIUMPH OF ORDER

Death Comes for the Archbishop is a hard book to criticize because as a nondramatic book it is so loosely constructed and contradictory in character that almost any statement taken from the text can be refuted by some other statement taken from another part of the text. However, certain themes are insisted upon more than their opposites, and of these the most frequently iterated is that of the return to the old ways, or the recovery of the past. This first appears in the Prologue in Rome in which several high churchmen are discussing the appointment of a bishop to New Mexico, which has newly been annexed to the territory of the United States. The problems he will meet arc outlined as follows:

> "Your Eminence, I beg you to follow me. This country was evangelized in fifteen hundred, by the Franciscan Fathers. It has been allowed to drift for nearly three hundred years and is not yet dead. It still pitifully calls itself a Catholic country, and tries to keep the forms of religion without instruction. The old mission churches are in ruins. The few priests are without guidance or discipline. They are lax in religious observance, and some of them live in open concubinage." [25]

The problem set for the new bishop is the reconversion of a people to their former ways from which they have backslid. This is a logical subject for an author who had become convinced that contemporary America had backslid and would do well to return to the virtues it had formerly practiced. The emphasis in this passage is on forms, on guidance, on discipline; what is wanted is ritual and the ordering of life which ritual brings with it. Thus the novel's second major theme is introduced: the necessity for and eventual triumph of order. This, too, is made explicit in the Prologue. In describing the qualifications which the new bishop will need, one of the churchmen says:

"The new Vicar must be a young man, of strong constitution, full of zeal, and above all, intelligent. He will have to deal with savagery and ignorance, with dissolute priests and political intrigue. He must be a man to whom order is necessary — as dear as life."

The Spaniard's coffee-coloured eyes showed a glint of yellow as he glanced sidewise at his guest. "I expect, from your exordium, that you have a candidate — and that he is a French priest, perhaps?"

"You guess rightly, Monsignor. I am glad to see that we have the same opinion of French missionaries."

"Yes," said the Cardinal lightly, "they are the best missionaries. Our Spanish fathers made good martyrs, but the French Jesuits accomplish more. They are the great organizers."

"Better than the Germans?" asked the Venetian, who had Austrian sympathies.

"Oh, the Germans classify, but the French arrange! The French missionaries have a sense of proportion and rational adjustment. They are always trying to discover the logical relation of things. It is a passion with them." [26]

As a result of their deliberations the choice lights upon a Frenchman, Father Jean Marie Latour, who thereupon becomes the hero of the book. His task is to restore order to the new diocese, and the rest of the narrative chronicles, albeit very intermittently, his efforts to impose a French pattern of religious culture upon a population which is quite mixed, since it consists partly of Indians who follow their own traditional religion, partly of Mexicans who have developed their own peculiar brand of Catholicism, and partly of Anglo-Americans of Protestant background. Throughout the long, rambling narrative the twin themes of order and recovery of the past are never very far from his thoughts. In fact, the very first time we see him with his new parishioners they are clamoring to have the lost gift of Catholicism restored to them. He has been traveling through the desert and is languishing of thirst when suddenly he comes upon a remote little Mexican settlement called Agua Secreta, or Hidden Water. The very name turns out to be symbolic, for the hidden water refers to a spiritual spring as well as a literal one; the natives beg him to renew the Catholic rites which have almost been forgotten since their grandfathers' time.[27] Father Latour meditates upon the significance of this at close of day, as he watches the sun go down behind the tiny hamlet:

> This settlement was his Bishopric in miniature; hundreds of square miles of thirsty desert, then a spring, a village, old men trying to remember their catechism to teach their grandchildren. The Faith planted by the Spanish friars and watered with their blood was not dead; it awaited only the toil of the husbandman.[28]

Later in the book his closest friend and confidant, Father Vaillant, reflects in a similar manner:

> "Down near Tucson a Pima Indian convert once asked me to go off into the desert with him, as he had something to show me. He took me into a place so wild that a man less accustomed to these things might have mistrusted and feared for his life. We descended into a terrifying canyon of black rock, and there in the depths of a cave, he showed me a golden chalice, vestments and cruets, all the paraphernalia for celebrating Mass. His ancestors had hidden these sacred objects there when the mission was sacked by Apaches, he did not know how many generations ago. The secret had been handed down in his family, and I was the first priest who had ever come to restore to God his own. To me, that is the situation in a parable. The Faith, in the wild frontier, is like a buried treasure; they guard it, but they do not know how to use it to their soul's salvation. A word, a prayer, a service, is all that is needed to set free those souls in bondage. I confess I am covetous of that mission. I desire to be the man who restores these lost children to God." [29]

The theme of recovery is intimately associated with that of ritualistic order, for in both these passages what the natives need is instruction in ritual — prayers, services, the catechism — before they can make use of their faith. We have entered into a new period in which Willa Cather's characters look to the past in hopes of recovering an order which they are unable to find in the present. Immediately after Father Latour's musing on the village of Agua Secreta (in the very next sentence, as a matter of fact) his thoughts turn toward the problem of imposing order upon his new bishopric, against the inclinations of some of the more rebellious of the local clergy:

> He was not troubled about the revolt in Santa Fé, or the powerful old native priest who led it — Father Martinez, of Taos, who

had ridden over from his parish expressly to receive the new Vicar
and to drive him away. He was rather terrifying, that old priest,
with his big head, violent Spanish face, and shoulders like a
buffalo; but the day of his tyranny was almost over.[30]

It has sometimes been suggested that in Father Latour Willa Cather
meant to present the ideal pioneer, one who was able to tame and at the
same time civilize a new land.[31] But Fathers Latour and Vaillant are
by no means the first Catholic missionaries to penetrate the region; the
ground had already been broken two centuries earlier, and all they have
to do is to reclaim their diocese. It is the seventeenth-century Spanish
Fathers who are the real pioneers; they are the ones who brought
European society to New Spain and are the literary equivalents of the
Nebraska pioneers of Willa Cather's earlier novels. All the two Frenchmen have to do is build on their predecessors' foundations. Willa Cather
recognizes this, for late in the book she has the Archbishop admit the
fact himself:

He had, indeed, for years, directed the thoughts of the young
priests whom he instructed to the fortitude and devotion of these
first missionaries, the Spanish friars; declaring that his own life,
when he first came to New Mexico, was one of ease and comfort
compared with theirs. If he had used to be abroad for weeks together on short rations, sleeping in the open, unable to keep his
body clean, at least he had the sense of being in a friendly world,
where by every man's fireside a welcome awaited him.
But the Spanish Fathers who came up to Zuñi, then went north
to the Navajos, west to the Hopis, east to all the pueblos scattered
between Albuquerque and Taos, they came into a hostile country,
carrying little provisionment but their breviary and crucifix. When
their mules were stolen by Indians, as often happened, they
proceeded on foot, without a change of raiment, without food or
water. A European could scarcely imagine such hardships. The
old countries were worn to the shape of human life, made into an
investiture, a sort of second body, for man. There the wild herbs
and the wild fruits and the forest fungi were edible. The streams
were sweet water, the trees afforded shade and shelter. But in the
alkali deserts the water holes were poisonous, and the vegetation
offered nothing to a starving man. Everything was dry, prickly,
sharp; Spanish bayonet, juniper, greasewood, cactus; the lizard,
the rattlesnake, — and man made cruel by a cruel life. Those early

missionaries threw themselves naked upon the hard heart of a country that was calculated to try the endurance of giants. They thirsted in its deserts, starved among its rocks, climbed up and down its terrible canyons on stone-bruised feet, broke long fasts by unclean and repugnant food. Surely these endured *Hunger, Thirst, Cold, Nakedness,* of a kind beyond any conception St. Paul and his brethren could have had.[32]

If anybody in the book is a pioneer, it is not Bishop Latour himself but his right-hand man Father Vaillant. It is he who goes to the Colorado gold fields after the strike on Cripple Creek and is the only person in the novel who actually does missionary work in non-Catholic territory. But Willa Cather very carefully keeps him subordinate to the less enterprising, more introverted Archbishop. She does not let him appear at all in the first thirty-five pages; she often has him disappear from the narrative for long stretches of time, and she makes him die before the Archbishop, although with the originals of Fathers Latour and Vaillant the reverse was true.[33] No doubt is left in the reader's mind as to which of the two is her main concern and her real hero. Formerly she had glorified the pioneer spirit as the highest expression of what was finest in human nature. Now she finds that spirit less interesting and less important than the quiet and orderly life epitomized by Jean Marie Latour.

THE INTERNATIONAL THEME AS ORDER AND THE OVERSIMPLIFICATION OF NATIONAL TYPES

Order is of fundamental importance in *Death Comes for the Archbishop,* and Willa Cather makes use of it in dealing with what had once been the great theme of her prairie novels: the coming of the European to America. The problem faced by the European immigrant was essentially that of imposing order on chaos, in the great conflict between nature and civilization which played such a vital role in nineteenth-century American thought. In *Death Comes for the Archbishop* the problem is more complicated because there are no less than five civilizations depicted in the book. First there are the Indians who maintain an almost impenetrable reserve and are extreme traditionalists;[34] when their traditions exalt order, Miss Cather admires them; when their traditions deviate from it, she does not. Then come the Spanish, represented in the book by the seventeenth-century Jesuit fathers who first colonized southwestern North America. Willa Cather describes them as intensely

vital and willing to sacrifice themselves for an ideal, but — and this is
a serious drawback in her eyes — they are not given to neatness or
order.[35] Next come the Mexicans whom she characterizes as violent,
colorful, melodramatic, and more than a little childlike.[36] These form
by far the largest part of the population over which the Bishop holds
ecclesiastical sway. Then come the Anglo-Americans, who figure less
prominently in the book than the other groups, although they were
rapidly coming to dominate the Southwest at the very time the action of
the book occurs. Aside from providing an unobtrusive background of
willing and co-operative fur traders and military officers, they usually
appear as "white trash," as in the case of the low-caste-Protestant family
that enslaves the Mexican woman Sada, and the degenerate murderer
Buck Scales, although occasionally they rise to nobility as in the case of
the gentlemanly but somewhat anemic portrayal of Kit Carson.[37]
Finally there are the French. These, represented by Father Vaillant and
his Bishop, stand for order in the highest degree, and it is of them that
Willa Cather most fully approves. For her at this stage of her life order
has become the very essence of civilization, and it is for this reason that
she regards the great civilizing force in the nineteenth-century Southwest as being not the Americans but the French.

Willa Cather's characterization of the five groups tends to reduce
each one to a single national trait: the Indians' silent reserve, the
Spaniards' passionate intensity, the childlike emotionalism of the Mexicans, the sordid greed of the Americans, and the civilized order and
logic of the French. Naturally this results in two-dimensional or "flat"
characters. This is especially true of the minor characters, of which
there are a great many. Consequently there is a tremendous falling-off
of richness in characterization as compared with previous works, a fact
which bodes no good to a book which already has eschewed some of
the main resources by which a novel can build and sustain interest.
Willa Cather's passion for order has led her to a greatly oversimplified
conception of character.

The greatest exemplar of order as the guiding principle of the European civilizing influence is of course the Archbishop himself. When we
first meet him he is traveling through an arid stretch of country in
central New Mexico: a desolate region where the thousands of conical
red hills present an aspect so uniform as to be a "geometrical night-
mare." This remote impersonal landscape is suddenly humanized by
the presence of a cruciform juniper tree: "Living vegetation could not
present more faithfully the form of the Cross."[38] Father Latour, recognizing how nature can mirror human aspirations, then gets down and

kneels before it. Willa Cather takes time out to describe his appearance:

> Under his buckskin riding-coat he wore a black vest and the
> cravat and collar of a churchman. A young priest, at his devo-
> tions; and a priest in a thousand, one knew at a glance. His
> bowed head was not that of an ordinary man, — it was built for
> the seat of a fine intelligence. His brow was open, generous, reflec-
> tive, his features handsome and somewhat severe. There was a
> singular elegance about the hands below the fringed cuffs of the
> buckskin jacket. Everything showed him to be a man of gentle
> birth — brave, sensitive, courteous. His manners, even when he
> was alone in the desert, were distinguished. He had a kind of
> courtesy toward himself, toward his beasts, toward the juniper
> tree before which he knelt, and the God whom he was addressing.[39]

Bishop Latour's politeness toward everyone and everything show him
to be both reasonable and humane; he is a great believer in dignity and
order in human relations. At first glance this passage might seem to
have been written by any one of half a dozen minor novelists of the
nineteenth century. But on closer inspection it turns out to contain, in
much watered-down form, several of the ideas found in Willa Cather's
previous works. Father Latour is at once identified as an exceptional individual (one in a thousand), but — and this is a great
change from the protagonists of the prairie novels — he is also a social
aristocrat (he behaved like a man of gentle birth). This characterization is further evidence of a transformation of Willa Cather's earlier
ideas of natural aristocracy: as she grew older she came to believe
more and more rigidly in the idea of blood and family.[40] Almost all the
characters she approved of in her later life had to be genteel. Even
the trapper and Indian fighter Kit Carson is toned down and made
into a gentleman in order to bring him within the confines of Willa
Cather's own special version of the genteel tradition. This emphasis on
blood coincides with her treatment of national stereotypes and tends to
make the characters flat and uninteresting.

ORDER AND PERSONALITY: TRADITION FOR ITS OWN SAKE

From all that is said in the book about the importance of order in the
life of a French Catholic bishop, one might suppose that the tradition
which Willa Cather considered as most likely to embody order was the
Catholic tradition. But this is not the case. This is made abundantly

clear by the attitude she has her hero take toward the Indians. At one point the Bishop defends them against the criticism of an old white trader who has said, "The things they value most are worth nothing to us. They've got their own superstitions, and their minds will go round and round in the same old ruts till Judgment Day." Willa Cather writes, "Father Latour remarked that their veneration for old customs was a quality he liked in the Indians, and that it played a great part in his own religion."[41]

Willa Cather's treatment of the young Indian boy Jacinto, who is Father Latour's companion on many of his journeys, is further evidence of the respect in which they are held:

> The Bishop seldom questioned Jacinto about his thoughts or beliefs. He didn't think it polite, and he believed it to be useless. There was no way in which he could transfer his own memories of European civilization into the Indian mind, and he was quite willing to believe that behind Jacinto there was a long tradition, a story of experience, which no language could translate to him.[42]

By balancing one against the other, the Bishop suggests that the Indian tradition is at least as worthy of respect as the European. Sometimes indeed he treats it as if it were more so. This is suggested by the passage describing Father Latour's reflections upon watching Jacinto bury the embers of a fire after they had had a meal together:

> Father Latour judged that, just as it was the white man's way to assert himself in any landscape, to change it, make it over a little (at least to leave some mark or memorial of his sojourn), it was the Indian's way to pass through a country without disturbing anything; to pass and leave no trace, like fish through the water, or birds through the air."[43]

The Indian, in other words, considers himself to be part of nature and not above it, and is the very antithesis of the Willa Cather pioneer:

> Moreover, these Indians disliked novelty and change. They came and went by the old paths worn into the rock by the feet of their fathers, used the old natural stairway of stone to climb to their mesa towns, carried water from the old springs, even after white men had dug wells. . . .
> They seemed to have none of the European's desire to "master" nature, to arrange and re-create. They spent their ingenuity in the

other direction; in accommodating themselves to the scene in which they found themselves. This was not so much from indolence, the Bishop thought, as from an inherited caution and respect. It was as if the great country were asleep, and they wished to carry on their lives without awakening it. . . . The land and all that it bore they treated with consideration; not attempting to improve it, they never desecrated it.[44]

In view of Willa Cather's interest in the recovery of the past in this book and her general animus against change, it is pretty clear that she regarded this attitude as praiseworthy. An even stronger expression of respect for Indian tradition as such is seen in her treatment of the Navajos:

Though this nomad people were much slower to adopt white man's ways than the home-staying Indians who dwelt in pueblos, and were much more indifferent to missionaries and the white man's religion, Father Latour felt a superior strength in them. There was purpose and conviction behind their inscrutable reserve; something active and quick, something with an edge.[45]

These last few lines show an association between tradition, reserve, and the ability to act effectively which perhaps explains why order became so important to Willa Cather in later life. To her mind the kind of order embodied in tradition helped organize personality; it determined not only what to do but what not to do. Thus tradition becomes both a guide to purposeful action and a safeguard against those spontaneous emotions of which she was so afraid.

Willa Cather's treatment of the Indian suggests still another conclusion which is helpful in evaluating the Catholic tone of the novel. It seems clear that on several occasions she has her hero indicate that he considers the Indian tradition every bit as admirable as the Catholic. This raises the interesting possibility that it is not really Catholicism at all that he is most interested in, but rather tradition for its own sake. To put it mildly, this is a strange position for an ecclesiastical protagonist to take, and one which casts doubts on the views of those who say that this is a Catholic novel.

ORDER *vs.* FERTILITY: TRADITION AS VITALITY DENIED

Of course Willa Cather does not have the Bishop approve of all branches of Indian tradition. There are stories about an undying fire kept burning in the mountains and a ceremonial snake to which babies were supposed to be fed. This darker side of Indian tradition is hinted at in the passage in which the Bishop and Jacinto, suddenly caught in a snowstorm, save their lives by taking refuge in a ceremonial cave:

> Looking up, the Bishop saw a peculiar formation in the rocks; two rounded edges, one directly over the other, with a mouthlike opening between. They suggested two great stone lips, slightly parted and thrust outward. Up to this mouth Jacinto climbed quickly by footholds . . . and helped the Bishop to clamber up. . . .
>
> He found himself in a lofty cavern . . . — the only light within was that which came through the narrow aperture between the stone lips. [46]

The air in the cave is glacial, and its fetid odor repels the Bishop until Jacinto lights a fire to freshen and purify it. Before doing this however, the boy plasters up an irregularly shaped hole in the back of the cavern, at which place the Bishop finds him later in the night, listening intently, as if waiting for something living to make a sound. No mention is made of snake worship, but the suggestion is there.[47] Another eerie feature of the cavern is an extraordinary vibration; "it hummed like a hive of bees, like a heavy roll of distant drums." [48] The Bishop mentions this to Jacinto, and the latter takes him into a tunnel far back into the mountain. By putting his ear against a crack in the floor the Bishop can hear "a great underground river flowing through a resounding cavern":

> The water was far, far below, perhaps as deep as the foot of the mountain, a flood moving in utter blackness under the ribs of antediluvian rock. It was not a rushing noise, but the sound of a great flood moving with majesty and power.
>
> "It is terrible," he said at last, as he rose.[49]

The meaning of the underground river is obscure; yet it would probably be fair to say it represents the primitive life forces at the base of all existence. The fact that Bishop Latour finds the fetid air highly disagreeable and calls the underground stream terrible suggests a feeling of discomfort and fear upon approaching the sources of vitality:

> The Bishop kept his word, and never spoke of Jacinto's cave to anyone, but he did not cease from wondering about it. It flashed

into his mind from time to time, and always with a shudder of repugnance quite unjustified by anything he had experienced there. It had been a hospitable shelter to him in his extremity. Yet afterward he remembered the storm itself, even his exhaustion, with a tingling sense of pleasure. But the cave, which had probably saved his life, he remembered with horror. No tales of wonder, he told himself, would ever tempt him into a cavern hereafter.[50]

One need not be a Freudian to sense that there is something quite peculiar in Willa Cather's handling of this episode. Lover of tradition as she was, she nevertheless veered away from that part of the Indian tradition that had to do with the fertility cult. The most vital part of Indian religious ceremonies, which exerted such a fascination over D. H. Lawrence and others, she has her protagonist regard with distrust and fear.

ORDER AND THE AESTHETIC RESPONSE:
TRADITION AND PHYSICAL SENSATION

So it appears that at this point Willa Cather is all for tradition when it stands for orderliness and all against it when it does not. In this book she goes so far as to give order domain even over physical sensation. This is most clearly seen in the case of two objects of aesthetic value that have crossed the Atlantic: namely the Angelus bell and the recipe for soup.

The first of these two more nearly fits the usual conception of what constitutes an object of aesthetic interest. Father Latour wakes up one morning under the pleasing delusion that he is in Rome, the reason being that he wakes to the sound of the Angelus ringing. This cannot be; there are no bells in New Mexico. But it turns out that he is wrong; his friend Father Vaillant has dug up an old bell in the basement of the church with an inscription in Spanish on it and the date 1356. Presumably it had been brought all the way up from Mexico City by oxcart — a task of heroic magnitude. Father Vaillant tells a story about it of how it had been pledged to St. Joseph in the wars with the Moors:

"... the people of some besieged city brought all their plate and silver and gold ornaments and threw them in with the baser metals. There is certainly a good deal of silver in the bell, nothing else would account for its tone."

The Bishop, however, is struck by the fact that the bell is somewhat
oriental in tone, and tries to account for that fact:

> Father Latour reflected. "And the silver of the Spaniards was
> really Moorish, was it not? If not actually of Moorish make,
> copied from their design. The Spaniards knew nothing about
> working silver except as they learned it from the Moors."
>
> "What are you doing, Jean? Trying to make my bell out to be
> an infidel?" Father Joseph asked impatiently. . . . "I notice that
> scholars always manage to dig out something belittling," he com-
> plained.
>
> "Belittling? I should say the reverse. I am glad to think there
> is Moorish silver in your bell. When we first came here, the one
> good workman we found in Santa Fé was a silversmith. The
> Spaniards handed on their skill to the Mexicans, and the Mexicans
> have taught the Navajos to work silver; but it all came from the
> Moors."[51]

This passage points up the temperamental difference between the two
men, inasmuch as Father Vaillant is concerned with the religious significance of the bell, whereas the Bishop is interested in its aesthetic
significance. For our present purposes however the passage makes two
important points. One is that it indicates a complex awareness on the
Bishop's part of the cosmopolitan interdependence of cultures — the
Christian on the non-Christian, the Spanish on the Moorish — so much
so that Father Vaillant objects to it as tending to make even Chris-
tendom look provincial. The other is that the Bishop obviously derives
pleasure from the thought that the bell descends from a long tradition
of craftsmanship. The very fact of its having had a long history is
almost made a condition for its enjoyment.

The second object of aesthetic consideration appears in the description of the dinner Father Vaillant prepares for himself and Father
Latour on Christmas Day. The latter has been writing home to his
brother that "we have no green vegetables here in winter, and no one
seems ever to have heard of that blessed plant, the lettuce. Joseph finds
it hard to do without salad oil, he always had it in Ohio, though it was
a great extravagance." [52] Father Joseph sets the table before his friend
and brings him a dark onion soup with croutons:

> The Bishop tasted it critically and smiled at his companion.
> After the spoon had travelled to his lips a few times, he put it
> down and leaning back in his chair remarked,

"Think of it, *Blanchet;* in all this vast country between the Mississippi and the Pacific Ocean, there is probably not another human being who could make a soup like this."

"Not unless he is a Frenchman," said Father Joseph. He had tucked a napkin over the front of his cassock and was losing no time in reflection.

"I am not deprecating your individual talent, Joseph," the Bishop continued, "but, when one thinks of it, a soup like this is not the work of one man. It is the result of a constantly refined tradition. There are nearly a thousand years of history in this soup."

Father Joseph frowned intently at the earthen pot in the middle of the table. . . . *"C'est ça, c'est vrai,"* he murmured.[53]

The case of Fray Baltazar, to be discussed later, is a different matter altogether; there gourmandizing is treated as the sin which brings about the hero's downfall, but here it is regarded as a positive virtue. Nor is this the only place in the book where good eating receives a surprising amount of attention; at one point Father Vaillant drives a Mexican cook out of the kitchen of a ranch house at which he is staying in order to prepare a lamb roast in such a way as not to offend his sense of taste.[54] The triviality of this literary treatment of food for its own sake shows how Willa Cather had degraded Pater's doctrine of beautiful sensations in her old age. But the real importance of this discourse on onion soup's antiquity lies in the fact that the exquisiteness of taste is seen to lie in the eater's consciousness that it comes out of a long tradition of soupmaking; in other words, even sensuous appetite is linked to the theme of recovery of the past. Not only the aesthetic response but even physical delight is now made dependent upon tradition.

THE ROCK AS SANCTUARY: ORDER AS SAFETY AND RETREAT

It is evident that tradition has come to play an overwhelmingly important role in Willa Cather's thought, and has managed to attract to itself a great many things which are not normally associated with it and do not belong with it. But the most revealing glorification of order and tradition in the book occurs in a chapter called "The Rock." During the course of a missionary journey, Bishop Latour and Jacinto come to two great mesas, the Enchanted Mesa and Acoma. The Bishop is intrigued. How, he asks, "did men first think of living on the top of naked rocks like these, hundreds of feet in the air, without soil or water?"

Jacinto shrugged. "A man can do a whole lot when they hunt him day and night like an animal. Navajos on the north, Apaches on the south; the Ácoma run up a rock to be safe."

All this plain, the Bishop gathered, had once been the scene of a periodic man hunt: these Indians, born in fear and dying by violence for generations, had at last taken this leap away from the earth; and on that rock had found the hope of all suffering and tormented creatures — safety. They came down to the plain to hunt and to grow their crops, but there was always a place to go back to. If a band of Navajos were on the Ácoma's trail, there was still one hope; if he could reach his rock — Sanctuary! On the winding stone stairway up the cliff, a handful of men could keep off a multitude. . . . The rock, when one came to think of it, was the utmost expression of loyalty in love and friendship. Christ himself had used that comparison for the disciple to whom He gave the keys of His Church. And the Hebrews of the Old Testament, always being carried captive into foreign lands, — their rock was an idea of God, the only thing their conquerors could not take from them.

Already the Bishop had observed in Indian life a strange literal-ness, often shocking and disconcerting. The Ácomas, who must share the universal yearning for something permanent, enduring, without shadow of change, — they had their idea in substance. They actually lived upon their Rock; were born upon it and died upon it.[55]

The rock is the same symbol of the enchanted mesa that we have seen before in Tom Outland's story, where it also served to protect civiliza-tion against the onslaught of marauding tribes.

No clearer statement could be made of Willa Cather's often des-perately felt need for some sort of bedrock security and shelter. The description of the Acomas being hunted down like animals recalls the fate of the cliff dwellers in "Tom Outland's Story," with its overtones of the creative and the good being annihilated by the destructive and the bad. Here, as there, the way in which the good life is to be preserved seems peculiarly negative and passive. Instead of staying to fight the enemy, the Indians withdraw.

But Willa Cather cannot find peace in her belief in sanctuary, nor forget for long her previous faith in all-conquering desire. Almost im-mediately she has her hero discover the less pleasant aspects of the rock, and find out that the concept of sanctuary has its limitations. The

Bishop is obliged to say Mass there in the "old war-like church of Acoma":

> That spacious interior depressed the Bishop as no other mission church had done. He held a service there before midday, and he had never found it so hard to go through the ceremony of the Mass. Before him, on the grey floor, in the grey light, a group of bright shawls and blankets, some fifty or sixty silent faces; above and behind them the grey walls. He felt as if he were celebrating Mass at the bottom of the sea for antediluvian creatures; for types of life so old, so hardened, so shut within their shells that the sacrifice on Calvary could hardly reach back so far. Those shell-like backs behind him might be saved by baptism and divine grace, as undeveloped infants are, but hardly through any experience of their own, he thought. When he blessed them and sent them away, it was with a sense of inadequacy and spiritual defeat.[56]

> Built upon the north-east corner of the cloister the Bishop found a loggia. . . . From this loggia he watched the sun go down; watched the desert become dark, the shadows creep upward. Abroad in the plain the scattered mesa tops, red with the after-glow, one by one lost their light, like candles going out. He was on a naked rock in the desert, in the stone age, a prey to home-sickness for his own kind, his own epoch, for European man and his glorious history of desire and dreams. Through all the centuries that his own part of the world had been changing like the sky at daybreak, this people had been fixed, increasing neither in numbers nor desires, rock-turtles on their rock. Something reptilian he felt here, something that had endured by immobility, a kind of life out of reach, like the crustaceans in their armor.[57]

The final result that the Indians of Acoma have on the Bishop is to make him feel like a strayed traveler lost in prehistoric time, and realize that too great a burden of armor leads to immobility.

By comparing the inhabitants of Acoma with crustaceans, rock turtles, and reptiles Willa Cather has indicated that while the rock may represent a tenacious and successful determination to survive, it does not represent very much that we know of as human.[58] Indeed the Bishop wonders whether mere survival alone is worth the price, whether all by itself it forms an adequate substitute for "European man and his glorious history of desire and dreams." Clearly he thinks that it is not. Thus Willa Cather undercuts the notion of withdrawal to sanctuary, as an ultimate goal in life, and reintroduces, by implication at least, the validity of the way of facing life exemplified by the heroic pioneers.

THE CLAIMS OF BEAUTY *vs.* MORAL RESPONSIBILITY

The chapter just described marks both the high tide of the book's glorification of order and the start of its ebb. For Willa Cather cannot maintain her faith in sanctuary for very long. In spite of its insistence on the triumph of order, *Death Comes for the Archbishop* shows a few signs of the same struggle we have seen occurring over and over in her previous works. Although the terms of the struggle vary from book to book, in general there is an opposition between responsibility to one's own personal development and responsibility to others; between the claims of beauty and the claims of humanity. One's own development may involve the erection of bridges, the pursuit of a career as creative or interpretive artist, the interpretation of the past, or simply devotion to the ideal of the comely life; responsibility to others may involve the claims of parents or husband or wife or lover. Except in *My Ántonia,* fulfillment is regarded as something which always runs counter to personal and social obligations, and Willa Cather never seems to be able to reconcile the conflict satisfactorily. With each new book she poses the problem in a different form. In *Death Comes for the Archbishop* the struggle is submerged. Nevertheless tension exists at various points between the comely life, which usually involves appreciation of the aesthetic aspects of Catholicism, and the necessity of meeting the ritual needs of a Catholic people.

The first example of this tension occurs in the Prologue, where the Spanish Cardinal relates the story of the lost El Greco to his Roman dinner guests:

> "Listen," said the host, "and I will relate a little story, while the Bishop does me the compliment to drink my champagne. I have a reason for asking this question which you have answered so finally. In my family house in Valencia I have a number of pictures by the great Spanish painters, collected chiefly by my great-grandfather, who was a man of perception in these things and, for his time, rich. His collection of El Greco is, I believe, quite the best in Spain. When my progenitor was an old man, along came one of these missionary priests from New Spain, begging. All missionaries from the Americas were inveterate beggars, then as now, Bishop Ferrand. This Franciscan had considerable success, with his tales of pious Indian converts and struggling missions. He

came to visit at my great-grandfather's house and conducted devotions in the absence of the Chaplain. He wheedled a good sum of money out of the old man, as well as vestments and linen and chalices — he would take anything — and he implored my grandfather to give him a painting from his great collection, for the ornamentation of his mission church among the Indians. My grandfather told him to choose from the gallery, believing the priest would covet most what he himself could best afford to spare. But not at all; the hairy Franciscan pounced upon one of the best in the collection; a young St. Francis in meditation, by El Greco, and the model for the saint was one of the very handsome Dukes of Albuquerque. My grandfather protested; tried to persuade the fellow that some picture of the crucifixion, or a martyrdom, would appeal more strongly to his redskins. What would a St. Francis, of almost feminine beauty, mean to the scalp-takers?

"All in vain. The missionary turned upon his host with a reply which has become a saying in our family: 'You refuse me this picture because it is a good picture. *It is too good for God, but it is not too good for you.*'

"He carried off the painting. In my grandfather's manuscript catalogue, under the number and title of the St. Francis, is written: *Given to Fray Teodocio, for the glory of God, to enrich his mission church at Pueblo de Cia, among the savages of New Spain.*

"It is because of this lost treasure, Father Ferrand, that I happen to have had some personal correspondence with the Bishop of Durango. I once wrote the facts to him fully. He replied to me that the mission at Cia was long ago destroyed and its furnishings scattered. Of course the painting may have been ruined in a pillage or massacre. On the other hand, it may still be hidden away in some crumbling sacristy or smoky wigwam. If your French priest had a discerning eye, now, and were sent to this Vicarate, he might keep my El Greco in mind." [59]

This passage embodies several of Willa Cather's themes, among them the transplanting of European civilization to America and the recovery of the past. But its chief interest lies in the fact that it opposes the aesthetic and moral impulses in a way that prefigures their opposition at various other points in the book. The Cardinal's grandfather thinks that the dictates of Christian morality have nothing at all to do with his enjoyment of his private art collection. He finds out that he is wrong. Responsibility to others very definitely can interfere with the aesthete's own private enjoyment, and since the latter is fundamentally self-regarding, if the two collide one must allow the former to triumph or else give up altogether any pretense of being civilized. It is easy to sympathize with the grandee's reluctance to give up the El Greco; surely if the picture went to the New World savages it would be a terrible waste. But the issues are so clearly drawn that the implications are inescapable, and the hairy Franciscan will not let the grandee evade the point. When he says: "You refuse me the picture because it is a good picture. *It is too good for God, but it is not too good for you,"* he is reminding the Cardinal's grandfather that in any rational scheme of things the aesthetic impulse must be subordinated to and work within a moral framework, or else leave its owner prey to the grossest kind of egoism and pride. So at last the grandee reluctantly relinquishes the picture. Willa Cather drives home the point by ending the incident here; the lost El Greco is never recovered. Commitment to the moral life, she seems to say, very frequently does necessitate the sacrifice of beauty.

A similar struggle and outcome occurs in the mind of the rich *ranchero* Manuel Lujon when he somewhat grudgingly makes Father Vaillant a gift of his two beautiful white mules. There is one story in the book, however, in which the struggle between the aesthetic impulse of one man and the moral feelings of a group becomes so aggravated as to lead to open war, and in the conflict the moral sense does not win, although retribution follows. The story recounts the legend of Fray Baltazar, the evil friar of Acoma.

Of all the stories woven into *Death Comes for the Archbishop,* this is the only one in which Willa Cather meets the problem of evil head on. Perhaps partly as a result of this it stands out head and shoulders above the rest. Briefly, it relates the history of an intelligent and powerful friar stationed all alone in an Indian pueblo on a rock in a remote part of New Mexico. Since he lives in the early eighteenth century and is responsible to no one within hundreds of miles of him, he is far removed from the civilizing force of the society of Europeans. He has a passion for eating and becomes more and more self-indulgent, tyrannizing over the native population and sending his Indian runner on as much as five days' journey to the nearest mountains to catch fish for his fast days. He is an expert on cooking and is particularly proud of one or two sauces he has managed to develop in the time that should have been spent in caring for his flock. One day while he is banqueting the priests from three other pueblos (themselves many days' journey distant), his serving boy, who is listening to their conversation, accidentally spills a stream of rich brown gravy on the head and shoulders of one of the visitors. In a fit of rage, Fray Baltazar hurls a pewter mug at the head of the boy and inadvertently kills him. The guests flee in terror, leaving the friar alone with the consequences of his anger, since he is too proud to follow. Nothing happens until moonrise, at which time the inhabitants of the pueblo file silently out and come up to Fray Baltazar's loggia, where they take him captive, tying his hands and feet together. They carry him over to the edge of the mesa, swing him back and forth over the brink a few times, and then drop him to the desert beneath.

The story is an interesting one. It deals with the problem of a superior person put in a position of absolute authority in a feudal society, with no restraints whatsoever to hold him in check. The result is, of course, that he becomes a tyrant. Seen from this point of view, the theme is similar to that of Conrad's *Heart of Darkness:* once we plunge into the wilderness and free ourselves from the restraints of civilization, there is a very real danger that our innate evil may get the upper hand; we are barbarians all. But the story has other implications as well. Like "Paul's Case," it is a good example of a "decadent" story: it shows how the aesthete, in his single-minded search for beauty, cuts himself off from all human relationships; a conflict develops between him and the people around him, and since he has broken the moral code by placing beauty above goodness and thus denying his kinship with mankind, he must pay the penalty. Here Willa Cather seems to be edging back to a vivid awareness of the tension existing between beauty and moral responsibility which made *The Professor's House* so interesting. Fray Baltazar is an extremely civilized man in the sense that his aesthetic perceptions are highly refined; he is extremely uncivilized in that he uses them for purely selfish purposes. The unhealthily specialized form the aesthetic impulse takes in him is gluttony, which itself suggests the narcissistic nature of pure aestheticism. Baltazar's aesthetic passion is greater than his moral passion; he cannot stand the thought of spilled sauce, so, in a moment of passion, accidentally kills the boy. Willa Cather has him punished with death, even though it means that his superior sensibilities will be obliterated. Thus she seems to be vindicating the moral force. His psychic imbalance is his tragic flaw; the legend might almost be called the aesthete's tragedy. But it does contain a certain triumph in that he was a brave man and accepts his fate once it is certain. He does not once cry out when the Indians swing him over the edge of the cliff. Willa Cather makes the point that aesthetes can have courage, whatever their other lacks.

Although morality emerges triumphant in the anecdote about the lost El Greco and the legend of Fray Baltazar, it will be noticed that both of these are stories from the past; they refer to conditions prevailing at a time considerably before that of the narrative. When Willa Cather tries to handle the conflicts arising between beauty and responsibility at the time of the novel itself, i.e., the mid-nineteenth century, she is considerably less successful. As might be expected, she has her same old trouble of wanting incompatibles, of being unwilling to compromise on them, and of nevertheless feeling obliged to resolve the tension in favor of one of the opposing value systems, even though this leads her to partial frustration. In *Death Comes for the Archbishop* Willa Cather develops a new way of dealing with the problem which seems to show signs of weakening and defeat. Formerly she had shown a single protagonist who tried to respond simultaneously to the call of beauty and claims of responsibility; this was true of characters as different as Bartley Alexander, Marian Forrester, Godfrey St. Peter, and Myra Henshawe. Now she divides the response to conflicting value systems between two different characters: Bishop Latour and Father Vaillant.

It is evident from the beginning that this pair form a sharp contrast to each other. Even their looks are antithetical, and Willa Cather considers physical appearance to be extremely revealing.[60] When the Bishop first makes his appearance we are told, "His brow was open, generous, reflective, his features handsome and somewhat severe." [61] But of Father Vaillant's first entrance Willa Cather writes, "His countenance had little to recommend it but kindliness and vivacity." [62] "My God, but he is ugly, the Padre!" comments an old Mexican woman whom he meets. "He must be very holy." [63] The difference in looks mirrors a difference in temperament, which Willa Cather points up in a charming little vignette:

> In his youth, Joseph had wished to lead a life of seclusion and solitary devotion; but the truth was, he could not be happy for long without human intercourse. And he liked almost everyone. In Ohio, when they used to travel together in stagecoaches, Father Latour had noticed that every time a new passenger pushed his way into the already crowded stage, Joseph would look pleased and interested, as if this were an agreeable addition—whereas he himself felt annoyed, even if he concealed it.[64]

Although the Archbishop and his cultivated temperament receive most of the praise in the novel, nevertheless Willa Cather occasionally makes him a little envious of his younger and more impetuous colleague: "In that first encounter," she writes, "he chose the lively, ugly boy for his friend. It was instantaneous. Latour himself was much cooler and more critical in temper; hard to please, and often a little grey in mood." [65] The two priests differ as much in their approach to religion as they do about everything else. Father Vaillant himself sums up the difference when he explains to Latour why he would prefer to go out and reclaim lost Catholics in the territory recently acquired from Mexico by the Gadsden Purchase to staying with the Bishop and helping him perform his parish duties at Santa Fe: "But you do not need me as much as they do!" he says.

> "Any one of our good French priests from Montferrand can serve you here. It is work that can be done by intelligence. But down there it is work for the heart, for a particular sympathy, and none of our new priests understand those poor natures as I do. I have almost become a Mexican! I have learned to like *chili colorado* and mutton fat. Their foolish ways no longer offend me, their very faults are dear to me. I am *their man!*" [66]

The distinction between work for intelligence and work for the heart reflects the romantic movement's characteristic opposition between heart and head. Willa Cather had often opposed the two to each other in her protagonists, but never before had she meted them out to separate people. Now she seems to be denying that a person can both think and feel at the same time: that he can have both a head and a heart.

The result of this split in sensibility is that instead of presenting a single character torn between the conflicting claims of beauty and moral responsibility, as she had done in her previous novels, she now has Bishop Latour respond almost exclusively to the one and Father Vaillant respond almost exclusively to the other. Nowhere is this more clearly seen than in the treatment of the cathedral at Santa Fe which the Bishop wishes to build as a monument to himself.[67]

Previous to this incident, Willa Cather has made it abundantly clear that, however many virtues Father Vaillant may possess, he is not an aesthete. "The ugly conditions of life in Ohio had never troubled Joseph," she writes. "The hideous houses and churches, the ill-kept farms and gardens, the slovenly, sordid aspect of the towns and the country-side, which continually depressed Father Latour, he seemed scarcely to perceive." [68] Now the Bishop calls Father Vaillant all the way back from Tucson to Santa Fe and wants to tell him his plans for

building a church. Without revealing the reason for it, he invites Father
Vaillant for a ride out into the desert, his intention being to surprise him
with the sight of the golden-ocher hill from which he intends to quarry
the stone for the church. When they get there, the two men's reactions
are significantly different:

> "It is curious, is it not, to find one yellow hill among all these
> green ones?" remarked the Bishop, stooping to pick up a piece of
> the stone. "I have ridden over these hills in every direction, but
> this is the only one of its kind." He stood regarding the chip of
> yellow rock that lay in his palm. As he had a very special way of
> handling objects that were sacred, he extended that manner to
> things which he considered beautiful. After a moment of silence
> he looked up at the rugged wall, gleaming gold above them. "That
> hill, *Blanchet,* is my Cathedral."
> Father Joseph looked at his Bishop, then at the cliff, blinking.
> *"Vraiment?* Is the stone hard enough?" [69]

As might be expected, the missionary priest thinks of the cathedral in
its relation to human needs, while the Bishop thinks of it as an art
object, an end in itself. Father Vaillant says:

> "I had no idea you were going in for fine building, when every-
> thing about us is so poor — and we ourselves are so poor."
> "But the Cathedral is not for us, Father Joseph. We build for
> the future — better not lay a stone unless we can do that. It
> would be a shame to any man coming from a Seminary that is one
> of the architectural treasures of France, to make another ugly
> church on this continent where there are so many already." . . .
> "I could hardly have hoped that God would gratify my personal
> taste, my vanity, if you will, in this way. I tell you, *Blanchet,* I
> would rather have found that hill of yellow rock than have come
> into a fortune to spend in charity." [70]

The Bishop's response to the stone is cultivated, but it is hardly Christian. Willa Cather has made her hero into an aesthete, and Father
Vaillant into the religious man of the two. Small wonder then that she
could write of the latter:

> As they rode home through the sage-brush silvered by moon-
> light, Father Vaillant was still wondering why he had been called

home from saving souls in Arizona, and wondering why a poor missionary Bishop should care so much about a building. He himself was eager to have the Cathedral begun; but whether it was Midi Romanesque or Ohio German in style, seemed to him of little consequence.[71]

Thus in *Death Comes for the Archbishop,* Willa Cather, instead of creating a single protagonist who possesses both a sense of beauty and a sense of responsibility, as she had striven to do in previous novels, simplified her task by creating a double protagonist. It is true that she had used double characters before, in the case of Ántonia Cuzak and Jim Burden in *My Ántonia* and Marian Forrester and Niel Herbert in *A Lost Lady.* But in each of these cases one of the two characters had considerably overshadowed the other, so that there was no doubt as to who was the book's real protagonist, and in each the main character possessed a psychic wholeness which Jean Marie Latour simply does not possess. For the Bishop is represented as being somewhat lost and lonely when he is separated from his beloved Father Vaillant. Willa Cather writes:

Father Latour needed his Vicar, who had so much tact with the natives, so much sympathy with all their short-comings. When they were together, he was always curbing Father Vaillant's hopeful rashness — but left alone, he greatly missed that very quality. And he missed Father Vaillant's companionship — why not admit it? [72]

The Bishop's ambivalent attitude toward the "hopeful rashness" of Father Vaillant mirrors the whole confusion in Willa Cather's mind about this time as to the value of heroic individualism. For what is that "hopeful rashness" but the same pioneer spirit which she celebrated in her prairie novels a dozen years before? Then it had been glorified as the last great expression of the human spirit. Now it is periodically criticized for being disorderly and rash.

From this and from other things Willa Cather has to say about him it appears that Father Vaillant is a truncated version of the Willa Cather pioneer: he has spiritual and physical energy but is neither aesthetic nor scholarly.[73] The Bishop feels that Blanchet is both better and worse than he; in a sense, he epitomizes life itself[74] much as the Bishop epitomizes art.[75] But he is everywhere subordinated to his rather remote but exceedingly civilized friend. At this stage in her career the author still has a place for the heroic individual, but he has been demoted several grades and is now operating within the hierarchal framework of the Catholic Church. Willa Cather is unwilling to discard the pioneer, but she now deprives him of several desirable qualities he formerly had possessed and makes him subservient to the man of thought.

In its treatment of the conflicting claims of beauty and responsibility, *Death Comes for the Archbishop* presents a new and narrower concept of beauty. Formerly Willa Cather had dealt with the active creation of beauty; now she describes the mere passive enjoyment of it. The Bishop cannot build his Midi Romanesque cathedral himself, and he sends for an architect from France to design it; he merely picks out the stone. In the story of the lost El Greco it is the pleasures of the connoisseur rather than the delights of painting which please the Cardinal's grandfather, and in the legend of Fray Baltazar it is not even artistic enjoyment which is celebrated, but mere gustatory sensation. Second, her use of twin protagonists to respond respectively to the claims of beauty and moral responsibility seems to represent an abandonment of the hope, still discernible in the characterization of Tom Outland, that both could be found in the same man.[76] Even while she recognizes the validity of both claims, she cannot help tipping the scales in favor of the Bishop and thus insuring the ultimate triumph of aestheticism as she had done so many times before. Third, and most ominous for her future development, she seems utterly unable to resolve convincingly the problems presented by her main characters; she is able to impose order neither on the world about her, nor on that about the Bishop, but only on the world of the remote past. This indicates a serious weakening of her hold upon the moral problems presented by her material. She could satisfactorily resolve the conflict between beauty and responsibility in the past for the minor characters of the inset stories; she could not resolve it in the present for the major characters of the narrative itself.

The Elimination of Conflict: Order Overcomes the Pioneer Spirit

Thus in *Death Comes for the Archbishop* Willa Cather not only fails to solve the problem which had absorbed her in the immediately preceding novels and was indeed the central problem of her entire literary career; for the most part she writes as if it did not exist. That very tension between the claims of beauty and moral responsibility which had lent so much interest to *A Lost Lady* and *The Professor's House* is notably lacking in *Death Comes for the Archbishop;* its place is taken by an almost unearthly calm. Now Willa Cather's chief interest seems to lie in polished descriptions of landscape and the minute delineation of human figures in clear bright colors; perhaps this is what she meant when she compared her work to the frescoes of Puvis de Chavannes.[77] But this calm certainly does not grow out of the material she uses; instead it gives the impression of being forcefully superimposed by the author herself. The narrative's detached, lucid tone is achieved at terrible expense; it entails the sacrifice of some of the story's most interesting implications and involves the almost complete elimination of conflict from the book.

Examples of this are almost too numerous to mention. The Bishop's fight to get his bishopric upon arriving in New Mexico is omitted; it is mentioned rather than described. Willa Cather summarizes this in a few words:

> On his arrival at Santa Fé, this was what had happened: The Mexican priests there had refused to recognize his authority. They disclaimed any knowledge of a Vicarate Apostolic, or a Bishop of Agathonica. They said they were under the jurisdiction of the Bishop of Durango, and had received no instructions to the contrary. If Father Latour was to be their Bishop, where were his credentials? [78]

The next time we hear of the Bishop, in connection with his flock, he has already been installed, owing to the services of Father Vaillant, of which we have heard nothing up to now:

> On his arrival he found amity instead of enmity awaiting him. Father Vaillant had already endeared himself to the people. The Mexican priest who was in charge of the pro-cathedral had gracefully retired. . . . Father Vaillant had taken possession of the priest's house, and with the help of carpenters and the Mexican women of the parish had put it in order. The Yankee traders and the military Commandant at Fort Marcy had sent generous contributions of bedding and blankets and odd pieces of furniture.[79]

Willa Cather uses the same method in disposing of Padre Gallegos, the fandango-dancing priest of Albuquerque. Since in addition to his terpsichorean activities he also drinks, hunts, and plays poker, he is obviously a threat to ecclesiastical decorum and the rule of good order, so Bishop Latour decides on strong measures: "There was but one course: to suspend the man from the exercise of all priestly functions, and bid the smaller native priests take warning." [80] Here again, conveniently enough for the Bishop, Willa Cather turns the actual meeting of the problem over to Father Vaillant, and again the conflict which develops is mentioned, not described:

> A month after the Bishop's visit to Albuquerque and Ácoma, the genial Father Gallegos was formally suspended, and Father Vaillant himself took charge of the parish. At first there was bitter feeling; the rich *rancheros* and the merry ladies of Albuquerque were very hostile to the French priest. He began his reforms at once. Everything was changed. The holy-days, which had been occasions of revelry under Padre Gallegos, were now days of austere devotion.[81]

Now it might be argued that Willa Cather was not interested in describing the struggle involved in re-establishing ecclesiastical discipline in the Southwest; that her real interest lay in the everyday life of the exceptional man on the frontier. This is what she herself claimed in the letter to *Commonweal* Magazine in which she tried to explain her purposes in writing the book.[82] But this argument does not explain her treatment of the Bishop's encounter with Padre Martinez, the rebel priest of Taos. In this incident, one of the few dramatic events in the book, the forces of civilization meet face to face with the forces of nature. As Willa Cather explicitly states: "Father Latour judged that the day of lawless personal power was almost over, even on the frontier." [83] The Bishop's visit to the Padre induces the latter's open defiance of him:

> "We have a living Church here, not a dead arm of the European Church. Our religion grew out of the soil, and has its own roots. We pay a filial respect to the person of the Holy Father, but Rome has no authority here. . . ."
> To this eloquence the Bishop returned blandly that he had not come to deprive the people of their religion, but that he would be compelled to deprive some of the priests of their parishes if they did not change their way of life.
> Father Martínez filled his glass and replied with perfect good humour. "You cannot deprive me of mine, Bishop. Try it! I will organize my own church. You can have your French priest of Taos, and I will have the people!"
> With this the Padre left the table and stood warming his back

at the fire, his cassock pulled up about his waist to expose his trousers to the blaze. "You are a young man, my Bishop," he went on, rolling his big head back and looking up at the well-smoked roof poles. "And you know nothing about Indians or Mexicans. If you try to introduce European civilization here and change our old ways, to interfere with the secret dances of the Indians, let us say, or abolish the bloody rites of the Penitentes, I foretell an early death for you. I advise you to study our native traditions before you begin your reforms. You are among barbarous people, my Frenchman, between two savage races. The dark things forbidden by your Church are a part of Indian religion. You cannot introduce French fashions here." [84]

The quarrel between the Frenchman and the Mexican begins when it becomes clear that the Padre had not the least intention of keeping the vows of celibacy he made upon entering the priesthood. The Bishop's sense of shock at Martinez's lechery and sensuality is balanced by his surprise when he hears the Padre sing the Mass next morning:

> The Bishop had never heard the Mass more impressively sung than by Father Martínez. The man had a beautiful baritone voice, and he drew from some deep well of emotional power. Nothing in the service was slighted, every phrase and gesture had its full value. At the moment of the Elevation the dark priest seemed to give his whole force, his swarthy body and all its blood, to that lifting-up. Rightly guided, the Bishop reflected, this Mexican might have been a great man. He had an altogether compelling personality, a disturbing, mysterious magnetic power.[85]

Finally the Bishop sensibly concludes that the Padre is getting too old to play the part of Don Juan much longer, and decides to leave him in charge of his parish for the time being. Yet in spite of the decision, he continues to have trouble with the old man, and finally is forced to excommunicate him. Again, as in the case of Padre Gallegos, Willa Cather does not dwell on the incident but is content to summarize it in a few brief lines.[86] One of the few vivid tension-producing incidents in the book is thus left dramatically unresolved.

Once again Willa Cather has shied away from the actual presentation of conflict, although the clash between the Bishop and Martinez is a major one, and she has aroused the reader's expectations by preparing for a climactic scene which never takes place. The reader finds it quite irritating to read, "The vigour and zeal of Bishop Latour's administra-

tion had already been recognized at Rome," [87] when he is constantly
being told about that vigor but never is given a chance to see it at
work. If her only interest in the book is in the Bishop's everyday life,
why make such an issue of Martinez in the first place? We have seen
how in her early novels Willa Cather had presented conflict but had
been unable to resolve it dramatically, and so had recourse to a third
person to relate the crucial action which had occurred off the stage. She
had used this device with telling effect on the description of the killing
of Emil and Marie in *O Pioneers!;* she had employed it with considerably less success in the description of Ántonia's illegitimate pregnancy in *My Ántonia.* Now, however, what she had once made use of
merely as a last resource becomes with her an habitual way of dealing
with problems; in *Death Comes for the Archbishop* the consequences of
almost all the conflicts are glozed over or suppressed.

The fact is that Willa Cather often starts out to do one thing and
ends up doing another. She said she wished to write about the everyday
life of a superior man in a rough country; yet Padre Martinez is by no
means typical of the Bishop's everyday life. He is quite unusual, since
he presents special problems of insubordination within the Bishop's
own diocese. Willa Cather pointedly ignores this by refusing to describe
its consequences except in the most perfunctory manner. She builds
up a dramatic clash between two opposing personalities, only to drop
the subject almost completely, leaving the reader with an irritating
awareness of unresolved tensions. If she really had wanted to do something "in the style of legend, which is absolutely the reverse of dramatic
treatment," she should never have written the scene in the first place.
This ambiguity is typical of her treatment of conflict in this book; she
detests it, but she simply cannot stay away from it.

Nowhere is the tendency to shrink from the direct presentation of
conflict more noticeable than in the book's final section, which culminates on the last page in the death of the Archbishop. Since the
section bears the same title as the book itself, one might expect it to
build up to a climax, even though this would go against the author's
avowed intention of writing "something without accent." Instead, she
makes the section into a hodgepodge leading nowhere. She begins with
a reference to the deaths of Father Vaillant and his sister, describes the
garden of the Bishop's villa outside Santa Fe, tells how in the good
old days he and the French architect he had sent for used to glory
together over the natural setting of the cathedral, relates his decision
to remain in New Mexico instead of returning to the Old World to die,
has him reflect on the hardships suffered by the seventeenth-century

Spanish Jesuits, takes him back in imagination to the time of his youth and the heartbreaking leave-taking Father Vaillant had to go through when he left his native town of Riom, brings him forward again in order to recall Father Vaillant's later career and funeral, describes his own gradual loss of interest in his present surroundings, backtracks once more to describe the expulsion of the Navajos from Canyon de Chelly, and then comes forward once again to describe a deathbed scene. She is almost always a good deal more successful in describing past events than present ones, and the result is that the reader's attention is distracted from the approaching death by the constant introduction of anecdotes and other irrelevant material from the more-or-less remote past. While it is true that the Bishop's mind is supposed to be wandering during the last few days of his life, this does not excuse Willa Cather's mind for wandering as well. What has happened is that her point of view has gone out of control; she makes no discrimination at all between what is important and unimportant, or even between herself and her characters. She says of the Bishop:

> Sometimes, when Magdalena or Bernard came in and asked him a question, it took him several seconds to bring himself back to the present. He could see they thought his mind was failing; but it was only extraordinarily active in some other part of the great picture of his life — some part of which they knew nothing.[88]

This is not the first time she has blurred the distinction between the thoughts of an omniscient author and those of her principal character, but in this book she becomes a habitual offender, another sign of her weakening hold on her materials. But the greatest symptom of decline of powers is her treatment of the death itself. If Willa Cather had really wanted to describe the Bishop's death quietly and without emphasis, in the manner of legend, or if on the other hand she was interested in preparing for a truly dramatic death scene, she should not have used the stock suspense-building devices of the bad nineteenth-century sentimental novel. And this is precisely what she does:

> On the last day of his life his condition was pretty generally known. The Cathedral was full of people all day long, praying for him; nuns and old women, young men and girls, coming and going. The sick man had received the Viaticum early in the morning. Some of the Tesuque Indians, who had been his country neighbours, came into Santa Fé and sat all day in the Archbishop's

courtyard listening for news of him; with them was Eusabio the Navajo. Fructosa and Tranquilino, his old servants, were with the supplicants in the Cathedral.

The Mother Superior and Magdalena and Bernard attended the sick man. There was little to do but to watch and pray, so peaceful and painless was his repose. Sometimes it was sleep, they knew from his relaxed features; then his face would assume personality, consciousness, even though his eyes did not open.

Toward the close of day, in the short twilight after the candles were lighted, the old Bishop seemed to become restless, moved a little, and began to murmur; it was in the French tongue, but Bernard, though he caught some words, could make nothing of them. He knelt beside the bed: "What is it, Father? I am here."

He continued to murmur, to move his hands a little, and Magdalena thought he was trying to ask for something, or to tell them something. But in reality the Bishop was not there at all; he was standing in a tip-tilted green field among his native mountains, and he was trying to give consolation to a young man who was being torn in two before his eyes by the desire to go and the necessity to stay. He was trying to forge a new Will in that devout and exhausted priest; and the time was short, for the *diligence* for Paris was already rumbling down the mountain gorge.[89]

Here it is obvious that Willa Cather is presenting a dramatic scene and is doing it badly. Although the style picks up somewhat toward the very end, the effect she produces is almost completely sentimental; it is not climax but bathos. The passage as a whole belongs to the "his-fingers-plucked-at-the-coverlet" school of deathbed description. Willa Cather is trying to write without using her emotions about things which involve a considerable understanding of the emotions; as a result she treats her material superficially and falls victim to stock responses and clichés.

The extent of Miss Cather's decline in artistry can be seen when one compares her handling of the Archbishop's death with her treatment of the deaths of Mr. Shimerda and of Emil and Marie. There, although she does not describe the death itself, she nevertheless accords it its full emotional value as registered in the minds of other people. Here, she attempts and fails to portray the very act of dying, and produces nothing but a sentimental effect.

The refusal to face conflict not only interferes with the presentation of certain scenes; it also has a definitely harmful effect on the book's overall organization. In spite of brilliant passages, it is the most poorly constructed of all Willa Cather's works. Whole episodes are given little or no relation to the lives of the chief protagonists. Thus the story of Padre Lucero, the miser of Arroyo Hondo, is tacked on to the powerful account of the Bishop's meeting with Padre Martinez. Not only has it little connection with the latter; it actually dissipates some of the energy generated by that episode by letting the account trail off indeterminately. The expulsion of the Navajos from their ancestral home, an event which took place during the Bishop's middle years, is described in detail just before the account of the Bishop's death. As a result the reader's mind is distracted from that impending event, which is thereby robbed of considerable power and significance. And the story of Doña Isabella, who doesn't want to confess her age even to win an inheritance, is a pointless digression which has nothing to do with what comes before or after it. As an anecdote it rates at best only a few lines, not the twenty-five pages devoted to it. Time and again in the course of the narrative Willa Cather will write passages of landscape description beautiful in themselves but which have only the flimsiest connection with what follows or precedes them. She tried to forestall all such criticism in her *Commonweal* letter by asserting that she was not trying to write a novel at all but a narrative, thereby presumably freeing herself from the shackles of plot and form.[90] This is all very well, but we have a right to judge the final product, whatever it may be called, by its overall effect. Because it is so poorly constructed *Death Comes for the Archbishop* can easily fail to hold the reader's interest and may even be boring when read straight through. As we have seen, this poor form is a result of Willa Cather's avoidance of conflict, which in turn is a result of failing to look squarely at life.

We are now in a position to look at the cool lucid tone of the book and decide where it comes from. It derives from the almost complete elimination from the book of anything resembling the clash and struggle which lie at the base of human problems and form the major part of our experience in life. Willa Cather either omits strife altogether or, if she does include it, she leaves it unresolved so that the issues are left hanging in mid-air. The greatest conflict of all in the minds of most men has to do with the fact of death, and it is precisely this conflict which Willa Cather seems at most pains to avoid. In the book's final section she evades it in every way possible, and far from making use of the fertility myth, as she had in treating the death of Mr. Shimerda, she employs the shabby and threadbare devices of the second-rate sentimental novel. The order which she imposes on the book is a specious order. It does not arise out of what she ostensibly took for her subject matter, the submission of nature to civilization. Willa Cather's great contribution in her early career had been to recognize that conflict lay at the root of all experience and to bring this truth home to the American experience by embodying it in descriptions of struggle on the frontier. Now, neglecting her earlier insight and the dramatic structure it entailed, she seeks order and coherence in other, lesser ways. The order which she here imposes in Procrustean manner is a spurious thing, since it does not represent any real transcendence of human strife.

SUBSTITUTES FOR CONFLICT: LANDSCAPE AND LOCAL COLOR

If Willa Cather carefully refrains from building her story around a single central conflict, such as serves as subject matter in most novels, the question arises as to just what it is she does do. She does several things. One of them is to write many inset stories relating the history and legends of the Spanish Southwest. Many of these are charming in the extreme, and at least one can stand as a work of art in its own right: the Legend of Fray Baltazar. Another device Willa Cather uses is the description of the home life of Father Vaillant and the Bishop. I have described one such domestic vignette in discussing the significance of the history of onion soup. Still a third thing Willa Cather does to lend interest to a novel which is episodic and plotless is to describe, often with great beauty, the landscape in which what action there is takes place.

Here Willa Cather writes some prose which is undeniably glorious. Her response to nature was that of a lyric poet, and some of her most successful passages involved nature description. One recalls the climactic impact of the plough against the sun in *My Ántonia* and of the white mulberry tree in *O Pioneers!* However weak the rest of *Death Comes for the Archbishop* may be, it is clear her hand had not lost its touch in the description of landscape:

> In all his travels the Bishop had seen no country like this. From the flat red sea of sand rose great rock mesas, generally Gothic in outline, resembling vast cathedrals. They were not crowded together in disorder, but placed in wide spaces, long vistas between. This plain might once have been an enormous city, all the smaller quarters destroyed by time, only the public buildings left, — piles of architecture that were like mountains. . . .

This mesa plain had an appearance of great antiquity, and of incompleteness; as if, with all the materials of world-making assembled, the Creator had desisted, gone away and left everything on the point of being brought together, on the eve of being arranged into mountain, plain, plateau. The country was still waiting to be made into a landscape.

Ever afterward the Bishop remembered his first ride to Ácoma as his introduction to the mesa country. One thing which struck him at once was that every mesa was duplicated by a cloud mesa, like a reflection, which lay motionless above it or moved slowly up from behind it. These cloud formations seemed to be always there, however hot and blue the sky. Sometimes they were flat terraces, ledges of vapour; sometimes they were dome-shaped, or fantastic, like the tops of silvery pagodas, rising one above another, as if an oriental city lay directly behind the rock. The great tables of granite set down in an empty plain were inconceivable without their attendant clouds, which were a part of them, as the smoke is part of the censer, or the foam of the wave.

Coming along the Santa Fé trail, in the vast plains of Kansas, Father Latour had found the sky more a desert than the land; a hard, empty blue, very monotonous to the eyes of a Frenchman. But west of the Pecos all that changed; here there was always activity overhead, clouds forming and moving all day long. Whether they were dark and full of violence, or soft and white with luxurious idleness, they powerfully affected the world beneath them. The desert, the mountains and mesas, were continually re-formed and re-coloured by the cloud shadows. The whole country seemed fluid to the eye under this constant change of accent, this ever-varying distribution of light.[91]

While they were ascending the rock, deafening thunder broke over their heads, and the rain began to fall as if it were spilled from a cloud-burst. Drawing into a deep twist of the stairway, under an overhanging ledge, they watched the water shaken in heavy curtains in the air before them. In a moment the seam in which they stood was like the channel of a brook. Looking out over the great plain spotted with mesas and glittering with rain sheets, the Bishop saw the distant mountains bright with sunlight. Again he thought that the first Creation morning might have looked like this, when the dry land was first drawn up out of the deep, and all was confusion.

The storm was over in half an hour. By the time the Bishop
and his guide reached the last turn in the trail, and rose through
the crack, stepping out on the flat top of the rock, the noontide
sun was blazing down upon Ácoma with almost insupportable
brightness. The bare stone floor of the town and its deepworn
paths were washed white and clean, and those depressions in the
surface which the Ácomas call their cisterns, were full of fresh
rain water. Already the women were bringing out their clothes, to
begin washing.[92]

A particularly interesting feature of the foregoing passages is the
use made of light. Early in the book's Prologue, when the Spanish
Cardinal and his guests are having dinner in the late afternoon, Willa
Cather writes, ". . . the vehemence of the sun suggested motion. The
light was full of action and had a peculiar quality of climax — of
splendid finish." [93] This gives us a hint as to how she used light imagery,
both in this book and in her previous works. Light is used to suggest
motion and climax; is used, in fact, to transfigure the scene being
described and endow it with a special significance. This is true in the
plough against the sun passage in *My Antonia*, where special illumina-
tion suddenly reveals the true significance of a whole agricultural civilization, which is thereby glorified by it. The same holds good in the
climactic murder scene of *O Pioneers!* where the two lovers both consummate their love and are destroyed by it under a light-drenched
mulberry tree. The passages from *Death Comes for the Archbishop*
quoted above also show Willa Cather using light to prepare for a
climax. In the first of them the ever changing patterns of the cloud
shadows suggest by their fleetingness the human desire for permanence
and stability which finds expression in the Bishop's reflections on the
Rock as sanctuary.[94] In the second passage the violent alternations of
rain and sunshine suggest the passionate mood of the Europeans, which
forms a complete contrast to the stolid immobility of the Acoma Indians
for whom the Bishop has come to perform the Mass; this in turn makes
him regret his present surroundings and long for "his own kind, his own
epoch, for European man and his glorious history of desires and
dreams." [95]

Although Willa Cather uses light as a transfiguring agent in novels
written both early and late, one important difference should be noted.
Formerly she had used light to symbolize the resolution of a conflict in
the previously occurring action. Thus in *My Antonia* the plough
against the sun indicates the resolution of the conflict in Jim Burden's

mind between the rival claims of country and city; in *O Pioneers!* the sun-drenched white mulberry tree stands for the resolution of Marie Shabata's conflict between passionate love and duty to her husband. But in *Death Comes for the Archbishop* Willa Cather uses effects of light more for their own sake. At most, she has them suggest some reflection or other to the mind of the Bishop. This effect is a good deal more passive and static than the previous effects obtained. She now uses tonal climaxes with light instead of emotional climaxes of action.[96]

There can be no doubt that the Bishop feels overwhelmed by the southwestern landscape in which he finds himself, and that this is something new to a Willa Cather protagonist. The question now arises as to why Willa Cather no longer subordinates the landscape to her characters, as she had done in her earlier novels. I would like to suggest that she is no longer interested in writing novels of the type exemplified by *My Ántonia*, or even *The Professor's House*, but wishes to write a local-color story instead; something resembling Sarah Orne Jewett's *Country of the Pointed Firs*, which she had always admired extravagantly.[97] Now local color is a relatively minor literary genre which can be described as having three characteristics: romanticized or sentimentalized characters, a realistic setting (which is, however, used romantically and exploited for its exotic qualities), and a generally escapist tone. This escape may take the form of describing scenes which are at a considerable distance from the audience in space, as in the case of Bret Harte (who wrote for Easterners), or at a considerable remove from them in time, as in the case of Mary Noailles Murfree and George Washington Cable. The plots are often trivial and the construction episodic, and moral problems arising from the action are often shuffled off, since they are not the author's main concern. Local color at its worst tended to depict characters who were flat and mawkishly sentimental; at its best, as in Miss Jewett's work, it tended to show the influence of environment on character, in which case it became something more than local color and passed over into the realm of regional realism.[98] Now Willa Cather had started off as a regional realist of disillusion in her early stories such as "On the Divide," "A Wagner Matinée," and "The Sculptor's Funeral." In the best work of her prairie period she had gone beyond regional realism and written realistic novels of the frontier. Now she has passed her peak and is dwindling down to the nostalgia of local color. *O Pioneers!* and *My Ántonia* are more than local color because Willa Cather shows something of the wild vitality of the land as passing into the heroines, who in turn use it to conquer the land. They are able to respond to the environment in an active way. But in *Death Comes for the Archbishop,* Bishop Latour is merely the percipient who registers sense impressions. Instead of feeling challenged by the land, as would a Willa Cather pioneer, he is content to enjoy the beauties of the scenery, like any tourist.

Since the book's main character is thus not related organically to the environment, it follows from the definition given above that the overall pattern of *Death Comes for the Archbishop* is that of a local-color story. But while this is true of the Bishop, it does not hold true for all the other personages involved in the book. Let us look at some of these other characters and see to what extent *Death Comes for the Archbishop* is a local-color story and to what extent it rises to the level of regional realism.

It might be expected that since Father Vaillant is in the direct line of descent from Willa Cather's pioneers, his personality would bear the imprint of his surroundings. This is true, but not in the way one would expect. Although he is supposed to be a loving shepherd to his flock, Willa Cather never shows him ministering to their needs although she frequently shows him talking about it. On the few occasions when she does portray him with his parishioners, he responds to them in a completely secular way. In one such incident he browbeats a rich rancher into giving him two beautiful white mules which he has taken a fancy to; in another the Mexican women of his parish out of sheer love for him make him six feather beds with pillowcases and sheets to match. So while Willa Cather does present Father Vaillant in organic relation to his background, it is not in his religious capacity that she finds him most interesting.

Willa Cather's treatment of the other characters can be discussed in terms of the ethnic group to which they belong. Her presentation of Anglo-Americans is almost uniformly vapid, with the single exception of the murderer Buck Scales, whom she deftly characterizes in a few swift lines of dialogue. The trapper and Indian guide Kit Carson, the Bishop's beloved "Christobal," is the merest pasteboard figure and bears little relation to the historical Kit Carson;[99] Willa Cather makes a genteel hero out of him.[100] Interestingly enough, she gives practically no indication of any struggle taking place between the Anglo-Americans and other groups, although this became the region's most pressing problem during the period of historical time covered by the book.[101] This is another example of her elimination of conflict. The Mexicans on the other hand receive more detailed treatment. Padre Martinez, the rebel priest of Taos, is exceedingly well rendered, as is his son Trinidad, who is every bit as sensual as his father and yet partakes of the bloody rites of the Penitentes and has himself crucified during Holy Week. In both cases Willa Cather makes it clear that they are very much people of their place and time.[102] She shows that the flamboyant nature of the country left its mark on the character of the people:

> When the Bishop dismounted to enter the church, the women threw their shawls on the dusty pathway for him to walk upon, and as he passed through the kneeling congregation, men and women snatched for his hand to kiss the Episcopal ring. In his own country all this would have been highly distasteful to Jean Marie Latour. Here, these demonstrations seemed a part of the high colour that was in landscape and gardens, in the flaming cactus and the gaudily decorated altars, — in the agonized Christs and the dolorous Virgins and the very human figures of the saints. He had already learned that with this people religion was necessarily theatrical.[103]

While this passage seems on the whole favorable, there are other places where Willa Cather condescends to the Mexicans and devalues them:

> The fickle Mexican population soon found as much diversion in being devout as they had once found in being scandalous. Father Vaillant wrote to his sister Philomène, in France, that the temper of his parish was like that of a boys' school; under one master the lads try to excel one another in mischief and disobedience, under another they vie with each other in acts of loyalty.[104]

> "The more I work with the Mexicans" [says Father Vaillant], "the more I believe it was people like them our Saviour bore in mind when He said, *Unless ye become as little children.* He was thinking of people who are not clever in the things of this world, whose minds are not upon gain and worldly advancement. These poor Christians are not thrifty like our country people at home; they have no veneration for property, no sense of material values." [105]

These passages reveal too much eagerness on the author's part to demonstrate the "quaintness" of her material and smack of literary slumming. They are at the farthest possible remove from her treatment of Bohemians and Scandinavians in her prairie novels.

Her treatment of the Indians is equally ambiguous. She has her hero admire them for their extreme traditionalism, but he does not understand them and does not think that he can.[106] Perhaps he and his creator too do not even want to understand them.[107] Although Willa Cather often praises the Indians, she also uses the Genesis myth [108] and geology[109] to devalue them (as seen in the previously quoted description of the uncompleted landscape around Acoma and the reference to the Indians as crustaceans). That she was afraid of the more vital aspects of the Indian religion we have seen in her description of the cave with the stone lips.[110] Jacinto and Eusabio, her two chief Indian characters, are flat in the extreme; she does not sufficiently differentiate between them, and the reader has difficulty in telling them apart. The one time in the book when the Indians really come to life is when they appear *en masse* and throw Fray Baltazar over the edge of a cliff. Willa Cather never does get inside the Indians, and although she has her hero admire them for not wanting to change the landscape through which they pass,[111] she nevertheless causes him to build a Midi Romanesque cathedral in the middle of Spanish Santa Fe.[112]

The successfully realized characters are almost always those who show the influence of the New Mexican environment; the others do not. In the cases of Padre Martinez and Fray Baltazar, Willa Cather rises to the level of regional realism. Most of the other characters however are of the shallow two-dimensional variety usually found in local color.

Local-color fiction, combining geographical and temporal escapism, lends itself to an extreme nostalgia. The writing of Sarah Orne Jewett had had as one of its chief traits a nostalgia for a preindustrial past, and the same nostalgia, always latent in Willa Cather, can now be seen in the form of intrusive direct statements which stand out from the surrounding prose like a mesa above a plain:

> The old town was better to look at in those days, Father Latour used to tell Bernard with a sigh. In the old days it had an individuality, a style of its own; a tawny adobe town with a few green trees, set in a half-circle of carnelian-coloured hills; that and no more. But the year 1880 had begun a period of incongruous American building. Now, half the plaza square was still adobe, and half was flimsy wooden buildings with double porches, scrollwork and jackstraw posts and banisters painted white. Father Latour said the wooden houses which had so distressed him in Ohio, had followed him.[113]

It is easy to understand why after the terrible agonies Willa Cather must have gone through in writing *The Professor's House* and *My Mortal Enemy* she should turn to local-color fiction as a relief. "Writing this book," she wrote, ". . . was like a happy vacation from life, a return to childhood, to early memories." [114]

> The writing of it took only a few months, because the book had all been lived many times before it was written, and the happy mood in which I began it never paled. It was like going back and playing the early composers after a surfeit of modern music.[115]

But it is precisely the escapist quality of local-color fiction which keeps it from being more than a minor literary genre. And the geographical and temporal escapism is as nothing compared with the evasion involved in the near-complete elimination of strife and struggle from the pages of the book.

THE RELIGIOUS TONE OF THE NOVEL EXAMINED

Of all the books Willa Cather ever wrote *Death Comes for the Archbishop* has the most obviously Catholic subject matter, since it describes the labors of two missionary priests. For this reason many people have assumed that the novel is Catholic in outlook, and even that Willa Cather herself became an actual convert. Catholic commentators themselves have praised the book for its sympathetic and understanding treatment of Catholicism.[116] With this in mind, let us examine the tone of the novel and see whether this view is borne out.

A good place to begin is the section entitled "December Night," in which Willa Cather describes the Bishop's supreme religious experience.[117] In it Bishop Latour, unable to sleep, gets up in the middle of the night and goes to his church to pray. Crouching in the doorway he comes upon a human figure, an old Mexican woman named Sada who is described as the slave of an American family who are militant Protestants and for nineteen years have not let her come to the church to pray or to hear Mass. Seeing her shivering in the midnight chilliness, the Bishop strips off the furred cloak he is wearing and throws it around the shoulders of the trembling woman. Then they enter the church to pray. Of Bishop Latour's reaction to this Willa Cather says: "Never, as he afterward told Father Vaillant, had it been permitted to him to behold such deep experience of the holy joy of religion as on that pale December night." [118] Unlike Fray Baltazar, his moral passion has triumphed over his aesthetic passion, and the problem which has vexed Willa Cather for so many years seems to be solved.

Unfortunately there is one thing wrong with Willa Cather's presentation of this supreme religious experience. I have said that just before entering the church the Bishop gives Sada his fur-lined cloak. Just before this Willa Cather has related the history of the cloak: how he had bought the material for it at Paris before starting for the New World, how it had been made into a riding cloak and lined with fox fur by a German tailor in Ohio, and how, before the Bishop had started for the Southwest, the same tailor had relined it with squirrel skin. Evidently Latour is quite attached to his garment, so that in giving it away he sacrifices something that is of real aesthetic value to him. But when Sada leaves the church, she starts to take the cloak off. He tries to restrain her, telling her to keep it for her own, but she is terrified at the thought of having her oppressors discover it: "No, no, Father! If they were to find it on me!" Whereupon Father Latour substitutes for it a little silver medal of the Virgin which he happens to have about him. Such a medallion would mean little or nothing to him, although Sada reveres it because it has been blessed by the Pope. In return for it he gets his own cloak back, thus undercutting the significance of his sacrifice.

Now there is no doubt that this is intended to be a spontaneously religious action. Willa Cather writes: "Her teeth struck together as she stood trying to control her shivering. With one movement of his free hand the Bishop took the furred cloak from his shoulders and put it about her." [119] Also, the Bishop's experience seems to be one of genuine self-abnegation:

> He was able to feel, kneeling beside her, the preciousness of the things of the altar to her who was without possessions; the tapers, the image of the Virgin, the figures of the saints, the Cross that took away indignity from suffering and made pain and poverty a means of fellowship with Christ. . . .
>
> He received the miracle in her heart into his own, saw through her eyes, knew that his poverty was as bleak as hers. When the Kingdom of Heaven had first come into the world, into a cruel world of torture and slaves and masters, He who brought it had said, *"And whosoever is least among you, the same shall be first in the Kingdom of Heaven."* This church was Sada's house, and he was a servant in it.[120]

But Willa Cather has made one serious technical mistake which blurs the significance of what she was trying to do. By having the Bishop know in advance who Sada was and what her lot was like, she has arranged things so that a moment's reflection would convince him that Sada couldn't possibly keep the cloak: thus she allows him to get credit for generosity when he has made no real sacrifice.

If the moral significance of the ending is blurred as the result of an error of technique, there is still no doubt of the passage's genuinely religious tone. But what are we to think of the episode in which Father Vaillant makes things so uncomfortable for the rich Manuel Lujon that the latter is forced to give him two beautiful white mules? After admiring Angelica and Contento, the stocky little priest tells the rancher, "What an easy gait this mule has, and what a narrow back! I notice that especially. For a man with short legs, like me, it is a punishment to ride eight hours a day on a wide horse. And this I must do day after day." [121] After some thought the Mexican makes him a present of Contento. The next day Father Joseph approaches his host once more:

> "Manuel," he said at once, "I cannot accept your present. I have thought upon it over night, and I see that I cannot. The Bishop works as hard as I do, and his horse is little better than mine." [122]

The wretched Manuel offers him a horse, but the vehement Frenchman will not be dissuaded. "I will raise the price of marriages until I can buy this pair from you," [123] he says, and finally:

> "If I were a rich *ranchero,* like you, Manuel, I would do a splendid thing; I would furnish the two mounts that are to carry the word of God about this heathen country, and then I would say to myself: *There go my Bishop and my Vicario, on my beautiful cream-coloured mules."* [124]

The rancher finally gives in.

Here is an example of a Willa Cather protagonist practicing "one-upmanship" by making use of the conventions of the society in which he lives. What Father Vaillant has done is to maneuver the Mexican into a position where he can't say no. It is all the more striking because he has just previously declined to buy a horse from the Indians, stating: "If we are to save their souls, we must make it clear that we want no

profit for ourselves. . . ." [125] It is hard to avoid the conclusion that
this is human selfishness passing itself off as religious need, for Father
Vaillant does not need a beautiful mule to carry him on his journeys;
all he needs is a sturdy one. If he uses the authority of the Church
in order to secure the beast for himself, he is perverting the power of
the Church to purely personal ends, as well as being guilty of covetous-
ness. If Willa Cather recognizes this fact, she fails to indicate it; for
her attitude is one of approval throughout. She ends her anecdote by
saying:

> . . . from his gate Señor Lujon watched them disconsolately
> until they disappeared. He felt he had been worried out of his
> mules, and yet he bore no resentment. He did not doubt Father
> Joseph's devotedness, nor his singleness of purpose. After all, a
> Bishop was a Bishop, and a Vicar was a Vicar, and it was not
> to their discredit that they worked like a pair of common parish
> priests. He believed he would be proud of the fact that they
> rode Contento and Angelica. Father Vaillant had forced his hand,
> but he was rather glad of it.[126]

Willa Cather does not often have her priests engage in sharp prac-
tices of dubious morality, but she does give other indications in the
book that Catholicism is not her main interest, but rather civilized
living. When gold is discovered under Pikes Peak and Father Vaillant
travels to Denver to become priest on the new frontier of Colorado, he
is shocked at the stupid, unnecessary discomforts found in mining
camps. "It was part of the Wild West attitude to despise the decencies
of life." [127] On a return trip to Santa Fe he tells his Mexican flock
about these deprivations:

> His dining-table was made of planks covered with oilcloth. He
> had no linen at all, neither sheets nor serviettes, and he used his
> worn-out shirts for face towels. . . . Nobody in Colorado planted
> gardens, Father Vaillant related; nobody would stick a shovel
> into the earth for anything less than gold. There was no butter,
> no milk, no eggs, no fruit. He lived on dough and cured hog
> meat.[128]

Whereupon the Mexican peasant women start making contributions to
Father Joseph, not for his congregation at Denver, but for himself. It
is this aspect of the incident which Willa Cather finds interesting; she

emphasizes, not the sufferings of the frontier community, but the personal tribute to the individual:

> Within a few weeks after his arrival, six feather-beds were sent to the Bishop's house for Father Vaillant; dozens of linen sheets, embroidered pillow-cases and table cloths and napkins; strings of chili and boxes of beans and dried fruit. The little settlement of Chimayo sent a roll of their finest blankets.[129]

Now if the life of renunciation is to mean anything at all, it must be accepted with the full consciousness that it *is* a life of renunciation. Willa Cather shows no sign of realizing this. There is nothing wrong in her having the Mexican women pay tribute to Father Vaillant in this tangible way because of their personal admiration for him. But it can hardly be argued that the way in which she treats the episode is in any sense religious; she places much more emphasis on Father Vaillant as a person than as a religious leader. I have shown that he is the only character in the book who has taken the risk of going to a new frontier which was not even civilized, let alone Catholic. The bestowal of luxury goods upon him materially diminishes the sacrifice he is making, and Willa Cather's handling of the situation undermines the spiritual significance she has been trying to give to his life.

There are times when the distinction between worldly and spiritual matters becomes very confused indeed. In this book Miss Cather's mind sometimes wanders, as it does in most of the books she was to write from now on; the point that she actually made was not always the point that she wished to make. One example occurs later in the book when Father Vaillant is about to take his final leave of the Bishop to do missionary work in the Colorado gold fields:

> Yes, he reflected, as he went quietly to his own room, there was a great difference in their natures. Wherever he went, he soon made friends that took the place of country and family. But Jean, who was at ease in any society and always the flower of courtesy, could not form new ties. It had always been so. He was like that even as a boy; gracious to everyone, but known to a very few. To man's wisdom it would have seemed that a priest with Father Latour's exceptional qualities would have been better placed in some part of the world where scholarship, a handsome person, and delicate perceptions all have their effect; and that a man of much rougher type would have served God well enough

as the first Bishop of New Mexico. Doubtless Bishop Latour's
successors would be men of a different fibre. But God had his
reasons, Father Joseph devoutly believed.[130] Perhaps it had pleased
Him to grace the beginning of a new era and a vast new diocese
by a fine personality. And perhaps, after all, something would
remain through the years to come, some ideal, or memory, or
legend.[131]

Now this passage is dramatically inappropriate when put in the mouth
of Father Vaillant, who for all his virtues is not a man of delicate
perception. Willa Cather has interrupted her character and is speaking
in her own person once more. But there are other things wrong with
the passage as well. It involves no recognition that the religious calling
often involves the giving up of worldly things; instead Willa Cather
seems to feel that the Bishop should have the best of everything,
whether sacred or profane. Furthermore the passage fails completely
as an attempt to analyze Bishop Latour's character. Willa Cather
writes, "But Jean, who was at ease in any society and always the
flower of courtesy, could not form new ties." This is self-contradictory;
if the Bishop cannot form new ties, he obviously is not at ease in all
societies. Apparently all he can do is to form superficial relations based
on politeness and formality.

The burden of this passage is that Father Vaillant can change and
adapt himself to new places and times, while Father Latour cannot.
The description of Father Latour shows a sense of waste, loss and un-
appreciated personality, which is all very well as a worldly judgment
but is quite out of place when attributed to someone who is supposed to
have devoted his life to God. Willa Cather tries to give a flattering
explanation of the Bishop's fate ("Perhaps it pleased Him to grace the
beginning of a new era and a vast diocese by a fine personality"), but
this is not very plausible, since such a person would not be likely to be
appreciated until much later on. She misses the point. It is not his
abilities but his limitations which make the Bishop unhappy; his
trouble is that he cannot form new ties. Willa Cather veers away from
the real issue.

Again, as the Bishop rides home from having seen Father Joseph
off, she has him reflect:

He was forty-seven years old, and he had been a missionary
in the New World for twenty years — ten of them in New Mexico.
If he were a parish priest at home, there would be nephews coming

to him for help in their Latin or a bit of pocket-money; nieces to run into his garden and bring their sewing and keep an eye on his housekeeping. All the way home he indulged in such reflections as any bachelor nearing fifty might have.[132]

Here the Bishop shows a perfectly natural longing for human relations within the family. Yet in the next paragraph he denies that such a longing in him exists — and Willa Cather, with her usual inability to maintain a detached point of view, shoulders her character aside and enthusiastically agrees with him:

> But when he entered his study, he seemed to come back to reality, to the sense of a Presence awaiting him. The curtain of the arched doorway had scarcely fallen behind him when that feeling of personal loneliness was gone, and a sense of loss was replaced by a sense of restoration. He sat down before his desk, deep in reflection. It was just this solitariness of love in which a priest's life could be like his Master's. It was not a solitude of atrophy, of negation, but of perpetual flowering. A life need not be cold, or devoid of grace in a worldly sense, if it were filled by Her who was all the graces; Virgin-mother, girl of the people and Queen of Heaven: *le rêve suprême de la chair.* The nursery tale could not vie with Her in simplicity, the wisest theologians could not match her in profundity.[133]

It is plain that Willa Cather doesn't want her hero to have to give up anything; she won't admit that people have to give things up and sometimes must make painful choices. When she says, "It was not a solitude of atrophy, of negation, but of perpetual flowering," she is saying not what she believes, but what she wishes to believe. We are given no reason at all why. We are simply asked to regard the statement as true. And when she says that such a life "need not be cold, or devoid of grace in a worldly sense," what can we do but declare this untrue unless the word "worldly" loses all its meaning? Here she is dealing with the same conflict between human ties and devotion to a calling which had formed the central problem of *The Professor's House.* But whereas in that book the agonizing tension between the two brought the novel to life, here she is denying that the conflict even exists. She tries to convince herself that rejection of human ties involves no real loss, that what the Bishop has given up, he has not given up. This is precisely what she had criticized Bartley Alexander for fifteen years before. The failure to recognize the existence of human limitations constitutes the great defect of Willa Cather's moral vision; it is this self-same lack that kept her from developing as an author and made everything she wrote after *The Professor's House* of minor importance. Charming as it is, *Death Comes for the Archbishop* is only too good an example of this; in it religion is made easy, and renunciation is robbed of its sting.

The escapist tendency of Willa Cather's mind is brought out clearly in the very next paragraph after the one previously quoted:

> Here in his own church in Santa Fé there was one of these nursery Virgins, a little wooden figure, very old and very dear to the people. De Vargas, when he recaptured the city for Spain two hundred years ago, had vowed a yearly procession in her honour, and it was still one of the most solemn events of the Christian year in Santa Fé. She was a little wooden figure, about three feet high, very stately in bearing, with a beautiful though rather severe Spanish face. She had a rich wardrobe; a chest full of robes and laces, and gold and silver diadems. The women loved to sew for her and the silversmiths to make her chains and brooches. Father Latour had delighted her wardrobe keepers when he told them he did not believe the Queen of England or the Empress of France had so many costumes. She was their doll and their queen, something to fondle and something to adore, as Mary's Son must have been to Her.[134]

Willa Cather has now dropped completely the painful idea of religious renunciation and gone on to something which is more to her liking. This passage has very little to do altogether with religion, but it has quite a bit to do with its artistic accoutrements. Enlarging on *le rêve suprême de la chair* and describing the little wooden image of the Virgin in the church at Santa Fe, once again her mind slides away from the issue at stake to something which is less ugly and more pleasing than the problem at hand. At the end of the paragraph the whole cult of the Virgin Mary is reduced to the image of a little girl playing with her doll.

It would seem that Willa Cather's interpretation of Catholicism is not a very profound one; as in other cases she takes only what interests her and leaves the rest behind. Just as her earlier treatment of the hero as the paragon to whom all ordinary people must submit themselves ignored the necessity for give-and-take in human relationships, so the portrayal of her ecclesiastical heroes fails to take into account the fact that religious calling demands the continuous subordination of the lower self to the higher self. In this book Willa Cather seems to have a bad case of wanting to have things both ways at once. She wants Bishop Latour to be both worldly *and* spiritual; she confuses the Catholic religion with the artistic objects with which it tends to surround itself, forgetting that, however lovely these may be, they are only a part of the story and not the whole. It is hard to interpret this as anything but another sign of her weakening hold on moral realities which was rapidly bringing her career as a serious artist to a close.

Having examined the foregoing incidents, we are now in a better position to evaluate the religious tone of the novel. It would appear that, although religious in spots, the book is only intermittently Catholic at best.[135] Therefore it is reasonable to ask what nonreligious use Willa Cather makes of religious material. The answer to this can be given in three parts: she regards the Church as a repository of tradition and ritual, as an art object, and as a larger projection of the family.

USES OF THE CHURCH: THE CHURCH AS RITUAL AND TRADITION

The moral teachings of the Church receive relatively little attention from Willa Cather. The reason for this is not any lack of good will on her part, but rather that her interest tends to center on other things than religion. She is becoming more and more an enthusiast for tradition and ritual, and she tends to like Catholicism because it puts a high premium on these things. But we have already seen that she admired Indian culture at least as much and for the very same reasons; there is nothing Catholic about her admiration of Eusabio's steadfast refusal to adopt Christianity. Moreover, although in her Catholic novels she talks at considerable length about ritual, it is usually not religious ritual which she describes but the domestic kind. Her interest seems to center around the kitchen rather than the cathedral. Thus while she mentions Father Vaillant's or Bishop Latour's celebrating Mass or the Novena, she never describes it. What she does describe is the carving of lamb, the preparing of salad oil, the making of soup.

USES OF THE CHURCH: THE CHURCH AS ART OBJECT

If Willa Cather was not primarily interested in Catholicism as Catholicism, just what was her interest in it? I have indicated one answer by noting her waning appreciation of forceful spontaneity and her growing interest in tradition and ritual, as exemplified by her relegation of Father Vaillant to the status of a subordinate and her portrayal of the opposed characters of Padre Martinez and Bishop Latour. But the chief way she regards the Church in this book is as a kind of gigantic art object; she loves Catholic Christianity for that religion's tendency to surround itself with beautiful things. In her earlier novels she had shown that she associated Catholicism with beauty and Protestantism with the deprivation of beauty; one need only contrast the role the Church played in the lives of the French and Bohemians in *My Ántonia* and *O Pioneers!* with the role played by evangelical Protestantism in *The Song of the Lark, My Ántonia, One of Ours,* and *The Professor's House.* One recalls Professor St. Peter's speech to his students on the glories of the medieval Catholic world drama in which he said: "Art and religion — they come to the same thing in the end — give men the only happiness they have ever had." [136] The Archbishop has very much the same response. The aesthetic importance of religion to Willa Cather is heightened by the fact that the responses of both the Archbishop and the Professor seem to have less to do with religion than they do with art. This is evident when we recall Willa Cather's description of how Father Latour came to build himself a cathedral:

> Bishop Latour had one very keen worldly ambition: to build in Santa Fé a Cathedral which would be worthy of a setting naturally beautiful. As he cherished this wish and meditated upon it, he came to feel that such a building might be a continuation of himself and his purpose, a physical body full of his aspirations after he had passed from the scene.[137]

And when the Bishop discovers his golden-ocher hill whose stone is of exactly the right color to build a Midi Romanesque cathedral like those of his native Clermont, he says to his companion, "I tell you, *Blanchet,* I would rather have found that hill of yellow rock than have come into a fortune to spend in charity . . . I hope you do not think me very worldly." [138] Worldly, of course, is exactly what this reveals him to be, and his desire to leave a thing of beauty as his own personal monument contrasts sharply with Father Vaillant's oft-repeated desire to do missionary work, which finally leads him to the Colorado frontier. I have shown that Father Vaillant certainly has more of the religious impulse in him. One would expect him to be the center of attention if the novel were genuinely Catholic. But since it is not Catholicism at all but a secular value associated with it which interests the author, Father Vaillant receives only a second place.

USES OF THE CHURCH: THE CHURCH
AS THE LARGER FAMILY

But there is another highly important aspect of the Church which Willa Cather makes use of in *Death Comes for the Archbishop*. This can be summed up in the phrase "religion as the larger family." I have shown that from the beginning of her career practically all of Willa Cather's values stemmed from the multigeneration family, which to her was the fundamental unit of society. In the novels dealt with in the section entitled "The World Dissolved" she noted that the close-knit familial organization she had grown up in was disintegrating, and saw this disintegration as being paralleled by the break-up of society itself. The question for her then became one of how social order could be reintroduced and how the family unit could be restored as the locus of values. Looking about her she thought she might find the answer in the ecclesiastical organization of the Catholic Church. The Church assumes the importance and sanctity of the family unit, and it considers itself to be a larger family, in which all men are brothers united under the leadership of a spiritual father. Bishop Latour's Great Diocese thus becomes his own family unit writ large; all the Catholics in the Southwest are his spiritual children. Moreover Willa Cather portrays the relation between Father Vaillant and Bishop Latour as being almost a familial one. As is the case with Ántonia and Cuzak, Father Vaillant is the active partner and the Bishop the cautious one, a combination we have seen more than once in Willa Cather's portrayal of married couples. What is more, Father Joseph keeps house for the Bishop, watches over his Mexican "children," attends to their needs, and does the cooking, taking care that suitable meals are served and that they are properly prepared. Further evidence of this aspect of their relationship is the fact that the Bishop's only real emotional struggle occurs when Father Joseph wants to leave Santa Fe to become a missionary in Colorado, while Bishop Latour wants him to stay at home with him.

So it was that Willa Cather saw the Catholic Church as an extension of the family unit, and it became for her a larger family immune to the harms and hurts to which private families are subject. This was her answer to the disintegration of the multigeneration family unit in the course of her lifetime. Not only were all the Catholics in the Southwest the Bishop's spiritual children; because of the Church's hierarchical organization, they were compelled to obey their spiritual father. This feature could hardly have failed to please the authoritarian bent in her temperament. At last she saw a possible way of harmonizing what for her had always been incompatibles: the claims of human relations and devotion to the calling of beauty, whether in religion or in art. The Catholic hierarchy provided a patterned society like the multigeneration family unit in which people played prescribed roles; it exemplified for her a way of accepting people — and of forcing them to accept you.

In view of the foregoing evidence I do not find that *Death Comes for the Archbishop* is more than incidentally Catholic. In all its three hundred and more pages Willa Cather makes hardly any mention of the passion and crucifixion of Jesus, and no mention of an afterlife. These are fairly important points in Catholic doctrine. It is true that there is repeated reference to the Virgin Mary, but Willa Cather continually stresses her qualities as a woman, not as the Mother of God. Her interest in Catholicism seems to be almost completely aesthetic rather than religious or moral. The Church has long held that religious instruction can be instilled through the senses as well as by other means; that is why it has so often served as patron to religious art. Willa Cather has misinterpreted the role played by artistic beauty in Catholicism and erected what was meant to be a means into an end. There is more to Catholicism than the enjoyment of artistic splendor. If Willa Cather realized that religion is discipline, she has not made her characters realize it.

Summary of *Death Comes for the Archbishop:* The Cathedral and the Stagecoach

I have remarked earlier that in her novels Willa Cather often employs a double protagonist, one of whom symbolizes the heart, the other the head, and that the two stand for different aspects of Willa Cather herself, and represent the sophisticate and the provincial dwelling side by side in her own breast. In Father Vaillant and Archbishop Latour she has presented the two different ways of life which interested her, the one in her youth, the other in her age. The two can be symbolized in the images of the cathedral and the stagecoach: the great stone pile by means of which the Bishop hopes to perpetuate his personality, and the rough jolting vehicle inside of which Father Joseph would lean forward to greet an incoming guest. The cathedral is beautiful but it is a little cold, a little remote from human needs (at least in the sense in which the Bishop envisions it); above all it is stationary and unchanging. The stagecoach is much humbler, rather ugly, but is designed for human needs and is warm with human life within; and most important of all, it is dynamic, constantly moving on to seek new places. These two images could serve as tropes not only for Willa Cather's two clergymen, but also for her conception of art and life themselves. Throughout most of her career Willa Cather had tried to combine the two and achieve some sort of balance. Here again she tries to combine them by having Father Vaillant and the Bishop set up a household together almost as if they were a married couple. Once Father Vaillant leaves for Colorado, however, the balance is upset, and the Bishop is exposed again to the pangs of loneliness. But Willa Cather quickly intervenes, insisting that the Bishop isn't really lonely at all. It is easy to see the Bishop in his solitude as a type of the author herself who has given up everything for art, and wondering whether after all the choice really was worth while. But the later Willa Cather is not so clear-headed as the younger one had been; she refuses to admit that any conflict between art and life exists; so she tells us that the Bishop's solitude is not solitude after all.

In her *Commonweal* letter Willa Cather writes of *Death Comes for the Archbishop:* "As a writer I had the satisfaction of working in a special genre which I had long wished to try." [139] This statement is highly revealing. For the genre she is writing in is that of local color; *Death Comes for the Archbishop* fits all the specifications for a local-color story which I have previously set up. Its characters are mostly stereotypes or, if not this, are (with a few notable exceptions) sentimentally rendered; even its two heroes are not related to their environment in any clear way, and, although Father Vaillant comes to life from time to time, the Bishop remains rather vague. The setting of the book is probably its best feature. Willa Cather gives a good realistic description of the Spanish Southwest, but uses it romantically; that is, she uses the landscape and the Catholic Church together as an exotic and exciting backdrop for what little action the book contains; she uses it the way local-color writers make use of their backgrounds. The book is permeated with a strong feeling of nostalgia for an earlier and, it is implied, a better time in which the problems of a commercial and industrial civilization simply had not arisen. The idea of recovery of the past can be found in Willa Cather's writing as far back as *My Ántonia;* one need only recall the note of Populist nostalgia on which that novel ended. But now it has become so important to Miss Cather that it forms the major theme of the entire book.

Now local-color fiction, charming as it may be, is a minor genre because it takes a limited view of things and one implying an escape from life. Thomas Love Peacock could have used it to justify his "mental rattle" theory of poetry. Since it is more concerned with the presentation of picturesque surroundings than of human problems, it very often neglects to describe struggle and conflict. This is just what Willa Cather tells us she wanted to do when she writes: "I had all my life wanted to do something in the style of legend, which is absolutely the reverse of dramatic treatment." [140] It is true that omitting conflict from a book is the reverse of dramatic treatment, but such a literary method loses more than it gains. Conflict is the essence of life, and it is the essence of nearly all novels. The reason that we can accept a work of literature as an interpretation of human experience is that the conflicts it portrays are in some sense an extension of our own. The absence of struggle, far from being a virtue, is a handicap in this narrative. It is precisely because of the lack of struggle that *Death Comes for the Archbishop* is less memorable than the prairie novels or *A Lost Lady*.

But leaving aside for the moment the value of what she is attempting, does Willa Cather accomplish in the book what she says she does? Does she consistently omit conflict and deal with the lives of the two fathers in the style of legend? The answer is no. Willa Cather doesn't treat *Death Comes for the Archbishop* like a fresco by Puvis de Chavannes; she doesn't give great and little happenings equal importance. On the whole she gives much more importance to little things: to chance sense impressions, the gold-ocher color of a hill, the delicate taste of a soup. This is neither medieval nor saintly. And in spite of what she says in the *Commonweal* letter we find her reverting to the novelistic technique she had practiced before. Her dialogue is like that in a realistic novel; even she realized that it resembled "the old trite phraseology of the frontier." [141] The aura of realism which surrounds the book contradicts her avowed intention of imitating legend. Moreover, although she says she wished to omit conflict entirely, she occasionally fails to do so; one can say of the book that when it's good, it's dramatic. A few parts of it are very dramatic indeed: for example, the legend of Fray Baltazar and the scene between Bishop Latour and Padre Martinez. But, except in the case of Fray Baltazar, she never shows the conflict resolved. Miss Cather's comments on her aims and ideas are frequently illuminating, but they do not always have much bearing on the work referred to. Her capacity for self-criticism was small.

Because of her tendency to eliminate conflict from the novel, one feels that the order which Willa Cather stresses so much is a spurious order; that human problems have been ignored rather than transcended. The realities of the situation she deals with are put on a Procrustean bed, and if any should fail to fit in with her ideas, so much the worse for them. It is this distortion of what life is like in favor of her pre-conceived view of what it should be like that makes her later fiction so much less interesting to read than her earlier work. She was very much interested in presenting an image of life without conflict, without tension between opposing claims, and this apparently is more than life has to offer. Evidence of this can be found even in her presentation of the things which now interest her, especially in her treatment of landscape. In her pioneer novels enjoyment of nature had been a reward for struggling with nature. Now nature is enjoyed tourist-fashion for its own sake. Her evasion of the serious problems she had treated in previous novels becomes most marked when she is dealing with ritual. Instead of the mysteries of life and death, Willa Cather invites us to consider the mysteries of the gourmet's dinner table. Instead of sowing and harvesting and the cycle of the seasons we find cooking and eating and the preparation of three meals a day. Religious ritual has given way to domestic ritual.

Thus the order which in earlier books had grown out of the material itself and had been based on a fairly frank confrontation of human conflict is here forcefully imposed by the author with no regard for the material because Willa Cather felt an extreme reluctance even to suggest the idea of conflict. In *Death Comes for the Archbishop* she gives a convincing picture of neither the inner discipline which constituted the strength of the pioneers nor the external discipline responsible for the functioning of the Catholic Church. This lack of any real order in her vision is emphasized by the loose episodic construction of the novel. The fact that Willa Cather wrote a poorly organized book extolling the virtues of order does not argue well for her insight. There is something inherently ludicrous in a disorderly praise of order. Discipline, one would think, should begin at home.

Of all the books Willa Cather ever wrote, *Death Comes for the Archbishop* is by far the most popular. It ran through eleven editions, was translated into eight languages, and is known to people who have never read anything else of Willa Cather's. Many consider it to be the crowning glory of her achievement. In spite of this, it is not a good book. The reason is that her anxiety for order stultified her creative urge and crippled her vision of life. *Death Comes for the Archbishop* falsifies the facts as she herself had previously seen them; for she asks us to admire the Bishop as both a pioneer and a deeply religious man,

whereas in the book he is neither. Pioneers have to struggle, but the
Bishop lets Father Vaillant do his struggling for him. Religious men
have to face the problem of evil and suffering, but this too is carefully
avoided. In *My Ántonia* she had used the vegetation myth as a means
of confronting and transcending the great problem presented by the
fact of death. Now the only allusion to the fertility myth occurs in
connection with Indian snake worship, and there it is found disgusting.

A great deal of Willa Cather's trouble with *Death Comes for the
Archbishop* seems to stem from her confusion of art with life. She does
not realize that things which are ugly in the living, such as intense conflict, suffering, and pain, can be rendered beautiful by the ordering
process which constitutes the essence of art. Instead, she forms her
own special variant of the genteel tradition by trying to avoid all mention of ugly things. The result is a vision of life which is pitifully
maimed and inadequate; at times it seems superficial and unconvincing,
at times downright dishonest in its ignoring of the issues raised. What
remains? Some beautiful description of landscape and a well-conceived
minor character or two. At the end of her most famous essay Willa
Cather remarks: "The elder Dumas enunciated a great principle when
he said that to make a drama, one needed one passion and four walls." [142]
She followed this principle in her prairie novels, but in *Death Comes for
the Archbishop* she has given us four walls and left the passion out.

Shadows on the Rock: From Acoma to Quebec

In *Shadows on the Rock* Willa Cather set herself a different task from
the one which had occupied her in *Death Comes for the Archbishop*.
What she was trying to do she expressed in a letter to Governor Wilbur
Cross of Connecticut, who had written an appreciative review of the
book in *The Saturday Review of Literature*.[143] Her letter is interesting
for what it reveals of her intention:

> You seem to have seen what a different kind of method I tried
> to use from that which I used in the *Archbishop*. I tried, as you
> say, to state the mood and the viewpoint in the title. To me the
> rock of Quebec is not only a stronghold on which many strange
> figures have for a little time cast a shadow in the sun; it is the
> curious endurance of a kind of culture, narrow but definite. There
> another age persists. . . . It is hard to state that feeling in
> language; it was more like an old song, incomplete but uncorrupted,
> than like a legend. . . . I took the incomplete air and tried to

give it what would correspond to a sympathetic musical setting; tried to develop it into a prose composition not too conclusive, not too definite: a series of pictures remembered rather than experienced; a kind of thinking, a mental complexion inherited, left over from the past, lacking in robustness and full of pious resignation.[144]

When we compare this letter with the *Commonweal* letter on *Death Comes for the Archbishop* written four years before, we notice an interesting change in Willa Cather's attitude. She no longer sounds as happy and contented as she had previously. "The mood is the thing," she had said in describing the former novel, and the same holds true of this one, but it is an entirely different mood. Of *Death Comes for the Archbishop* she had written, "Writing this book . . . was like a happy vacation from life, a return to childhood, to early memories." What interests her in her Quebec story is "the endurance of a kind of culture . . . there another age persists." Now she is much more on the defensive. In *Death Comes for the Archbishop* she had "wanted to do something in the style of legend" and had tried to imitate in prose the frescoes of Puvis de Chavannes. In *Shadows on the Rock* she is trying to describe a feeling about life which reminded her of an incomplete old song which she tried to set down in a series of pictures which would correspond to a musical setting. In short, her conception of art has shifted from the pictorial to the musical

As Willa Cather continues her letter, she sounds even more defensive than before. She writes:

Now, it seemed to me that the mood of the misfits among the early settlers (and there were a good many) must have been just that. An orderly little French household that went on trying to live decently, just as ants begin to rebuild when you kick their house down, interests me more than Indian raids or the wild life in the forests. . . . And really, a new society begins with the salad dressing more than with the destruction of Indian villages. Those people brought a kind of French culture there and somehow kept it alive on that rock, sheltered it and tended it and on occasion died for it, as if it really were a sacred fire — and all this temperately and shrewdly, with emotion always tempered by good sense.[145]

There is a good deal of transferred self-pity in this description of the orderly little French household that tries to go on living decently;

Willa Cather has a chip on her shoulder against the modern world. Two
other qualities of the passage stand out. In her *Commonweal* letter
Willa Cather wrote that *Death Comes for the Archbishop* sprang from
her interest in two different things: the history of the Church in the
Southwest and the personality of Bishop Latour's prototype, Archbishop
Lamy. The Church's history attracted her because of the way in which
local customs had shaped religious habits. This is shown in the case
of Padre Martinez and his son Trinidad; by showing the positive influence of environment on character she had affirmed the environment.
But in the *Saturday Review* letter she emphasizes "the mood of the
misfits." This negative attitude shows fear of the environment, as seen
in the case of the apothecary M. Auclair. Similarly what interested her
in Archbishop Lamy was the possibility of living the comely life on the
frontier. What interested her in her Quebec story is the life of the
household, of which she makes salad dressing the symbol. As I suggested
in discussing the onion soup interlude in *Death Comes for the Archbishop*, the preparation of food may be an inadequate symbol of the
comely life.

The two letters reflect a difference in the two novels inasmuch as
they show an increased sense of alienation on the author's part as well
as an increasingly narrow scope. In passing from one book to the
other, the rediscovery of the past becomes a hanging-on to the past; the
larger family of the Bishop's Great Diocese shrinks to the personal
family of the Auclair household; the administration of the religious
affairs of the entire Southwest gives place to the tending of the family
hearthfire.

There are personal reasons for the subdued tone of *Shadows on the
Rock*. At the time Willa Cather was writing it her mother was suffering
from her last illness, and, as E. K. Brown says, "So great was Willa
Cather's involvement in what her mother was undergoing that she
could scarcely continue the writing of *Shadows on the Rock*." [146] In
addition her father had just died, a blow which she had taken extremely
hard; his spirit hovers over the pages of the novel and finds embodiment
in the character of M. Auclair, the gentle apothecary. This helps explain
the nostalgic tone of the story; Willa Cather was trying to re-create
the warmth and security of a family group which now had vanished
forever. Perhaps this is the reason why the story is seen through the
eyes of a twelve-year-old girl. [147] The one group of people with whom
she had had really close emotional ties was now broken up, and Willa
Cather was left alone in the world with her art.

The residue of this emotion is a certain dreamlike quality which pervades the book and is suggested by the title. Human life consists but of passing shadows, she seems to say, and the title itself is reminiscent of Plato's cave. But although she admits that for her the rock is "a stronghold on which many strange figures have for a little time cast a shadow in the sun," her main interest is in the rock as sanctuary. What had been a single incident in the previous book now forms the subject of an entire novel; the Rock of Acoma has become the Rock of Quebec.

Any discussion of the Rock's meaning should go back to Father Duchene's remarks on the findings at Blue Mesa in "Tom Outland's Story." This contains the idea of the Rock as sanctuary in miniature:

> "Like you I feel a reverence for this place. Wherever humanity has made that hardest of all starts and lifted itself out of mere brutality, is a sacred spot. Your people were cut off here without the influence of example or emulation, with no incentive but some natural yearning for order and security. They built themselves into this mesa and humanized it." [148]

Willa Cather had expressed the same idea in *Death Comes for the Archbishop,* remarking that the Acoma Indians actually lived on their rock, and that there was something strange about such complete literalness. Now, instead of peopling her Rock with primitive Indians who could not respond to "European man and his glorious history of desires and dreams," she peoples it with civilized Frenchmen who transplant the best there is in France to the wilds of Canada and try to leave the evil behind. She still wants to make life safe, but she wants it to be a little more exciting than that of the Acoma Indians, and thus tries to combine bedrock security with "European man and his glorious history of desire and dreams."

Like *Death Comes for the Archbishop, Shadows on the Rock* shows the author's strong resistance to change. As in the previous book, Willa Cather does her best to eliminate all conflict, and underplays the stormy careers of the Comte de Frontenac and Monsignor Laval. But before the book is over there is a withdrawal from this position, and the author's spokesmen are made to feel regret for the old days when, as they believe, heroic action was still possible. Both Laval and Frontenac are shown as heroic individualists who live on into an age of trivialities; so is the now dead Chevalier Robert de la Salle. It is easy to see in this the Willa Cather of the nineteen-twenties and thirties longing for the rugged individualism of the pioneer period. As in *Death Comes for the Archbishop* she tries to submit life to the strictest order; as in *Death*

Comes for the Archbishop she is unable to forget the memory of past glories performed by individual heroes and looks back on them with mournful regret.

TRIUMPH OF THE CITY: FEAR OF THE FRONTIER

One indication of Willa Cather's resistance to change is her new attitude toward the wild land. The frontier has now become an enemy. Formerly her protagonists had regarded it with awe, to be sure, but still as a challenge, with all the exhilaration that that implies. Now it is regarded with revulsion, as something to flee from which is deadly to man. Willa Cather writes:

> On the opposite shore of the river, just across from the proud rock of Quebec, the black pine forest came down to the water's edge; and on the west, behind the town, the forest stretched no living man knew how far. That was the dead, sealed world of the vegetable kingdom, an uncharted continent choked with interlocking trees, living, dead, half-dead, their roots in bogs and swamps, strangling each other in a slow agony that had lasted for centuries. The forest was suffocation, annihilation; there European man was quickly swallowed up in silence, distance, mould, black mud, and the stinging swarms of insect life that bred in it. The only avenue of escape was along the river. The river was the one thing that lived, moved, glittered, changed, — a highway along which men could travel, taste the sun and open air, feel freedom, join their fellows, reach the open sea . . . reach the world, even![149]

The inhabitants of Quebec cling to their Rock just as the Indians at Acoma clung to theirs; Willa Cather still tends to regard the Rock as the utmost expression of human need. A fairly typical although somewhat exaggerated attitude toward the forest is shown by Blinker, the poor misshapen friend of the Auclairs who tends the oven fires of the baker next door:

> He had such a horror of the forest that he would not even go into the nearby woods to help fell trees for firewood, and his fear of Indians was one of the bywords of Mountain Hill. Pigeon used to tell his customers that if the Count went to chastise the Iroquois beyond Cataraqui, Blinker would hide in his cave in Quebec. Blinker protested that he had been warned in a dream that he would be taken prisoner and tortured by the Indians.[150]

In *Shadows on the Rock,* in marked distinction to *Death Comes for the Archbishop,* there is always fog between earth and heaven, between Quebec and the sun, between the real and the ideal. This is one of the meanings of the title. In the earlier book the role of light had been a major one; it served as a transfiguring agent to lend significance to moments of insight; the light of heaven had been so important that nothing was allowed to interpose itself between the land and the brilliance of the sky. But in Quebec the inhabitants are always conscious of being cut off from heaven by the clouds, just as they are cut off by the ocean from France and civilization. This sense of alienation which the colonists feel makes them think that even the angels are farther from them in Quebec than they were in France; only Blinker thinks that they are actually much nearer.[151]

In contrast to their fear of the frontier, the Quebec colonists feel a love for the Rock, for their town, and specifically for the household of the apothecary M. Euclide Auclair, which symbolizes the other two for them. Willa Cather writes:

> The colonists liked to drop in at his house upon the slightest pretext; the interior was like home to the Frenchborn. On a heavy morning, when clouds of thick grey fog rolled up from the St. Lawrence, it cheered one to go into a place that was like an apothecary's shop at home; to glimpse the comfortable sitting-room through the tall cabinets and chests of drawers that separated without entirely shutting it off from the shop.[152]

The homelike atmosphere of the household is the work of the apothecary's wife, Mme. Auclair, who has died before the book began. Of her Willa Cather says:

> Madame Auclair had brought her household goods, without which she could not imagine life at all, and the salon behind the shop was very much like their old salon in Paris. . . . As long as she lived, she tried to make the new life as much as possible like the old. After she began to feel sure that she would never be well enough to return to France, her chief care was to train her little daughter so that she would be able to carry on this life and this order after she was gone.[153]

This attitude on the part of a Willa Cather mother should come as no surprise. Alexandra Bergson's mother had felt precisely the same way:

Habit was very strong with Mrs. Bergson, and her unremitting
efforts to repeat the routine of her old life among new surroundings
had done a great deal to keep the family from disintegrating
morally and getting careless in their ways. . . .

She had never quite forgiven John Bergson for bringing her to the
end of the earth; but, now that she was there, she wanted to be
let alone to reconstruct her old life in so far as that was possible.[154]

In *Shadows on the Rock,* the center of the whole novel is the Auclair
household, which a moment's thought reveals to be another form of the
room of one's own, or image of sanctuary. All the emphasis on home,
household goods, and undisturbed continuance of domestic customs is
simply another expression of the anxiety for order which had preoccupied Miss Cather in *Death Comes for the Archbishop:*

Madame Auclair never spoke of her approaching death, but
would say something like this:

"After a while, when I am too ill to help you, you will perhaps
find it fatiguing to do all these things alone, over and over. But
in time you will come to love your duties, as I do. You will see
that your father's whole happiness depends on order and regularity,
and you will come to feel a pride in it. Without order our lives
would be disgusting, like those of the poor savages. At home, in
France, we have learned to do all these things in the best way, and
we are conscientious, and that is why we are called the most
civilized people in Europe and other nations envy us." [155]

Triumph of the Group: Submission of the Individual

No novel Willa Cather ever wrote better illustrates the change her
values underwent late in life when, having lost faith in the ability of
the heroic individual to triumph against all odds, she came to place
more and more emphasis on the group. This involved the abandonment
of her former highly individualistic view of human relations and society
for a view that comes very close to being organic. In *Shadows on the
Rock* these new values are apparent at three different levels: the
familial, the social and political, and the religious. Instead of the
individual protagonist she emphasizes the family; instead of the democratic open society, the feudal hierarchy; and instead of the spontaneous
nature worship of her earlier novels, the institutionalized ritual of the
Catholic Church.

On the family level, the book is the story of the apothecary Euclide Auclair and his twelve-year-old daughter Cécile. They have come across the ocean from France with their patron, the great Comte de Frontenac, and are now established in a little shop on a steep stony street halfway up the hill of the great rock of Quebec. Euclide is not by any stretch of the imagination a pioneer or heroic character; in fact he is quite the reverse. Willa Cather remarks, "He was not of the proper stuff for a colonist, and he knew it," words which remind us of her own father. "He was clearly not a man of action, no Indian-fighter or explorer. The only remarkable thing about his life was that he had not lived it to the end exactly where his father and grandfather had lived theirs, — in a little apothecary shop on the Quai des Célestins, in Paris."[156] Later she writes:

> Euclide was a natural city-dweller; one of those who can bear poverty and oppression, so long as they have their old surroundings, their native sky, and the streets and buildings that have become part of their lives . . . he was a creature of habit and derived an actual pleasure from doing things exactly as he had always done before.[157]

Euclide's rather compulsive character is diametrically opposed to that of earlier Willa Cather protagonists such as Bartley Alexander. His wife on the other hand is more familiar. As we have seen, she is reminiscent, not of the heroine Alexandra but of Alexandra's immigrant mother.

> During the last winter of her illness she lay much of the time on her red sofa, that had come so far out to this rock in the wilderness. The snow outside, piled up against the window-panes, made a grey light in the room, and she could hear Cécile moving softly about in the kitchen, putting more wood into the iron stove, washing the casseroles. Then she would think fearfully of how much she was entrusting to that little shingled head; something so precious, so intangible; a feeling about life that had come down to her through so many centuries and that she had brought with her across the waste of obliterating, brutal ocean. The sense of "our way," — that was what she longed to leave with her daughter. She wanted to believe that when she herself was lying in this rude Canadian earth, life would go on almost unchanged in this room with its dear (and, to her, beautiful) objects; that the proprieties

would be observed, all the little shades of feeling which make the common fine. The individuality, the character, of M. Auclair's house, though it appeared to be made up of wood and cloth and glass and a little silver, was really made, of very fine moral qualities in two women: the mother's unswerving fidelity to certain traditions, and the daughter's loyalty to her mother's wish.[158]

This passage has several interesting qualities. It shows the now familiar idea of woman as cultural conservator and transmitter of tradition; poor M. Auclair is left quite out of it. The emphasis on preserving the proprieties reminds one of Willa Cather's description of the quality of life lived at Mrs. James T. Fields' at 148 Charles Street. The assumption that for a feeling about life to be centuries old is somehow a point in its favor reminds one of the treatment of tradition in *Death Comes for the Archbishop*. Such a feeling of course is not new in Willa Cather, but what is new is the urgency of its presentation, the extreme force with which it is pressed home. Finally, the sense of "our way," of loyalty to household traditions and especially to the head of the household, points to that preoccupation with her own family which was so characteristic of the older Willa Cather, and finds expression in her emphasis on the group. When placed beside passages from her prairie novels, the above quotation shows clearly the change that has taken place in the later Willa Cather. Here we have no even balance between tradition and innovation, as we had in her golden period, but an emphasis on tradition alone. In it the heroic individual does not even appear; the individual now exists only to serve tradition, and the traditions served are those of the family group. This attitude first became noticeable in the conclusion of *My Mortal Enemy;* now it is immeasurably stronger. The days of the movement of her protagonists away from the family are ended; from now on her heroines will move toward the family. The group has finally replaced the individual as the center of attention and the locus of all value.

As might be suspected, the ritual element is strong in *Shadows on the Rock,* and, although religious ritual is occasionally mentioned, it is domestic ritual which is stressed. Again Willa Cather shows her preoccupation with food, this time to an even more marked degree:

Dinner was the important event of the day in the apothecary's household. The luncheon was a mere goûter. Breakfast was a pot of chocolate, which he prepared very carefully himself, and a fresh loaf which Pigeon's oldest boy brought to the door. But his dinner

Auclair regarded as the thing that kept him a civilized man and a Frenchman.[159]

Willa Cather's interest in food dates far back. As early as in *O Pioneers!* she had written of Alexandra's mother:

> Alexandra often said that if her mother were cast upon a desert island, she would thank God for her deliverance, make a garden, and find something to preserve. Preserving was almost a mania with Mrs. Bergson. Stout as she was, she roamed the scrubby banks of Norway Creek looking for fox grapes and goose plums, like a wild creature in search of prey.[160]

But whereas in *O Pioneers!* Willa Cather had regarded this avid interest in food as almost a mania, she takes it quite seriously in *Shadows on the Rock*, devoting many pages to it:

> "What are we having for dessert tonight, my dear?"
> "We have the cream cheese you brought from market yesterday, and which ever conserve you prefer; the plums, the wild strawberries, or the gooseberries."
> "Oh, the gooseberries, by all means, after chicken."
> "But, Papa, you prefer the gooseberries after almost everything! It is lucky for us we can get all the sugar we want from the Count. Our neighbours cannot afford to make conserves, with sugar so dear. And gooseberries take more than anything else."
> "There is something very palatable about the flavour of these gooseberries, a bitter tang that is good for one. At home the gooseberries are much larger and finer, but I have come to like this bitter taste." [161]

> Sometimes on a very bitter night, when the grip of still, intense cold tightened on the rock as if it would extinguish the last spark of life, the pharmacist would hear his daughter softly stirring about, moving something, covering something. He would thrust his nightcap out between the curtains and call:
> *"Qu'est-ce que tu fais, petite?"*
> An anxious, sleepy voice would reply:
> *"Papa, j'ai peu pour le persil."*
> It had never frozen in her mother's time, and it should not freeze in hers.[162]

This lust for preserving and passion for parsley suggest that Willa Cather was not entirely free of the sin of Fray Baltazar which she had described so feelingly. One remembers her remark that "a new society begins with salad dressing more than with the destruction of Indian villages."

So much for Willa Cather's treatment of values with respect to the family. On the political and social level she replaces the anarchistic society of spontaneously co-operating heroes found in the prairie novels with a hierarchal feudal society. This is reflected in the very geography of the city of Quebec itself. On top of the rock stands the Château Saint-Louis, home of the Comte de Frontenac, Governor of the province, and near it the seminary of the old Bishop Laval. Two hundred feet below, on a narrow strip of beach along the river's edge, lies the Lower Town, inhabited by poor people such as the prostitute 'Toinette Gaux, mother of Cécile's little friend Jacques. The apothecary Euclide Auclair has his shop on a street halfway up the rock, between the spiritual and temporal lords who are perched on the rock's summit and the common people of the Basse Ville who dwell beneath. It is his business to mediate between top and base of the rock, between rich and poor. Middle class himself, he shuttles back and forth in his necessary calling, attempting to weave the social fabric which shall bind rich and poor together.[163] An example of this is his daughter's intercession with the Count to get him to buy shoes for the barefoot Jacques Gaux, an instance of benevolent paternalism which turns out to be successful.

Auclair in his role of social unifier rather resembles Father Latour: his secular duties as apothecary roughly correspond to the latter's religious duties as pastor; both men move in a feudal-hierarchical framework and in both cases people have to do as they say, or live to regret it. The Count is the apothecary's patron, and they are loyally devoted to each other. This is the feudal bond and represents solidarity between the social classes; it is the same kind of loyalty between a social superior and social inferior that we have seen in the case of Bishop Latour and Father Vaillant. But, as we shall see, although the Count may have respect for people beneath him in the social scale, such as Auclair, Cécile has no respect at all for the poor Harnois family. It seems that social sympathy does not extend below the middle class.

On the religious level Willa Cather has replaced her earlier nature worship with the institutionalized worship of the Catholic Church. This is a part of the general submission of the individual to common forms which seemed so important to her in her later career. And yet the older leaders, like the railroad and empire builders of her pioneer novels, remind one of the superb arrogance and self-confidence of the nine-teenth-century rugged individualist. Bishop Laval, locked in mortal feud with the Comte de Frontenac, is as authoritarian a personality as was old John Driscoll:

> The Bishop got up at four o'clock every morning, dressed with-out a fire, went with his lantern into the church, and rang the bell for early mass for the working people. Many good people who did not want to go to mass at all, when they heard that hoarse, frosty bell clanging out under the black sky where there was not even a hint of daybreak, groaned and went to church. Because they thought of the old Bishop at the end of the bell-rope, and because his will was stronger than theirs. He was a stubborn, high-handed, tyrannical, quarrelsome old man, but no one could deny that he shepherded his sheep.[164]

But such throwbacks to the pioneer period are relatively rare. Willa Cather's usual picture of religious life stresses the satisfactions which result from its collective and communal nature. She is apt to suggest certain superiorities it has over profane existence because of its freedom from certain worries which harass M. Auclair:

> Fear for the sick and old so far away, sorrow for those who died last year — five years ago — many years ago, — memories of fam-ilies once together and now scattered; these things hung over the rock of Kebec on this day of the dead like the dark fogs from the river. The cheerful faces were those in the convents. The Ursulines and the Hospitalières, indeed, were scarcely exiles. When they came across the Atlantic, they brought their family with them, their kindred, their closest friends. In whatever little wooden vessel they had laboured across the sea, they carried all; they brought to Canada the Holy Family, the saints and martyrs, the glorious company of the Apostles, the heavenly host.
>
> Courageous these Sisters were, accepting good and ill fortune with high spirit, — with humour, even. They never vulgarly exag-gerated hardships and dangers. They had no hours of nostalgia, for they were quite as near the realities of their lives in Quebec as in Dieppe or Tours. They were still in their accustomed place in the world of the mind (which for each of us is the only world), and they had the same well-ordered universe about them: this all-important earth, created by God for a great purpose, the sun which He made to light it by day, the moon which He made to light it

by night, — and the stars, made to beautify the vault of heaven like frescoes, and to be a clock and compass for man. And in this safe, lovingly arranged and ordered universe (not too vast, though nobly spacious), in this congenial universe, the drama of man went on at Quebec just as at home, and the Sisters played their accustomed part in it. There was sin, of course, and there was punishment after death; but there was always hope, even for the most depraved; and for those who died repentant, the Sisters' prayers could do much, — no one might say how much.[165]

In the last paragraph one senses the same fascination of the medieval world-drama felt by Godfrey St. Peter in *The Professor's House*. Willa Cather contrasts the secular world of death and decay with the formal, unchanging world of religion; the fleeting with the eternal, the shadows with the rock. She pictures religion as forming that world of permanent and unchanging essences which lies above the clouds which hide the face of the sun from the people of Quebec. But upon looking closely we see that religious verities are not the main thing being stressed; what really attracts Willa Cather is the warmth and comfort derived from membership in a group which turns out to be just another example of the larger family.

Triumph of the Genteel: The Bourgeois Family as Transmitter of the Comely Life

From the Ursulines let us turn back to the Auclairs, that apotheosis of the bourgeois family. I have said that in writing this book Willa Cather was influenced by her feelings for her own family, which was rapidly passing away. Something of their aristocratic disdain for all members of social classes beneath their level is transmitted to the Auclairs, who sometimes play a benevolent paternal role in relation to the lower classes, but never regard them as equals. This attitude is vividly portrayed in the episode of the Harnois. All her life Cécile Auclair had wanted to visit the Ile d'Orléans, that island in the St. Lawrence River lying four miles below the city of Quebec. A friend of her father's, Pierre Charron the trapper, knows a farmer on the island named Harnois, and makes arrangements for Cécile to visit him for a few days. When she goes there she is charmed by the natural beauty of the island; it is the loveliest place she has ever seen. But she is considerably less taken by the Harnois family and its four daughters. The family is a dirty one, although kindly; they eat greasy food, and during mealtime they keep the windows tight closed even in hot weather to keep the mosquitoes out; the little girls make indelicate remarks about the sexual behavior of the farm animals, and when it turns out that all five of them are to sleep in one bed on dirty linen without even bothering to wash their bodies, it is too much for Cécile. Rather than rest her head on a greasy bolster, she gets up and sits by the window all night, looking at the river and thinking of her father:

> She thought a great deal about her mother, too, that night, how her mother had always made everything at home beautiful, just as here everything about cooking, eating, sleeping, living, seemed repulsive. The longest voyage on the ocean could scarcely take one to conditions more different.[166]

After the second night she can stand it no longer and asks Pierre Charron to take her home again to her father. This he obligingly does, to her great content. When she arrives home, she and Euclide have the following interchange:

> "Father, Pierre took it on himself, but it was my fault we came home. I didn't like country life very well. I was not happy."
>
> "But aren't they kind people, the Harnois? Haven't they kind ways?"
>
> "Yes, they have." She sighed and put her hand to her forehead, trying to think. They had kind ways, those poor Harnois, but that was not enough; one had to have kind things about one, too. . . .
>
> But if she was to make a good dinner for Pierre, she had no time to think about the Harnois. She put on her apron and made a survey of the supplies in the cellar and kitchen. As she began handling her own things again, it all seemed a little different, — as if she had grown at least two years older in the two nights she had been away. She did not feel like a little girl, doing what she had been taught to do. She was accustomed to think that she did all these things so carefully to please her father, and to carry out her mother's wishes. Now she realized that she did them for herself, quite as much. Dogs cooked with blueberries [an Indian dish] — poor Madame Harnois' dishes were not much better! These coppers, big and little, these brooms and clouts and brushes, were tools; and with them one made, not shoes or cabinet-work, but life itself. One made a climate within a climate; one made the days, — the complexion, the special flavour, the special happiness of each day as it passed; one made life.

Suddenly her father came into the kitchen. "Cécile, why did you not call me to make the fire? And do you need a fire so early?" "I must have hot water, Papa. It is no trouble to make a fire." She wiped her hands and threw her arms about him. "Oh, Father, I think our house is so beautiful!" [167]

This passage reveals many preferences of the later Willa Cather. It shows the triumph of the city and the triumph of the comely life, here identified with the surrounding- of oneself with beautiful household objects. The comely life not only becomes the life of the bourgeois (reversing the judgment made in "Paul's Case"); as in *Death Comes for the Archbishop* it is defined largely in terms of domestic ritual. Willa Cather now seems to expect the practitioners of the comely life to be less likely to spring from common clay than from the middle and upper levels of a social hierarchy, her former Jeffersonian social ideals being replaced by a view of society considerably more aristocratic.

An interesting contrast results if we set this passage side by side with passages from *My Ántonia*. Just as she had the Middle West, Willa Cather sets the Ile d'Orléans up as an earthly paradise — but it turns out to be a paradise inhabited by near-imbeciles. The fact that they shut all their doors and windows even in the hottest weather to keep out the mosquitoes instead of making a smudge of eucalyptus balls to drive them off as does M. Auclair shows the difference between an intelligent and brainless way of attacking problems, of living life itself. Willa Cather could have been expressing her own feelings when she wrote, "They had kind ways, those poor Harnois, but that was not enough; one had to have kind things about one, too. . . ."

There is a certain complacency and smugness about the section's final paragraph which suggests a lack of human understanding. We can sympathize with Cécile for not liking greasy food or dirty pillows, but it is harder to forgive her self-gratulatory tone as she contemplates the gulf between herself and the Harnois family. The division between the right people and the wrong people is now a little too neat. Formerly Willa Cather had shown intelligence and stupidity existing within the same family, as in the case of Alexandra and her brothers. One wonders how she would have presented the Scandinavian and Bohemian heroines of her early novels if she had come across their originals in later life instead of her girlhood. The chances are that the Shimerdas would not have received much better treatment from her pen than did the Harnois.

Triumph of the Aesthete:
Religion Subordinate Again

Not only is the outlook of this novel bourgeois and genteel; it also is definitely secular. In contradistinction to *Death Comes for the Archbishop*, Willa Cather makes it plain that she now sees the secular life rather than the religious as yielding the greater aesthetic satisfaction. While Cécile and her father are visiting the Hôtel Dieu to attend the Reverend Mother Juschereau, the latter tells the young girl a Norman saint's story of how Marie la Pécheresse, a run-of-the-mill sexual sinner, was saved from the fires of purgatory by the intercession of the Blessed Virgin:

> Here Mother Juschereau glanced down at the young listener, who had been following her intently. "And now from this we see — " she went on, but Cécile caught her hand and cried coaxingly,
> *"N'expliquez pas, chère Mère, je vous en supplie!"*
> Mother Juschereau laughed and shook her finger.
> "You always say that, little naughty! *N'expliquez pas!* But it is the explanation of these stories that applies them to our needs."
> "Yes, dear Mother. But there comes my father. Tell me the explanation some other day."
> Mother Juschereau still looked down into her face, frowning and smiling. It was the kind of face she liked, because there was no self-consciousness in it, and no vanity; but she told herself for the hundredth time: "No, she has certainly no vocation." Yet for an orphan girl and one so intelligent, there would certainly have been a career among the Hospitalières. She would have loved to train that child for the Soeur Apothicaire of her hospital. Her good sense told her it was not to be. When she talked to Cécile of the missionaries and martyrs, she knew that her words fell into an eager mind; admiration and rapture she found in the girl's face, but it was not the rapture of self-abnegation. It was something very different, — almost like the glow of worldly pleasure.[168]

N'expliquez pas! With this phrase Cécile specifically rejects the religious life, and she is after all the heroine of the novel. This is the remark of an artist made by one who is Willa Cather's spokesman. This reinforces the idea I have already discussed that, in the Catholic novels as elsewhere, it is not religion at all but aestheticism that interested Willa Cather first, last, and always.

The Decline of Rugged Individualism
and the Void It Leaves

I have tried to show that in later life a change occurred in Willa Cather's values which amounts to almost a direct reversal. On the family level the heroic individual is replaced by the self-effacing individual subordinated to the family; on the social level the spontaneously co-operating society of heroes gives way to a highly stratified feudal society; on the religious level spontaneous worship of nature yields to the hieratic sanctities of Catholicism. Yet for all her emphasis on order and regularity and submission of the individual to the group, Willa Cather cannot refrain from casting a wistful backward glance at the era of rugged individualism, the age of the pioneers. In the novel this refers to the generation that came just before Euclide Auclair's — the generation of the Comte de Frontenac and his great ecclesiastical opponent Bishop Laval. These have long passed their prime at the time the story takes place; they are bowed down but not beaten by life. Together they embody the theme of the heroic individualist, but they are aging heroes; they seem to show the later Willa Cather's idea of what happens to spontaneity and the will in this world. They form a natural foil to Auclair, who has never dared as they have but has always believed in order and domestic ritual. On the surface this might seem a telling blow at the doctrine of spontaneity and an admission that it leads to failure. And yet all the glory lies with Frontenac and Laval. They are treated throughout the book as being the real heroes; M. Auclair himself regards them as such, and confesses that he could have wished to have been like them:

> Her father went on sadly: "The Count and the old Bishop were both men of my own period, the kind we looked up to in my youth. Saint-Vallier and Monsieur de Champigny are of a different sort. Had I been able to choose my lot in the world, I would have chosen to be like my patron, for all his disappointments and sorrows; to be a soldier who fought for no gain but renown, merciful to the conquered, charitable to the poor, haughty to the rich and overbearing. Since I could not be such a man and was born in an apothecary shop, it was my good fortune to serve such a man and to be honoured by his confidence." [169]

Just before this he has said of the Count:

> "He belonged to the old order; he cherished those beneath him

and rendered his duty to those above him, but flattered nobody, not the King himself. That time has gone by. I do not wish to outlive my time." [170]

Thus the prime exemplar of the ordered and tranquil life admits the natural superiority of the life of heroic endeavor while at the same time asserting that such a life is a thing of the past. These sentiments remind us of Gabrielle Longstreet and of Judge Pommeroy talking about Captain Forrester. But these men belong to an older generation which is already passing from the scene. Is there anybody like them in the current generation? There is, and his name is Pierre Charron. He is the hunter and trapper friend of the Auclair family, and Willa Cather describes him thus:

> To both Auclair and Madame Auclair, Pierre Charron had seemed the type they had come so far to find; more than anyone else he realized the romantic picture of the free Frenchman of the great forests which they had formed at home on the bank of the Seine. He had the good manners of the Old World, the dash and daring of the New. He was proud, he was vain, he was relentless when he hated, and quickly prejudiced; but he had the old ideals of clan-loyalty, and in friendship he never counted the cost. His goods and his life were at the disposal of the man he loved or the leader he admired [171]

Pierre sounds a good deal like the natural aristocrats of the prairie novels. Like them, he is able to combine the best features of the Old World and the New, and achieve a perfect balance between tradition and innovation. And although he lives in a society that is feudal and hierarchical, he manages to escape most of its restrictions by leading a free-ranging life in the forest. As he puts it, "Very well; religion for the fireside, freedom for the woods." [172]

Pierre Charron is an interesting character because his very existence in the book is an implicit denial of everything the Auclair family stands for. Just as in *O Pioneers!* Willa Cather was unable to come to any convincing resolution of the city-country conflict, so in *Shadows on the Rock* she fails to satisfactorily resolve the tension between the heroic individualism of Pierre Charron and the group emphasis of the Auclairs. As in *O Pioneers!* she attempts to resolve the problem by bringing about a marriage between the representatives of country and town (for Pierre eventually marries Cécile), but as in the case of Alexandra and Carl Linstrum, the union is unconvincing. Like Ántonia's baby, the marriage is not presented but described; two pages from the end of the book Euclide Auclair mentions it casually to a visitor in his shop.

Whether or not it raises more problems than it settles, Pierre Charron's presence in the novel is a sign that Willa Cather has not completely abandoned her belief in the need for individual heroic action in any society. Individualism was always her ideal, and the family circle a poor second best. She shows this by the role she assigns to Pierre upon the death of the old Count Frontenac, who had been M. Auclair's friend and benefactor all his life. When during the dark days following the Comte de Frontenac's death, deprived of a strong arm to lean on, the Auclair family is helpless to the point of not even bothering to prepare meals for themselves, it is to Pierre that they turn for the comfort and sustenance that they had formerly drawn from the Count. His timely entrance brings them back to themselves and renders them able to resume the natural functions of living. Before his arrival, Cécile had reflected:

> That sense of a strong protector had counted in her life more than she had ever realized. To be sure, they had not called upon the Count's authority very often; but to know that they could appeal to him at any moment meant security, and gave them a definite place in their little world.[173]

This dependence of Cécile and her father on the Count resembles a child's dependence on its parents; when the prop is gone, panic is likely to result. But their mood changes completely after Pierre arrives:

> . . . she had once more that feeling of security, as if the strong roof were over them again; over her and the shop and the salon and all her mother's things. For the first time she realized that her father loved Pierre for the same reason that he had loved the Count; both had the qualities he did not have himself, but which he most admired in other men.[174]

Here we have a statement on the part of a group-centered protagonist that group-centeredness is a poor second best when compared with heroic individualism. Willa Cather's thinking has come full circle; she has now come back to affirming the natural aristocrats of her pioneer period. A little later she makes this even more explicit:

> Cécile, in her upstairs bedroom, turned to slumber with the weight of doubt and loneliness melted away. Her last thoughts

before she sank into forgetfulness were of a friend, devoted and fearless, here in the house with them, as if he were one of themselves. He had not a throne behind him, like the Count (it had been very far behind, indeed!), not the authority of a parchment and seal. But he had authority, and a power which came from knowledge of the country and its people; from knowledge, and from a kind of passion. His daring and his pride seemed to her even more splendid than Count Frontenac's.[175]

So the book ends with more than a partial reaffirmation of the very values which Willa Cather had been trying to discard. The natural aristocrat has come into his own again, even if only within the framework of the seventeenth-century French colonial political and religious institutions, which were essentially feudal. Willa Cather's rage for order no longer completely overwhelms her faith in the exceptional individual; consequently we are not surprised when in the epilogue, fifteen years later, we hear that Cécile Auclair has married Pierre Charron and has had four lusty children by him.

But this is not the only evidence we have that the later Willa Cather's insistence on order fails to satisfy all the demands she makes upon life. On the social as well as the individual level she sometimes shows a longing for the values she had previously held, a desire to find a place for them even in her turn to the values of an ordered and group-centered society. Recurrent throughout the book is her belief that, despite her horror at the new land's wildness, she still considers America to be a haven of refuge where the crimes of Europe will not be perpetrated again. Feudal institutions Willa Cather may admire very greatly, but that admiration is tempered by the knowledge that feudal institutions had their dark side. She is not so much a feudalist that she is willing to accept, for instance, the torture chamber. Near the beginning of the novel we are told that Euclide Auclair

> . . . could not shut his eyes to the wrongs that went on about him, or keep from brooding upon them. In his own time he had seen taxes grow more and more ruinous, poverty and hunger always increasing. People died of starvation in the streets of Paris, in his own parish of Saint-Paul, where there was so much wealth. All the while the fantastic extravagances of the Court grew more outrageous. The wealth of the nation, of the grain lands and vineyards and forests of France, was sunk in creating the pleasure palace at Versailles. The richest peers of the realm were ruining

themselves on magnificent Court dresses and jewels. And, with so many new abuses, the old ones never grew less; torture and cruel punishments increased as the people became poorer and more desperate. The horrible mill at the Châtelet ground on day after day. Auclair lived too near the prisons of Paris to be able to forget them. In his boyhood a poor old man who lodged in their own cellar was tortured and put to death at the Châtelet for a petty theft.[176]

This reads like a page from one of the nineteenth-century liberal historians such as Saint-Simon or Lecky. Willa Cather illustrates and drives the point home by telling the story of Bichet, the old knife grinder who is tortured and put to death for the theft of two small brass kettles, and of their next-door Quebec neighbor, Blinker, who in the old country had been torturer in the King's prison at Rouen. Blinker tells his own tale to M. Auclair, with bitterness and loathing. He had indeed been brought to his trade by his father, who was torturer before him. He used to fill his son up with brandy, all he could hold, so that he would be indifferent to the screams of the victims. One day Blinker had had a terrible experience. He had helped to torture and put to death a washerwoman who had supposedly killed her son after a violent family squabble. But suddenly the son returned and walked on the streets of Rouen. It turns out that after the brawl he had stowed away on a boat and shipped on a voyage to the West Indies, which he had only just then completed. Blinker could not bear the thought of being party to such injustice and cruelty any longer:

> He had only one hope; that miserable boy's adventure had put a thought into his head. If he could get away to a new country, where nobody knew him for the executioner's son, perhaps he would leave all that behind and forget it. That was why he had come to Kebec.[177]

America for him had proven a haven of refuge by the very fact that in it a man could make a fresh start. That is why he disagrees with the settlers' idea that in Quebec they are farther from civilization and heaven itself than in France; he knows they are much closer.

In all of this there is something of Willa Cather's earlier optimistic nineteenth-century belief that America is the hope of the world. But owing to her later disillusionment with life even this belief is given a pessimistic twist. America turns out to be superior to Europe, not because it is changing into something better, but because it fails to change into something worse. This emerges very clearly in the Epilogue, which takes place during the old age of Louis XIV and mirrors the bitterness and disappointment which attended the last years of that monarch's reign. In it Europe is pictured as decaying while America stands still. This is brought out in a conversation the new Bishop has with M. Auclair at the story's end:

> "Monsieur," began the Bishop sadly, "we are in the beginning of a new century, but periods do not always correspond with centuries. At home the old age is dying, but the new is still hidden. . . . There is now no figure in the world such as our King was thirty years ago. The changes in the nations are all those of the old growing older. You have done well to remain here where nothing changes. Here with you I find everything the same." [178]

Here, as in "The Old Beauty," Willa Cather expresses the belief that the great age is past and that the present age is one of brass. For her protagonist M. Auclair himself expresses the same attitude in the book's final paragraph:

> While he was closing his shop and changing his coat to go up to his daughter's house, he thought over much that his visitor had told him, and he believed that he was indeed fortunate to spend his old age here where nothing changed; to watch his grandsons grow up in a country where the death of the King, the probable evils of a long regency, would never touch them.[179]

It is hard not to conclude that this ending reflects Willa Cather's own growing pessimism and dissatisfaction with the United States of the nineteen-thirties. She no longer thinks the social order can be changed for the better; instead, she is afraid lest it change of its own accord for the worse; in her disenchantment she ignores growth and sees only decay. One recalls the implications of the pessimistic theory of history Willa Cather had expressed; as I have previously said in my discussion of *The Professor's House:*

> Her problem will soon become one of trying to freeze the social order exactly as it is in order to slow down and put off as long as possible the destruction which inevitably attends on beauty. Western civilization is interpreted as being in its death throes and

breathing its last gasp; the immediate problem is to postpone as long as possible the approach of the undertaker.[180]

DEVOTION TO CALLING QUESTIONED AGAIN: THE CONFLICT RENEWED

If Willa Cather is uncertain whether to accord honors to the heroic individual or the group, she is also equally uncertain about whether an individual can find his greatest satisfactions in human relations or in work. In *Shadows on the Rock* the whole question of devotion to a calling versus human claims is raised once more. Here again Willa Cather presents two contradictory views. One she exemplifies in Father Hector Saint-Cyr, who has made the same choice as Professor St. Peter or supposedly Bishop Latour and devoted all his energies to his calling:

Father Hector smiled, but shook his head. "Ah, no. Thank you, but no. I have taken a vow that will spoil your plans for me. I shall not return to France."

Auclair had put his glass to his lips, but set it down untasted. "Not return?" he echoed.

"Not at all, Euclide; never."

"But when my wife was here, you both used to plan — "

"Ah, yes. That was my temptation. Now it is vanished." He sat for a moment smiling. Then he began resolutely:

"Listen, my friend. No man can give himself heart and soul to one thing while in the back of his mind he cherishes a desire, a secret hope, for something very different. You, as a student, must know that even in worldly affairs nothing worth while is accomplished except by that last sacrifice, the giving of oneself altogether and finally. Since I made that final sacrifice, I have been twice the man I was before." [181]

This sounds like the younger Willa Cather who had decided to give up everything for art. But she presents just the opposite view in the stories of Noël Chabanel, the missionary priest to the Hurons, and of Jeanne Le Ber, known to the people of New France as the Recluse of Montreal. The story of the Recluse is the more moving of the two. She is the daughter of Jacques Le Ber, the famous merchant, and is the richest heiress in all Canada. She is the apple of her father's eye, and he sees a gorgeous worldly career in store for her. He promises her suitors a dowry of fifty thousand gold écus, and it looks as if this princely sum is going to go to Pierre Charron, who lives next door to her and has been her playfellow since childhood. But at the age of seventeen, imitating the domestic retreat of St. Catherine of Siena, she takes the vow of chastity for five years, shutting herself up in a chamber of her father's house. Her parents think that she will get over it, doubting that a girl so affectionate and tender can keep so harsh a rule. But when the five years are up Jeanne renews her vows of seclusion for another five years. During this period her mother dies after calling for her daughter to attend her deathbed, but "Tell her I am praying for her night and day" is the only answer she gets. After nearly ten years of this solitary existence one of Jeanne's dearest hopes comes true; she is able to persuade her grief-stricken father to devote the money from her dowry to building a chapel for the Sisters of the Congregation of the Blessed Virgin. She has a special cell constructed for herself behind the high altar, and, taking final vows, enters it with the intention of never coming forth alive. From then on she is known as the Recluse of Montreal.

Thenceforth, no matter how sultry the summer's heat or bitter the winter's cold, she stays within her cell, emerging only at midnight to enter the deserted church and pray for an hour. One burning summer, when her confessor urges her to emerge from her confinement after sunset and take the air in the convent garden, she replies to him:

> *Ah, mon père, ma chambre est mon paradis terrestre: C'est mon centre; c'est mon élément. Il n'y a pas de lieu plus délicieux, ni plus salutaire pour moi; point de Louvre, point de palais, qui me soit plus agréable. Je préfère ma cellule à tout le reste de l'univers.*[182]

The Recluse sounds very much like the Willa Cather of the nineteen-thirties, who had deliberately cut herself off from most of her contemporaries and lived a life of seclusion in a great Park Avenue apartment, a hermit consecrated to the religion of art. If so, the rest of Jeanne's story may be a parable revealing the bitter fruits of a life devoted too exclusively to art for art's sake. Pierre Charron, disappointed of his bride, takes to the woods and becomes a trapper in true romantic fashion. Years later, while being entertained at the fireside of his old friend Euclide Auclair, he tells the sequel to the story. It seems that Jeanne Le Ber is not so happy as she has represented; in fact, he says, she is no better than dead, or even worse:

"It was like this," he went on presently. "You know, because of my mother, this year I got back to Montreal early, months before my time. There is not much to do there, God knows, except to be a pig, and I never behave like dirt in my mother's town. We live so near the chapel of the Congregation that I can never get the recluse out of my mind. You remember there were two weeks of terrible cold in March, and it made me wretched to think of her walled up there. No, don't misunderstand me!" Charron's eyes came back from their far-away point of vision and fixed intently, distrustfully, on his friend's face. "All that is over; one does not love a woman who has been dead for nearly twenty years. But there is such a thing as kindness; one wouldn't like to think of a dog that had been one's playfellow, much less a little girl, suffering from cold those bitter nights. *You see, there are all those early memories; one cannot get another set; one has but those.*" Pierre's voice choked, because something had come out by chance, thus, that he had never said to himself before. The candles blurred before Auclair a little, too. God was a witness, he murmured, that he knew the truth of Pierre's remark only too well.

After he had relit his pipe and smoked a little, Charron continued. "You know she goes into the church to pray before the altar at midnight. Well, I hid myself in the church and saw her. It is not difficult for a man who has lived among the Indians; you slide into the chapel when an old sacristan is locking up after vespers, and stay there behind a pillar as long as you choose. It was a long wait. I had my fur jacket on and a flask of brandy in my pocket, and I needed both. *God's Name, is there any place so cold as churches?* I had to move about to keep from aching all over, — but, of course, I made no noise. There was only the sanctuary lamp burning, until the moon came round and threw some light in at the windows. I knew when it must be near midnight, you get to have a sense of time in the woods. I hid myself behind a pillar at the back of the church. I felt a little nervous, sorry I had come, perhaps. — At last I heard a latch lift, — you could have heard a rabbit breathe in that place. The iron grille beside the altar began to move outward. She came in carrying a candle. She wore a grey gown, and a black scarf on her head, but no veil. The candle shone up into her face. *It was like a stone face; it had been through every sorrow.*"

Charron stopped and crossed himself. He shut his eyes and dropped his face in his hands. "My friend, I could remember a face! — I could remember Jeanne in her little white furs, when I used to pull her on my sled. Jacques Le Ber would have burned

Montreal down to keep her warm. *He meant to give her every joy in the world, and she has thrown the world away.* . . . She put down her candle and went toward the high altar. She walked very slowly, with great dignity. At first she prayed aloud, but I scarcely understood her. My mind was confused; *her voice was so changed, — hoarse, hollow, with the sound of despair in it. Why is she unhappy, I ask you?* She is, I know it! When she prayed in silence, such sighs broke from her. And once a groan, such as I have never heard; *such despair — such resignation and despair!* It froze everything in me. *I felt that I would never be the same man again. I only wanted to die and forget that I had ever hoped for anything in this world.* [Above italics are mine.]

"After she had bowed herself for the last time, she took up her candle and walked toward that door, standing open. I lost my head and betrayed myself. I was well hidden, but she heard me sob.

"She was not startled. She stood still, with her hand on the latch of the grille, and turned her head, half facing me. After a moment she spoke.

"Poor sinner, she said, *poor sinner, whoever you are, may God have mercy upon you! I will pray for you. And do you pray for me also.*

"She walked on and shut the grille behind her. I turned the key in the church door and let myself out. No man was ever more miserable than I was that night." [183]

There are several factors at work here. One is probably a Protestant protest against the ascetic ideal as such; another is a sense of guilt at the rejection of all human ties which we have already seen embodied in the characters of Professor St. Peter and Tom Outland; a third is the pure waste from a worldly point of view of the ideal to which Jeanne Le Ber had given her life. Most important of all, Willa Cather is talking about the terrible isolation and loneliness of the artist who has given her all for art: "God's Name, is there any place so cold as churches?" Pierre in telling the story is definitely on the side of old Jacques Le Ber, who never was the same after his daughter took vows. What his story adds up to is an explicit repudiation of the exalted saint's legend which had been built up around the Recluse of Montreal. Willa Cather is saying that devotion to a calling is intolerable if it excludes all human warmth.

In somewhat the same vein is the story of Noël Chabanel, the missionary priest to the Hurons. Chabanel had been a professor of rhetoric before he came to America; he was a cultivated and learned man who was a master of Hebrew and Greek as well as of Italian and Spanish. But after five years of painstaking study among the Hurons he was still unable to master their tongue or that of any other Indian tribe. Moreover he was revolted by all their ways: the dirt and degradation, the filth and squalor. The story of his martyr's life is told by another of Auclair's friends, Father Hector Saint-Cyr:

"His humiliating inability to learn the language was only one of poor Chabanel's mortifications. *He had no love for his converts.* Everything about the savages and their mode of life was utterly repulsive and horrible to him; their filth, their indecency, their cruelty. *The very smell of their bodies revolted him to nausea. He could never feel toward them that long-suffering love which has been the consolation of our missionaries.* He never became hardened to any of the privations of his life, not even to the vermin and mosquitos that preyed upon his body, nor to the smoke and smells in the savage wigwams. In his struggle to learn the language he went and lived with the Indians, sleeping in their bark shelters, crowded with dogs and dirty savages. Often Father Chabanel would lie out in the snow until he was in danger of a death self-inflicted, and only then creep inside the wigwam. *The food was so hateful to him that one might say he lived upon fasting.* The flesh of dogs he could never eat without becoming ill, and even corn-meal boiled in dirty water and dirty kettles brought on vomiting; so that he used to beg the women to give him a little uncooked meal in his hand, and upon that he subsisted.

"*The Huron converts were more brutal to him than to Father Garnier.* They were contemptuous of his backwardness in their language, and *they must have divined his excessive sensibility, for they took every occasion to outrage it.* In the wigwam they tirelessly perpetrated indecencies to wound him. Once when a hunting party returned after a long famine, they invited him to a feast of flesh. After he had swallowed the portion in his bowl, they pulled a human hand out of the kettle to show him that he had eaten of an Iroquois prisoner. He became ill at once, and they followed him into the forest to make merry over his retchings.

"But through all these physical sufferings, which remained as sharp as on the first day, the *greatest of his sufferings was an almost continual sense of the withdrawal of God.*" [Italics are mine.] [184]

Nevertheless, in spite of all these hardships and in spite of the freely offered chance to return to France and resume his former dignified position, in the fifth year of his labors he took a "vow of perpetual stability" among the Huron missions, which committed him to remain among the squalor he hated for the rest of his life. Father Saint-Cyr says of him: "No man ever gave up more for Christ than Noël Chabanel; many gave all, but few had so much to give." [185] He did not have long to suffer, for two years later he perished in the great Iroquois raid of 1649.

Chabanel's revulsion at the Hurons reminds us of Cécile's reaction to the Harnois; it is also a melodramatic version of Thea Kronborg's reaction to her townspeople: the Indians are those same old stupid faces under another name. Willa Cather treats Noël Chabanel's vow of perpetual stability among the missions in such a way as to make it seem a gratuitous act of self-degradation. M. Auclair, who is the author's spokesman, thinks it unlikely that Chabanel was serving the Hurons, despising them as he did and being unable to feel any sort of Christian love toward them:

> After Auclair had disappeared behind his bed-curtains that night, he lay awake a long while, regretting that a man with Father Hector's gifts should decide to live and die in the wilderness, and wondering whether there had not been a good deal of misplaced heroism in the Canadian missions, a waste of rare qualities which did nobody any good.
>
> "Ah, well," he sighed at last, "perhaps it is the box of precious ointment which was acceptable to the Saviour, and I am like the disciples who thought it might have been used better in another way."
>
> This solution allowed him to go to sleep.[186]

The passage ends with a submission to orthodoxy, and yet one wonders if the apothecary's rationalist doubts have been quieted. Earlier in the book he has taken an extremely skeptical attitude toward a supposedly miraculous conversion thought to have been effected by the eating of ground bone from a saint's skull.[187] The last two sentences do not sound as if M. Auclair was fully convinced of the solution he proposes. In fact, he finally adopts a religious interpretation only as a pragmatic solution to the problem of insomnia.[188]

SUMMARY OF *Shadows on the Rock:* CIVILIZATION
ON THE WANE, THE THEORY OF HISTORY ONCE MORE

Earlier in this chapter I have shown how in *Death Comes for the Archbishop* Willa Cather departed from the vegetation myth and did so at dire peril to her artistic success. In *Shadows on the Rock* she returns to the myth once more, even though she still tends to leave conflict out. This book, like the prairie novels, is based on the cycle of the seasons; as in those books, the ultimate reality is the long, hard winter, which represents the death of the year and also the dangers of life. At the beginning of the novel the last of the summer ships sail home for France, not to return from the outside world until the following spring:

> Now for eight months the French colony on this rock in the North would be entirely cut off from Europe, from the world. This was October; not a sail would come up that wide waterway before next July. No supplies; not a cask of wine or a sack of flour, no gunpowder, or leather, or cloth, or iron tools. Not a letter, even — no news of what went on at home. There might be new wars, floods, conflagrations, epidemics, but the colonists would never know of them until next summer.[189]

Toward the end of the book the ships return, and this is an occasion for great rejoicing; the sailors become symbols of the pioneer spirit struggling against the elements and are treated in much the same manner as is Pierre Charron. A glance at the table of contents reveals the book's dependence on the vegetation myth. In the first section, entitled "The Apothecary," the ships leave; Willa Cather describes Euclide Auclair's nonheroic nature, emphasizes the importance of the family group, and has Cécile reject the religious view of life. In the next section, "Cécile and Jacques," again emphasizing the group, she describes the feudal social relations and benevolent paternalism that characterize life on the Rock. Then comes "The Long Winter," in which all the worst stories about human misery are told: the self-immolation of Jeanne Le Ber, the agonized renunciation of Noël Chabanel, and the sufferings of Blinker. In "Pierre Charron," the individualist hero appears once more, although he does not take over until later on. "The Ships from France" deals with the rebirth of the year and of hope, since it describes the return of the sailor-pioneers and the celebrations which follow. "The Dying Count" describes both death and rebirth, since it deals with the death of the old hero, Comte de Frontenac, and the assumption of the heroic role by Pierre Charron. His rescue of the Auclair family makes Cécile think his daring and pride "even more splendid than Count Frontenac's." [190] Finally, the Epilogue concentrates on death again. The aged Louis XIV is dying, the new Bishop who came after Laval is broken by life, and America is represented as a haven of refuge because it does not change. The whole continent has turned into a sanctuary.

So, unlike *Death Comes for the Archbishop, Shadows on the Rock* is based on the vegetation myth, although somewhat narrow use is made of it. The succession of generations is shown by the decline of the aging Bishop and the Count, on the one hand, and the rise of Pierre Charron and the sailors on the other. The pioneer spirit of the latter emerges in Willa Cather's description of them when they return to Quebec in the spring:

> It brought tears to the eyes to think how faithful they were, and how much they had endured and overcome in the years they had been beating back and forth between Canada and the Old World. What adverse winds those sails had been trimmed to, what mountains of waves had beaten the sides of those old hulls, what a wilderness of hostile, never-resting water those bows had driven through! Beaten southward, beaten backward, out of their course for days and even weeks together; rolling helpless, with sails furled, water over them and under them, — but somehow wearing through. On bad voyages they retraced their distance three and five times over, out-tiring the elements by their patience, and then drove forward again — toward Kebec. . . .
>
> Many a time a boat came in wracked and broken, and it took all summer to make repairs, before the captain dared face the sea again. And all summer the hardships and mischances of the fleet were told over and over in Quebec. The greater part of the citizens had made that voyage at least once, and they knew what a North Atlantic crossing meant: little wooden boats matched against the immensity and brutality of the sea; the strength that came out of flesh and blood and goodwill, doing its uttermost against cold, unspending eternity. The colonists loved the very shapes of those old ships. Here they were again, in the roadstead, sending off the post-bags. And tomorrow they would give out of their insides food, wine, cloth, medicines, tools, fire-arms, prayer-books, vestments, altars for the missions, everything to comfort the body and the soul.[191]

The battered ship becomes a symbol of the human will to survive; the sailors themselves represent energy directed against the indifference of nature. By perseverance they succeed in conquering nature, just like the protagonists of the prairie novels. And it is interesting that while Frontenac and the Bishop, although heroic, are of noble blood and have the full force of social aristocracy behind them, Captain Pondaven of *Le Faucon* is a self-made man,[192] as Pierre Charron apparently is.

We now are able to put Willa Cather's theory of history as she developed it in *The Professor's House* into the larger framework of the vegetation myth. In arguing the inevitable destruction of high civilizations she was concentrating on the death part of the cycle. In *Shadows on the Rock* too she asserts that civilization is on the wane, but she also gives some hope for its future rebirth. The old Count dies, but the mantle falls on Pierre Charron, and in the meantime the family group represented by the Auclairs is ready to carry on the traditions of the old order and keep things from deteriorating too much. Thus *Shadows on the Rock* shows a kind of qualified optimism when compared with *The Professor's House*. Some of this same optimism appears in a short story she wrote in 1942 called "Before Breakfast," in which an elderly businessman who has become discouraged by having brought home to him man's geological insignificance takes hope again after seeing a young girl brave the tides of the icy North Atlantic in order to enjoy an early-morning dip. He decides that "Plucky youth is more bracing than enduring old age," and concludes, "Anyhow, when that first amphibious frog-toad found his water-hole dried up behind him, and jumped out to hop along till he could find another — well, he started on a long hop." [193] Like parts of *Shadows on the Rock,* this seems to indicate a recurrence of Willa Cather's original belief that desire *is* all. But such a mood is not characteristic of her in later life; most of the time she was quite discouraged and pessimistic.

The fact that Pierre Charron takes over at the end of the book and marries Cécile Auclair may show a qualified return on Willa Cather's part to the individualism of her earlier novels, but it does not represent in any sense a solution of the conflict between nature and civilization. Pierre is like Leatherstocking in the James Fenimore Cooper novels; he flees civilization and the sound of the axe; if forced to dwell within a town he would be miserable. Willa Cather never does solve this problem, and in this novel she does not even face it; if she had, it is hard to imagine whether she could have done any more with it than repeat with Pierre, "Very well; religion for the fireside, freedom for the woods."

Shadows on the Rock resembles the other "Catholic" novel in that it too is a local-color story and is saturated with nostalgia for the past. At the very beginning of the book Euclide Auclair stands on the tip of Cap Diamant and watches the summer supply ships of the Quebec fleet leave for France. Since they are freighted with memories, the apothecary stands gazing after them long after they have disappeared from sight. This incident might serve as a trope for the whole novel, which is in effect one long, backward, nostalgic look. More than this, it symbolizes the author's emotional outlook during the last period of her creative life: a regretful backward glance at a way of life which she felt had departed forever and had taken so many lovely things with it.

Shadows on the Rock is, however, a more honest book than *Death Comes for the Archbishop*, even though it, too, omits conflict. The reason is that Willa Cather has now confined herself to doing what she set out to do. In dealing with her protagonists she does not claim to be writing about heroes; she never for a moment tries to convince the reader that Euclide Auclair is anything other than what he is: a rather timid ineffectual man who knows he is not the stuff of which pioneers are made. In addition to being more honest, the book is also more artistic. All of Willa Cather's novels can be considered to be extended lyrics in prose; on this basis *Shadows on the Rock* is better constructed than the previous novel because in it the unity of lyric tone is consistently maintained. It is not a lyric prose poem containing unassimilated fragments of material dramatically handled, as is *Death Comes for the Archbishop*. Its overall effect is slight but charming, reminding one of Gautier's *Émaux et Camées*. Although less famous than its predecessor, it is a purer work of art.

THE MIDDLE WEST REVISITED

After her "Catholic" novels Willa Cather seems to have grown tired of searching for exotic locales to use as settings for local-color stories. Perhaps she felt that she was acquiring too much of a tourist view of life; it is more likely, however, that the illness and death of both of her parents rudely interrupted her search for beautiful sensations and turned her mind back on childhood experiences, pointing up for her the importance of the family in human affairs. Whatever the cause, the result is that her next two books show two characteristics, one new and one old: a nostalgic return to writing about that part of the country with which she was most familiar, the American Middle West, and the previously seen emphasis on the group rather than the individual together with the standards and traditions adhered to by the group. In these two books Willa Cather revisits the Middle West, but it no longer interests her as raw material for the creative pioneer spirit; instead it seems to her to be the environment in which the values of the multigeneration family unit can best be maintained. She now looks at the Middle West through the spectacles of tradition, maintaining roughly the same attitude that she had shown in her "Catholic" novels.

Obscure Destinies (1932) demonstrates this attitude very clearly. The very title forms a contrast with those of her earlier prairie volumes; unlike her earlier self, she is now content to describe "the short and simple annals of the poor." The book invites comparison with Flaubert's *Trois Contes,* upon which she apparently modeled it. Like that book, it starts with the present and moves backward in time (although of course with a much shallower historical reference, since the farthest back she goes is to the turn of the century); like that book it is a tacit criticism of the present in its implied praise of the past. Something of Flaubert's quiet, cadenced prose is to be found in the volume too. As in *Shadows on the Rock,* she concentrates on the death part of the life cycle; the first two stories end in the death of a person, the last in the death of a friendship. John Randul points out that

The first story, "Neighbour Rosicky," was written during the final months of Charles Cather's illness, and is probably a tribute to her father.[194] In it she comes to grips with the fact of death as she was unable to do (at least at the time) in her own life. Although she deals with the same pioneers whose lives she had described in heroic terms in her prairie novels, she now adopts a completely different tone. This is a tired story; even the landscape is passively enjoyed as it was in *Death Comes for the Archbishop.*

"Neighbour Rosicky" has for its hero the man who in real life was the husband of "my Ántonia." In it Willa Cather describes the last days and death of this pioneer farmer; and in so doing she chronicles the end of an epoch, depicting Nebraska as it was after the passing of the pioneer period. The story of the earthly paradise, the yeoman's fee-simple empire founded in the garden of the Middle West, is thus finally brought to a close.

"Neighbour Rosicky" is about an old man who at the end of his life feels he has much to cherish and little to regret. He goes to a doctor in the fall and learns that he has a bad heart, an ailment that kills him the following spring. But, much to his doctor's surprise, he is not at all worried about his condition; death can claim him any time it wants to; he has had a good life and is satisfied. The reason for Rosicky's content is that he has had a happy married and family life. This is the result of the ministrations of his wife, the Ántonia of the prairie novel, here called Mary. The only real worry he has concerns Polly, his "American" daughter-in-law; he is uncertain as to how happy she will be at having married into a "foreign" family.

Into the story Willa Cather pours many of her feelings about the source of human happiness in general and the Rosickys' in particular. We are told that unlike their neighbors they are not money-minded; they are comfortably out of debt, although they never seem to get ahead very far. The doctor muses, "May be you couldn't enjoy your life and put it into the bank too." [195] But according to Willa Cather the real secret of their success is that they have learned that the life of the country is preferable to the life of the town. Rosicky's opinion on the subject is based on his own experience, since he has lived in five different places in three countries; aside from a village and farm in his native Czechoslovakia he has been down and out in London and well-to-do in New York. But he finally decided to spend the rest of his life on a farm. He has a vivid memory of the day he made that decision:

> Rosicky, the old Rosicky, could remember as if it were yesterday the day when the young Rosicky found out what was the matter with him. It was on a Fourth of July afternoon, and he was sitting in Park Place in the sun. The lower part of New York was empty. Wall Street, Liberty Street, Broadway, all empty. So much stone and asphalt with nothing going on, so many empty windows. The emptiness was intense, like the stillness in a great factory when the machinery stops and the belts and bands cease running. It was too great a change, it took all the strength out of one. Those blank buildings, without the stream of life pouring through them, were like empty jails. It struck young Rosicky that this was the trouble with big cities; they built you in from the earth itself, cemented you away from any contact with the ground. You lived in an unnatural world, like the fish in an aquarium, who were probably much more comfortable than they ever were in the sea. [196]

Several interesting attitudes are expressed here. First, the idea of cities' being empty is a curious concept, especially for one who has seen Nebraska. It is definitely not the reaction of a city man. Second, the feeling that a life led close to nature is also close to the ultimate realities is acceptable only to somebody who rejects the theory of the stages of civilization as outlined by Condorcet and accepts some form of primitivism. This, of course, is nothing new in Willa Cather. Third, Neighbor Rosicky (and with him the author) has failed to realize that civilization is not identical with physical comfort; those who think it is are missing the point. After affirming the town in *Shadows on the Rock*, Willa Cather definitely and finally resolves the city-country conflict in favor of the country, a solution which will hold good for the rest of her career.[197] This represents a return to the values of her childhood, especially of the years between eight and fifteen.

Willa Cather continues:

> After that Fourth of July day in Park Place, the desire to return to the country never left him. To work on another man's farm would be all he asked; to see the sun rise and set and to plant things and watch them grow. He was a very simple man. He was like a tree that has not many roots, but one tap-root that goes down deep.[198]

It need hardly be pointed out that this is not the heroic spirit which tamed the soil. Rosicky is no Ántonia; he would be quite content to play the passive spectator's role; to work on another man's farm, to see the sun rise, and to plant things and watch them grow. It might be argued that this is the attitude of old age were it not for the fact that these thoughts are attributed to the young Rosicky. Actually, it is not Neighbor Rosicky's old age which is speaking at all but Willa Cather's.

Willa Cather's view of the superiority of country life is buttressed by two anecdotes, one told by Rosicky himself and the other by his wife Mary. They contrast the relative severity of poverty in the city and in the country. Hard times in the city are illustrated by Rosicky's story of how once in London on a Christmas Eve he was forced to beg from strangers for money to buy a Christmas goose to replace the one he had ravenously eaten which belonged to his poverty-stricken landlord.[199] Hard times in the country, on the other hand, are recalled by Mary's anecdote of how the family had celebrated a Fourth of July picnic in defiance of fate, in spite of the fact that a scorching hot wind had just destroyed their entire corn crop along with that of all their neighbors.[200] As Rosicky muses on the fate of his children and their probable happy future, it seems to him that mere subsistence in the country is better than anything the city has to offer:

> They would have to work hard on the farm, and probably they would never do much more than make a living. But if he could

think of them as staying here on the land, he wouldn't have to
fear any great unkindness for them. Hardships, certainly; it was a
hardship to have the wheat freeze in the ground when seed was so
high; and to have to sell your stock because you had no feed. But
there would be other years when everything came along right, and
you caught up. And what you had was your own. You didn't have
to choose between bosses and strikers, and go wrong either way.
You didn't have to do with dishonest and cruel people. They were
the only things in his experience he had found terrifying and
horrible; the look in the eyes of a dishonest and crafty man, of a
scheming and rapacious woman.

In the country, if you had a mean neighbour, you could keep
off his land and make him keep off yours. But in the city, all the
foulness and misery and brutality of your neighbours was part of
your life. The worst things he had come upon were human, —
depraved and poisonous specimens of man. To this day he could
recall certain terrible faces in the London streets. There were
mean people everywhere, to be sure, even in their own country town
here. But they weren't tempered, hardened, like the treacherous
people in cities who live by grinding or cheating or poisoning their
fellow-men. . . .

It seemed to Rosicky that for good, honest boys like him, the
worst they could do on the farm was better than the best they
could be likely to do in the city. If he'd had a mean boy, now,
one who was crooked and sharp and tried to put anything over on
his brothers, then town would be the place for him. But he had
no such boy. . . . What Rosicky really hoped for his boys was
that they could get through the world without ever knowing much
about the cruelty of human beings. "Their mother and me ain't
prepared them for that," he sometimes said to himself.[201]

In these passages Willa Cather seems to have succumbed completely
to nostalgia. She sentimentalizes the countryside, totally distorting
the picture she had painted of the Middle West in her prairie novels.
When she says that on the farm one didn't have to deal with dishonest
or cruel people, one wonders whether she ever remembered Krajiek or
Wick Cutter or Ivy Peters; they could be kept off one's land, too, but
they were still a threat. Rosicky's notion of shipping mean boys off
to the city because they would not be out of place there is the old
rural-evangelical Populist view of the big town put in milder form.
And when Rosicky hopes his children will never realize the full cruelty

of human beings because he and Mary had never prepared them for it, the escapist impulse in Willa Cather seems to come close to the surface. His desire for cloistered virtue makes one wish that either he or his creator had studied *Areopagitica*.

I have said that "Neighbour Rosicky" was written during the period of Willa Cather's father's final illness. Perhaps this is the reason why in it she resolves the old, old conflict between the claims of a calling and human claims in a human direction once more. Neighbor Rosicky is an artist in living; he leads his own particular version of the comely life, which is based ultimately on his capacity to love. Even his "American" daughter-in-law, who feels peculiar at having married a "foreigner," realizes this. Willa Cather writes:

> She had a sudden feeling that nobody in the world, not her mother, not Rudolph, or anyone, really loved her as much as old Rosicky did. . . . It was as if Rosicky had a special gift for loving people, something that was like an ear for music or an eye for colour. It was quiet, unobtrusive; it was merely there. You saw it in his eyes, — perhaps that was why they were merry.[202]

No doubt is left in the reader's mind that it is his talent for loving that makes Rosicky's family such a happy one. In this and the other stories written during the period of her parents' final illnesses, Willa Cather affirms human relations once more.

Rosicky finally dies as a result of overexerting himself on behalf of the land. He takes a buggy-rake and starts weeding out the Russian thistles that have sprung up in his son Rudolph's alfalfa field. He has a heart attack, and is saved from immediate death only by the help of Polly, Rudolph's wife, who gets him to the house and makes him lie down.[203] Before the end of the story all conflict arising from differences in background are resolved as he and Polly come completely to understand and love each other; they are reconciled when faced with the ultimate realities. Rosicky's death when it comes is beneficent and peaceful; he accepts it much as the cowboy Otto Fuchs had accepted the idea of death in *My Ántonia*. Willa Cather indicates his attitude toward his end by the quiet tone she uses in describing it:

> After he had taken a few stitches, the cramp began in his chest, like yesterday. He put his pipe cautiously down on the window-sill and bent over to ease the pull. No use, — he had better try to get to his bed if he could. He rose and groped his way across

the familiar floor, which was rising and falling like the deck of a ship. At the door he fell. When Mary came in, she found him lying there, and the moment she touched him she knew that he was gone.[204]

In the end we are left with the feeling that Rosicky understands death because he understands life. He displays a complete acceptance of death as timely and welcome when it comes after a full life, in its proper place in the sequence of the vegetation cycle.

The second story to be found in *Obscure Destinies* is entitled "Old Mrs. Harris." This piece constitutes a retelling of Thea Kronborg's story but with a difference; it has for its heroine, not a high-spirited young girl, but her group-centered grandmother. The story has a young girl in it, to be sure, in the person of Vickie Templeton, but it is the self-effacing old Mrs. Harris who is the center of emphasis and receives all our sympathy. "Old Mrs. Harris" embodies among other things the theme of the ungrateful child and in this respect is a kind of truncated *Père Goriot* or *King Lear*. For Vickie's mother, Mrs. Victoria Templeton, is inconsiderate of her aged parent, being a vain, frivolous, and self-centered Southern belle. She had been the toast of the Tennessee town from which she had come, and continued her self-centered and demanding ways once she reached the Nebraska frontier. Old Mrs. Harris, on the other hand, is just the opposite. She lives for others only. She is seen through the eyes of Mrs. Rosen, the cultivated Jewish neighbor who comes from a different and more sophisticated culture than the Templetons and is the only adult around who really appreciates Mrs. Harris. "You know I care more about the old folks than the young," [205] she tells her. Miss Cather notes:

> But she had observed that whenever Mrs. Harris's grandchildren were about, tumbling all over her, asking for cookies, teasing her to read to them, the old lady looked happy.[206]

To keep Victoria different from these "ordinary" women meant everything to Mrs. Harris. She realized that Mrs. Rosen managed to be mistress of any situation, either in kitchen or parlour, but that was because she was "foreign." Grandmother perfectly understood that their neighbour had a superior cultivation which made everything she did an exercise of skill. . . .
Grandmother's own lot could improve only with the family

fortunes — any comfort for herself, aside from that of the family, was inconceivable to her; and on the other hand she could have no real unhappiness while the children were well, and good, and fond of her and their mother. . . .

Sometimes, in the morning, if her feet ached more than usual, Mrs. Harris felt a little low. . . . But the moment she heard the children running down the uncarpeted back stairs, she forgot to be low. Indeed, she ceased to be an individual, an old woman with aching feet; she became part of a group, became a relationship. She was drunk up into their freshness when they burst in upon her, telling her about their dreams, explaining their troubles with buttons and shoe-laces and underwear shrunk too small. The tired, solitary old woman Grandmother had been at daybreak vanished; suddenly the morning seemed as important to her as it did to the children, and the mornings ahead stretched out sunshiny, important.[207]

The only other adult who pays any attention to Mrs. Harris is the hired girl Mandy who rubs her feet for her when the circulation gets poor. For the rest, all of them are half indifferent to her and take her services for granted. Vickie, the adolescent young girl of the family, resembles her mother more than her grandmother: she too is self-centered, inconsiderate, and vain.

Willa Cather takes the family through a series of incidents designed to reveal its members' characteristics and show them in a good light or bad. Most prominent is the Methodist ice-cream social at which Victoria is publicly criticized for letting her old mother slave for her in the kitchen. It takes some time for Victoria to recognize the thrust for what it is, but when she does she gets in a huff, for she cannot bear criticism. This calls forth some remarks from Willa Cather on the contrast between Nebraska and Tennessee, between the Western and Southern modes of living, which result in the following summary:

> Mrs. Harris was no longer living in a feudal society, where there were plenty of landless people glad to render service to the more fortunate, but in a snappy little Western democracy, where every man was as good as his neighbour and out to prove it.[208]

Another author might have written a comedy of manners on the subject, but Willa Cather does not choose to make comedy of it. She is pretty impartial in her handling of the conflict between Western and

Southern manners. The issue involved seems to be whether or not a "lady" can do housework and still be a lady:

> [The Westerners] who belonged to clubs and Relief Corps lived differently, Mrs. Harris knew, but she herself didn't like the way they lived. She believed that somebody ought to be in the parlour, and somebody in the kitchen. She wouldn't for the world have had Victoria go about every morning in a short gingham dress, with bare arms, and a dust-cap on her head to hide the curling-kids, as these brisk housekeepers did. To Mrs. Harris that would have meant real poverty, coming down in the world so far that one could no longer keep up appearances.[209]

The phrase "snappy little Western democracy" and the fact that the one Westerner presented, Mrs. Jackson, is rude enough to publicly insult Victoria Templeton seem to indicate an antipathy for the democratic ideal as opposed to the feudal one. But on the other hand Mrs. Rosen, who represents European civilization and is the most sophisticated character in the whole tale, is closer to the Western point of view than to the Southern one.[210]

The portrait of the Templetons is interesting as the first sign of Willa Cather's renewed interest in the South of her extreme childhood (before the age of eight) which she was later to use in the last novel she wrote, *Sapphira and the Slave Girl*. The picture she paints of Southern middle-class manners (with aristocratic pretensions) is not very savory. It involves a sense of clannishness (the Templetons do not like it when somebody else sits down at their picnic table) and an excessive admiration of superficial qualities (respectability and the keeping up of appearances are far more important to them than they should be, and the Templeton children have an extravagant admiration for their mother's good looks). But more serious is Victoria's reaction to the insult hurled at her by Mrs. Jackson:

> Mrs. Templeton didn't at once take it in. Her training was all to the end that you must give a guest everything you have, even if he happens to be your worst enemy, and that to cause anyone embarrassment is a frightful and humiliating blunder. She felt hurt without knowing just why, but all evening it kept growing clearer to her that this was another of those thrusts from the outside which she couldn't understand. The neighbours were sure to take sides against her, apparently, if they came often to see her mother. . . .

Nothing ever made Victoria cross but criticism. She was jealous
of small attentions paid to Mrs. Harris, because she felt they were
paid "behind her back" or "over her head," in a way that implied
reproach to her. Victoria had been a belle in their own town in
Tennessee, but here she was not very popular, no matter how
many pretty dresses she wore, and she couldn't bear it. She felt as
if her mother and Mr. Templeton must be somehow to blame; at
least they ought to protect her from whatever was disagreeable —
they always had! [211]

These passages not only show Victoria to be lacking in insight and
unable to take criticism; they also show her as given to indiscriminate
politeness which makes her helpless before those who are impolite. The
fact of her wanting to blame someone else for her troubles reveals a
rather frightening conception of a woman as a spoiled child who must
always be pampered and petted. This particular Southern tradition is a
foolish tradition; and the Templetons are victims of immature social
standards. Willa Cather shows her awareness of this by the mordant
portrait she paints of Victoria. The neglected Mrs. Harris is the unsung
heroine of the piece, but it is not the standards she adheres to but the
unswerving fidelity to her family whatever their standards that Mrs.
Rosen and Willa Cather herself find admirable.

Another sign of Mrs. Harris's superiority is her acceptance of pain
as an inescapable consequence of life. This comes out in the description
of the death of Blue Boy, the tomcat. Blue Boy, who has been likened
to Mrs. Harris and whose death foreshadows her own, comes down
with distemper, to the consternation of the entire family. The Templeton twins have never seen suffering before, and are aghast as he begins
to froth at the mouth and goes into spasm after spasm. "Oh, Gram'ma,
can't you do anything?" they ask. But Mrs. Harris only replies, "Everything that's alive has got to suffer." [212] This attitude is completely
different from Victoria's escapist reaction to the same thing: "I'm
sorry about your cat, boys," she said. "That's why I don't like to have
cats around; they're always getting sick and dying." [213] This amounts
to a saying no to life because of the danger it involves.

A little later in the story the granddaughter Vickie wins a long-
coveted scholarship to go to college at Ann Arbor, but doesn't have the
money to go. Her father lets her down by failing to find any way of
raising the necessary cash, and for a while Vickie thinks the whole world
is against her and feels herself to be a solitary rebel, like Willa Cather's
early heroines. Here she becomes another Thea Kronborg — but with-

out eliciting the sympathy that Thea got when Miss Cather too was young and ardent for success. Finally the necessary three hundred dollars is lent to her by Mrs. Rosen's husband through the intercession of old Mrs. Harris, who keeps her role in the affair a strict secret. Vickie never even knows who her benefactor is.

Meanwhile other members of the family are having troubles of their own. Mrs. Templeton discovers that she is pregnant once more, and just can't stand the thought of going through another confinement. Using the excuse of a business trip, Mr. Templeton runs out on her, just as he always does in times of trouble. In the midst of these domestic crises Mrs. Harris realizes her time has come to die, and, self-effacing to the last, resolves to do so as quietly and unobtrusively as possible. She recalls a passage from *Pilgrim's Progress,* where Christiana and her band come to the arbor on the Hill of Difficulty: *"Then said Mercy, how sweet is rest to them that labour,"* [214] a quotation which sums up her entire life. The bound girl Mandy tries to rub the cold out of her legs, but Mrs. Harris is under no illusions about the meaning of that cold. Her final lapse into unconsciousness is quite peaceful:

> Grandma fell to remembering the old place at home: what a dashing, high-spirited girl Victoria was, and how proud she had always been of her; how she used to hear her laughing and teasing out in the lilac arbour when Hillary Templeton was courting her. Toward morning all these pleasant reflections faded out. Mrs. Harris felt that she and her bed were softly sinking, through the darkness to a deeper darkness.
>
> Old Mrs. Harris did not really die that night, but she believed she did. Mandy found her unconscious in the morning. Then there was a great stir and bustle; Victoria, and even Vickie, were startled out of their intense self-absorption. Mrs. Harris was hastily carried out of the play-room and laid in Victoria's bed, put into one of Victoria's best nightgowns. Mr. Templeton was sent for, and the doctor was sent for. . . . But Grandmother was out of it all, never knew that she was the object of so much attention and excitement. She died a little while after Mr. Templeton got home.[215]

"Old Mrs. Harris" compresses a great deal of the history of Willa Cather's own family into a short space: Victoria Templeton being Willa Cather's mother; Vickie, Willa herself. It shows quite clearly some of the less pleasant aspects of the multigeneration family: the oppressive claustrophobic atmosphere of a crowded house and the inability of the generations to understand each other until it is too late. The story is a tribute to Willa Cather's grandmother, and the main impulse behind it seems to be a regret that she had not appreciated her forebear earlier, while there still was time to express her gratitude to her. This idea is borne out by the story's concluding paragraph:

> Thus Mrs. Harris slipped out of the Templetons' story; but Victoria and Vickie had still to go on, to follow the long road that leads through things unguessed at and unforeseeable. When they are old, they will come closer to Grandma Harris. They will think a great deal about her, and remember things they never noticed; and their lot will be more or less like hers. They will regret that they heeded her so little; but they, too, will look into the eager, unseeing eyes of young people and feel themselves alone. They will say to themselves: "I was heartless, because I was young and strong and wanted things so much. But now I know." [216]

"Old Mrs. Harris" is the second story in the book to chronicle a timely and kindly death coming at the end of a long honorable life. However, its heroine is much more self-effacing than "Neighbour Rosicky" ever was; she bears a much closer resemblance to Euclide Auclair. This story's treatment of life in Nebraska is at the opposite pole from that found in the prairie novels; here unbridled individualism is severely criticized, and subordination to the family is praised. In her loyalty, strength, and simple enduring qualities Grandma Harris resembles Félicité in Flaubert's *"Un Coeur Simple,"* and, like Félicité, she is a kind of saint. Willa Cather's sympathies are completely with the unassertive grandmother who gives her loyalty to the South and the feudal order rather than to the West and democracy. The story thus restates the theme of *Shadows on the Rock* but in a Middle Western setting; as in *Shadows on the Rock* the group is all-important. Finally, the story is a convincing one, and not particularly sentimentalized, as are the next stories with which we will have to deal.

Not much need be said about the short story entitled "Two Friends"; of all the stories in *Obscure Destinies* it is the weakest. It describes through the eyes of a child the friendship of Mr. Trueman the cattle rancher and Mr. Dillon the banker and businessman, and the break-up of that friendship due to a political argument over the nomination of William Jennings Bryan. It is tempting to see the story as an allegory of the split between commerce and agriculture, business and creativity, fact and value, but more likely it represents the break-up of Willa Cather's childhood world, her first realization that the adult world contains conflict and pain. It is interesting because it shows vividly her own peculiar interpretation of conflict. According to her view, people either agree completely or else completely break off with each other — there is no conception of compromise or of people agreeing to disagree. Needless to say, this is not a very mature view. Not only does she not sufficiently motivate Trueman to break off a lifelong friendship on the basis of a political argument; she insists that "After that rupture nothing went well with either of my two great men." [217] Dillon dies within three years of that time; Trueman moves out of town and presumably leads a frustrated life until his demise within a decade of the quarrel. The concluding passage voices a regret for lost human relationships that makes one sympathize with Willa Cather's old age and reminds one of the remorse of Tom Outland:

> When that old scar is occasionally touched by chance, it rouses the old uneasiness; the feeling of something broken that could so easily have been mended; of something delightful that was sense-lessly wasted, of a truth that was accidentally distorted — one of the truths we want to keep. [218]

The next step in Willa Cather's reconsideration of the Middle West is mawkishly sentimental. Into this group falls the novel *Lucy Gayheart* (1935) and the short story "The Best Years," written in 1945 but first published in the posthumous collection of short stories called *The Old Beauty and Others*, published in 1948. The tone of *Lucy Gayheart* is best indicated by Willa Cather's original title for it, *Blue Eyes on the Platte*. It tells of a young Nebraska girl at the turn of the century who goes to Chicago to study music and falls in love with the singer Clément Sebastian, whose accompanist she has become. In the best Cather tradition, Clément is unhappily married and given to brooding over his lost youth and the unsatisfactory nature of life in general. They have the habit of standing in the doorway for long periods of time, embracing and kissing; but we are carefully given to understand that there is no further involvement. The older Willa Cather seems as afraid as ever of passion:

> When she gave him a quick shy look and the gold sparks flashed in her eyes, he read devotion there, and the fire of imagination;

but no invitation, no appeal. In her companionship there was never the shadow of a claim. On the contrary, there was a spirit which disdained advantage.[219]

This rather extraordinary love affair comes to an end when Clément Sebastian, on a European concert tour, takes up small-boat sailing and is drowned in a storm on Lake Como. Brokenhearted, Lucy returns to her Nebraska home and leads a life of solitary seclusion, broken only by her periodic attempts to strike up a friendly but not inviting relationship with the young town banker, whom she has previously jilted. Quite understandably he gives her little encouragement. Finally, angered at his refusal to pick her up on the road in his sleigh, she goes skating on rotten ice in the river, falls in, and is drowned. The book ends with an epilogue twenty-five years later during which everyone mournfully loves Lucy.

In treatment of its theme, this book is far inferior to *O Pioneers!*, which it to some extent parallels. The difference between *O Pioneers!* and *Lucy Gayheart* is a measure of the distance Willa Cather has traveled in a little over twenty years. A discouraged tone prevails throughout the latter book. Both novels show the lives of young people blighted by disappointment, but *O Pioneers!* at least looks forward to a future; whereas in *Lucy Gayheart* there is nothing to look forward to at all. The meaning of the book, insofar as it has a serious meaning, is that of a mournful dirge for the passing of youth and hope. Desire is all, it seems to say; accomplishment is impossible. The famous Clément and the unknown Lucy alike go down to defeat and death, in unfulfillment.

It is hard not to read this book as a projection of the older Willa Cather's own discouragement and disillusionment. This is certainly seen in the attitude of Clément Sebastian who, like Willa Cather, was personally dissatisfied although a popular success:

Nothing had ever made Sebastian admit to himself that his youth was forever and irrevocably gone. He had clung to a secret belief that he would pick it up again, somewhere. This was a time of temporary lassitude and disillusion, but his old feeling about life would come back; he would turn a corner and confront it. He would waken some morning and step out of bed the man he used to be. Now, all in a moment, it came over him that when people spoke of their dead youth they were not using a figure of speech. The thing he was looking for had gone out into the wide air, like a volatile essence, and he was staring into the empty jar. . . .

The lid once off, he began remembering everything, and everything seemed to have gone wrong. Life had so turned out that now, when he was nearing fifty, he was without a country, without a home, without a family, and very nearly without friends. Surely a man couldn't congratulate himself upon a career which had led to such results. He had missed the deepest of all companionships, a relation with the earth itself, with a countryside and a people. That relationship, he knew, cannot be gone after and found; it must be long and deliberate, unconscious. It must, indeed, be a way of living. Well, he had missed it, whatever it was, and he had begun to believe it the most satisfying tie men can have.[220]

This pessimistic view is seen not only in the author's tone but in the incidents of the story itself. The two deaths upon which the plot hinges are completely accidental; neither of them grows with any inevitability out of the novel's action. The treatment of the relation between Clément and Lucy is unmitigatedly pessimistic, too. Willa Cather makes some strange reflections on Lucy's feeling which seem to suggest that the idea of love terrifies her:

She was struggling with something she had never felt before. A new conception of art? It came closer than that. A new kind of personality? But it was much more. It was a discovery about life, a revelation of love as a tragic force, not a melting mood, of passion that drowns like black water. As she sat listening to this man the outside world seemed to her dark and terrifying, full of fears and dangers that had never come close to her until now.[221]

Her forebodings on that first night had not been mistaken; Sebastian had already destroyed a great deal for her. Some peoples' lives are affected by what happens to their person or their property; but for others fate is what happens to their feelings and their thoughts — that and nothing more.[222]

In addition, it is painfully obvious that Willa Cather cannot come to grips with a physical relation between a man and a woman. What should be the central human situation in the book is simply not credible. Lucy has an indeterminate relationship with Clément Sebastian: he is neither lover nor friend, but a baffling mixture of both. Once again

Willa Cather's inability to portray a believable love relation leads her
to an impasse; there is a hollow center to be found where the real
meaning of the book should be.

An example of the kind of writing in which Willa Cather all too
often indulges herself in *Lucy Gayheart* is the following, which occurs
after Clément's death, when Lucy has retreated to her home town:

> How often she had run out on a spring morning, into the orchard,
> down the street, in pursuit of something she could not see, but
> knew! It was there, in the breeze, in the sun; it hid behind the
> blooming apple boughs, raced before her through the neighbour's
> gardens, but she could never catch up with it. Clément Sebastian
> had made the fugitive gleam an actual possession. With him she
> had learned that those flashes of promise could come true, that
> they could be the important things in one's life. . . .
>
> Suddenly something flashed into her mind, so clear that it must
> have come from without, from the breathless quiet. What if —
> what if Life itself were the sweetheart? It was like a lover waiting
> for her in distant cities — across the sea; drawing her, enticing
> her, weaving a spell over her. She opened the window softly and
> knelt down beside it to breathe the cold air. She felt the snow-
> flakes melt in her hair, on her hot cheeks. Oh, now she knew!
> She must have it, she couldn't run away from it. She must go back
> into the world and get all she could of everything that had made
> him what he was. Those splendours were still on earth, to be
> sought after and fought for. . . .
>
> She crouched closer to the window and stretched out her arms to
> the storm, to whatever might lie behind it. Let it come! Let it
> all come back to her again! Let it betray her and mock her and
> break her heart, she must have it.[223]

Thea Kronborg had sounded like this in *The Song of the Lark*, but
at least Thea had known that she wanted to be an opera singer. Lucy
Gayheart does not know what she wants to do. Apparently Willa
Cather had fallen back on describing the emotions of her childhood,
which were, naturally, childish. The trouble here lies in the extreme
vagueness of the emotions concerned. Such generalized and objectless
emotion as Lucy expresses can lead only to emptiness and frustration.
Lucy herself sounds like an adolescent schoolgirl, and she never gets
beyond this stage. No wonder Willa Cather can think of nothing else
to do with her than to have her die.

A similar kind of sentimentality mars "The Best Years." In this story, which takes place in Nebraska in the year 1899, Miss Evangeline Knightly, a rural superintendent of public schools, drives out to see her favorite schoolteacher, Miss Lesley Ferguesson. The latter has obtained a position by lying about her age — she is fourteen instead of the legal sixteen — and Miss Knightly, because of her friendship for Lesley, has tacitly acquiesced in her lie. After listening to her pupils recite, Miss Knightly offers to take the delighted Lesley home to visit her family over the weekend, and there follows a touching description of her reunion with her parents and brothers. Some time later Miss Knightly learns that a tremendous blizzard has occurred, and that Lesley, in a heroic effort to help her pupils escape from the snowbound schoolhouse, has caught pneumonia and died. There follows the usual twenty-years-after epilogue in which Miss Knightly returns to visit with Mrs. Ferguesson and talk about her daughter with her. Here again, as in *Lucy Gayheart,* the heroine's death is completely accidental and unmotivated. Willa Cather plays it for all the pathos she can get out of it, and the reader is left with the general impression that in Willa Cather's mind a malignant universe sees to it that the good die young.

Lucy Gayheart and "The Best Years" both show how bad Willa Cather could be when dealing with the same Middle West about which she had written her finest novels. Both of them are sentimental in much the same way. Willa Cather's use of accidental death in these stories seems to be a sign of self-pity; she apparently felt that anything she valued or cared for was bound to be destroyed by a cruel cosmos. This attitude is just as immature as that of Vickie Templeton, who when unable to dig up money to go to college on had felt that the whole world was her enemy; and moreover it compares unfavorably with that presented in *O Pioneers!,* where accidental death was much more subtly and believably handled, and embodies a seriously held view of man's fate. The big difference between her present protagonists and those of her prairie novels is that those were heroic, while these are only pathetic. Formerly she had written about young people brimming over with vitality, who had a tremendous will to succeed. Now her ideal seems to be a much more passive one; the young people she chooses as heroines are improbably good and impossibly sweet.

THE PROTESTANT PAST: *Sapphira and the Slave Girl*

During the course of this study I have tried to trace Willa Cather's development, to show how she started out by portraying heroic individualists who struggle successfully to master their environment, then, under the influence of personal and social events in the twenties and thirties, gradually evolved a way of looking at the world which was traditional and hierarchic. I have also tried to show how she was unable to maintain this latter view for any length of time and kept drifting back from an affirmation of feudal social arrangements to an exaltation of the individual, although in such stories as *Lucy Gayheart* and "The Best Years" the individualist view she expresses is a sentimentalized and debased version of that which had formed the basis of her prairie novels. Now, at the end of her career, she writes a novel in which both versions of the ideal life and society are inconsistently mixed. For *Sapphira and the Slave Girl* starts out as an affirmation of individualism; then it completely reverses its values and ends up by strongly affirming both feudal hierarchy and the authority of the group.

I have suggested earlier that after her parents' deaths Willa Cather seemed to be shocked out of her preoccupation with Catholic culture; at any rate, following her father's death and the completion of *Shadows on the Rock* she never treated Catholic themes again. The break-up of her family carried her mind back to her own past and reawakened an interest in the scenes of her childhood and adolescence, as we saw in the short stories of *Obscure Destinies* and in *Lucy Gayheart*. But, apparently feeling that she had worked that vein out (certainly a reader feels so), in the autumn of 1937 she began a new novel which was entirely different from any other she had written, with a setting which went back even farther into her past, to her very early childhood, to the mountains of Virginia which she had left at the age of eight. The story takes place in her grandparents' time before the Civil War, and is about that radical Protestant movement, abolitionism. She had long intended to write a story about her Virginia memories as a favor to her father.[224] At about the same time as the publication of the book she told a newspaper reporter who questioned her about what religion she held, "I'm an Episcopalian and a good one, I hope!" [225] Thus it seems quite likely that Willa Cather intended the book to be a tribute to her family's Protestant heritage.

The story tells how Sapphira Dodderidge, a Loudoun County aristocrat who is afraid of becoming an old maid, takes "a long step downward" to marry Henry Colbert, who is a miller by profession, a "foreigner" by extraction (his grandfather came from Flanders), and a democrat in his manners. To escape from the stigma that must ensue from such a poor match she and her husband move across the mountains to a farm she owns on the edge of the wilderness. There they resume their separate occupations, he being the only miller in the district, and she the only practicing aristocrat.

A lapse of twenty-five years finds them somewhat estranged from each other: Henry now sleeps down at the millhouse, while Sapphira stays on at the manor. Because she is afflicted with dropsy and has been unable to get out of a wheelchair alone for four years, Sapphira's suspicions are easily aroused, and she becomes extremely jealous of the young yellow girl Nancy who keeps Henry's room down at the mill for him. Thinking that Nancy and her husband are having an affair, she determines to ruin the girl. She invites Henry's wild young nephew Martin Colbert, "the worst rake in the country," to visit them and then takes every opportunity possible to throw Nancy in Martin's way. Harried beyond endurance, Nancy finally appeals to Sapphira's daughter Rachel Blake, who never has been sympathetic with her mother's slaveholding mentality and autocratic temperament. Rachel helps Nancy escape to Canada via the Underground Railroad. The money needed for the venture is supplied by the miller, but, although he is firmly convinced that slavery is wrong, he does not think he has the right to interfere with his wife's personal property. Instead of facing the issue squarely and realizing he must make a decision, he adopts the equivocal course of leaving his coat hanging overnight by an open window with a hundred dollars in its pocket, telling Rachel in advance that he is going to do so. Nancy escapes successfully and returns twenty-five years later after the Civil War to visit with her old friends, who include Willa Cather's father and mother. For some reason Willa Cather includes herself in the story as a child of five who is all agog to see the yellow girl she had heard so much about. Later she rightly considered this to be an artistic error, and regretted having included the episode.[226]

The main conflict in the book is that between Sapphira on the one hand and her husband and daughter on the other, arising from the former's jealous persecution of the slave girl Nancy; a persecution which outrages every moral feeling the other two possess. She is able to undertake her cruel scheme only because of the abuses possible under the institution of slavery. This is not the first time she has abused her position as mistress of her establishment; she had done wrong to Nancy's mother Till a generation earlier by marrying her to a "capon man" because Till was a lady's maid and because, in the words of the Negro cook, she didn't want a lady's maid to be "havin' chillun all over de place, — always a-carryin' or a-nussin' 'em." [227] Now she inflicts grievous wrong on the daughter Nancy by forcing her into a position where her rights as a human being are completely abrogated. The situation is well summed up by Rachel's reflections at a crucial point just before she makes up her mind to help Nancy escape:

> Mrs. Colbert had turned on Nancy; that was well known. Now she had the worst rake in the country staying in her house, and she was sending the girl up into the woods alone, after giving him fair warning. Did her mother really want to ruin Nancy? Could her spite go so far as that?
>
> Rachel Blake closed her eyes and leaned her head and arms forward on her dresser top. She had known her mother to show great kindness to her servants, and, sometimes, cold cruelty. But she had never known her to do anything quite so ugly as this, if Nancy's tale were true.[228]

This is not the only criticism of the "peculiar institution" voiced in the book. Willa Cather informs us that Rachel had been openly opposed to slavery since the time she was twelve years old and had overheard a conversation between the abolitionist postmistress of their village and her father, who had wanted to buy a slave for her.[229] Miss Cather writes:

> A feeling long smothered had blazed up in her — had become a conviction. She had never heard the things said before, never put into words. It was the *owning* that was wrong, the relation itself, no matter how convenient or agreeable it might be for master or servant. She had always known it was wrong. It was the thing that made her unhappy at home, and came between her and her mother. How she hated her mother's voice in sarcastic reprimand to the servants! And she hated it in contemptuous indulgence.[230]

And later in the book:

> Ever since she could remember, she had seen her mother show shades of kindness and cruelty which seemed to her purely whimsical.[231]

The miller, being of Flemish extraction and thus an alien to the Loudoun County aristocracy from which his wife came, does not share her slaveholding views, and the daughter takes after him rather than her mother. But there is another level of conflict between husband and wife which has to do with religious differences; Sapphira is an Anglican, while her husband and daughter have strong Baptist connections. Willa Cather makes this clear very early in the book when describing the miller's courtship:

> With his father he regularly attended a dissenting church supported by small farmers and artisans. He was certainly no match for Captain Dodderidge's daughter.[232]

And later, in speaking of Sapphira's attendance at the Anglican communion, she remarks:

> The miller, of course, did not accompany her. Although he had been married in Christ Church, by an English rector, he had no love for the Church of England.[233]

So the conflict between Henry Colbert and his wife is among other things a conflict of social and religious traditions: between the Episcopalian slaveholding hierarchy of Virginia and a radical Protestant egalitarianism and abolitionism.

The struggle between Henry and Sapphira is apparent from the very first chapter. In a scene which serves as a trope for the whole novel the miller is having breakfast with his wife when she casually mentions the possibility of selling Nancy to a friend. Immediately a strong feeling of resentment and hostility appears beneath the customary veneer of good manners and domestic courtesy:

> Her husband pushed back his plate. "Nancy least of all! Her mother is here, and old Jezebel. Her people have been in your family for four generations. You haven't trained Nancy for Mrs. Grimwood. She stays here."
>
> The icy quality, so effective with her servants, came into Mrs. Colbert's voice as she answered him.
>
> "It's nothing to get flustered about, Henry. As you say, her mother and grandmother and great-grandmother were all Dodderidge niggers. So it seems to me I ought to be allowed to arrange Nancy's future. Her mother would approve. She knows that a proper lady's maid can never be trained out here in this rough country."
>
> The miller's frown darkened. "You can't sell her without my name on the deed of sale, and I will never put it there. You never

seemed to understand how, when we first moved up here, your troup of niggers was held against us. This isn't a slave-owning neighbourhood. If you sold a good girl like Nancy off to Winchester, people hereabouts would hold it against you. They would say hard things." [234]

The same kind of hostility is discernible in the relations between Rachel and Sapphira. A strong undercurrent of antagonism existed between Rachel and her mother; she had always been unhappy as long as she had lived at home,[235] and Willa Cather reflects: "Rachel had always been difficult, — rebellious toward the fixed ways which satisfied other folk. Mrs. Colbert had been heartily glad to get her married and out of the home at seventeen." [236] Their conflicting attitudes are dramatized in the passage in which Rachel is identified with the spirit of radical Protestantism, so important in the abolition movement:

Her daughter sometimes felt a kind of false pleasantness in the voice. Yet, she reflected as she listened to the letter, it was scarcely false — it was the only kind of pleasantness her mother had, — not very warm.

As Mrs. Colbert finished, Mrs. Blake said heartily: "That is surely a good letter. Aunt Sarah always writes a good letter."

Mrs. Colbert took off her glasses, glancing at her daughter with a mischievous smile. "You are not put out because she makes fun of your Baptists a little?"

"No. She's a right to. I'd never have joined with the Baptists if I could have got to Winchester to our own Church. But a body likes to have some place to worship. And the Baptists are good people."

"So your father thinks. But then he never did mind to forgather with common people. I suppose that goes with a miller's business."

"Yes, the common folks hereabouts have got to have flour and meal, and there's only one mill for them to come to." Mrs. Blake's voice was rather tart. She wished it hadn't been, when her mother said unexpectedly and quite graciously:

"Well, you've surely been a good friend to them, Rachel."

Mrs. Blake bade her mother good-bye and hurried down the passage. At times she had to speak out for the faith that was in her; faith in the Baptists not so much as a sect (she still read her English Prayer Book every day), but as well-meaning men and women.[237]

So far so good; *Sapphira and the Slave Girl* starts out to be a very readable and powerful novel. But then Willa Cather does a disconcerting thing. About three-quarters of the way through she completely reverses the values upon which the book is based, so that instead of the democratic Rachel being the heroine, the protagonist now becomes the autocratic and imperious Sapphira. Sticking up for the underdog gives way to acceptance of a social system which Willa Cather has already admitted to be unjust. The result is a blurring and a complete loss of definition of the moral issues involved. For the first two hundred and thirty pages the book's main center of interest is Nancy, and the story is concerned with her growth from slavery to freedom, from innocence to experience. She is another in the long line of Cather protagonists who have to struggle to free themselves from a hostile environment:

> She was to go out from the dark lethargy of the cared-for and irresponsible; to make her own way in this world where nobody is altogether free, and the best that can happen to you is to walk your own way and be responsible to God only. Sapphira's darkies were better cared for, better fed and better clothed than the poor whites in the mountains. Yet what ragged, shag-haired, squirrel-shooting mountain man would change places with Sampson, his trusted head miller? [238]

Here slavery is clearly equated with being cared for and freedom with taking care of oneself. This is exactly the attitude of Thea Kronborg and other early Cather heroines for whom the process of growing up includes breaking away from the family; it is at once self-reliant, Puritan, and individualistic. But later in the same book Willa Cather includes episodes which completely contradict this attitude. She shows Nancy going to pieces as a result of persistent molestation by Martin ("I'm goin' to throw myself into the millpawnd, I am!" [239] she makes her say at one point) and later has her doze off in the wagon in which she is being rescued because, as she says, "The girl seemed worn out and dulled by the day's excitement." [240] Later still Willa Cather makes Nancy lose her courage completely and beg to be taken back to her family and friends.

> "Oh, Miz' Blake, please mam, take me home! I can't go off amonst strangers. It's too hard. Let me go back an' try to do better. I don't mind Miss Sapphy scoldin'. Why, she brought me

up, an' now she's sick an' sufferin'. Look at her pore feet. I ought-a
borne it better. Miz' Blake, please mam, I want to go home to the
mill an' my own folks."

"Now don't talk foolish. What about Martin?"

"I kin keep out-a his way, Miz' Blake. He won't be there always. I can't bear it to belong nowheres!" [241]

After building her character up in the first part of the novel, Willa
Cather whittles it down again. Actions such as these diminish Nancy's
stature, and completely disrupt what seems to be the original moral
purpose of the story.

The same process of building up a character only to undercut her
later on can be seen in the characterization of Rachel Blake. In the
early part of the book Rachel is the only one with a mind of her own,
who is not afraid to speak out against injustice and who stands up for
Nancy's rights as a human being when the latter is being persecuted
by Martin and Sapphira. But toward the end of the book we hear
strangely little of her. After her part in the escape has become known
there is a complete break between her mother and her. She receives a
letter containing the following message:

> Mistress Blake is kindly requested to make no further visits at
> the Mill House.
>
>   Sapphira Dodderidge Colbert [242]

Then Willa Cather, apparently at a loss as to how to resolve the conflict she has set up, has recourse to a *deus ex machina* once more. A
diphtheria epidemic comes along and carries off one of Rachel's children;
Sapphira hears about it and invites Rachel and the remaining child
to spend the winter at her house, and then, strangely enough, it is the
mother who forgives the daughter instead of the other way around. The
miller, who had formerly been at least passively on Rachel's side,
switches around and comes to admire Sapphira. Then we suddenly
discover that family insubordination is wrong and that Willa Cather
is all for autocracy:

> He seemed in a moment to feel sharply so many things he had
> grown used to and taken for granted: her long illness, with all its
> discomforts, and the intrepid courage with which she had faced the
> inevitable. He reached out for her two hands and buried his face
> in her palms. She felt his tears wet on her skin. For a long while

he crouched thus, leaning against her chair, his head on her knee.

He had never understood his wife very well, but he had always been proud of her. When she was young, she was fearless and independent, she held her head high and made this Mill House a place where town folks liked to come. After she was old and ill, she never lowered her flag; not even now, when she knew the end was not far off. He had seen strong men quail and whimper at the approach of death. He, himself, dreaded it. But as he leaned against her chair with his face hidden, he knew how it would be with her; she would make her death easy for everyone, because she would meet it with that composure which he had sometimes called heartlessness, but which now seemed to him strength. As long as she was conscious, she would be mistress of the situation and of herself.

After this long silence, in which he seemed to know that she followed his thoughts, he lifted his head, still holding fast to her hands, and spoke falteringly. "Yes, dear wife, do let us have Rachel here. You are a kind woman to think of it. You are good to a great many folks, Sapphy."

"Not so good as Rachel, with her basket!" She turned it off lightly, tweaking his ear.

"There are different ways of being good to folks," the miller held out stubbornly, as if this idea had just come to him and he was not to be teased into letting go of it. "Sometimes keeping people in their place is being good to them." [243]

As a work of art the book, however interesting, is a failure. Henry Colbert's final acceptance of his wife's ethical and social ideas is, of course, a complete espousal of hierarchy and "the great principle of subordination" and completely undercuts the novel's chief significant action, the freeing of Nancy by Rachel Blake. As it stands, the book simply will not hold together. Willa Cather starts the book as if it were a novel of her early period and ends up writing in her later vein. The shift from emphasis on the individual (Rachel) to emphasis on the group (Sapphira's feudal establishment) here occurs within the confines of a single novel, thus recapitulating the author's entire development. But however convenient this complete inversion of values may be for the literary historian, it completely wrecks the story as a work of art by knocking out its moral center. We are presented with two contradictory views of human nature: one, having Rachel as its exponent, consists in the belief that equality is a moral requirement and that some measure of dignity and respect is due to every man as a human right; the other, represented by Sapphira, holds that equality consists of treating equals as equals and unequals as unequals. There is a complete confusion of values between a feudal Episcopalian hierarchy and a democratic Puritan individualism. The two are clearly incompatible, and Willa Cather makes no effort to show that the state of tension between the two is a tension which exists in life itself. Instead she veers from all-out rugged individualism to complete group conformity, and we are left in no doubt as to the fact that it is Sapphira who gets Willa Cather's final approval.[244]

The necessity which Willa Cather apparently felt for a happy ending, however unbelievable, for a reconciliation between mother and daughter and restoration of peace within the family fold, completes the ruin of what starts out to be a powerful and dramatic novel. Everything in the novel points to a tragic ending, for the way its structure is set up there can be no reconciliation if Nancy is to go free. But Willa Cather does not have the courage to follow out the logical implications of the situation and bring the story to its inevitable conclusion. It is evident that her later view of life definitely interfered with her handling of the novel, and by undercutting its moral realism, reduced its artistic worth.

Miss Elizabeth Sergeant, in her remarks about the writing of the novel, throws some interesting light on its curious reversal of values. She says of Willa:

> She was then [1939] engaged with Sapphira, and told us that she had discarded some six pounds of manuscript dealing with the Shenandoah Valley background.[245]

> . . . in her zest for the novel démeublé, she threw out many pages and chapters to give Sapphira the central place.[246]

So it seems that Willa Cather herself had trouble making up her mind who the real heroine was, although she finally decided in favor of the authoritarian Sapphira. There must have been complete confusion in her mind as to which of the opposing value systems claimed her final allegiance. In this book more than in any other the conflict between value systems destroys her vision of reality and makes a hash of her art. It seems clear that all the ambiguities and uncertainties implicit in her view of life come out in her treatment of Sapphira. For Sapphira is a projection of Willa Cather's own mother, the gay, laughing, imperious Virginia Boak Cather; the early Rachel is the young Willa Cather striving to break away from the family and find a place of her own in the world; the later Rachel is the older Willa Cather who, filled with remorse at her parents' deaths, wanted nothing so much as to be accepted back again into the now nonexistent family group; and the older Willa Cather is also seen in Henry Colbert, who buries his face in the palms of his wife's hands and doggedly admits that she is right. For whether consciously or not, in this story Willa Cather has given us an allegory of her whole life, from the young adolescent's departure from the bosom of her parents to the frustrated elderly lady's defeated return. If she ends the novel with the triumph of the mother-figure, it is because for her that was the only ending that was psychologically possible, however unconvincing it may appear to the reader.

CHAPTER VI

WINTER AT DELPHI

When they saw all that was sacred to them laid waste, the Navajos lost heart.
They did not surrender; they simply ceased to fight, and were taken.
— *Death Comes for the Archbishop*

THE COUNT'S DREAM AND WILLA CATHER'S
SEARCH FOR SANCTUARY

Toward the end of *Shadows on the Rock* Willa Cather includes an episode which is not at all clearly related to its context but which is extremely revealing of its creator; in fact it might serve as a fable for Willa Cather's entire life. It concerns a dream which the Count de Frontenac has shortly before his death and runs as follows:

> The Count de Frontenac awoke suddenly out of a curious dream — a dream so vivid that he could not at once shake it off, but lay in the darkness behind his bed-curtains slowly realizing where he was. The sound of a church-bell rang out hoarse on the still air: yes, that would be the stubborn old man, Bishop Laval, ringing for early mass. He knew that bell like a voice. He was, then, in Canada, in the Château on the rock of Kebec; the St. Lawrence must be flowing seaward beneath his windows.
>
> In his dream, too, he had been asleep and had suddenly awakened; awakened a little boy, in an old farmhouse near Pontoise, where his nurse used to take him in the summer. He had been awakened by fright, a sense that some danger threatened him. He got up and in his bare feet stole to the door leading into the garden, which was ajar. Outside, in the darkness, stood a very tall man in a plumed hat and huge boots — a giant, in fact; the little boy's head did not come up to his boot-tops. He had no idea who the enormous man might be, but he knew that he must not come in, that everything depended upon his being kept out. Quickly and cleverly the little boy closed the door and slid the wooden bar, —

he had no trouble in finding it, for he knew the house so well. But there was the front door, — he was sleeping in the wing of the cottage, and that front door was three rooms away. Still barefoot, he went softly and swiftly through the kitchen and the living-room to the hallway behind that main door, which could be fastened by an iron bolt. It was pitch-dark, but he did not fumble, he found the bolt at once. It was rusty, and stuck. He felt how small and weak his hands were — of that he was very conscious. But he turned the bolt gently back and forth in its hasp to loosen the rust-flakes, and coaxed it into the iron loop on the door-jamb which made it fast. Then he felt suddenly faint. He wiped the sweat from his face with the sleeve of his nightgown, and waited. That terrible man on the other side of the door; one could hear him moving about in the currant bushes, pulling at the rose-vines on the wall. There were other doors — and windows! Every nook and corner of the house flashed through his mind; but for the moment he was safe. The broad oak boards and the iron bolt were between him and the great boots that must not cross the threshold. While he stood gathering his strength, he awoke in another bed than the one he had quitted a few moments ago, but he was still covered with sweat and still frightened. He did not come fully to himself until he heard the call of the old Bishop's bell-clapper. Then he knew where he was.

Of all the houses he had slept in over the world, in Flanders, Holland, Italy, Crete, why had he awakened in that one near Pontoise, and why had he remembered it so well? His bare feet had avoided every unevenness in the floor; in the dark he had stepped without hesitation from the earth floor of the kitchen, over the high sill, to the wooden floor of the living-room. He had known the exact position of all the furniture and had not stumbled against anything in his swift flight through the house. Yet he had not been in that house since he was eight years old. For four summers his nurse, Noémi, had taken him there. It was her property, but on her son's marriage the daughter-in-law had become mistress, according to custom. Noémi had taken care of him from the time he was weaned until he went to school. His own mother was a cold woman and had little affection for her children. Indeed, the Count reflected, as he lay behind his bed-curtains recovering from his dream, no woman, probably, had ever felt so much affection for him as old Noémi. Not all women had found him so personally distasteful as his wife had done; but not one of his mistresses had felt more than a passing inclination for him. Tenderness, un-calculating, disinterested devotion, he had never known. It was in his stars that he was not to know it. Noémi had loved his fine strong little body, grieved when he was hurt, watched over him when he was sick, carried him in her arms when he was tired. Now, when he was sick indeed, his mind, in sleep, had gone back to that woman and her farm-house on the Oise. . . .

Of late the physical sureness and sufficiency he had known all his life had changed to a sense of limitation and uncertainty. He had no wish to prolong this state. There was no one in this world whom he would be sorry to leave. His wife, Madame de la Grange Frontenac, he had no desire to see again, though he would will to her the little property he had, as was customary. Once a year she wrote him a long letter, telling him all the gossip of Paris and informing him of the changes which occurred there. From her accounts it appeared that the sons of most of his old friends had turned out badly enough. He could not feel any very deep regret that his own son had died in youth, — killed in an engagement in the Low Countries many years ago.

The Count himself was ready to die, and he would be glad to die here alone, without pretence and mockery, with no troop of expectant relatives about his bed. The world was not what he had thought it at twenty — or even at forty.

He would die here, in this room, and his spirit would go before God to be judged. He believed this, because he had been taught it in childhood, and because he knew there was something in himself and in other men that this world did not explain. Even the Indians had to make a story to account for something in their lives that did not come out of their appetites: conceptions of courage, duty, honour. The Indians had these, in their own fashion. These ideas came from some unknown source, and they were not the least part of life.[1]

The peculiar intensity of the description of this dream suggests that the emotions it embodies may be of special importance to Willa Cather. As a matter of fact, the dream and the Count's reflections which follow it embody an entire vision of life. In it a great deal of Willa Cather's fear of life finds expression in symbolic form. Four points are worth noting: First, it shows a fear of overwhelming force; the enormous giant in huge boots must not come in; he must be kept out at all costs. Second, although this is an anxiety dream about childhood, in this passage childhood is regarded as being the only happy time. The Count believes that no one had ever cared for him as his old nurse Noémi had done. Third, the Count stresses his lack of any satisfactory adult emotional relationships. In speaking of women, he reflects, "Tenderness, uncalculating, disinterested devotion, he had never known," and in pondering his approaching death he remarks, "There was no one in this world whom he would be sorry to leave." He does not regret the death of his son, which seems odd, and Willa Cather remarks rather maliciously that "the sons of most of his old friends had turned out badly enough." Fourth and last, the Count feels disappointed with life; "The world was not what he had thought it at twenty — or even at forty." (Interestingly, Willa Cather herself had been just forty when she published her first prairie novel.) But although the Count is discontented, he knows there is more to life than mere gratification of self, even though he himself may not have found it: "He knew there was something in himself and in other men that this world did not explain . . . conceptions of courage, duty, honour. . . . These ideas came from some unknown source, and they were not the least part of life." These four points describe traits we have already seen in Willa Cather herself. The fear of overwhelming force fits in with her search for a sanctuary to which one can withdraw to escape conflict. The feeling that childhood is the only happy time we have seen over and over again in her writing; it is implicit in everything she wrote about the garden of the world and the golden age of her own childhood in the Middle West. The feeling that there is no such thing as real satisfaction in adult emotional relationships shows up in the myriad unhappy marriages she pictures in her fiction, and the fact that she was unable to portray directly a permanently satisfying love relationship between a man and a woman. Finally, the disappointment with life colors everything Willa Cather wrote or said after the First World War; her retreat to the past as the final sanctuary is a direct expression of this disappointment. It accounts for her theory of history, just as her feeling that there might be more to life than she had experienced accounts for her occasional intimations that a new age of great men may arrive and that the cycle of history may begin once more.

WILLA CATHER'S DREAM OF SOCIETY: THE FELLOWSHIP OF HEROES

At her best and most hopeful, Willa Cather pictures society as consisting at least potentially of a fellowship of heroes. For even when she was group-centered, the group represented to her a kind of temporary sanctuary; rugged individualism was always her ideal, even though she didn't always believe it was possible of fulfillment. For her the ideal society is one in which the heroes keep the little people in line, the relations between the heroes themselves being guided by courage, loyalty, and generosity. This ideal seemed to be opposed by all the abstract impersonal forces which condition (and largely govern) modern life. Politics, economics, and industrialization impose severe limitations on the human will which are difficult enough to recognize, let alone accept. What she did not want to admit was that the heroic ideal is impossible in the age of the machine; this was the real source of her animus against science, technology, and the industrial revolution. For the limitation of the heroic ideal is that it gives the hero no clue as to how to act when faced by bands of organized little men who do not choose to abide by the aristocratic code. Willa Cather believed that when faced by such a situation, a man like Captain Forrester has only two choices: he can either take over the code of the little men, in which case he is no longer a natural aristocrat; or he can stick to his own principles, in which case he is undone by his own generosity and goes down to defeat at the hands of men who are less principled than he. There is a third possibility, which twenty-five hundred years of Western civilization have striven to inculcate: namely, that man lives best when he obeys some sort of moral law which he regards as existing outside of himself. But to adopt this alternative would mean giving up heroic vitalism, the essence of which is that the creative hero must be bound by no law except that of his own will. Willa Cather was unwilling to give up her belief in hero worship; when she saw it failing in the modern world, rather than adopt some other view she made a villain of life.

THE DREAM OF ART: THE STRENGTH OF HER VIEW

At its best, Willa Cather's art represented an escape into reality instead of an escape away from it. The desire to create an imperishable masterpiece which will say something about human life long after its creator is dead is one of the prime reasons for the existence of art in the first place. Because of Willa Cather's aversion to conflict and because the whole impulse of her being tended toward the expression of a single unified emotion or mood, I have regarded her novels as being not novels at all in the conventional sense but extended lyrics in prose. One can apply to them the type of criticism which Walter Pater applied to various authors and painters in his *Renaissance* and attempt to find the essence or "virtue" of each one. Just as Pater felt he could define the essence of each artist in a single sentence or phrase, so it seems to me that the reader can do the same thing with the novels of Willa Cather. *O Pioneers!* for instance is an impure lyric since it describes two emotions: the joy of taming the soil and the impossibility of youthful romantic love. *The Song of the Lark* describes the ruthless force of the all-conquering will, the sheer drive to succeed. *My Ántonia* is a hymn to fruition and the contentment arising from abundance, a celebration of the earth-goddess in the garden of the world. *A Lost Lady* mourns the evanescence of beauty, the frailty of the gracious life. Then come the two novels in which Willa Cather describes supermen driven into a corner. The mood of *The Professor's House* is that life becomes unbearable unless one's own will prevails; the mood of *My Mortal Enemy* is that upon growing old even one's own passions become unbearable. In these two and the following books the feeling expressed is highly idiosyncratic and individual to the author. In *Death Comes for the Archbishop* Willa Cather was apparently trying to abolish conflict and found that the only way to do this was to abolish time and turn to something which she felt to be eternal, such as light; hence the innumerable descriptions of the landscape of the Southwest under the late afternoon sun. The essence of the book is the dissolution of time into an eternity of light. *Shadows on the Rock* is simpler; it affirms the importance of domestic order to the social fabric and holds that society's image is the home. The mood of *Lucy Gayheart* is that of nostalgia for lost adolescence and the first awakening to the possibilities of life. Here and in subsequent stories Willa Cather shows a tendency to kill off her heroines before they have a chance to get disillusioned with life as she herself had been. Finally, in *Sapphira and the Slave Girl* the family becomes the alpha and omega of all experience, and all roads leading away from it eventually lead back to it.

THE DREAM OF ART: THE WEAKNESS OF HER VIEW

While the strengths of Willa Cather's view of art are very great indeed, its weaknesses are many. All of her weaknesses come to a head, of course, in her refusal to face the contemporary world and her turning to the past for solace and escape. Her turn to the past was caused by two factors, the one external, the other internal. The external factor is the one with which we can more easily sympathize, since it has to do with the rise of modern mass man, the degradation of democracy, and the downgrading of standards of values. The internal factor is much more peculiar to Willa Cather herself and much less likely to gain our acceptance. First of all, it is an intellectual failure. For Willa Cather had no adequate concept of society; she failed to understand that people must live in groups. The only group she understands is the family unit, which is not a sufficiently broad basis for understanding society as a whole, at least not the way she envisages it; people must live in other groups besides. The omnipotent will does all very well until her heroes run afoul of social organization; they can handle mass man individually or in crowds, but not when they are organized into groups. The superior individual holding a mob of awed little people at bay is mostly a thing of the past; Captain Forrester may have been able to quiet by his mere presence the men in the construction gangs of the labor camps, but he would not have been able to do so had they been unionized. It was perfectly predictable that Willa Cather would hate the New Deal.[2]

Another symptom of Willa Cather's intellectual failure is her use of scapegoats to blame for things which she did not like about the modern world. Her anti-Semitism is one example of this; her bias against industrialism and science is another. Few people would pretend that the problems raised by the Industrial Revolution have been solved, but Willa Cather is too apt to condemn what she does not understand. In this way she followed the oversimplified Populist version of the social struggle as taking place between the forces of light and the forces of darkness.

Another major failing on Willa Cather's part is an emotional failure. It would be hard to dispute the fact that she had a naïve moral view. The bitterness of her later years only increased a tendency long apparent in her to divide the world too simply into the good and the bad. Unable to hold to the realization that the worst evil that occurs to human beings comes not from without but from within, she approached a vision and acceptance of life and then retreated from it into mere pessimism, thus ruining what might have been her best novel, *The Professor's House.* Another sign of emotional immaturity is her abandonment of adult standards and return to childhood values in her later years. We have seen that Professor St. Peter rejects his family and Myra Henshawe rejects her husband, while both of them try their best to return mentally to childhood. If the protagonist of *Shadows on the Rock* does not try to return to childhood it is only because she has never left it; the heroine is a twelve-year-old girl.

The result of Willa Cather's intellectual and emotional failure is ultimately an artistic failure. More and more often in her later novels her bitterness against the modern world results in repeated direct statements about the superiority of the past to the present, and such direct statements can be the reverse of artistic when they short-circuit the more powerful effects attainable through dramatic indirection and symbolism. The deterioration of her style over the years is also evident in her growing inability to maintain an aesthetic distance from her characters, a detached point of view. She had been able to maintain an aesthetic distance in "Paul's Case" and in *O Pioneers!*, *My Ántonia*, and *A Lost Lady* (in the last book she is detached from Marian Forrester although not from Niel), but after *A Lost Lady* she increasingly identifies her own ideas with those of her protagonists until finally the barrier between them breaks down almost completely.

In all fairness to Willa Cather it should be said that many of her weaknesses are weaknesses of the art-for-art's-sake movement which so influenced her. It was the fault of the movement that it was given to making exorbitant demands; it insisted on an impossible upgrading of life by trying to make life into an art and art into a religion. This can be seen in all Willa Cather's writings, and especially in that most agonized of all her novels, *The Professor's House*. It encouraged her to distort reality in a manner to which she was already prone since hers was a personality which put too high a premium on order; she did not want to look on life as the unfinished struggle that it is but as a realized art object. Her version of art for art's sake is incompatible with giving a complete and accurate representation of life as it is because it is based upon the search for beautiful sensations, and much of life is not beautiful. Willa Cather did not want to admit this. In a larger sense many of Willa Cather's weaknesses are the weaknesses of the nineteenth century. It was the fault of that century that it demanded of life that it constantly be at its highest pitch; hence Matthew Arnold's emphasis on "high seriousness." That apparently is more than life can bear. The nineteenth century tended to demand the impossible of human nature in hopes that it would do its best; that seemed to be the moral equivalent of unlimited competition and economic laissez-faire. This was very stimulating to some people, but it could be paralyzing to others, especially when they ran into difficulties that could not be solved by a simple exertion of the will.

FAILURE TO LEARN FROM EXPERIENCE: THE DREAM UNFULFILLED

In my first chapter I pointed out that there were three great influences on the writing of Willa Cather: the art-for-art's-sake movement, the

Populist mythology, and the peculiar configuration of her own personality. I now must point out that she ignored the implications of all
three things that influenced her. She ignored Walter Pater's gradual
development from an aesthetic to a moral outlook; at the end of his
life he was working on a book on Plato. She ignored the fact that the
Populist movement and especially its mythology was a failure because
the world it conceived of was dead and because it ignored the commercial and industrial, and especially the intellectual, realities of its
own time. The "Great Commoner's" career that was launched with the
"Cross of Gold" speech favoring free silver ended with the tragi-comic
farce of the Scopes trial. Finally she too often ignored the fact that
monklike devotion to a calling exacts a terrible toll; that artistic
creativity cannot be indefinitely substituted for human relations without
grave psychic consequences. Elizabeth Shepley Sergeant sometimes
hints at this in her gentle way; to the careful student of Willa Cather's
life and art it is obvious.

In her memoir of Willa Cather, Elizabeth Shepley Sergeant quotes
her as saying, "Life began for me . . . when I ceased to admire and
began to remember." [3] It might also be said that her serious artistic
career ended when she ceased to observe and began to regret. Because
she is such an autobiographical novelist it is easy to characterize her
from her own writings. In *Obscure Destinies* she had said of Neighbor
Rosicky, "He was like a tree that has not many roots, but one tap-root
that goes down deep." [4] Willa Cather is like this herself; her one deep
root is the response of the heroic and imaginative individual to the
challenge of his environment. She is even more explicit and precise
about the nature of her gift in *The Song of the Lark*, which is one of
the most autobiographical of all her novels. She writes:

> The faculty of observation was never highly developed in Thea
> Kronborg. A great deal escaped her eye as she passed through the
> world. But the things which were for her, she saw; experienced
> them physically and remembered them as if they had once been a
> part of herself. [5]

Thea, like her creator, is narrow, but what she knows she knows well.
At the very end of that novel, when Thea is discussing her now highly
successful career with her old friend Dr. Archie, she voices sentiments
characteristic of the author, showing that both by temperament and
training Willa Cather exhibited the romantic movement's glorification
of childhood at the expense of maturity in its most extreme form:

"A child's attitude toward everything is an artist's attitude. I am more or less of an artist now, but then I was nothing else. . . .

"Wagner says, in his most beautiful opera, that art is only a way of remembering youth. And the older we grow the more precious it seems to us, and the more richly we can present that memory. When we've got it all out, — the last, the finest thrill of it, the brightest hope of it," — she lifted her hand above her head and dropped it, — "then we stop. We do nothing but repeat after that. The stream has reached the level of its source. That's our measure." [6]

Other artists have had other attitudes toward experience, but for this one experience stopped with childhood. "Art is but a way of remembering youth," she wrote, and for Willa Cather that is exactly what art was.

NOTES AND

REFERENCES

THE FOLLOWING ABBREVIATIONS ARE
USED IN THE NOTES

AB Alexander's Bridge, Boston, 1922

Bennett Mildred Bennett, The World of Willa Cather, New York, 1951

Brown E. K. Brown, Willa Cather, A Critical Biography, New York, 1953

DCA Death Comes for the Archbishop, New York, 1927

Hofstadter Richard Hofstadter, The Age of Reform, New York, 1955

LG Lucy Gayheart, New York, 1935

LL A Lost Lady, New York, 1923

MA My Ántonia, Boston, 1918

MME My Mortal Enemy, New York, 1926

NUF Not Under Forty, New York, 1936

OB The Old Beauty and Others, New York, 1948

OD Obscure Destinies, New York, 1932

OO One of Ours, New York, 1922

OP O Pioneers!, Boston, 1913

OW Willa Cather on Writing, New York, 1949

PH The Professor's House, New York, 1925

SSG Sapphira and the Slave Girl, New York, 1940

Sergeant Elizabeth Shepley Sergeant, Willa Cather, a Memoir, Philadelphia, 1953

SR Shadows on the Rock, New York, 1931

SL The Song of the Lark, Boston, 1915

TG The Troll Garden, New York, 1905

YBM Youth and the Bright Medusa, New York, 1920

NOTES AND REFERENCES

CHAPTER I
FORMATIVE INFLUENCES

1. OW, p. 18.
2. OW, p. 19.
3. OW, p. 20.
4. Oscar Wilde, "The Critic as Artist."
5. The Portable Oscar Wilde (New York, 1953), p. 139.
6. Walter Pater, *The Renaissance* (New York, 1888), p. 250.
7. Sergeant, p. 23.
8. OW, p. 40.
9. OW, p. 41.
10. Cf. the essay entitled "A Chance Meeting" in NUF, especially pp. 16 and 23.
11. Needless to say, this was also the view of the man who influenced them both — Flaubert.
12. Quoted in Brown, p. 66. The superficially comic but essentially serious use of the marriage service to apply to the relations between an author and his art is significant in view of the denial of human relations implicit in the characterization of so many of Willa Cather's protagonists. One need only think of Bartley Alexander, Alexandra Bergson, Thea Kronborg, Professor St. Peter, and Myra Henshawe. The echo of religious phraseology toward the end of the paragraph is equally significant, since it suggests what her whole career shows — that she tended to treat art as if it were religion.
13. Oscar Wilde, "The Critic as Artist," quoted in Holbrook Jackson, *The Eighteen Nineties* (Harmondsworth, Middlesex, 1950), pp. 106-107.
14. Cf. PH, p. 75: "It struck him that the seasons sometimes gain by being brought into the house, just as they gain by being brought into painting, and into poetry. The hand, fastidious and bold, which selected and placed it was that which made the difference. In Nature there is no selection."
15. See section of this study on hero worship, pp. 66 ff. See also Sergeant, p. 127, "By August Willa had gone to Red Cloud . . . [where she was] among country people dear to her from childhood. They were

to Willa like characters in a story that rolled on like *War and Peace,* always more dramatic and interesting than anything she could have made up in her head."

16. Cf. Sergeant, p. 120: "She said that the air was totally different where fields had never been cleared and harvested nor virgin forest cut. When I thought about this, I saw that her intimacy with nature lay at the very root of her relation to *O Pioneers!* — and indeed of her power to work at all." Also p. 212: "They had certain things in common — there were likenesses in their differences. Frost had never thrown off the effect of having been born in San Francisco in a rough-and-tumble age. Nor Willa Cather the starkness of her migration at the age of nine from a soft green valley to wild red earth. To both, the hardness of the basic struggle for existence was a long memory that purified their approach to the life of the artist. The usual trappings and self-indulgences seemed to them both effete. Both thought of themselves, if I were to believe them, as "roughnecks" who had more or less happened into fame. Both liked a rather bare and timeless world. Both were suspicious of their own emotional, singing side, and imposed on it an elegant and sober line."

17. This stems from the notion prevalent in the romantic movement that while the artist's task is to put his revelation of the Divine Idea in a form apprehensible by the senses, the artist himself is a somewhat clearer revelation of the Idea. Cf. Shelley's *A Defence of Poetry:* "A man cannot say, 'I will compose poetry.' The greatest poet even cannot say it; for the mind in creation is as a fading coal, which some invisible influence, like an inconstant wind, awakens to transitory brightness," quoted in *Criticism, the Foundations of Modern Literary Judgment,* ed. Mark Schorer, Josephine Miles, and Gordon McKenzie (New York, 1948), p. 468, column 1.

18. Sergeant, p. 16: "But one year on the Divide — as the region was called — had been enough to make an indelible impression on a nine-year-old."

19. OW, pp. 125-126.

20. Quoted in Brown, p. 3.

21. Brown, p. 65. The essay was written for a symposium entitled *These United States,* ed. Ernest Gruening (New York, 1923), pp. 141-153.

22. Brown, p. 65.

23. Hofstadter, pp. 62 ff.

24. Hofstadter, p. 62.

25. Quoted in Vernon L. Parrington, *Main Currents in American Thought* (New York, 1927), vol. 1, p. 347.

26. Hofstadter, pp. 24-25.

27. MA, p. 387.

28. Hofstadter, p. 62.

29. OP, p. 118.

30. LL, pp. 168-169.
31. Hofstadter, p. 63.
32. Quoted in Hofstadter, p. 64.
33. OO, p. 419.
34. Hofstadter, p. 78.
35. YBM, p. 191.
36. YBM, p. 198.
37. PH, pp. 48-49.
38. PH, p. 78.
39. Hofstadter, p. 71.
40. Hofstadter, p. 74.
41. LL, pp. 106-107.
42. Dixon Wector, *The Hero in America* (New York, 1941), p. 373.
43. 1910 was the date of Willa Cather's first meeting with Elizabeth Sergeant; she did not resign her editorship at *McClure's Magazine* until 1912.
44. Sergeant, p. 33.
45. Sergeant, p. 34.
46. Sergeant, pp. 48-49.
47. Sergeant, p. 34; cf. the description of Thea Kronborg in SL, p. 442: "But, clearly, she knew only one way of being really kind, from the core of her heart out; and there was but one way in which she could give herself to people largely and gladly, spontaneously. Even as a girl she had been at her best in vigorous effort . . . ; physical effort, when there was no other kind at hand. She could be expansive only in explosions."
48. Sergeant, p. 40.
49. Cf. Sergeant, p. 117: "When Willa talked of what she hated, her whole personality changed. Her chin hardened, her shoulders pushed forward, and one felt that the rigors of her life had made her tough or touchy. Her emotional nature was disciplined on the surface; but not far below burned a fiery furnace. When the wrong kind of person — for her — approached her with seeming kindness, an uncontrollable antagonism flashed out."
50. *Writings from Willa Cather's Campus Years,* ed. James R. Shively (Lincoln, Nebraska, 1950), p. 37.
51. Quoted in Brown, p. 68. Brown also quotes on the same page a retrospective editorial written in 1921 describing the impact made by her dramatic columns contributed to the Nebraska *State Journal* at Lincoln while she was still attending the university there (1891–1895): "Many an actor of national reputation wondered on coming to Lincoln what would appear next morning from the pen of the meat-ax young girl of whom all of them had heard. Miss Cather did not stand in awe of the greatest actors, but set each one in his place with all the authority of a veteran metropolitan critic." Of the dramatic criticism written

while she was a reporter for the Pittsburgh *Daily Leader* (1897–1900) he says on page 86: "Dramatic criticism for her was still often the wielding of a sharp hatchet rather than of an urbane pen: she could still describe a play as "awful" or "terrible." What she lacked in finesse, however, she made up in vigor and conviction; and she never lacked the capacity to formulate and frame her strong opinions with complete clarity and often with charm."

52. Cf. Sergeant, p. 37: "She finished with an aggrieved sound as if I'd spoiled her fun and good humor by forcing her to look into those obscene tenements that crowded up to the Hotel Judson."

Cf. Sergeant, p. 50: ". . . she laughed, with a dig at this continued involvement of mine with 'home-workers' and the contests between exploiters and social workers that raged around them.

" 'I understand your Chief S.S. — who is *not* scared of reformers — ' I got back at her, 'considers the Bible "the greatest piece of journalism ever written! Take the headlines alone," he said to a friend of mine. "In six days God made Heaven and Earth!" '

"Miss Cather seemed annoyed. It was unfortunate that in a magazine, cheap writing, patterns of popular success, forced even an honest editor to keep looking through dross for gold."

53. Sergeant, p. 46. Cf. Sergeant, p. 111: "Willa could interpose a marble-hard wall between herself and whomever or whatever she wanted to ignore — . . ."

Cf. Sergeant, p. 118: "There were so many people and things she ignored or disdained, and she was so armored against them."

54. Cf. Sergeant, pp. 124-125: "These people, she supposed, were rivals of *The Nation?* They were doubtless Wilsonians, Bull Moosers and such? Indeed they were! After all, said I, you yourself worked on a new kind of magazine created out of exactly nothing but brilliant hunches by a man, who like these editors-to-be regarded our America as an unfinished affair, which needs constant remaking to help its growth.

"Willa abruptly changed the subject, asking me if I had been reading the *Autobiography* of S. S. McClure. . . ."

This trait is sometimes seen in her heroes and heroines. Cf. Professor St. Peter during a quarrel with his wife, PH, pp. 47-48. " 'It all comes down to this, my dear: one likes the florid style, or one doesn't. You yourself used not to like it. And will you give me some more coffee, please?' "

55. This is implicit in both E. K. Brown's and Elizabeth Sergeant's discussions of her later life. Cf. Bennett, pp. 222-223: "In 1931, when she was in Red Cloud for Christmas, she arranged her crèche and told the Christmas story to a group of children. One of Willa's friends had asked a photographer to come because she wanted a picture for each of the children; but when Willa saw the camera, she ran upstairs and refused to come down. Her friend found her crouched with her arm

over her face as if expecting a blow; but when she was assured that the man wasn't from a newspaper, she came down."

Cf. her refusal to walk to the microphone upon receiving an honorary degree at Princeton, as told in Sergeant, p. 246: "In 1931 Miss Cather received an honorary Litt.D. from Princeton University. This pleased her partly because she was in very good company: Charles A. Lindbergh, Robert Frost, two great admirations. She told me about the occasion, about how much she had enjoyed meeting Mrs. Lindbergh. But there had been a bit of trouble about the loud speaker.

"Every recipient of an honorary degree, after accepting his parchment roll, was expected to walk to the microphone and respond. When it came to Willa Cather's turn she refused to go! So the microphone must and did go to her instead. Her subjective recoil from the devices of publicity was automatic."

56. Arthur Mizener, *The Far Side of Paradise* (Boston, 1951), p. 3.
57. This is the attitude of most of her protagonist spokesmen. Cf. Captain Forrester's after-dinner speech, LL, pp. 54-55. Also cf. Dr. Wunsch in SL, pp. 75-76: "Nothing is far and nothing is near, if one desires. The world is little, people are little, human life is little. There is only one big thing — desire. And before it, when it is big, all is little. It brought Columbus across the sea in a little boat, *und so weiter.*"

Cf. also Dr. Archie, SL, p. 243: " 'Thea,' he said slowly, 'I won't say that you can have everything you want — that means having nothing, in reality. But if you decide what it is you want most, *you can get it.*' His eye caught hers for a moment. 'Not everybody can, but you can. Only, if you want a big thing, you've got to have nerve enough to cut out all that's easy, everything that's to be had cheap.' "

Cf. also Captain Forrester's philosophy-of-life speech in LL, pp. 54-55.
58. Cf. Sergeant, pp. 121-122, giving Willa Cather's comments to Elizabeth Sergeant in the spring of 1914 on Miss Cather's being taken to a hospital for the treatment of a scalp infection resulting from a minor hatpin scratch: "Declaring that there was no place in her philosophy for the unlucky, Willa raged at the foolish kind of illness that separated her from her book [that she was then writing]. She made sardonic comments on the price of wearing a new hat. . . . Her comments on her illness sounded the note of 'The Profile.' Willa went so far as to say she deserved derision, such as was given to lunatics in Dickens' time!"

Cf. Sergeant, p. 90: "I had shepherded her back from Boston on a Pullman in this typical down-hearted state of mind in which through physical illness, she had, in a way that was baffling to me, lost her own self-respect."

But cf. also her sympathy with such artistic defeated souls as Carl Linstrum, Dr. Archie, Mr. Shimerda, Emil Bergson, Professor Wunsch, Jim Burden, etc.

59. Although it was specifically the present which she rejected, the feeling seems to have carried over to life itself. Bennett, p. 147, quotes her as saying: "New things are always ugly. New clothes are always ugly. A prima donna will never wear a new gown upon the stage. She wears it first around her apartment until it shapes itself to her figure; or if she hasn't time to do that, she hires an understudy to wear it. A house can never be beautiful until it has been lived in for a long time. An old house built in miserable taste is more beautiful than a new house built and furnished in correct taste."
    Cf. also her running from a photographer (footnote 55).

60. Cf. Sergeant, p. 48, description of her knowledge of music and opera: "It had been a regret to her that she had not been born into an inheritance of musical scholarship and linguistic gifts like the Viennese. There were gaps, she said ironically, that youthful temerity and native flair and assiduity could never fill."

61. Sergeant, p. 48: "But now we had reached the Fifties, and I was again surprised by her delight in the false French chateau architecture of the Smart Set; her comment on the Astors and Vanderbilts with their French art collections and their boxes in the Diamond Horseshoe. Since she was so really simple herself I was unprepared to find her so respectful of wealth and swagger — it was as if she turned to the drama and the panoply of capitalism in spite of, or because of, her daily association with reformers and muckrakers; who were, after all, so grey and so boringly narrow."
    Cf. Sergeant, p. 53: "As the French and British writers know, money and success are unrelated to art. 'But one must have simple tastes — to give up a good salary,' she blurted out, and made for the restaurant door."

62. Cf. quotation on p. 5, this study.

63. Brown, p. 187. Cf. Willa Cather's preface to the 1932 revision of SL, pp. v-vi: "The life of nearly every artist who succeeds in the true sense (succeeds in delivering himself completely to his art) is more or less like Wilde's story, *The Picture of Dorian Gray*. . . . The Thea Kronborg who is behind the imperishable daughters of music becomes somewhat dry and preoccupied. . . . Her artistic life is the only one in which she is happy and free, or even very real."
    Cf. NUF, p. 73: " 'With a great gift,' I once heard [Mrs. James T. Fields] murmur thoughtfully, 'we must be willing to bear greatly, because it has already greatly borne.' "

64. Cf. Sergeant, p. 271: "Willa feared and hated the psychological repercussions of change, even in peacetime, and was increasingly troubled by the heroic and tragic disasters of the war. Moreover, she was increasingly subject to illness, and the limitations resulting from illness. With her dearest friends in and out of her family, dying and taking with them irreplaceable values, she had little spiritual margin with which

to resist physical weakness and sorrow. Her seeming withdrawal from vital participation into a mold of almost rigid quietness resulted. She is saving herself for her work, I thought, and I believe she tried to do just that. Nevertheless, no other new books appeared in her lifetime."

65. Sergeant, pp. 115-116. Compare this with another impassioned outburst, this time on the part of Willa Cather to Miss Sergeant, Sergeant, p. 63: " 'But to do this paradoxical thing, one must have the power to refuse most of the rest of life. Could *you* do it — give yourself, dedicate yourself to your art, you who love life and find human beings so fascinating? Are you perchance thinking of getting married?' She hesitated and I think just avoided a warning that art was all.

"What was she driving at? This importunate urge in my friend that was insisting on being listened to had nothing to do with marriage and children. Art *was* all, to her, it seemed. Though obviously she enjoyed and cared for men, they did not pose the problem known to most unmarried women under forty."

66. Cf. quotation from Brown on p. 15 of this study.

67. Cf. the remarks in Brown, pp. 274-275, on the genesis of SR.

68. Cf. Brown, p. v: "It had always been Miss Cather's way to decide instantly and irrevocably whether she would give her confidence. . . ."

Cf. Sergeant, p. 133: "Willa's mature judgments were final and never revoked."

69. Sergeant, p. 39.

70. Cf. Brown, p. 89: "The element of hero-worship is strong. Willa Cather never overcame it."

Cf. Sergeant, p. 41: "It seemed very Western of her to be such a hero-worshipper."

71. PH, p. 172.

72. Cf. footnote 17 of this chapter.

73. Brown, p. 86.

74. Sergeant, p. 18.

Cf. also Bennett, p. 153: "On the day for music lessons, the professor stopped at the Cathers'. Although 'Willie' hungered to hear music and stories about it, she did not want to play and she would interrupt her lesson constantly with questions about the cities, the customs, the languages of the old country. By the time her hour was finished, the poor old man would be exhausted and exasperated."

75. These strong female characters are often offset by sensitive, intelligent, but rather ineffectual male characters such as Carl Linstrum, Dr. Archie, Jim Burden and Cuzak, Claude Wheeler, Niel Herbert, Oswald Henshawe, Euclide Auclair, and Henry Colbert.

76. MME, p. 97. It is significant that Myra Henshawe puts more emphasis on crushing an enemy than on helping a friend.

77. Cf. footnote 54 of this chapter.

78. SL, pp. 455-456.

79. LL, pp. 54-55.

80. SL, p. 472.

81. MME, p. 22. Cf. also Thea Kronborg in SL, p. 194: "When she went into the city she used to brave the biting winds and stand gazing in at the displays of diamonds and pearls and emeralds; the tiaras and necklaces and earrings, on white velvet. These seemed very well worth while to her, things worth coveting."

Cf. also Thea's conversation with Dr. Archie, SL, p. 242: " 'I'm still chasing the elusive metal, Thea,' — he pointed to the papers before him, — 'I'm up to my neck in mines, and I'm going to be a rich man some day.' "

" 'I hope you will; awfully rich. That's the only thing that counts.' "

Cf. SL, p. 406, Dr. Archie's reply to questioning by Thea's mother: " 'She doesn't look like she was beholding to anybody, does she?'

" 'She isn't, Mrs. Kronborg. She never has been. That was why she borrowed the money from me' [to study in Germany]."

82. Cf. Sergeant, p. 131, the description of Willa Cather's writing a novel about an opera singer: "She had consulted nobody, no musician anyhow, about the musical problems of a technical nature she had inevitably run into. She had had to work them out in her own fashion. So it was reassuring to find that the [music] critic [who was reading her book in page proof] could forecast the nature and quality of Thea's voice (nowhere described) from her early lessons."

83. See treatment of concept of art as sanctuary, Chapter II, pp. 51-57.

84. NUF, p. 82.

85. Sergeant, pp. 46, 117, 118; Brown, pp. 68, 86, 306-307; Bennett, pp. 222-223.

86. Bennett, p. 149.

87. Captain Forrester's philosophy-of-life speech, LL, pp. 54-55.

88. Cf. "Light on Adobe Walls," OW, p. 123: "[The artist] is never free, and the more splendid his imagination, the more intense his feeling, the farther he goes from general truth and general emotion."

89. NUF, p. 82.

90. Cf. Lionel Trilling, "Willa Cather," *New Republic*, XC (February 10, 1937), 10-13.

91. NUF, p. v.

92. Cf. opening remarks of Chapter V, pp. 247-253.

CHAPTER II
THE WORLD OF ART

1. Cf. Curtis Bradford, "Willa Cather's Uncollected Short Stories," *American Literature*, XXVI (January, 1955), pp. 537-551.

2. I am here considering only the *Hesperian* stories which have to do with Nebraska. The first two are her earliest and best contributions to that magazine; her later contributions deal with remote times and distant lands and are more conventionally romantic.

3. Peter's suicide is the prototype of the more famous suicide of Mr. Shimerda in *My Ántonia*, written more than twenty-five years later.

4. Willa Cather, "On the Divide," *Overland Monthly*, XXVII (January, 1896), p. 65.

5. *Ibid.*, p. 67.

6. *Ibid.*, p. 66.

7. YBM, p. 253.

8. YBM, p. 264.

9. YBM, p. 266.

10. YBM, pp. 268-271 *passim*.

11. YBM, p. 272.

12. YBM, pp. 246-247.

13. YBM, p. 261.

14. Cf. Sergeant, p. 61: " 'What is so hard to find — though seemingly simple — as four walls within which one can write?' Willa Cather mourned gloomily. Her father in Red Cloud had wanted to build her a little 'studio' in his backyard — but heaven knew she could never write there. . . . Many and better things to do in Nebraska — such as going up to the Divide to get the gossip of the year saved by old neighbors on their farms."

15. DCA, p. 101

16. Cf. E. K. Brown's remark, p. 121, on "Paul's Case": "One might almost as well have lived in the small Western town of 'The Sculptor's Funeral,' as in Red Cloud."

17. YBM, pp. 208-209.

18. YBM, p. 209.

19. YBM, p. 205.

20. YBM, pp. 216-217.

21. YBM, pp. 215-216. Cf. Paul's arrival in New York during a snow flurry and his fascination with the florists' stands (YBM, p. 224): ". . . whole flower gardens blooming behind glass windows, against which the snow-flakes stuck and melted . . . somehow vastly more lovely and alluring that they blossomed thus unnaturally in the snow."

22. YBM, p. 203.

23. YBM, p. 228.

24. YBM, pp. 199-200.

25. YBM, p. 202: " 'I don't really believe that smile of his comes altogether from insolence; there's something sort of haunted about it. The boy is not strong, for one thing. There is something wrong about the fellow.' "

26. YBM, p. 206.

27. YBM, pp. 218-219.
28. YBM, p. 230.
29. YBM, p. 234.
30. YBM, p. 226.
31. YBM, p. 232.
32. Lionel Trilling, *The Liberal Imagination* (New York, 1950), p. 258.
33. YBM, p. 213.
34. YBM, pp. 225-226.
35. YBM, p. 231.
36. Brown, p. 61.
37. NUF, p. 16.
38. YBM, pp. 205-206.
39. Francis Steegmuller, *Flaubert and Madame Bovary* (New York, 1939), p. 38.
40. Cf. description of her trip to Europe in 1902 in Brown, p. 102: "Willa Cather's report was sharply personal: 'Late in the day we arrived at Rouen, the well-fed, self-satisfied town built upon the hills beside the Seine, the town where Gustave Flaubert was born and worked and which he so sharply satirized and bitterly cursed in his letters to his friends in Paris. In France it seems that a town will forgive the man who curses it if only he is great enough.' She might be writing of Rouen, but she seems to have thought of Red Cloud. 'The Sculptor's Funeral' was already in her pen."
41. A partial exception is "A Death in the Desert," of which E. K. Brown says, p. 119: "It is like the other two stories about art and the prairies in the rendering of the foreground; but in the background is the world of 'Flavia and Her Artists.'" This story was omitted from the authoritative "Library Edition" of her works (1937–1941).
42. TG, p. 165.
43. TG, p. 190.
44. TG, p. 171.
45. TG, p. 173.
46. TG, p. 163.
47. *The Great Short Novels of Henry James,* ed. Philip Rahv (New York, 1944), p. 445.
48. TG, p. 188.
49. Willa Cather gave orders that her own unfinished Avignon story be burnt after her death. Cf. George N. Kates in his essay on Willa Cather in *Five Stories by Willa Cather* (New York, 1956), p. 178.
50. Willa Cather's treatment of the Jewish art dealer shows evidence of the kind of grass-roots anti-Semitism which was found in the Populist movement (see section entitled "The Populist Movement" in Chapter I of this study). The following description (TG, pp. 179-180) is an example: "This Jew, an Austrian by birth, who had a large business in Melbourne, Australia, was a man of considerable discrimination, and at once selected

the *Marriage of Phaedra* as the object of his especial interest. When, upon his first visit, Lichtenstein had declared the picture one of the things done for time, MacMasters had rather warmed toward him and had talked to him very freely. Later, however, the man's repulsive personality and innate vulgarity so wore upon him that, the more genuine the Jew's appreciation, the more he resented it and the more base he somehow felt it to be. It annoyed him to see Lichtenstein walking up and down before the picture, shaking his head and blinking his watery eyes over his nose glasses, ejaculating: 'Dot is a chem, a chem! It is wordt to gome den dousant miles for such a bainting, eh? To make Eurobe abbreciate such a work of ardt it is necessary to take it away while she is napping. She has never abbreciated until she has lost, but,' knowingly, 'she will buy back.' "

51. TG, p. 185. The character of James may have been suggested by the servant described in Henry James's "Brooksmith."

52. TG, p. 192.

53. In OW, p. 91, Miss Cather remarks on *Alexander's Bridge,* which deals with much the same kind of milieu: "My first novel, *Alexander's Bridge,* was very like what painters call a studio picture. It was the result of meeting some interesting people in London. Like most young writers, I thought a book should be made out of 'interesting material,' and at that time I found the new more exciting than the familiar. The impressions I tried to communicate were genuine, but they were very shallow."

54. AB, pp. 15-16.

55. AB, pp. 48-49.

56. AB, p. 46.

57. AB, p. 52.

58. See OP, pp. 258-264, in which Emil and Marie are discovered and shot the only time that they ever make love.

59. Cf. Bradford, *Willa Cather's Uncollected Short Stories,* p. 545.

60. Cf. Brown, p. 189.

61. Although we are told in the epilogue that Thea married Fred Ottenburg, whenever we see them together in the text she is always rejecting him.

62. SL, pp. 200-201.

63. Thomas Carlyle, *Sartor Resartus,* ed. Charles Frederick Harrold (New York, 1937), p. 168.

64. Tille Kronborg, Thea's simple-minded aunt, is sympathetic to her but doesn't understand her.

65. SL, p. 239.

66. SL, pp. 75-76.

67. The 1932 edition was shortened by about a tenth of its length. See Brown, p. 189.

68. SL, p. 422.

69. SL, p. 449.

70. SL, p. 78.
71. SL, p. 477.
72. SL, p. 307.
73. SL, p. 62.
74. SL, p. 306.
75. SL, p. 308.
76. SL, pp. 303-304.
77. SL, p. 448.
78. Brown, pp. 184 ff.
79. Brown, p. 187.
80. The last was omitted from the collected Library Edition of her works (New York, 1938). See Brown, p. 318.
81. YBM, p. 77.
82. YBM, p. 134.
83. YBM, p. 99.
84. YBM, pp. 82, 88.
85. YBM, pp. 88-89.
86. YBM, pp. 144, 145, 148.
87. YBM, p. 191.
88. YBM, p. 195.
89. YBM, p. 196.
90. YBM, p. 198.
91. Cf. Bradford, *Willa Cather's Uncollected Short Stories.*
92. NUF, p. 82.

CHAPTER III
THE WORLD OF NATURE

1. OW, pp. 91-92, 93-94.
2. Sergeant, p. 57: "Mrs. Fields was all eagerness to adorn her young friend with sophistication. But Miss Jewett thirsted to revive in her a positive love of her own region, Nebraska."
3. Although the decision to leave *McClure's* was made under the influence of Sarah Orne Jewett, it was an influence exerted from the grave, so to speak, since by the time Willa Cather resigned Miss Jewett had been dead three years. See Sergeant, pp. 54-71 *passim.*
4. Quoted in Nora Lewison, "The Achievement of Willa Cather," unpublished doctoral dissertation, University of Iowa, 1944.
5. Preface to 1922 edition of AB, p. vii.
6. Bennett, caption of the photograph facing p. 196.
7. AB, pp. viii-ix.
8. AB, p. vii.

9. Cf. Sergeant, pp. 182-183: "Willa herself had the poet's response to life, including the typical sense of the lyric poet that youth and the emotions of youth, because of their great intensity and simplicity, surpass all other emotions."

10. MA, pp. 397-398.

11. NUF, pp. 78-79.

12. OP, p. 1.

13. OP, p. 15.

14. OP, p. 20.

15. OP, pp. 21-22.

16. OP, p. 65.

17. OP, pp. 47-48.

18. OP, p. 67.

19. OP, p. 68.

20. OP, pp. 68-69.

21. OP, p. 75.

22. OP, pp. 75-76.

23. OP, p. 76.

24. OP, p. 84.

25. Henry Nash Smith, *Virgin Land* (Cambridge, 1950), pp. 123-124.

26. OD, p. 59.

27. OP, p. 118.

28. See Brown, p. 179: "There is nothing of the tightness of organization, the cold clearness of style, that were so right for the story of Bartley Alexander. The structure of *O Pioneers!* has a happy looseness and the style an easy strength that belong in a story where the great values are the land, the large nature of Alexandra, and the warm love of Emil."

And Sergeant, p. 86: "The cold Swedish story she had written in the autumn of 1911, Alexandra's story, had entwined itself with the Bohemian story, 'The White Mulberry Tree,' and somehow she had on her hands a two-part pastoral: the most foolish endeavor imaginable, she mourned. She now thought of calling the book by Whitman's line: '*O Pioneers!*' "

29. Sergeant, p. 91.

30. OP, pp. 76-77.

31. OP, p. 77.

32. OP, p. 217.

33. OP, p. 222.

34. MME, p. 97.

35. SL, p. 550.

36. OP, pp. 127-128.

37. OP, p. 305.

38. OP, p. 249.

39. OP, pp. 163-164.

40. OP, p. 157.
41. OP, pp. 152-153.
42. OP, p. 41.
43. OP, p. 37.
44. OP, p. 36.
45. OP, p. 33.
46. OP, p. 37.
47. OP, p. 38.
48. OP, pp. 37-38.
49. OP, p. 34.
50. OP, pp. 270-271.
51. OP, p. 296.
52. OP, p. 231.
53. OP, p. 277.
54. OP, p. 277.
55. OP, p. 119.
56. OP, p. 307.
57. OP, p. 293.
58. OP, p. 295.
59. OP, p. 298.
60. OP, pp. 277-278.
61. Maxwell Geismar, *The Last of the Provincials* (Boston, 1947), pp. 208-209.
62. NUF, p. 136.
63. OP, p. 294.
64. OP, pp. 205-207.
65. OP, pp. 206-207.
66. OP, pp. 282-283.
67. OP, p. 307.
68. OP, pp. 307-308.
69. OP, p. 308.
70. See the ending of *The Professor's House,* in which Godfrey St. Peter withdraws all his emotions from the world around him because he too sees emotion as leading only to pain.
71. OP, p. 309.
72. OP, pp. 163-164.
73. OP, pp. 236-238.
74. This was generally although not absolutely true. Willa Cather managed to find a good deal of cultural stimulation in the Red Cloud of the eighties — perhaps more than she would find in the same region today.
75. OP, p. 117.
76. OP, pp. 238-239.
77. Willa Cather, "Nebraska: the End of the First Cycle," *These United States* (second series), ed. Ernest Gruening (New York, 1925), pp. 147-148.

78. An exception exists in the case of Captain Forrester, but Willa Cather makes it plain that he is a natural aristocrat and by that very fact able to rise superior to his culture. The same thing is true of Grandfather and Grandmother Burden in *My Ántonia;* significantly enough their grandson Jim is neither a natural aristocrat nor a success in life. He is one of a long line of Willa Cather's sympathetic weak people who resemble Carl Linstrum in *O Pioneers!*

79. OP, p. 51.
80. OP, pp. 122-124.
81. OP, p. 91.
82. OP, pp. 91-92.
83. OP, p. 92.
84. OP, pp. 92-93.
85. OP, p. 94.
86. OP, p. 95.
87. SL, p. 66.
88. MA, p. xiv.
89. MA, p. xiv.
90. See Willa Cather's remark reported in Brown, p. 202: "A comment on *My Ántonia* that Willa Cather made in an interview she gave in Lincoln a few years after the book came out shows that in her use of Jim as narrator she had been trying to achieve two effects that were not really compatible: Jim was to be fascinated by Ántonia as only a man could be, and yet he was to remain a detached observer, appreciative but inactive, rather than take a part in her life." This clearly implies that Willa Cather considered Ántonia to be the central subject.
91. MA, pp. 74-75.
92. MA, pp. ix-x.
93. MA, pp. 197-198.
94. Brown, p. 17.
95. Brown, pp. 13-14.
96. Brown, p. 13.
97. Sergeant, p. 23.
98. MA, p. 219.
99. MA, p. 300.
100. MA, p. 8.
101. MA, p. 9.
102. MA, p. 9.
103. MA, p. 35.
104. OP, pp. 28-29.
105. MA, p. 98.
106. MA, p. 70.
107. MA, p. 43.
108. MA, pp. 164-165.
109. MA, p. 241.

110. MA, p. 354.
111. MA, p. 355.
112. MA, p. 388.
113. Bennett, p. 47.
114. MA, p. 202.
115. MA, pp. 204-205.
116. Cf. the episode of the tramp in the standpipe in SL, pp. 135-139, when the subject is also changed and the problem of evil evaded.
117. MA, p. 271.
118. MA, p. 102.
119. MA, p. 118.
120. MA, p. 113.
121. Willa Cather makes no reference to Ántonia's emotions until she describes the day of the funeral, MA, p. 131.
122. MA, pp. 124-125.
123. MA, p. 125.
124. MA, p. 127.
125. MA, p. 117.
126. MA, p. 131.
127. MA, p. 137.
128. MA, p. 200.
129. MA, p. 205.
130. MA, pp. 225-226.
131. MA, p. 226.
132. MA, p. 229.
133. MA, p. 237.
134. MA, p. 231.
135. MA, p. 250.
136. MA, pp. 248-249.
137. MA, pp. 277-279.
138. MA, pp. 296-297.
139. MA, pp. 298-299.
140. MA, p. 306.
141. MA, p. 156.
142. MA, p. 205.
143. MA, p. 370.
144. MA, p. 394.
145. MA, p. 396.
146. MA, p. 403.
147. MA, p. 404.
148. MA, p. 413.
149. MA, p. 269.
150. MA, p. 384.
151. MA, p. 385.
152. MA, p. 398.

153. MA, p. 416.
154. MA, p. 419.
155. MA, p. 419.
156. Cf. Smith, *Virgin Land,* pp. 59-71. See especially his discussion of *The Pioneers.*
157. On the other hand, it may explain Willa Cather's close and continuing friendship with the Menuhins, parents of the violinist Yehudi, in the nineteen-thirties.
158. OP, p. 84.
159. See "Human Relations: The Case Against Spontaneity," pp. 76-95, this chapter.

CHAPTER IV
THE WORLD DISSOLVED

1. Sergeant, p. 166.
2. Cf. Bernard Baum, "Willa Cather's Waste Land," *South Atlantic Quarterly,* XLVIII (October, 1949), 589-601.
3. "Nebraska: the End of the First Cycle," in *These United States,* pp. 144-145.
4. Brown, p. 226.
5. Brown, pp. 226-227.
6. Sergeant, pp. 163-164.
7. SL, p. 244.
8. NUF, prefatory note, p. v.
9. OO, p. 52.
10. OO, p. 53. Claude's friend Ernest takes him to task for this: "You Americans are always looking for something outside yourselves to warm you up, and it is no way to do. In old countries, where not very much can happen to us, we know that, — and we learn to make the most of little things."
11. OO, p. 90.
12. OO, p. 10.
13. OO, p. 20.
14. OO, p. 101.
15. OO, pp. 101-102.
16. OO, p. 102.
17. OO, p. 166.
18. OO, p. 236.
19. OO, pp. 167-168.
20. Cf. Sergeant, pp. 174-180, Willa Cather's comments on David Hochstein, the original of David Gerhardt.
21. See Brown, p. 224.

22. OO, p. 356.

23. OO, p. 390.

24. OO, p. 358.

25. OO, p. 375.

26. This is my statement, not Willa Cather's. The only specific piece of music mentioned in the text is the Saint-Saëns Violin Concerto, which is French, of course.

27. OO, p. 419.

28. OO, pp. 457-459.

29. OO, p. 312.

30. Edith Lewis, quoted in Brown, pp. 228-229.

31. LL, p. 10.

32. OP, p. 3.

33. LL, p. 9.

34. LL, p. 9.

35. LL, pp. 9-10.

36. LL, p. 10.

37. LL, p. 11.

38. LL, p. 53.

39. LL, p. 11.

40. LL, p. 13.

41. LL, p. 13.

42. LL, p. 87.

43. OW, p. 41.

44. LL, p. 35.

45. LL, p. 13.

46. LL, p. 20.

47. LL, p. 20.

48. LL, pp. 22-25.

49. LL, p. 32.

50. LL, pp. 45-46.

51. LL, p. 46.

52. LL, p. 19.

53. LL, p. 68.

54. LL, p. 78.

55. LL, pp. 78-79.

56. A similar point of view is expressed directly by the author in "Neighbour Rosicky," OD, p. 60.

57. LL, pp. 48-49.

58. LL, pp. 81-82.

59. LL, pp. 85-87.

60. LL, pp. 88-93 *passim*.

61. LL, p. 125.

62. LL, pp. 125-126.

63. LL, p. 111.

64. LL, pp. 104-105.
65. LL, pp. 105-106.
66. LL, pp. 106-107.
67. LL, pp. 152-153.
68. LL, p. 170.
69. LL, p. 171.
70. LL, p. 174.
71. LL, pp. 168-169.
72. Cf. Bernard Baum, *Willa Cather's Waste Land.*
73. Cf. LL, pp. 85-87, quoted in this chapter on pp. 188-189.
74. Cf. Miss Cather's remarks on the composition of OP in OW, p. 92.
75. Cf. Sergeant, 108-109. Also see Edith Lewis, *Willa Cather Living* (New York, 1953), pp. 126-127.
76. OW, p. 31.
77. OW, p. 32.
78. PH, pp. 201-202.
79. PH, p. 213.
80. PH, pp. 219-220.
81. PH, p. 194.
82. PH, p. 243.
83. PH, p. 244.
84. PH, p. 251.
85. PH, p. 258.
86. PH, p. 95.
87. PH, p. 106.
88. PH, p. 119.
89. PH, pp. 260-261.
90. PH, pp. 219-221 *passim.*
91. *The Complete Essays and Other Writings of Ralph Waldo Emerson,* ed. Brooks Atkinson (New York, 1950), p. 146.
92. OW, p. 53.
93. Don Watson, *Cliff Dwellers of the Mesa Verde,* Mesa Verde Museum Association, no date or place of publication, *passim.*
94. PH, p. 160.
95. PH, p. 58.
96. It apparently does not occur to the Professor, or, rather, to Willa Cather, that out of consideration for his friend he might leave the bottle of claret off the table for one evening.
97. PH, pp. 242-243.
98. PH, p. 244.
99. PH, p. 246.
100. PH, pp. 247-248.
101. PH, p. 244.
102. PH, p. 239.
103. PH, p. 247.

104. PH, p. 248.
105. PH, pp. 250-251.
106. PH, p. 253.
107. PH, p. 47.
108. PH, p. 35.
109. PH, p. 159.
110. PH, p. 162.
111. PH, pp. 162-163.
112. PH, p. 11.
113. PH, p. 16.
114. Brown, p. 30.
115. Willa Cather, "The Enchanted Mesa," *Five Stories,* ed. George N. Kates (New York, 1956), pp. 67-69.
116. PH, pp. 67-69.
117. PH, p. 162.
118. PH, pp. 263-264.
119. PH, pp. 264-265.
120. PH, pp. 266-267.
121. PH, pp. 265-266.
122. PH, p. 276.
123. PH, p. 280.
124. PH, p. 280.
125. PH, p. 281.
126. PH, p. 281.
127. PH, p. 29.
128. PH, p. 272.
129. PH, p. 282.
130. See Brown, p. 245: "It was profound, unconscious preparation for death, for the last house of the professor." See Brown, p. 246: "Not by any answers it proposes, but by the problems it elaborates, and by the atmosphere in which they are enveloped, *The Professor's House* is a religious novel."
131. PH, p. 282.
132. Jonathan Swift, "Thoughts on Various Subjects," *The Prose Works of Jonathan Swift,* ed. Temple Scott (London, 1907), I, 277.
133. MME, p. 113.
134. PH, p. 267.
135. MME, pp. 90-91.
136. MME, p. 83.
137. MME, p. 88. "I'd love to see this place at dawn. . . . That is always such a forgiving time. When that first cold, bright streak comes over the water, it's as if all our sins were pardoned; as if the sky leaned over the earth and kissed it and gave it absolution."
138. MME, p. 45.
139. MME, p. 68.

140. MME, p. 115.
141. MME, p. 104.
142. MME, p. 109.
143. MME, p. 111.
144. MME, pp. 25-27.
145. MME, p. 20.
146. MME, p. 91.
147. MME, p. 97.
148. MME, p. 22.
149. MME, pp. 98-99.
150. MME, p. 113.
151. MME, p. 113.
152. MME, p. 38.
153. MME, p. 41.
154. MME, p. 122.
155. OB, p. 68.
156. OB, p. 7.
157. OB, p. 10.
158. OB, p. 30.
159. OB, p. 32.
160. OB, p. 33.
161. OB, p. 46.
162. Brown, p. 162.
163. OB, p. 31.
164. OB, p. 58.
165. Edmund Burke, *Reflections on the Revolution in France, Works*, Vol. II (London and New York, 1844), p. 348.
166. OB, p. 5.
167. OB, p. 25.
168. LL, p. 112.
169. OB, p. 49.
170. OB, p. 50.
171. OB, p. 49.
172. OB, p. 56.
173. But she was not completely consistent about this. In later life she became the devoted friend of the Knopf family and the Menuhins, who evidently meant something else to her than the anti-Semitic stereotype found in her writings.
174. OB, p. 53.
175. OB, pp. 65-66.
176. OB, p. 67.
177. OB, p. 67.
178. OB, p. 68.
179. Brown, pp. 304-305.

CHAPTER V

THE WORLD OF THE PAST

1. Sergeant, p. 261: "When I [visited Miss Cather] I was sometimes led into discussing values I saw in the New Deal that Willa condemned. I told her what it had been like in my New Mexico valley in the autumn of 1933: all the men from the Mexican village standing idle on the bridges; if working at all, paid by the ranchers only in produce — in fresh meat or milk. A whole family of brothers depended on the few dollars I paid their little sister for housework. But by the time I left, all the men were laboring on needed highways at WPA wages.

   "No good! Willa believed in the early American virtues, courage, sturdiness, tough endeavor. Nobody, young people especially, should be helped, no artist or writer either. Endowments, frescoes for public buildings, travelling fellowships be damned. During the ten years before she received the Pulitzer Prize, she said, she did plenty of pot-boiling articles and average short magazine stories — let them be forgotten."

2. Sergeant, p. 261: "It was harder and harder, I discovered, for professionals in her own literary world to see Willa. Henry Canby of *The Saturday Review of Literature* would try, only to find her guarded by lions of every description."

3. NUF, p. 57.

4. NUF, pp. 73-74.

5. Cf. NUF, pp. 50-51: "Literalness, when applied to the presenting of mental reactions and of physical sensations, seems to be no more effective than when it is applied to material things. A novel crowded with physical sensations is no less a catalogue than one crowded with furniture. A book like *The Rainbow* by D. H. Lawrence sharply reminds one how vast a distance lies between emotion and mere sensory reactions. Characters can be almost dehumanized by a laboratory study of the behaviour of their bodily organs under sensory stimuli — can be reduced, indeed, to mere animal pulp. Can one imagine anything more terrible than the story of *Romeo and Juliet* rewritten in prose by D. H. Lawrence?"

6. Cf. Claude Wheeler's essay on Jeanne d'Arc, OO, pp. 61-64.

7. NUF, pp. 92-94.

8. For an extreme expression of her revulsion against the present, see footnote 59, Chapter I.

9. For a conflicting view, see Edith Lewis, *Willa Cather Living* (New York, 1953), pp. 136-137 *passim*.

10. Brown, pp. 289-290.

11. Sergeant, pp. 209-210.

12. Sergeant, p. 114.
13. Sergeant, p. 194.
14. Sergeant, p. 209, but see Brown, pp. 290-291: "The new paths of fiction in the 1930's did not seem to her to lead anywhere worth going, though she kept all her interest in what was written by those who seemed to her genuine artists, Ernest Hemingway, Thornton Wilder, Scott Fitzgerald, and, somewhat to one's surprise, Sinclair Lewis, whose pictures of Midwestern towns and cities seemed to her not only authentic but full of suggestion. There was no critic of power writing in these years, she felt: the last of the great American critics was Henry James, and the last of the good ones W. C. Brownell and H. L. Mencken."
15. Sergeant, pp. 226-227.
16. Sergeant, p. 237.
17. Sergeant, p. 227.
18. Brown, p. 275.
19. Bennett, pp. 27-28.
20. Brown, p. 289.
21. OW, p. 9.
22. *Saturday Review of Literature*, VIII (August 22, 1931), 6-7.
23. *New York Times,* August 2, 1931, p. 1.
24. Archibald MacLeish, "Frescoes for Mr. Rockefeller's City," quoted in Cleanth Brooks and Robert Penn Warren, *Understanding Poetry* (New York, 1952), p. 451.
25. DCA, p. 5.
26. DCA, p. 7.
27. DCA, p. 19: "The long main street began at the church, the town seemed to flow from it like a stream from a spring."
28. DCA, p. 30.
29. DCA, p. 207.
30. DCA, pp. 30-31.
31. Cf. Brown, pp. 261-262: ". . . what Willa Cather was trying to tell was the story of man's capacity to establish dominion over the immutable, as the farmers had done in Nebraska." Also see Sergeant, p. 241: "But by contrast with her nineteenth century missionaries the late seventeenth century French exiles on the rock of Quebec looked minute, fixed, immobile, almost puny; in a state of suspension. They were conservationists, not builders or discoverers."
32. DCA, pp. 278-279.
33. Brown, p. 253; Sergeant, p. 233.
34. DCA, pp. 138, 212.
35. DCA, p. 7.
36. See footnotes 104 and 105 on page 293 of this chapter.
37. DCA, p. 76.
38. DCA, p. 16.
39. DCA, p. 16.

40. MME, pp. 98-99.
41. DCA, pp. 137-138. Cf. DCA, p. 236.
42. DCA, pp. 92-93.
43. DCA, pp. 235-236.
44. DCA, pp. 236-237.
45. DCA, pp. 295-296.
46. DCA, pp. 128-129.
47. DCA, pp. 135-137.
48. DCA, p. 131.
49. DCA, p. 132.
50. DCA, p. 135.
51. DCA, pp. 44-45.
52. DCA, pp. 35-36.
53. DCA, p. 38.
54. DCA, p. 57.
55. DCA, pp. 97-99.
56. DCA, pp. 101-102.
57. DCA, p. 104.
58. Geismar, *Last of the Provincials*, p. 193.
59. DCA, pp. 10-11.
60. Her heroes and heroines are almost invariably handsome. Cf. Ántonia, Alexandra, Thea Kronborg, Marian Forrester, Professor St. Peter.
61. DCA, p. 16.
62. DCA, p. 37.
63. DCA, p. 55.
64. DCA, p. 229.
65. DCA, p. 227.
66. DCA, p. 208.
67. Cf. passage quoted on page 304.
68. DCA, pp. 229-230. It is true that the three following sentences are: "One would have said he had no feeling for comeliness or grace. Yet music was a passion with him. In Sandusky it had been his delight to spend evening after evening with his German choir-master, training the young people to sing Bach oratorios." Yet this is the only mention of his love for music in the entire novel.
69. DCA, pp. 241-242.
70. DCA, pp. 244-245.
71. DCA, p. 245.
72. DCA, p. 225.
73. Cf. DCA, p. 228: "His Vicar was one of the most truly spiritual men he had ever known, though he was so passionately attached to many of the things of this world." See also p. 227: "During their Seminary years he [Father Latour] had easily surpassed his friend in scholarship, but he always realized that Joseph excelled him in the fervour of his faith."

74. Padre Martinez is also presented in this light; he breaks all the rules, but he brings more passion to the singing of the Mass than the Bishop feels he can muster. Cf. DCA, p. 150.

75. Cf. DCA, p. 230: "Nothing one could say of Father Vaillant explained him. The man was much greater than the sum of his qualities."

76. Cf. the struggle in *A Lost Lady, The Professor's House,* and Bishop Latour's envy of Father Vaillant (DCA, p. 227).

77. Willa Cather apparently was attempting (unsuccessfully, in my opinion) the same kind of effect that Flaubert successfully produced in "La Légende de Saint-Julien-L'Hospitalier."

78. DCA, p. 20.

79. DCA, p. 32.

80. DCA, p. 83.

81. DCA, p. 118.

82. Cf. Willa Cather's comment on the historical prototype of Bishop Latour in OW, p. 7: "What I felt curious about was the daily life of such a man in a crude frontier society."

83. DCA, p. 141.

84. DCA, pp. 147-148.

85. DCA, pp. 150-151.

86. DCA, pp. 160-161, 164: "Father Martínez continued at the head of his schismatic church until, after a short illness, he died and was buried in schism, by Father Lucero."

87. DCA, p. 157.

88. DCA, p. 293.

89. DCA, pp. 302-303.

90. OW, p. 12.

91. DCA, pp. 95-97.

92. DCA, pp. 99-100.

93. DCA, p. 2.

94. See the discussion in this chapter under "The Rock as Sanctuary." This passage may have been the germ for Willa Cather's next novel, *Shadows on the Rock.*

95. DCA, p. 104.

96. Willa Cather may have derived this technique from either Stephen Crane or Henry James, both of whom were influenced by the French Impressionist painters. It also seems to have Neo-Platonic overtones.

97. OW, p. 58: "If I were asked to name three American books which have the possibility of a long, long life, I would say at once: *The Scarlet Letter, Huckleberry Finn,* and *The Country of the Pointed Firs.* I can think of no others that confront time and change so serenely."

98. Bernard Bowron, Jr., "Realism in America," *Comparative Literature,* III (Summer, 1951, No. 3), 274.

99. Smith, *Virgin Land,* p. 86.

100. DCA, p. 76: "This Carson was not so tall as the Bishop himself, was

very slight in frame, modest in manner, and he spoke English with a soft Southern drawl. His face was both thoughtful and alert; anxiety had drawn a permanent ridge between his blue eyes. Under his blond moustache his mouth had a singular refinement. The lips were full and delicately modelled. There was something curiously unconscious about his mouth, reflective, a little melancholy, — and something that suggested a capacity for tenderness. The Bishop felt a quick glow of pleasure in looking at the man. As he stood there in his buckskin clothes one felt in him standards, loyalties, a code which is not easily put into words but which is instantly felt when two men who live by it come together by chance."

101. An exception is the account of Kit Carson's part in the expulsion ot the Navajos, in DCA, pp. 295 ff.

102. DCA, p. 154: "He was passionately attached to that old village under the pyramidal mountain. All the while he had been in Taos, half a lifetime now, he made periodic pilgrimages on horseback back to Abiquiu, as if the flavour of his own yellow earth were medicine to his soul. Naturally he hated the Americans. The American occupation meant the end of men like himself. He was a man of the old order, a son of Abiquiu, and his day was over."

103. DCA, p. 142.

104. DCA, p. 118.

105. DCA, p. 206.

106. See the first quotation on page 264 of this study.

107. See Sergeant, p. 207: ". . . now that she was so immersed in the art of writing and had given her own conception of the Indian in her own book, she wanted no news about him from the outside — so I surmised.

"In the nineteen forties, I gave Willa a little story that had delighted me, about the experience of two white boys on an Arizona reservation during some secret ceremonial. Willa returned it, saying:

" 'Don't you remember I am not interested in this sort of thing?' "

108. See p. 289 of this study.

109. See p. 271 of this study.

110. See p. 266 of this study.

111. See the quotation beginning "Moreover, these Indians . . ." on pages 264–265 of this study.

112. See Mary Austin's comment quoted in Sergeant, p. 235: ". . . after Willa Cather came to write *Death Comes for the Archbishop,* and I had to go to the hospital, Miss Cather used my house to write in, but she did not tell me what she was doing. When it was finished, I was very much distressed that she had given her allegiance to the French blood of the Archbishop; she had sympathized with his desire to build a French cathedral in a Spanish town. It was a calamity to the local culture. We have never got over it. It dropped the local mystery plays almost out of use, and many other far-derived Spanish customs."

113. DCA, p. 271.
114. OW, p. 11.
115. OW, p. 10.
116. Cf. Michael Williams, "Willa Cather's Masterpiece," *The Commonweal*, VI (September 28, 1927), 490-492, quoted in OW, p. 13: "Her [Willa Cather's] book is a wonderful proof of the power of the true artist to penetrate and understand and to express things not part of the equipment of the artist as a person. Miss Cather is not a Catholic, yet certainly no Catholic American writer that I know of has ever written so many pages so steeped in spiritual knowledge and understanding of Catholic motives and so sympathetically illustrative of the wonder and beauty of Catholic mysteries, as she has done in this book."
117. This section, apparently modeled on Flaubert's "La Légende de Saint-Julien-L'Hospitalier," was so well thought of by its author that she had it reprinted separately as a Christmas gift offering.
118. DCA, p. 218.
119. DCA, p. 214.
120. DCA, pp. 218, 219.
121. DCA, p. 60.
122. DCA, pp. 60-61.
123. DCA, p. 62.
124. DCA, p. 63.
125. DCA, p. 58.
126. DCA, pp. 63-64.
127. DCA, p. 262.
128. DCA, p. 262.
129. DCA, p. 262.
130. Actually, Father Latour is chosen Bishop by a group of cardinals at Rome, who make their choice as a result of discussion, and more specifically due to the pleading of the missionary bishop Father Ferrand with the Cardinal de Allande (DCA, p. 9). In other words, his appointment is the result of pull, not prayer.
131. DCA, p. 255.
132. DCA, p. 257.
133. DCA, pp. 257-258.
134. DCA, p. 258.
135. Some of the inset stories seem to show genuine religious feeling; for example, the story of the lost El Greco (DCA, pp. 10-11), and the legends of Our Lady of Guadaloupe [sic.] (pp. 47-49), and the Entertainment by the Holy Family (pp. 281-284). But here she was using traditional material whose interpretation had already been supplied to her by other people.
136. PH, p. 69.
137. DCA, p. 175.
138. DCA, p. 245.

139. OW, pp. 11-12.
140. OW, p. 9.
141. OW, p. 9.
142. OW, p. 43.
143. Wilbur Cross, "Shadows on the Rock," *Saturday Review of Literature,*
     VIII (August 22, 1931), 67-68.
144. OW, pp. 14-15.
145. OW, p. 16.
146. Brown, p. 277.
147. Cf. Brown, p. 280.
148. PH, p. 221.
149. SR, pp. 6-7.
150. SR, p. 16.
151. SR, p. 129.
152. SR, p. 22.
153. SR, p. 23.
154. OP, pp. 28-29, 30.
155. SR, pp. 24-25.
156. SR, p. 7.
157. SR, pp. 31-32.
158. SR, pp. 25-26.
159. SR, pp. 16-17.
160. OP, p. 29.
161. SR, p. 13.
162. SR, pp. 26-27.
163. SR, p. 9.
164. SR, p. 74.
165. SR, pp. 96-97.
166. SR, p. 192.
167. SR, pp. 197-198.
168. SR, pp. 39-40.
169. SR, p. 261.
170. SR, p. 261.
171. SR, pp. 171-172.
172. SR, p. 175.
173. SR, p. 263.
174. SR, pp. 265-266.
175. SR, pp. 267-268.
176. SR, p. 32.
177. SR, p. 161.
178. SR, p. 277. See quotation referred to in footnote 180 of this chapter.
179. SR, pp. 279-280.
180. This study, p. 219.
181. SR, p. 149.
182. SR, p. 136.

183. SR, pp. 181-183.
184. SR, pp. 151-152.
185. SR, p. 153.
186. SR, pp. 154-155.
187. SR, p. 126: "The sacred relics are all very well, my dear, and I do not deny that they work miracles, — but not through the digestive tract. Mother de Saint-Augustin meant well, but she made a mistake. If she had given her heretic a little more ground bone, she might have killed him."
188. Pierre Charron, the individualist hero who takes over at the end of the book, is also in religious matters a skeptic and a rationalist. Cf. SR, p. 224.
189. SR, pp. 3-4.
190. SR, p. 268.
191. SR, pp. 207-209.
192. SR, p. 218.
193. OB, p. 166.
194. Cf. Brown, pp. 275-276.
195. OD, p. 15.
196. OD, pp. 30-31.
197. With the exception of "The Old Beauty."
198. OD, p. 32.
199. OD, p. 51 ff.
200. OD, p. 46 ff.
201. OD, pp. 58-60.
202. OD, p. 66.
203. OD, p. 63.
204. OD, p. 69.
205. OD, p. 169.
206. OD, pp. 81-82.
207. OD, pp. 135-137.
208. OD, p. 133.
209. OD, p. 134.
210. Cf. first paragraph of the quotation in footnote 207 on p. 347.
211. OD, pp. 127-128, 129.
212. OD, p. 141.
213. OD, p. 146.
214. OD, p. 184.
215. OD, pp. 188-189.
216. OD, p. 190.
217. OD, pp. 226-227.
218. OD, p. 230.
219. LG, pp. 80-81.
220. LG, pp. 77-78.
221. LG, pp. 30-31.

222. LG, p. 32.
223. LG, pp. 183-185.
224. Brown, p. 308: "She had long intended to make a novel from her recollections of Virginia and from the countless stories about a yet earlier time she had heard of from older members of the family and their friends. She had promised her father she would do so."
225. Quoted in Rosemary and Stephen Vincent Benét's "Willa Cather: Civilized and Very American," *Books*, XVII (December 15, 1940), 6.
226. Cf. Sergeant, p. 270.
227. SSG, p. 43.
228. SSG, p. 169.
229. SSG, pp. 134-137.
230. SSG, p. 137.
231. SSG, pp. 219-220.
232. SSG, p. 23.
233. SSG, p. 29.
234. SSG, p. 8.
235. SSG, p. 134.
236. SSG, p. 15.
237. SSG, pp. 15-17.
238. SSG, pp. 228-229.
239. SSG, p. 216; cf. Geismar, *The Last of the Provincials*, p. 216.
240. SSG, p. 233.
241. SSG, pp. 236-237.
242. SSG, p. 245.
243. SSG, pp. 267-268.
244. Brown, p. 316: "The tract from the past rendered in *Sapphira* has upon it the great spreading stain of slavery, and from the stain the action arises. The reader is often persuaded to forget the stain — the picture of slavery is framed in leisure, grace, peace, and happiness."
245. Sergeant, p. 265.
246. Sergeant, p. 270.

CHAPTER VI
WINTER AT DELPHI

1. SR, pp. 243-247.
2. Cf. OD, p. 59: "[In the country] you didn't have to choose between bosses and strikers, and go wrong either way."
3. Sergeant, p. 107.
4. OD, p. 32.
5. SL, p. 301.
6. SL, pp. 460-461.

BIBLIOGRAPHY

BIBLIOGRAPHY

Primary Sources

Cather, Willa. *Alexander's Bridge.* Boston and New York: Houghton Mifflin Company, 1922. Copyright, 1912, by Willa Sibert Cather.

———. *Death Comes for the Archbishop.* New York: Alfred A. Knopf, Inc., 1927. Copyright 1926, 1927, by Willa Cather.

———. *Five Stories by Willa Cather,* ed. George N. Kates. New York: Vintage Books, 1956. Copyright 1905, 1909, 1920, 1932, 1948 by Willa Cather.

———. *A Lost Lady.* New York: Alfred A. Knopf, Inc., 1923. Copyright 1923 by Willa Cather.

———. *Lucy Gayheart.* New York: Alfred A. Knopf, Inc., 1935. Copyright 1935 by Willa Cather.

———. *My Ántonia.* Boston and New York: Houghton Mifflin Company, 1918. Copyright 1918 by Willa Sibert Cather.

———. *My Mortal Enemy.* New York: Alfred A. Knopf, Inc., 1926. Copyright 1926 by Alfred A. Knopf, Inc.

———. "Nebraska: the End of the First Cycle." *These United States* (second series), ed. Ernest Gruening. New York: Boni and Liveright, 1925. Copyright, 1924, by Boni & Liveright, Inc.

———. *Not Under Forty.* New York: Alfred A. Knopf, Inc., 1936. Copyright 1922, 1933, 1936, by Willa Cather.

———. *Obscure Destinies.* New York: Alfred A. Knopf, Inc., 1932. Copyright 1930, 1932 by Willa Cather.

———. *The Old Beauty and Others.* New York: Alfred A. Knopf, Inc., 1948. Copyright 1948 by Alfred A. Knopf, Inc.

———. "On the Divide." *Overland Monthly,* XXVII, 65-74 (January, 1896).

———. *On Writing.* New York: Alfred A. Knopf, Inc., 1949. Copyright 1920, 1924, 1925, 1926 by Alfred A. Knopf, Inc. Copyright 1936 by Willa Cather. Copyright 1927, 1931, 1938, 1949 by the Executors of the Estate of Willa Cather.

———. *One of Ours.* New York: Alfred A. Knopf, Inc., 1922. Copyright 1922 by Alfred A. Knopf, Inc.

———. *O Pioneers!* Boston and New York: Houghton Mifflin Company, 1913. Copyright, 1913, by Willa Sibert Cather.

——. *The Professor's House.* New York: Alfred A. Knopf, Inc., 1925. Copyright, 1925, by Willa Cather.

——. *Sapphira and the Slave Girl.* New York: Alfred A. Knopf, Inc., 1940. Copyright 1940 by Willa Cather.

——. *Shadows on the Rock.* New York: Alfred A. Knopf, Inc., 1931. Copyright 1931 by Willa Cather.

——. *The Song of the Lark.* Boston and New York: Houghton Mifflin Company, 1915. Copyright, 1915, by Willa Sibert Cather.

——. *The Troll Garden.* New York: McClure, Phillips & Co., 1905. Copyright, 1905, by McClure, Phillips & Co.

——. *Writings from Willa Cather's Campus Years,* ed. James R. Shively. Copyright by University of Nebraska Press, Lincoln, Nebraska, 1950.

——. *Youth and the Bright Medusa.* New York: Alfred A. Knopf, Inc., 1920. Copyright 1920 by Willa Cather.

Secondary Sources

Baum, Bernard. "Willa Cather's Waste Land." *South Atlantic Quarterly,* XLVIII, 589-601 (October 1949).

Benét, Rosemary and Stephen Vincent. "Willa Cather: Civilized and Very American," *Books,* XVII, 6 (December 15, 1940).

Bennett, Mildred. *The World of Willa Cather.* New York: Dodd, Mead, 1951.

Bowron, Bernard, Jr. "Realism in America." *Comparative Literature,* III, 268-285 (Summer 1951).

Bradford, Curtis. "Willa Cather's Uncollected Short Stories." *American Literature,* XXVI, 537-551 (January 1955).

Brown, E. K., and Leon Edel. *Willa Cather, a Critical Biography.* New York: Alfred A. Knopf, Inc., 1953.

Carlyle, Thomas. *Sartor Resartus,* ed. Charles Frederick Harrold. New York: Odyssey Press, 1937.

Cross, Wilbur. "Shadows on the Rock." *Saturday Review of Literature,* VIII, 6-7 (August 22, 1931).

Emerson, Ralph Waldo. *The Complete Essays and Other Writings of Ralph Waldo Emerson,* ed. Brooks Atkinson. New York: Modern Library, 1950.

Geismar, Maxwell. *The Last of the Provincials.* Boston: Houghton Mifflin, 1947.

Hofstadter, Richard. *The Age of Reform, from Bryan to FDR.* New York: Alfred A. Knopf, Inc., 1955.

James, Henry. *The Great Short Novels of Henry James,* ed. Philip Rahv. New York: Dial Press, 1946.

Lewis, Edith. *Willa Cather Living.* New York: Alfred A. Knopf, Inc., 1953.

MacLeish, Archibald. "Frescoes for Mr. Rockefeller's City," quoted in

Cleanth Brooks and Robert Penn Warren, *Understanding Poetry*. New
    York: Henry Holt, 1952.
Mizener, Arthur. *The Far Side of Paradise*. Boston: Houghton Mifflin, 1951.
Parrington, Vernon L. *Main Currents in American Thought*. New York:
    Harcourt, Brace, 1927.
Pater, Walter. *The Renaissance*. New York: Macmillan, 1888.
Schorer, Mark, Josephine Miles and Gordon McKenzie. *Criticism, the
    Foundations of Modern Literary Judgment*. New York: Harcourt
    Brace, 1948.
Sergeant, Elizabeth Shepley. *Willa Cather, a Memoir*. Philadelphia and
    New York: Lippincott, 1953.
Smith, Henry Nash. *Virgin Land*. Cambridge: Harvard University Press,
    1950.
Steegmuller, Francis. *Flaubert and Madame Bovary*. New York: Viking
    Press, 1939.
Swift, Jonathan. "Thoughts on Various Subjects." *The Prose Works of
    Jonathan Swift*, ed. Temple Scott. London: George Bell and Sons, 1907.
Trilling, Lionel. *The Liberal Imagination*. New York: Viking Press, 1950.
———. "Willa Cather." *New Republic*, XC, 10-13 (February 10, 1937).
Watson, Don. *Cliff Dwellers of the Mesa Verde*. Mesa Verde Museum
    Association. [No date or place of publication given.]
Wector, Dixon. *The Hero in America*. New York: Scribner's, 1941.
Wilde, Oscar. *The Portable Oscar Wilde*, ed. Richard Aldington. New York:
    Viking Press, 1953.

INDEX

INDEX

AEF, W.C.'s portrayal of, 166-174
Aesthetic movement, 2-3
  influence of, on W.C., 5-6, 27, 229, 275
Agrarian Garden of Eden, 7-8, 9, 19, 74-76, 181. *See also* Garden image
Alexander's Bridge (1912), 21, 54, 64, 255
  analysis of, 38-42
  Cather's estimate of, 59, 62-63
America, as represented by W.C., 97, 99-100, 102, 145, 210, 330. *See also* European in America
Anderson, Sherwood, 132
Anti-Semitism, of Populists, 10, 244
  of W.C., 10-11, 36, 55, 243-244, 374
Arnold, Matthew, 375
Art, Populist view of, 99
  as sanctuary, 1, 51-57, 218, 223, 225
  as subject for W.C.'s fiction, 42, 47-51, 61, 146, 151
  as substitute for human relations, 15, 38, 39, 54, 57, 73, 375, 376
Art-for-art's-sake movement, 1-6, 42, 57, 99, 375

Bank Street (New York), W.C.'s home on, 252
Baudelaire, 228
"Before Breakfast" (1942), 340
Bennett, Mildred, quoted, 252-253

"Best Years, The" (1945), 254, 353, 358
  analysis of, 357
Blue Eyes on the Platte, 353
Brown, E. K., quoted, 7, 15, 16, 33, 51, 156-157, 250, 252, 312
Bryan, William Jennings, 10, 216
Burke, Edmund, 242

Cable, George Washington, 291
Carlyle, Thomas, 45, 70, 104
Cather, Charles, *see* Cather, Willa— father; Family
Cather, Willa (biographical details)
  as autobiographical novelist, 376
  Bank Street home, 252
  at college, 21
  as dramatic critic, 13-14, 16
  as editor, 13, 16, 42, 58-59, 60
  emotional immaturity of, 18, 374, 377
  family, *see* Family
  father, 111
    death of, 252-253, 312, 343, 346, 358
    as "M. Auclair," 312
  formative influences on, 1-20, 42
  incapacity of, for self-criticism, 308
  longing for acceptance, 15-16
  moral views of, 272-280, 374
  mother, 111, 252, 312, 351, 366
  negativism, of, 12, 225, 230, 234, 240. *See also* Rejection
  parents, death of, 251, 341, 346, 358, 367

419